The Danish Directors 3

The Danish Directors 3
Dialogues on the New Danish Documentary Cinema

Edited by Mette Hjort, Ib Bondebjerg, and Eva Novrup Redvall
Translated by Mette Hjort

intellect Bristol, UK / Chicago, USA

First published in the UK in 2014 by
Intellect, The Mill, Parnall Road, Fishponds, Bristol, BS16 3JG, UK

First published in the USA in 2014 by
Intellect, The University of Chicago Press, 1427 E. 60th Street,
Chicago, IL 60637, USA

A catalogue record for this book is available from the
British Library.

Cover designer: Holly Rose
Copy-editor: Michael Eckhardt
Cover image: Søren Solkær Starbird, courtesy of Danish Documentary
Production manager: Jelena Stanovnik
Typesetting: Contentra Technologies

Print ISBN: 978-1-78320-041-2
ePDF ISBN: 978-1-78320-325-3
ePUB ISBN: 978-1-78320-326-0

Printed and bound by Hobbs, UK

For Arne Bro

Contents

Acknowledgements   ix

Introduction   1

Chapter 1:   Phie Ambo   29

Chapter 2:   Dola Bonfils   49

Chapter 3:   Dorte Høeg Brask   67

Chapter 4:   Mads Brügger   87

Chapter 5:   Pernille Rose Grønkjær   107

Chapter 6:   Jesper Jargil   125

Chapter 7:   Torben Skjødt Jensen   143

Chapter 8:   Max Kestner   163

Chapter 9:   Mikala Krogh   181

Chapter 10: Simone Aaberg Kærn   205

Chapter 11: Asger Leth   225

Chapter 12: Janus Metz   243

Chapter 13: Eva Mulvad   263

Chapter 14: Michael Noer   283

Chapter 15: Katia Forbert Petersen   303

Chapter 16: Jeppe Rønde   321

Chapter 17: Sami Saif   339

Chapter 18: Anne Wivel   359

Chapter 19: Anders Østergaard   379

Glossary   401

Index of Titles and Names   411

Index of the Institutional Landscape and Central Topics   423

Acknowledgements

All of the directors included in this volume have been very supportive of our project. They have been generous with their time, have lent us films, and have provided feedback on the edited transcripts of the interviews, as well as on their translations. We are deeply grateful for their enthusiasm for the project, and for their generosity.

Madeleine Schlawitz, Christian Hansen, and Henrik Fuglsang, all at The Danish Film Institute Stills & Posters Archive, helped us to secure portraits for each of the directors. Susanna Neimann, head of communication and press at The Danish Film Institute, also offered her kind assistance with images. The support of producers Sigrid Dyekjær and Katrine A. Sahlstrøm, and production assistants Minna Kirstine Katz and Ida Marie Gedbjerg, at Danish Documentary is gratefully acknowledged. Photographers credited in the captions throughout the book have graciously granted us permission to reproduce their work. Lars Ølgaard and his colleagues at the DFI Library have helped us to retrieve relevant newspaper clippings and, in some instances, films.

We are happy to acknowledge a publication subsidy from The Danish Film Institute, which has helped to reduce the cost of the book, and thus to make it more readily available to readers.

The team at Intellect Press, including May Yao and Jelena Stanovnik, has, as always, been a joy to work with.

The Danish Directors 3: Dialogues on the New Danish Documentary Cinema is dedicated to Arne Bro, in recognition of his tireless efforts as an educator, on behalf of documentary filmmaking in Denmark.

Introduction

Ib Bondebjerg, Mette Hjort, and Eva Novrup Redvall

In the two previous volumes in this series of practitioner interviews with Danish directors, documentary cinema has had a minor, but not always insignificant, role to play. Several of the directors featured in the first interview book, entitled *The Danish Directors: Dialogues on a Contemporary National Cinema* (Hjort & Bondebjerg 2000), have made important contributions to both fiction and non-fiction filmmaking, and this was necessarily reflected in the discussions. A case in point is director Henning Carlsen, for not only did this central filmmaker launch his filmmaking career with documentary films, he is also widely regarded as having helped, in the 1960s, to take Danish documentary filmmaking in new directions often described as 'modern.' Similar remarks are relevant with reference to filmmakers such as Jørgen Leth, Jon Bang Carlsen, and Jytte Rex, who first began exploring the possibilities of more poetic and reflexive approaches to documentary filmmaking several decades ago. Whereas the interviews with these filmmakers in *The Danish Directors: Dialogues on a Contemporary National Cinema* included some discussion of relevant documentary issues, and this within the context of a comprehensive evocation of the filmmakers' oeuvres, documentary filmmaking is virtually entirely absent from the second book, as its full title suggests: *The Danish Directors 2: Dialogues on the New Danish Fiction Cinema* (Hjort, Jørholt, & Redvall 2010). Only in the interviews with Jacob Thuesen and Omar Shargawi did documentary filmmaking impose itself as a necessary focus for discussion.

Motivating this third book of practitioner interviews is the aim of giving Danish documentary cinema, and especially *new* Danish documentary cinema, its due. Although many of the directors whom we have interviewed have ventured onto the terrain of fiction (often successfully so), their main contributions to the thriving post-80s milieu that has produced what counts as a *new* Danish cinema (Hjort 2005) lie in the (interconnected) areas of documentary film and television. The emphasis here is very much on *new* documentary cinema, for the vast majority of filmmakers included in this third volume of interviews belong to the generation that was born in the 1970s. Date of birth is by no means negligible in this context, for it was during this very same time frame that documentary filmmaking became part of the curricula offered by the National Film School of Denmark (NFSD). Many of the interviewees, although not all of them, were trained at the School's now legendary Department of Documentary & TV, which is closely associated with the untiring efforts of Arne Bro (Hjort 2013a), to whom this volume is respectfully dedicated.

The fact that thinking along generational lines is a defining feature of the new Danish documentary cinema is clearly suggested by the filmmakers themselves. Selected observations by Eva Mulvad and Michael Noer help to substantiate this point:

> My generation was simply carpet-bombed with black-and-white documentaries about WWII during secondary school. And those films created that dusty feeling of obligation that has been such a feature of the [documentary] genre. We feel a certain obligation to shake that off. […] my generation clearly dreams of making films that will be shown in the cinema. Our desire is to make films that are at once cinematic and entertaining.
>
> (Mulvad, this volume)

> What was missing [amongst documentary filmmakers at the Film School around 2000] was that sense of new beginnings, of a new generation making its mark. Ten years on, it's clear that the situation has changed completely. Now it's actually possible to talk about the impact that a new generation has had on the aesthetics and practices of filmmaking.
>
> (Noer, this volume)

The term 'new' references the impact of a generation, and of the Department of Documentary & TV, but also captures tendencies that cut across the work of the interviewees. These include the aspiration to draw on the full spectrum of cinematic tools and formal/stylistic/aesthetic possibilities, to think carefully about audience appeal, and, through intense collaboration with other film practitioners, to produce films that meet professional standards with respect to such areas as sound, cinematography, and editing. The realities about which the filmmakers in question make assertions through their documentary filmmaking also reflect a generational specificity. For filmmakers born in the 1970s, globalization and internationalization are inevitable aspects of everyday life, and this common ground has clear implications for their films.

Yet, not all of the names listed in the 'Table of Contents' can be neatly captured by this generational way of framing things. As will be clear, we have also opted to interview a number of filmmakers who, having demonstrated a capacity for innovation and renewal, can legitimately be seen as having helped to shape the contours of the new Danish documentary cinema. Directors such as Anne Wivel (b. 1945), Dola Bonfils (b. 1941), Jesper Jargil (b. 1945), and Torben Skjødt Jensen (b. 1958) have mostly followed paths quite different from those that have led a younger generation into documentary filmmaking. In several instances, for example, it has been a matter of 'learning by doing' in an industry context, as compared with the younger generation's typical exposure to a more formal process of film education at the Copenhagen-based conservatoire-style school that defines its profile in terms of a strong commitment to film as art. The documentary work of these filmmakers is crucial, however, in the context of any discussion of new Danish documentary cinema, and not merely for reasons relating to issues of continuity and renewal. More important still is the role that these filmmakers have played, as teachers and creative consultants, in inspiring filmmakers belonging to that younger generation that is so central to the new Danish documentary film phenomenon.

Like all of the programmes delivered by the National Film School of Denmark, those offered by the Department of Documentary & TV rely heavily on the ongoing involvement of a group of trusted practitioner-teachers. The interview with Anne Wivel in *The Danish Directors 3* provides insight into the emergence of this key department, but also into the role that well established documentary filmmakers (among them Wivel herself) play in sustaining it. Indeed, her reflections suggest a causal narrative about the emergence of the new Danish documentary cinema, one that points to the decisive vision of key practitioner-teachers, as well as to certain mentorship practices. As Wivel remarks, the current success of the new Danish documentary cinema, with its characteristic emphasis on depicting life in ways that preserve its inherent vitality, is anything but a chance occurrence. The new Danish documentary cinema, rather, finds at least some of its conditions of possibility in the decisive steps taken toward the development of a particular kind of milieu; one giving aspiring documentary filmmakers who possess a unique perspective the freedom to develop as practitioners of documentary film art. Often situated on the very boundary of fiction and non-fiction (much like Jørgen Leth and Lars von Trier's much acclaimed film, *De fem benspænd* [*The Five Obstructions*, 2003]), yet without compromising on the ethical duties and epistemic commitments that both constrain and enable the documentary film practitioner's work, the new Danish documentary cinema undoubtedly owes its existence to cogent decisions made several decades ago in the context of deliberations about practice-based film education.[1]

Perspectives on documentary film: Scholars and practitioners

For present purposes, scholarly writing on documentary film can be divided into two broad categories: one historical, the other theoretical. Being as it is a research-driven interview book rooted in clear theoretical convictions and focusing on a specific empirical context, *The Danish Directors 3* has insights to offer that are relevant to our understanding of the history of documentary film, but also the project of conceptualizing the specificity of documentary film. Regarding historically oriented writings on documentary film, it is fair to say that some of the most pioneering works present a general historical narrative about documentary film that stops short of thick descriptions of what it means to be a practitioner of the art of documentary filmmaking. The field-defining efforts of such figures as Eric Barnouw (*Documentary: A History of the Non-Fiction Film*, 1974), Richard Barsam (*Non-Fiction Film: A Critical History*, 1973), and Jack Ellis and Betsy McLane (*A New History of Documentary Film*, 2005) have been complemented in recent times by the work of film scholars who have devoted welcome energy to the writing of detailed national histories of documentary film. Nora Alter's *Projecting History: German Nonfiction Cinema,*

1967–2000 (2002) is a case in point, as is Sarah Brinch and Gunnar Iversen's (2001) edited book *Virkelighetsbilder. Norsk dokumentarfilm gjenom hundre år* ('Images of Reality: 100 Years of Norwegian Documentary Film'), which deals with Norwegian film history. Also warranting mention here is Ib Bondebjerg's (2008) *Virkelighedens Fortællinger. Den danske tv-dokumentarismes historie* ('Narratives of Reality'), the first book-length study of the history of Danish TV documentaries. 'Narratives of Reality' was followed in 2012 by Bondebjerg's *Virkelighedsbilleder. Den moderne danske dokumentarfilm* ('Images of Reality'), which takes a close look at Danish documentary film in its various 'modern' incarnations.

Although all of these works on documentary film help to deepen our understanding of the history of documentary cinema, of the features of specific documentary genres, and of the role that documentary films play in society, they do not (purport to) give us the story of documentary filmmaking through the actual articulations of filmmakers' self-understandings. And yet such self-understandings, as captured in the preferred concepts and terms of the practitioners themselves, surely have a role to play in any attempt to refine and amplify our historically oriented understandings of documentary filmmaking. Inasmuch as it is an interview book, rather than a work of full-blown scholarship, *The Danish Directors 3: Dialogues on the New Danish Documentary Cinema* cannot provide a fully developed historical account of the new Danish cinema. Yet, in the wide-ranging stories told by its nineteen practitioners, historians of documentary film will find clear elements and suggestions of such a narrative, and, we believe, insights that help to nuance claims based on a more 'externalist' perspective, understood here as one bypassing the articulated self-understandings of the practitioner.

Let us return to the second category of writing on documentary film evoked above – one comprising works aimed at conceptual clarification. We see work belonging to this category as being generally divided between a position that is sceptical of the idea of documentary filmmaking having its own specificity, and another, quite different position involving a reasoned defence of the notion of specificity. In our view, the practitioner-oriented approach underwriting the genre of the interview book more generally – and *The Danish Directors 3* in particular – is one that works in synergy with various cognitivist film scholars' attempts to defend and define the specificity of documentary filmmaking. The practitioner-oriented interview book about documentary filmmaking and cognitivist-oriented theorizations of documentary film may be very different discursive phenomena, but beneath the discursive differences there is a shared commitment to a concept of filmmakers' intentions as constitutive of the specificity of documentary filmmaking.

Scholars and philosophers who are inspired by analytic and cognitive approaches to film tend to believe that there is a distinction to be drawn between fiction and non-fiction films, and that documentaries belong squarely in the latter category. Scholars, on the other hand, who are influenced by poststructuralist and postmodernist ways of thinking about the world, maintain that the boundary between fiction and non-fiction films cannot be defended, and that documentaries or non-fiction films should not be viewed as fundamentally different from fiction films. The sceptics who deny the fiction/non-fiction distinction claim that films classified as non-fiction necessarily involve a subjective – and thus, less than truthful – dimension. Sceptics note how the non-fiction filmmaker necessarily makes a whole range of choices that can only – so the argument goes – stand in the way of any properly objective account of reality. The filmmaker must choose her film stock, her camera angles and lenses, and a certain editing style. In some cases – as in certain films focusing on historical figures from earlier centuries – the non-fiction filmmaker has no choice but to make use of actors and re-enactments when exploring the events that occurred. Sceptics also point out that films identified as works of 'non-fiction' often tell stories that organize aspects of reality in such a way as to create the kind of suspense with which we are familiar from fiction films. Such suspense may even be heightened by a certain use of music, one designed to prompt a specific mood or emotion. As far as the sceptics are concerned, non-fiction films are best thought of as having been shaped by a subjective take on reality and, typically, by a whole arsenal of cinematic devices involving invention; that is, by the kind of creative impulses that drive the very process of fiction-making. Sceptics also like to note that viewers cannot always tell the difference between fiction and non-fiction films simply by watching them.

Cognitivists have had quite a lot to say, much of it very insightful in our view, in response to the sceptics' proposed blurring of the boundaries between fiction and non-fiction. Scholars such as Trevor Ponech (1997), Carl Plantinga (1997, 2005), and Noël Carroll (1997) all accept the sceptics' contention that we may not always be able to decide whether a film is a work of fiction or non-fiction simply by looking at what's onscreen – by looking at what Carroll calls the 'manifest textual properties' of a film. They also agree that non-fiction films make use of all kinds of cinematic techniques, including re-enactments with actors, soundtracks that work on our emotions, editing techniques that create a highly cinematic experience quite different from how we usually experience the world, and so on. However, they do insist that fiction and non-fiction films are genuinely different sorts of phenomena, and that if we look elsewhere, to the intentions of those who make them, we begin to see this. Carroll, for example, would want to say that when Anders Østergaard makes a film like *Burma VJ: Reporter i et lukket land* (*Burma VJ – Reporting from a Closed Country*, 2008) in collaboration with Burmese video journalists, he is not interested in getting us to enter into a game of make-believe in which we simply entertain, in a 'suppose that' and uncommitted sort of way, a series of thoughts about the protests of monks and the risks taken by video journalists who support them. Østergaard, Carroll would argue, wants us to understand that the thoughts about protest, solidarity, and the violation of basic rights are ones to which the filmmaker is genuinely committed 'by way of belief.'

As we see it, Carroll, Ponech, and Plantinga are right to insist that non-fiction film involves an assertoric stance: the filmmaker makes a series of assertions about a given reality, and expects us to respond the way we would when assertions are made in other contexts. We might assess the evidence we have been given, and wonder whether it is the right kind of evidence. We might ask whether the overall argument makes sense. In some cases we might feel that the filmmaker has failed fully to respect the norms that accompany assertions. The point is that non-fiction films work with belief (rather than make-belief), assertions, and with the norms and expectations that accompany them. So when we are trying to figure out how best to respond to a given film, we should be asking questions about what Carroll (1997) calls the filmmaker's 'categorical intentions', as distinct from 'meaning intentions'. Categorical intentions – I see my work as belonging to *this* particular category of documentary, or non-fiction, films as opposed to *that* category of fiction films – are quite easy to ascertain once we think of films, not as isolated works that we encounter 'cold', without any kind of prior information, but as part of a whole system that conveys filmmakers' categorical intentions to us in all sorts of ways: through production companies' and distributors' promotional materials; through interviews with directors and cinematographers; through film critics' research-based reviews; and so on.

The Danish Directors 3 is part of a larger project (encompassing, in addition to the Danish Directors interview book series, the Nordic Film Classics series) that aims to make room within Film Studies for what Hjort (2010) calls 'practitioner's agency'.[2] As such, the volume in question reflects efforts to clarify the *subjective* rationality of documentary filmmakers' reasoning about their work through a process of dialogue and articulation. What Carroll calls 'categorical intentions' are central to this process, but so are some of the other categories of intention that are constitutive of agency more generally, and thus of practitioner's agency. Coined to draw attention to the need to incorporate a properly empirical dimension into research on cinematic authorship, the term 'practitioner's agency' is linked to the premise that the nature of cinematic authorship cannot be determined at a purely conceptual or speculative level. To be robust and convincing, claims about cinematic authorship, we contend, must make substantial reference to practitioners' *actual* reasoning about the cinematic practices in which they are involved.[3]

While *The Danish Directors 3* is part of a series focusing on Danish filmmaking as seen through the eyes of its practitioners, it is also part of a larger tradition involving exchanges between academics and filmmakers. Internationally-oriented contributions to this tradition include Maxine Baker's *Documentary in the Digital Age* (2005) (featuring twelve interviews with prominent, internationally-known documentary filmmakers) and Liz Stubbs' *Documentary Filmmakers Speak* (2002) (offering thirteen interviews with American-British documentary film directors). A variation on the genre of the interview book can be found in Jane Chapman's *Documentary in Practice* (2007), where a systematic approach to the different aspects of documentary film practice is informed by interviews with, and statements by, film directors. Each of these volumes is shaped by methodological choices and emphases, and the same is, of course, true for *The Danish Directors 3*.

Remarks on method

Interviewing, as Andrea Fontana and James H. Frey point out, 'has a wide variety of forms and a multiplicity of uses' (1994: 361). The interview may, for example, involve a 'face-to-face' exchange with a single interlocutor, but may also 'take the form of face-to-face group interviewing, mailed or self-administered questionnaires, and telephone surveys' (1994: 361). Further distinctions are typically made between so-called 'structured, semistructured, or unstructured' interviews, with the first type emphasizing 'preestablished questions with a limited set of response categories' (1994: 363) and the interviewer adopting a role that is 'neutral' and 'impersonal' (1994: 364). The unstructured interview, in contrast, is qualitative in nature, and sees the interviewer adopting a role that 'deviates from the "ideal" of a cool, distant, and rational interviewer' (1994: 366). As Fontana and Frey see it, the aims of the unstructured interview are to establish a 'human-to-human relation with the respondent' (1994: 366), and to achieve some form of understanding rather than to produce a quasi-scientific explanation of a particular phenomenon. In the context of unstructured interviews, the interviewee's 'presentational self' is seen as critical, and as having a decisive impact on the 'success (or failure) of the study' (1994: 367). For an unstructured interview to succeed, the relation between the interviewer and interviewee has to be defined by a certain level of trust. For this reason, Fontana and Frey regard the process of building rapport with the interviewee as integral to the conducting of unstructured interviews:

> Because the goal of unstructured interviewing is *understanding*, it becomes paramount for the researcher to establish rapport. He or she must be able to put him- or herself in the role of the respondents and attempt to see the situation from their perspective, rather than impose the world of academia and preconceptions upon them.
>
> (Fontana & Frey 1994: 367)

The approach adopted when preparing *The Danish Directors 3* emphasized trust and understanding in the context of face-to-face interviews on a one-to-one basis, usually at the filmmaker's home, office, or favourite café. Inasmuch as all three interviewers have been actively engaged with Danish film for many years, it was not difficult to establish the kind of trust that builds on expertise and knowledge, but also on some broad sense of shared purpose. Early on in the project, the three interviewers jointly identified the themes or questions that were seen as likely to be highly relevant in most cases. Each interviewee was interviewed once, for somewhere between 90 and 180 minutes. The interviews were subsequently transcribed and significantly shortened. The edited Danish texts were then submitted to the filmmakers who vetted them before Hjort undertook the process of translating them into English. The interviewees were also given an opportunity to comment on the English translations and, where necessary, to update the interview. In some cases, responses given by the interviewees were deemed by the interviewers as a group to be overly quick or insufficiently attentive to the deeper issues motivating the question. In such cases, the original interviewer was asked to revert to the interviewee with follow-up questions by phone or by e-mail.

The questions guiding the interviews were articulated with reference to ongoing discussions relating to research focusing on cinematic creativity, cinematic authorship, film policy, and the development of sustainable film milieus, among others. The point was to use the practitioners' interviews as a means of generating empirical data that could bring another dimension to the debates. We do not regard the practitioners' interviews as a set of research findings, but we do see the questions that drive them as informed by research questions, and the interviews themselves as having implications for scholarly work on film. Inscribed within this conception of the project is an understanding of the audience for *The Danish Directors 3*. The audience that we have in mind is a capacious one, for it includes filmmakers, cinephiles, policymakers, and researchers, with none of the categories in question limited to the Danish context.

The Danish Directors 3 features exchanges with nineteen of the most important and successful film directors from the world of new Danish documentary cinema. While these exchanges are necessarily wide-ranging, there are also recurring emphases. The interviews reflect an interest, for example, in getting the various practitioners to articulate their perspectives on the institutional conditions that have shaped their practices. It is a matter of trying to identity some of the defining features of the specific kind of practice-based education that they have received as documentary filmmakers, and of grasping the nature of the networks in which they operate through collaborative undertakings involving editors and cinematographers, among others. The institutional parameters shaping the actual production of the films, as well as their modes of distribution, were seen as important during the exchanges, as was the role of policies pertaining to both film and TV, and various funding schemes. The interviewers have not hesitated to probe areas that are seen as problematic, and as a source of recurring or growing conflicts. Many of the interviews evoke the Danish Film Institute's involvement in co-financing and co-producing documentaries in partnership with TV channels, be they defined in terms of public service or profit. The practitioners' accounts of their lived experiences of such collaborative ventures underscore the extent to which TV remains the most significant window for documentary films, but also draw attention to the problems that arise when distinct milieus, each with its own institutional culture, are required to join forces.

Shaping the exchanges in *The Danish Directors 3* is a further interest in providing a space where filmmakers are able to reflect on various creative processes. Included in such processes are conceptions of the very definition of documentary film and influences derived from various genres and traditions. Equally important are the filmmakers' thoughts about how they develop their ideas for documentary films, and about the sources to which they typically turn for inspiration. As far as the filmmakers who represent the new Danish documentary cinema in *The Danish Directors 3* are concerned, their practices are very much a question of redefinition of, even struggle against, the standard definition of documentary film as closely tied to traditions in journalism and to a wholly serious-minded depiction of 'the facts'. The directors have a lot at stake in developing creative strategies for telling reality-based stories or, as Eva Mulvad compellingly puts it, 'stories from life'. In each of the interviews, the interviewee was asked to think about the reasons for the success that the new Danish documentary cinema currently enjoys. The responses were remarkably convergent, with many of them pointing to skill and craftsmanship, but also to a central commitment to do justice to those 'stories from life'. We heard again and again how creative strategies are what allow the vitality and relevance of such stories to touch those who engage with the films of the new Danish documentary cinema.

A third and fourth area of interest providing focus for the discussions are those having to do with globalization and new digital technologies. Whereas the framework for Danish documentary filmmaking was once mostly national, this is no longer the case. Many of the documentary filmmakers in question have taken their cameras well beyond the borders of the nation-state of Denmark. They speak insightfully about the dynamics of a global film festival circuit, and about the nature of international distribution systems. Digital technologies have in some instances affected the very nature of cinematic authorship, inflecting it in new transnational directions (as in the case of Anders Østergaard's *Burma VJ*). And many of the interviewees evoke the need for new forms of distribution, and the potential, however unexplored at this stage, that digital technologies offer in this regard. Globalization is also relevant as an indicator of success. It is fair to say that the new Danish documentary cinema has made a mark internationally. The prizes that have been won by the films and their filmmakers are, of course, encouraging in many respects. Yet, these prizes, won with such regularity in recent years, are not merely a cause for celebration, but an opportunity to ask questions, such as: 'What are the conditions that have allowed the Danish documentary filmmaking milieu to thrive?'; 'How sustainable is the milieu in question?'; and 'Is there a model underwriting the success of this milieu; one that is potentially transferable, if only partially, to other national or sub-national contexts?'

What follows is a list of questions that illustrate the kind of thinking and research that informed the interviewers' preparation for the interviews, and indeed the interview/ practitioner exchanges themselves:

1. What are the established paths leading to a career as a documentary filmmaker in Denmark? To what extent are those paths accessible to all Danes, including aspiring filmmakers from the provinces, and from immigrant backgrounds?
2. What are the key institutions providing points of access to the profession of documentary filmmaker in Denmark? How interconnected are these different institutional sites? What is the nature of filmmakers' relation and connection to these sites once they emerge from them?
3. What are the factors that explain the relatively high number of women filmmakers in the documentary field, as compared with the relatively low number of women filmmakers in the domain of fiction filmmaking?
4. How do documentary filmmakers see the institutional field that exists as a result of government-mandated collaboration between the Danish Film Institute and the TV sector?
5. How do documentary filmmakers construe the attitudes toward risk and risk-taking of different players within the sphere of Danish documentary filmmaking?
6. How do documentary filmmakers 'manage' the bureaucratic constraints that are integral to the provision of state support?

7. What sorts of conceptions of creativity and creative processes are prevalent in the Danish documentary filmmaking milieu?

8. Following the transformation of the Danish Film Institute in 1997 and new leadership under then CEO Henning Camre, film commissioners have increasingly been drawn from the sphere of cinematic practice (compared with earlier periods when academic, and especially literary, backgrounds were the norm). What are the benefits, on an individual basis but also for the documentary milieu more generally, of documentary filmmakers being able to move between the role of practicing filmmaker and that of film commissioner; between the milieus of documentary practice and policy-making/policy implementation?

9. How have the different interviewees met the challenge of making the decision to become a documentary filmmaker personally sustainable?

10. What are the reasons motivating documentary filmmakers to establish their own filmmaking companies in the Danish context? How viable are such initiatives, and what are the decisive success factors?

11. What is the place of collaboration and networks in the context of new Danish documentary filmmaking practice? How do the relevant partnerships emerge? What do the different instances of collaboration tell us about the nature of cinematic authorship, whether generally or in a specific case?

12. How do the new Danish documentary filmmakers reason about the ethical challenges of their work? Are there specific challenges associated with the aspiration to make documentaries that are cinematic and entertaining, and thus have the potential to secure a theatrical release?

13. Danish filmmakers enjoy considerable freedom of movement beyond their national borders, and increasingly rely on this aspect of their first-world reality in their filmmaking projects. Given this, how do they prepare for filmmaking in contexts remote from those they know well? How do they reason about the deficiencies of knowledge and understanding that are likely to be a feature of their situation? What is their thinking about the ethical implications of such deficiencies?

14. Distinctions between documentary journalism and documentary proper, and between personal documentary filmmaking and documentary filmmaking focused on the purely private, are recurring elements in popular discussions of contemporary Danish documentary filmmaking. How do the practitioners themselves understand these distinctions?

While such questions reference the Danish context, their comprehensibility, as stated here, does not depend on an awareness of specific features of the Danish film and media world. Contextual knowledge is, however, a factor when interpreting the narratives that emerge from the filmmakers' responses. The aim here cannot be to provide a detailed picture of the developments that have shaped the environment within which the filmmakers operate. In what follows we offer a brief description of the landscape in question, keyed to a few suggestive examples of practitioners' reasoning about their filmmaking practices. It is our hope that this narrative, however brief, will be of use to readers who may have a strong interest in Danish documentary films, but very little knowledge of Danish film policies, among other things.

Birth of a modern Danish film culture

Around 1960, the cultural contexts of film and media underwent a number of fundamental changes in most European countries, and Denmark was no exception. In the cultural context of film, TV's emergence as the new visual mass medium was a challenge. But it was also an opportunity, for it brought new means of getting films, including documentaries, out to a much wider audience. In Denmark, as in many other European countries, television was defined as a public service medium, supported by public monies and licenses as opposed to income generated by commercials. With radio and then TV becoming the focus for cultural policy initiatives alongside the development of a modernizing welfare state, it soon became clear that film also warranted efforts along similar lines. The need for cultural policies pertaining to film was underscored by the rapid decline of the cinemas, by the fact that documentary films were no longer an integral part of a wider cinema culture, and by observations that saw these two developments as jointly posing a clear threat to the very survival of a national film culture.

In 1964, the first Film Act envisaging direct support for film production was passed. Whereas the tendency up until 1964 had been to see cinema as a form of pure, or mere, entertainment, the act in question defined film as an art form deserving support of the kind given to other art forms. There were clear implications for documentary films, which had previously been seen primarily as a vehicle for factual information. When the minister for culture, social democrat Julius Bomholt, presented the new Film Act in parliament, he said: 'The importance of the documentary film and short film as an independent art form and as one of the most important tools for enlightenment in the broadest sense of the word, has not been sufficiently recognized for many years in this country' (Bondebjerg 2012: 75). It is worth noticing the balance between art and information in this quote. On the one hand, documentary filmmaking was still tied to a demand for information about, depictions of, and reflections on a common reality. Yet, on the other hand, Bomholt's statement also links documentary film to the kind of artistic freedom that was a central feature of the Free Cinema movement in the UK, of Direct Cinema in the US, and of *cinéma vérité* in France. In this sense, his perspective is indicative of a more general tendency: with the development of a modern film culture and of new cultural policies in Europe, the documentary film moved in the direction of greater freedom of expression, and towards a wider variety of genres and ways of representing reality.

Danish film policy and film culture achieved their modern institutional form with the new Film Act of 1972. This Act established the Danish Film Institute (DFI) as the central funding body for fiction films, and the National Film Board of Denmark (Statens Film Central, SFC) as the central funding body for documentary films. These two institutions were completely separate, but their structures were quite similar, and their funding principles much the same. The key element in both cases was the commissioner system: three commissioners – two for films for adults and one for films for children – made the decisions regarding funding for individual films. The commissioners were replaced every three years, and a film director could apply for funding from another commissioner if the first one turned down an application for funding. The system has survived until today, despite recurring discussions about whether the system is too dependent on personal taste. The system has seen the gradual introduction of new support mechanisms pertaining to both fiction and documentary filmmaking. In the area of documentary filmmaking, change has been especially noticeable in the last ten years or so, with the development, for example, of co-production schemes involving TV.

In the wake of the 1972 Film Act, film policy was in many ways based on two different principles: on the one hand, the commissioner system was supposed to secure a professional production of documentary films, and also a diversity of genres and aesthetic forms; on the other hand, there was the principle of supporting grass-roots cultures and movements so as to foster a democratization of the media. As a means of supporting documentary film productions capable of enhancing a democratic use of the media, the so-called workshops were established: the Film Workshop in Copenhagen and the Video Workshop in Haderslev. Whereas the Film Workshop in Copenhagen gradually developed into a more experimental place, the workshop in Haderslev had a broader and more regional function and profile. In 1978, a Film Workshop in Aarhus was also established. The workshops produced a lot of films between 1960 and 1997 (when the system was changed), and it is clear from the interviews (in *The Danish Directors 3*, but also *The Danish Directors 2*) that the workshops provided an important institutional space for the development of new creative talents, and for the experimentations of more established directors. Many of the directors interviewed in this book have used the workshops as a platform for developing their creative talents, and a director like Torben Skjødt Jensen talks about how the workshop system effectively became his 'film school.' What is more, he points out that he has continued to use the workshop system well beyond the point of his having established himself as a filmmaker. The system, it appears, is especially hospitable to the filmmaker's work in a more experimental vein.

Film and TV: A difficult tango

In Denmark, the relationship between TV and film was problematic from the moment TV was introduced in 1951, and for at least a further fifteen years (and arguably even longer than that). In the case of documentary film, the problems did not appear to be that acute, with documentary filmmakers being far less concerned, for example, about the competition that TV represented than their colleagues who had something at stake in fiction film. Until around 1975, in-house production of documentaries at the TV stations was not especially well developed, and TV schedules thus revealed a need for the documentary films that the SFC produced (Bondebjerg 2008: 53ff). But the idea of creative collaboration between film and TV was not really developed in the period from 1960–97, and the first co-production agreement from 1969 did not amount to much. In 1988, when the new semi-public service channel TV 2 was established – bringing with it a new element of competition – the Danish Broadcasting Corporation (DR) decided to increase the volume of its in-house documentary productions. While TV 2 emphasized the commissioning of relevant works, it worked with very few companies. Initially, non-fiction programmes were produced in collaboration with Skandinavisk Filmkompagni, with Nordisk Film also becoming involved at a later stage (Bondebjerg 2008: 421f).

During the 1970s, 1980s, and 1990s there seems to be a certain distance, even hostility, between the film and TV milieus. While certain programme strands on DR and TV 2 – *DR-Dokumentar*, *Fak2eren*, and *Reportageholdet*, for example – met with success during prime-time slots and drew large numbers of viewers (Bondebjerg 2008: 383f), the independent film sector had a harder time finding an audience, whether in the cinemas or on TV. This created a tendency to stereotype on both sides: TV was seen as the place for journalistic documentary efforts dealing with important social and public issues; film was seen as the domain of subjective art documentaries that lacked the capacity to provoke debate or find an audience (Bondebjerg 2012: 11ff). The contrast and the stereotypes tended to stick, in part because the people belonging to the two production cultures rarely worked together. But the reality was much more complex and nuanced; documentary films did in fact find an audience on television, just as a number of the directors from both the older and the younger generations actually worked in TV, although not so much in the relevant documentary departments. The Children & Youth Department at DR established a reputation as an especially creative and innovative place as early as the 1970s, and many of the documentary film directors interviewed for *The Danish Directors 3* have worked there. The same goes for DR's Radio Documentary Department. A director like Mads Brügger developed his very personal style as a documentary film director through his work for DR's Children & Youth Department, and also through his involvement with DR's Radio Documentary Department. Dorte Høeg Brask and Max Kestner are other examples of directors who spent their formative years working for DR's Children & Youth Department. For Brask, this led to a keen interest in creating documentaries for children, both as a director and currently as a film commissioner at the DFI. Kestner was at the relevant department in the late 1990s, and developed elements of his poetic-ironic style while there.

Reasons for film and TV having developed as almost separate cultures during certain periods can be found in the structural characteristics of documentary film production in Denmark up until around 1990. With the introduction of a conception of documentary film as art around 1964, documentary filmmakers saw themselves as essentially freed from the task of delivering commissioned works to a range of public or private institutions, and from the demands of purely factual information. At the same time, filmmakers felt little or no inclination to join the TV sector, for in those days TV was widely seen as a very journalistically oriented field. The introduction of government support for documentary films led to the creation of new production companies with a new agenda for documentary filmmaking. At the same time, older, already established companies oriented themselves in new directions. These companies did at times cooperate with TV, but what is clear is that neither the film producers nor the directors wanted the TV stations to have too much of a say. This was true for both the formal properties of the films, and for their topics. Some of the large, traditional production companies – Minerva Film, Teknisk Film Co., and Laterna Film, for example – did manage to develop a comprehensive independent profile, and for a while at least their activities offered a framework for a range of different types of documentary projects. Yet, it was the small- and medium-size companies that dominated the scene, and their working conditions involved very little security. They essentially managed one production at a time, and none of them had anything resembling a stable, income-generating connection to the TV milieu.

Documentary film directors did not see TV as a medium giving them the kind of freedom that the new Film Act of 1972 had promised. Meanwhile, TV was seen as the new master replacing those private and public institutions that had once paid for the films and imposed limiting criteria on their form and content. Henning Carlsen provides a good example of how changes leading towards a more independent documentary film culture in the 1960s played out. Carlsen started his career at Minerva, one of the biggest production companies, where he made industrial films and informational films aimed at housewives. Inspired by the French *cinéma vérité* movement, Carlsen went on to develop a number of observational films about life in Denmark (*Familiebilleder* [*Family Portraits*, 1964] and *Ung* [*Young*, 1965]), and these in turn prompted him to establish his own film company. The point of creating Henning Carlsen Film, quite simply, was to be able to exercise artistic control over the documentary filmmaking process.

The new forms of public support for documentary film from 1964 onwards can thus be seen as having created a new dynamic, and the basis for a degree of independence for documentary filmmakers. But the economics of all this involved considerable vulnerability in spite of the combination of public support and private funding. What is more, in those instances where TV was part of the financing mix, the stations inevitably failed to deliver as much as the companies had hoped for. For the most part, TV put money into in-house productions up until 1997. Even with the creation of TV 2 in 1988, a station that was not authorized to engage in in-house productions, expectations in the independent film sector proved to be much too high. Many medium-size companies like Film & Lyd, Hanne Høyberg Film, and Ebbe Preisler Film got very few TV contracts because the lion's share of the money went to only one company, Skandinavisk Film Kompagni. TV 2 wanted production security above all else, and not a series of products coming from a wide range of different companies. From 1997 onwards, co-production agreements were developed to a significant degree, and collaboration between the film and TV sectors on various projects became prevalent. What is more, new companies were established, some of them with both a unit focusing on TV productions on an ongoing basis, and a unit devoted to more independent film productions. Cosmo Doc (1994–), Koncern TV & Film (1998–), Easy Film (1995–), Barok Film (2001–), Final Cut (1995–), and Bastard Film (2004–) are just some of the most successful examples.

Institutional changes and globalization

The relationship between film and TV had changed fundamentally by the end of the 1990s, although some of the old conflicts and mentalities lingered on. The change in question is linked to the emergence of what we might call a new Danish film culture, and was clearly expressed in various institutional innovations. An example is the decision made in 1996 by the National Film School of Denmark to establish a Documentary & TV Department, the aim being to train, educate, and cultivate documentary film directors and producers. The launch of the Department's programmes effectively created the conditions for a new merging of cultural forms previously associated with either film or TV. Inasmuch as the TV documentary – in its earlier incarnations – had been shelved by both DR and TV 2 by around 2000 (Bondebjerg 2008: 363f), practitioners with a commitment to documentary filmmaking as art discovered an open space hospitable to their practices, and to expanded efforts on their part. In his foreword to the first annual report on the Department's new programmes, the Head, Arne Bro, outlined the contours of a new and open type of documentary that clearly challenged the traits of a then still dominant made-for-TV type of journalistic documentary:

> The documentary works with what is self-contradictory, unpredictable, and hard to define, and this in the context of dynamic, complex situations. It is attuned to the full constellation of character traits that human beings bring to these situations […]. [T]he documentary takes its formal and expressive forms from fiction and from the inbuilt tendency in fiction to defend subjectivity as the essential, communicative concept.
>
> (Arne Bro 1997, quoted in Bondebjerg 2012: 115)

A programmatic statement like this might appear to be at odds with the sorts of tests that TV stations administer with an eye to ensuring respect for the norms of journalism and a commitment to factuality. Yet many of the most successful directors in the new Danish documentary culture, spanning the spheres of independent filmmaking and TV production, have been taught and/or mentored by Arne Bro, and profoundly influenced by the ethos of the new documentary film education offered by the Film School.

Directors like Eva Mulvad, Phie Ambo, Sami Saif, Max Kestner, and Michael Noer are all graduates, not only of the Film School, but of the specific department in question. What is more, they have consistently demonstrated a striking ability to produce innovative and effective films and programmes for TV, but also more independent films that evidence precisely the kind of expressive freedom and formal explorations to which Bro's various pronouncements over the years point.[4] Articulating his own philosophy of documentary filmmaking, director Max Kestner effectively gestures towards the philosophy of the School's Documentary & TV Department: 'We don't recount reality. We tell stories about it. Reality isn't itself a story. It's endless, so a lot choices about inclusion and especially exclusion have to be made in order to tell a story. And those choices require something as complicated and sophisticated as awareness' (Kestner 2005). Eva Mulvad makes a similar point: 'I felt it was important to be able to say: "I'm not doing journalism. I'm doing reality filtered through a gaze." Generally speaking I feel more inspired by fiction than journalism' (this volume). And Anne Wivel's comments provide the larger historical context for these younger filmmakers' remarks:

> My view was that since reality – and all the material it has to offer – can be grasped, interpreted, and filmed in such endlessly different ways, there was no reason why the Film School shouldn't relate to it in a thoughtful and considered way. [...] So I and a number of like-minded friends – including Arne Bro, who was my partner for many years – came up with the idea of establishing an entire programme devoted to documentary film [...]. So many of the developments and tendencies that are current today are exactly what Arne and I hoped for [...]. If you look at the younger generation of Danish documentary filmmakers, many of whom are enjoying a lot of success these days, it's clear that this refusal to trace a boundary between fiction and non-fiction filmmaking comes very naturally to them. They're very proud to be making documentaries that have a strong narrative drive, and that draw on visual styles resembling those of fiction films. I think that's just wonderful.
>
> (this volume)

This underlining of subjectivity, or at least expressive freedom, with reference to reality-based stories is not at odds with the goal of making powerful films with agenda-setting qualities. Films by Eva Mulvad provide evidence in support of such a claim, as does the work of Christoffer Guldbrandsen (who is not actually a graduate of the Film School, but was trained as a journalist, both in Denmark and abroad). In her TV documentary *Den sidste dans* (*The Last Dance*, 2005) Eva Mulvad combines an observational portrait of old age with a visual language that is highly expressive and symbolic. In her more international, political documentary *Enemies of Happiness* (2006), concerning Malalai Joya, the first female politician to be elected in Afghanistan, Mulvad uses landscapes and music in a very dynamic way. Christoffer Guldbrandsen has made several political documentaries, including *Præsidenten* (*The President*, 2011), which deals with the election of the European Union's first president in 2009. In this documentary work, elements of drama and comedy are combined to great effect, with a very precise documentation of political processes. We thus note that documentary filmmakers with a background in journalism or related academic fields have also responded to the opportunities afforded by an environment more conducive to the documentary's exploration of an expressive cinematic language. Janus Metz, who specialized in Communications and International Development Studies at Roskilde University, is a good example here. Focusing on Denmark's military involvement in Afghanistan, Metz' *Armadillo* (2010) played a significant role in the Danish public sphere. *Armadillo* was the first film to effect the Danish public's engagement with the realities of Denmark as a warring nation. The film's role in the context of public debate is without a doubt linked to its dual source of inspiration: observational cinema and the well-established American tradition for independent war movies.

The above-mentioned films were all made with a mix of support from the DFI and either DR or TV 2, and also, in some cases, with money from ministries or private companies. The Danish sources of funding for Mulvad's *Enemies of Happiness* were the DFI and DR, DANIDA, and the Ministry of Education; Guldbrandsen's *The President* was supported by the DFI, DR, and the Ministry of Education; while Metz' *Armadillo* was financed by the DFI and TV 2. At the same time, it is important to note that one of the salient traits of the new Danish documentary cinema is its tendency to rely on both Scandinavian and European co-production and co-distribution agreements. Such agreements are crucial, in terms of the films' intrinsic properties, but also the works' impact beyond Denmark, and through this, paradoxically enough, within Denmark. More specifically, the regional and European dimensions of the relevant processes help to secure higher production values, as well as significantly enhanced visibility for the films by means of a more internationally oriented system of distribution. The films by Mulvad, Guldbrandsen, and Metz that serve as examples here also received funding from the Nordic Film & TV Fond, and from Nordic public service broadcasters such as NRK, YLE, and SVT. Also, *Armadillo* managed to get further European support from ZDF/Arte. There is a clear trend, starting around 1997, for Danish documentary films to involve a much higher degree of international co-production activity, and inclusion in a far more global distribution network. The complexities in question are clearly evident in the work of Anders Østergaard, especially such films as *Tintin og mig* (*Tintin and I*, 2004) and *Burma VJ* (2008). Providing a complex, poetic portrait of Hergé, the first of these films has one of the most diverse co-production profiles of any of the films belonging to the new Danish documentary cinema category. France 2 and 5, DR, SVT, YLE, NRK, DFI, TV Suisse, EURIMAGES, MEDIA, NFTF, Centre National de la Cinématographie, the Flemish Film Fund, and Ciné Tirol were among the many financial partners for this film. What is more, the 'reach' of the film's financing is mirrored in the film's pattern of international distribution. *Burma VJ*, which was less expensive than *Tintin and I*, nonetheless involved co-financing by the DFI, DR, DANIDA and British Channel 4. While the financing of this film may have been less international, the unique transnational, collaborative dimension of its production history, not to mention the global significance of its topic – the Saffron Revolution in Burma – combined to make the film the most widely distributed Danish documentary in the entire history of Danish documentary film. *Burma VJ* is widely available on DVD, has been shown at numerous international festivals, and broadcast by TV stations around the world. The film has won 35 international prizes, and clearly exemplifies the interest shared by many of the new Danish documentary filmmakers in engaging with realities embedded in parts of the world that are geographically remote, yet proximate in terms of their implications for an increasingly interconnected world.

The new Danish documentary cinema finds its conditions of possibility in educational innovations, in enhanced professionalization of the relevant sectors, in growing collaboration between these sectors, and in more internationally oriented practices in the areas of funding and distribution. References to the various Film Acts have helped to signal high-impact institutional changes underpinning some of these developments. Even in the context of what can only be a summary, introductory narrative, some of these institutional elements deserve more than a mere passing mention.

The 1997 Film Act called for the creation of a new Danish Film Institute that would incorporate within one integrated institution the following three previously autonomous entities: the Danish Film Institute (specializing in fiction film up until 1997); the National Film Board of Denmark (SFC, specializing in documentary film up until 1997); and the Danish Film Museum. The newly established institution retained the name of the first of the autonomous bodies mentioned above: the Danish Film Institute. The main reasons for amalgamating these institutions were reflected in various cultural arguments made in the context of the 1997 Film Act. Emphasis was placed on professionalization and efficiency in the delivery of support at the national level, but also on developing a national film and media culture that would be well equipped to take advantage of opportunities arising from enhanced cooperation at the European level, and capable of contending with growing competition on a global scale. In the account of cultural policy work provided by the government to parliament at a time coinciding with the introduction of the 1997 Film Act (*Regeringens redegørelse til Folketinget om kulturpolitik*, November 4, 1997), a key theme was the need to strengthen Danish film culture domestically and in relation to growing international challenges. Moreover, cultural policy statements made around this time reflected an acute awareness of developments in the area of digital technology. Indeed, they called for an exploration of possibilities for convergence between the media and cultural sectors as a means of creating synergy, sustainability, and growth. Although the basic logic informing a national, cultural policy is intimately linked to support for national culture, politicians and policymakers were operating with a clear understanding of what was at stake in the establishing of a European and international presence, among other things, through collaboration.

Some fifteen years later, the situation is much changed; international financing is now commonplace, and Danish documentary filmmaking has a well-established profile and track record, both nationally and internationally. These factors bring direct benefits for directors, who are able to work with larger budgets and can reasonably aspire to reach larger audiences than was once the case. Yet, the changed terrain on which the new Danish documentary filmmaker works also requires new skills and commitments. Several of the directors interviewed in *The Danish Directors 3* foreground the need to develop a talent for pitching projects at international financing events and festivals, as well as a skill for communicating their ideas for films in efficient and persuasive ways. The production company known as Danish Documentary Production provides one example of how documentary filmmakers are responding to the challenges in question. Danish Documentary Production consists of four directors who have teamed up with producer Sigrid Dyekjær with an eye to helping each other creatively. The idea is to be able to pitch several projects simultaneously as team members travel to, and speak at, various forums. The point, in short, is to help each other get projects off the ground in a field that can no longer be construed as purely national.

New platforms – new forms of production

The new DFI and 1997 Film Act called for more synergy and collaboration between sectors and institutions, partly with reference to digital and global developments. Two initiatives point to an increased awareness of the implications of digital platforms for both production and distribution: 1) computer games and other digital genres became an integral part of the support system; and 2) the interrelated goals of getting various productions into the DFI's archives, and of facilitating the public's access to feature films (especially documentaries), led to the digital streaming initiative known as 'Filmstriben' in 2007. Whereas documentaries and other films had previously been distributed on video through public libraries, the public distribution of films became digital with Filmstriben. Films were now streamed, with the libraries functioning as the official portal to this service. Another example of a growing awareness of the significance of new digital platforms and production formats is 'Doxwise', a collaborative project involving Bombay Film, the DFI, and, eventually, the daily newspaper *Politiken*. The aim with Doxwise was to create an online youth documentary via MySpace. The result was a kind of video diary with four young people reporting on their own lives within the context of an interactive website.

It is worth noting that the international distribution of Danish documentaries remains something of a challenge, although practitioners are exploring various approaches. Thus, for example, the impetus for the creation of the now successful production company Danish Documentary Production was actually problems relating to distribution, as experienced by its founding filmmakers. The aim was to create a platform that would help to make the directors' films more readily available to international audiences. Many of the directors in *The Danish Directors 3* address themselves to problems relating to distribution, and to the issue of who exactly owns the rights to distribute specific titles on various platforms. In addition to the matter of rights, there's the issue of interest or commitment: producers and directors, it turns out, may have varying degrees of interest in vigorously pursuing a documentary film's wider, and more international, distribution. Since the potential profits are often quite limited, many directors find that they themselves need to drive the process of getting their films to audiences, whether by distributing the films themselves or by devoting a substantial amount of time to travelling with them. Artist/filmmaker Simone Aabærg Kærn is especially eloquent on this point, with reference to her experiences with *Smiling in a Warzone: The Art of Flying to Kabul* (2006).

In 1998, the new DFI (led by then CEO Henning Camre, in partnership with a board chaired by Ib Bondebjerg) launched the first of a series of four-year plans. In that same year, government support for film production was doubled, both for feature films and documentary films. The discourse focusing on the need to strengthen Danish film culture with reference to global developments was thus backed up by action and increased economic powers. A significantly changed economic environment must thus be seen as a key factor that helps to explain not only the increase in the number of documentary films being made from 1998 onwards, but also the success of these films. Critical mass, quite simply, has had very significant implications for the milieu in question. What is more, the budget for film production was further increased by new collaborative arrangements involving the film and TV sectors, and through intensified efforts on the international co-production front. Since 2000, the number of documentary films being produced on an annual basis has been somewhere between 40 and 45. The public's interest in these films is being nurtured in various ways, as part of a concerted effort on the part of various institutions to engage in audience building. In 2003, for example, the DFI used some of its resources to launch most new documentaries on DVD, with copies of the films being sent to schools and libraries. The films could also been seen in the DFI Videotheque, and, from 2007 onwards, on Filmstriben. However, the DFI only holds those rights that pertain to the non-commercial market. Some documentary films do end up being released on DVD on a commercial basis, but it is clear that this possibility is one that many directors would like to see emphasized more. Producers and directors, it would appear, have not always seen eye to eye on precisely this point.

In Denmark, documentary films rarely become box office hits in the cinemas, and so the audiences for these works must be reached through TV or by means of digital platforms. At the same time, the fact that a number of documentaries have achieved great success in the cinemas has had implications for the filmmakers' aspirations, and thus also, it could be argued, for some of their decision-making regarding form and content. Examples of successes that have helped to transform shared understandings of what is possible in the domain of documentary filmmaking are Anders Østergaard's *Gasolin'* (2006) and Janus Metz's *Armadillo* (2010). *Gasolin'* sold 250,000 tickets at the Danish box office, and *Armadillo* sold 150,000 tickets; Metz's film reached a further one million viewers through TV. The growing interest in documentaries amongst cinemagoers no doubt reflects the enhanced overall quality of the films, as well as the increase in the number of films being produced. Yet the figures being reported by the cinemas have also been bolstered by the profile and success of a key festival initiative, CPH:DOX, and by an equally significant initiative launched by the cinemas, DOXBIO. Based in Copenhagen and established in 2003, CPH:DOX is an international film festival devoted to documentary films. Within less than a decade, CPH:DOX has emerged as one of the major European festivals for documentary film. The fact that it was possible to create this recurring event, and to turn it into the both local and international success that it has become, has without a doubt helped to fuel interest in the new Danish documentary cinema on a worldwide basis. DOXBIO is a kind of national film club devoted to documentary film, with six documentaries (both Danish and foreign) premiering in the cinemas annually. DOXBIO has also helped to bring documentary films into the cinemas, and, just as importantly, into those that are not located in the greater Copenhagen area. The initiative plays an especially crucial role in the less urban areas, where it helps to ensure that selected films reach the many small cinemas that exist throughout the country.

Another important part of the story about the various ways in which the new Danish documentary cinema is thriving has to do with changes in the TV sector. More specifically, this sector now demonstrates a deeper commitment to documentary film, and a growing awareness of the need to support new talent. The result is that efforts along these lines are now linked to goals that are no longer sector- or milieu-specific. Established in 2003, the high-impact support scheme known as 'New Danish Screen' is, for example, based on collaboration between the DFI, DR, and TV 2. Government support totalling 100 million Danish crowns was disbursed through the DFI and the two TV stations from 2003–06; the DFI was responsible for identifying recipients for 70% of this amount, and the two TV stations the projects to be supported with the remaining 30% of the monies. New Danish Screen provides a mechanism and context for supporting talented professional filmmakers. In this sense, the Workshops (in Copenhagen and Haderslev), both of which have a clear pre-professional dimension, retain their traditional functions within a larger system. The links being built between film and TV, and the opportunities being created for professionally trained graduates from the Film School, provide evidence of attempts within the system as a whole to remove barriers between different production cultures. Intensified collaboration between film and TV has had the effect of increasing co-production activity within the context of the commissioner-based system for film support, and has led to a number of large, thematically defined co-production projects.

In *The Danish Directors 3*, Dola Bonfils talks about her experience as a film commissioner in the post-2004 period, when collaboration with TV was considerably intensified. Bonfils was part of the large ten-film project involving the DFI and DR called 'Magtens billeder' ('Pictures of Power', 2004). She recalls the experience as having been quite problematic, inasmuch as the absence of a shared language and culture made decision-making difficult. As she sees it, the difficulties point to a still vigorous age-old conflict between journalistic, and more properly cinematic, conceptions of the documentary genre. Yet it is perhaps telling that Dola Bonfils and Anders Østergaard nonetheless were able to make films consistent with their artistic visions within the context of this large-scale project. An experiment involving the film milieu and TV 2, 'Follow the Money,' helps to evoke the range of types of co-production activity. The intention with 'Follow the Money' was to create a new kind of business documentary by getting a journalist and a more experimental film director to join forces. The project seems to be assessed very differently, depending on whether people from the film industry or from TV 2 are asked to pronounce on it. TV 2 was dissatisfied with the number of viewers that the films attracted, having perhaps expected higher numbers, as the focus was very much on scandals and well-known charismatic people from the field of business.

A number of directors in *The Danish Directors 3* speak to the issue of whether it is a good idea for commissioners to initiate collective projects such as these, the thought being that investing in projects of a more director-driven nature might ultimately make better sense. The point is that aspects of the current funding schemes are somewhat contentious. At the same time, what emerges from the various interviews is an apparent consensus regarding the existence of unique support for documentary filmmaking in Denmark. Filmmakers see themselves as being able to produce work based on ideas that would be unlikely to prevail in a purely market-driven film culture. While disagreement regarding specific decisions made by individual commissioners is inevitable, the commissioners' scheme is identified as one of the central pillars underpinning the production of documentary films that are formally innovative and consistent with an understanding of film as art. Some of the interviewees do, however, foreground the dangers of a further professionalization of the system. These directors would like to see a system that remains somewhat hospitable to fragile ideas conceived during the early stages of a creative process, when defining the core of the film is still a matter of exploration. Emphasis on a great deal of elaboration and documentation, they point out, can be counter-productive, inasmuch as it thwarts rather than promotes creativity.

Going global

Co-production activity on an international level, global distribution, and projects defined by a global agenda have all had a decisive impact on the individual filmmakers whose films collectively define the contours of a new Danish documentary cinema. The four films in the DR/DFI project 'Cities on Speed' (2009) were primarily funded by Danish sources, yet their themes are global inasmuch as the focus is on problems arising in the context of four of the world's mega cities (Cairo, Mumbai, Shanghai, and Bogotá). Projects like 'Why Democracy?' (2009) and 'Why Poverty?' (2012) are also examples of global projects with global themes, both of them involving traditional modes of circulation, but also an innovative use of the Internet and digital resources. The first project was spearheaded by Mette Hoffmann Meyer at DR in collaboration with the BBC, ARTE, ZDF, YLE, and the non-profit organization Steps International (Hjort 2009). The project encompasses ten documentaries by ten directors from very different countries, as well as a number of short fiction films, and an interactive web page. Taking into account the reality of the digital divide, with some groups unable to access the Internet, the people driving the project have worked hard to develop outreach initiatives that take the films to some of the more remote parts of the developing world. Launched by 70 broadcasters around the world in 2012, 'Why Poverty?' relies on many of the same strategies that underpin 'Why Democracy?', but shifts the focus of attention to the global issue of poverty. While major collective projects such as these are designed to garner attention on an international scale, some of the most popular Danish documentary films in recent years have been stand-alone films by individual directors. Yet, these films have not only required an openness to realities well beyond Denmark, but have in many ways helped to underscore the extent to which the realities with which documentary filmmakers might wish to engage are shaped by the intricacies of global networks and alliances, and by forces from well beyond the boundaries of the nation state.

Danish directors have taken their cameras to a significant number of countries around the world, at times to document unfolding political realities with wider implications (as in Eva Mulvad's *Enemies of Happiness*). In other cases, the emphasis has been not so much on politics, but on more personal life stories. In Eva Mulvad's *The Good Life* (2010), for example, viewers are given insight into the values and decision-making of a mother and daughter, both of them Danish women living as once affluent and now impoverished expatriates in Portugal. The point of such a film is to ask crucial questions, most importantly perhaps: 'What does it mean to raise a child well?' Evoking much wider issues regarding wealth and poverty, the film offers a good example of how the best of the new Danish documentary filmmakers are managing to explore issues with universal relevance, and in ways that are at once highly cinematic and engaging. In some instances, the questions being explored are pursued across a range of persons and contexts, as for example, in *Mechanical Love* (Phie Ambo, 2007), which asks whether it's possible to love a robot. A similar approach is adopted in *Love Addict* (Pernille Rose Grønkjær, 2011), which looks at the phenomenon of love addiction in the United States.

While an engagement with realities that are anything but local or national is a feature of the new Danish documentary cinema, many of the filmmakers continue to deal with Danish realities. Yet the nature of the stories being told is different from those developed several decades ago; Danes now live their lives in a society that is increasingly multicultural, and with a growing awareness of the dynamics of various globalizations. Anne Wivel's portrait of her husband, former leader of the Social Democratic party Svend Auken (*Svend*, 2011), cannot be described as a depiction of a purely national figure, for the environmental issues about which he was so passionate throughout his political career are now truly matters of global concern. The shift from a more local/national framework to a more transnational/international/global one is nicely encapsulated in a recent instance of the remake phenomenon. In 2003, Jørgen Leth's documentary classic *Det perfekte menneske* (*The Perfect Human*, 1967) was remade, through a series of collaborative/obstructive sparrings with Lars von Trier, as *The Five Obstructions* (2003). Whereas the first film can be described as Danish in a variety of ways, the remakes that are constitutive of *The Five Obstructions* were shot in Belgium, Cuba, and India. What we have here is a kind of global meta-film, but also a reminder that the cool reality of the 1960s Danish welfare state is no more.

The Danish Directors 3 brings the voices of nineteen directors into play. Were it not for the inevitable constraints of time and space, many other voices would have been included, for directors such as Andreas Koefoed, Mira Jargil, Christian Sønderby Jepsen, and Christoffer Guldbrandsen are all producing remarkable films. In this sense, *The Danish Directors 3* should be seen as anything but exhaustive. The voices included here are varied and distinctive, and articulate a range of approaches. At the same time, they bring to light certain threads, continuities, synergies, and patterns. The interviews provide a picture, however incomplete, of the documentary filmmaking milieu in Denmark more than ten years into the new millennium. The hope is that this picture will have many roles to play. The documentary filmmaking milieu in Denmark is one that is thriving. To provide a portrait of that milieu is, at least as we see, it, to acknowledge the achievements of the practitioners in question, but also to create something of a cultural resource. It is our hope that *The Danish Directors 3* will provide inspiration in contexts where the reality of being a documentary filmmaker still falls short of certain aspirations, and where arguments are needed to persuade policy-makers to provide greater levels of support for independent documentary filmmaking.[5] In this sense, *The Danish Directors 3*, like the films it is about, is shaped by perspectives that extend well beyond the merely national.

References

Alter, Nora M. (2002), *Projecting History: German Nonfiction Cinema, 1967–2000*, Ann Arbor, MI: University of Michigan Press.

Baker, Maxine (2005), *Documentary in the Digital Age*, Oxford: Focal Press/Elsevier.

Barnouw, Erik (1974), *Documentary: A History of the Non-Fiction Film*, Oxford: Oxford University Press.

Barsam, Richard M. (1992), *Non-Fiction Film: A Critical History*, Bloomington, IN: Indiana University Press. First published 1973.

Bondebjerg, Ib (2008), *Virkelighedens fortællinger. Den danske tv-dokumentarismes historie*, Frederiksberg: Forlaget Samfundslitteratur.

——— (2012), *Virkelighedsbilleder. Den moderne danske dokumentarfilm*, Frederiksberg: Forlaget Samfundslitteratur.

Brinch, Sara and Iversen, Gunnar (2001), *Virkelighetsbilder. Norsk dokumentarfilm gjenom hundre år*, Oslo: Universitetsforlaget.

Carroll, Noël (1997), 'Fiction, Non-fiction, and the Film of Presumptive Assertion: A Conceptual Analysis', in Richard Allen and Murray Smith (eds), *Film Theory and Philosophy*, Oxford: Oxford University Press, pp. 173–202.

Chapman, Jane (2007), *Documentary in Practice: Filmmakers and Production Choices*, London: Polity Press.

Ellis, Jack C. and McLane, Betsy A. (2005), *A New History of Documentary Film*, New York: Continuum.

Fontana, Andrea and Frey, James H. (1994), 'Interviewing: The Art of Science', in Norman K. Denzin (ed.), *The Handbook of Qualitative Research*, Thousand Oaks, CA: Sage Publications, pp. 361–76.

Hjort, Mette (2005), *Small Nation, Global Cinema*, Minneapolis, MN: University of Minnesota Press.

——— (2009), 'Living with diversity: What difference can film-making make?', *Northern Lights*, 7, pp. 9–27.

——— (2010), *Lone Scherfig's 'Italian for Beginners'*, Seattle & Copenhagen: University of Washington Press & Museum Tusculanum.

——— (ed.) (2013a), *The Education of the Filmmaker in Africa, the Middle East, and the Americas*, New York: Palgrave Macmillan.

——— (ed.) (2013b), *The Education of the Filmmaker in Europe, Australia, and Asia*, New York: Palgrave Macmillan.

Kestner, Max (2005), 'Jeg er en af dem, der tror, at sandheden er min', *Ekko*, 28, http://www.ekkofilm. dk/artikler/jeg-er-en-af-dem-der-tror-at-sandheden-er-min/, accessed June 14, 2013.

Plantinga, Carl R. (1997), *Rhetoric and Representation in Nonfiction Film*, Cambridge: Cambridge University Press.

——— (2005), 'What a Documentary Is, After All', *Journal of Aesthetics and Art Criticism*, 63: 2, pp. 105–17.

Ponech, Trevor (1997), 'What is Non-fiction Cinema?', in Richard Allen and Murray Smith (eds), *Film Theory and Philosophy*, Oxford: Oxford University Press, pp. 203–20.

Rabiger, Michael (2009), *Directing the Documentary*, Oxford: Elsevier.

Stubbs, Liz (2002), *Documentary Filmmakers Speak*, New York: Allworth Press.

Notes

1   *The Education of the Filmmaker in Europe, Australia and Asia* and *The Education of the Filmmaker in Africa, the Middle East, and the Americas*, edited by Mette Hjort, offer a global, comparative context for understanding the significance of the specific programmes developed by the National Film School of Denmark.

2   Another collective initiative undertaken with a similar aim in mind is the Nordic Film Classics series, published by the University of Washington Press and Museum Tusculanum. 'Practitioner's agency' is a key pillar for this series, with authors contributing to it being encouraged to undertake empirical work on cinematic authorship. Practitioner interviews conducted with clear research questions in mind are central to the envisaged approach, offering data that clarifies the central features of individual oeuvres, group styles, and national traditions, but also the extent to which conceptions of cinematic authorship developed on a more abstract and speculative basis – without any engagement with actual milieus of practice – are cogent.

3   Michael Rabiger's *Directing the Documentary* (Oxford: Elsevier, 2009) is also very helpful in the context of a discussion of the agency of documentary practitioners.

4   See Hjort's chapter in *The Education of the Filmmaker in Africa, the Middle East, and the Americas* for an account of the language used to describe 'one (wo)man' filmmaking assignments in the Middle East, required of students halfway through their programmes.

5   One such context is that of post-handover Hong Kong.

Chapter 1

Phie Ambo

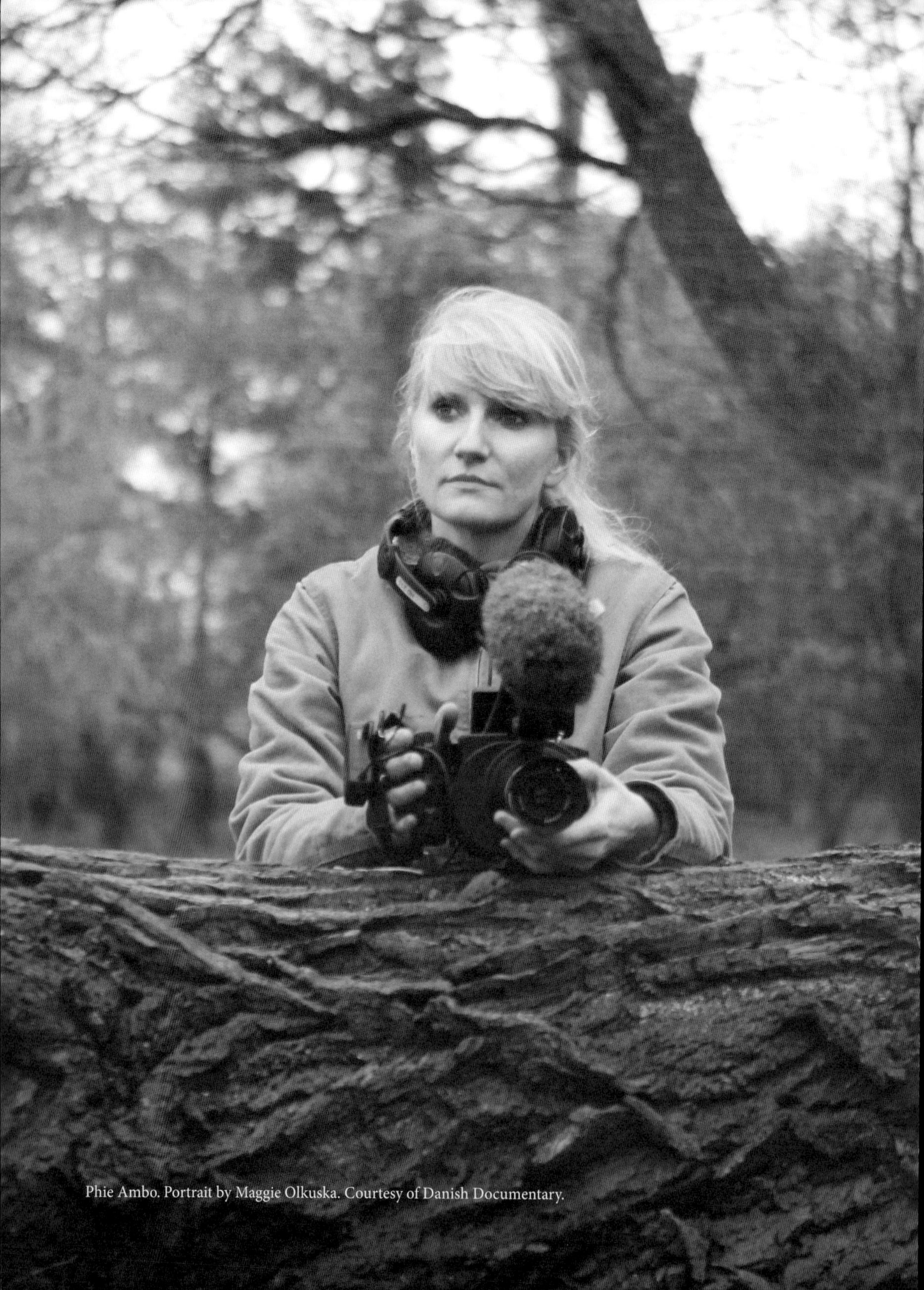

Phie Ambo. Portrait by Maggie Olkuska. Courtesy of Danish Documentary.

Born 1973. Phie Ambo holds a BA in Nordic Philology from the University of Copenhagen. She was subsequently trained at the National Film School of Denmark, graduating as a documentary film director in 2003. Phie Ambo released her first documentary film, entitled *Family* (2001), while still in film school. Co-directed with Sami Saif, *Family* won the prestigious Joris Ivens Award at the International Documentary Film Festival Amsterdam (IDFA). The film follows Saif's trip to the Middle East in search of his father. Like most of Ambo's films, *Family* was shot in CinemaScope. At the same time, however, the film has much of the intimacy of a documentary diary film. *Family* was one of the first Danish documentaries to achieve a noteworthy theatrical release. Having graduated from film school, Ambo made *Gambler* (2005), a thought-provoking account of Nicolas Winding Refn's efforts, against all odds, to complete *Pusher 2* (2004) and *Pusher 3* (2005). *Gambler* looks closely at the creative process of Refn's filmmaking, while also documenting the many economic battles in which the director was involved during the production of the second and third films in his trilogy. Ambo's more recent films include *Hjemmefronten – fjenden bag hækken* (*The Home Front*, 2010), which looks at the hostility that exists between neighbours who share hedges in suburban Denmark; and *Fever* (2010), a documentary short about the artist Julie Nord. In recent years, Ambo has been especially interested in pursuing work of a more thematic nature, and this in the form of a trilogy focusing on big existential issues. In *Mechanical Love* (2007), which travelled widely on the international festival circuit, Ambo explored the relationship between human beings and robots, and the nature of emotion itself. Released in 2012, *Free the Mind* deals with the impact that thoughts have on both the mind and the body. The last film in the trilogy, *Ripples at the Shore*, is about consciousness, and is scheduled for release in 2014. Ambo is also working on a film called *Kongens Foged* ('The Bailiff'), which takes a close look at the social system that shapes Danish realities. Phie Ambo co-owns the production company Danish Documentary with directors Pernille Rose Grønkjær, Mikala Krogh, and Eva Mulvad, and producer Sigrid Dyekjær.

Documentary features:

2014   *Bondemand Niels* ('Farmer Niels')
2014   *Ripples at the Shore* (working title)
2012   *Kongens Foged* ('The Bailiff')
2012   *Free the Mind*
2010   *Fever – En film om Julie Nord* (*Fever: A Film about Julie Nord*)
2007   *Mechanical Love*
2005   *Gambler*
2003   *The Diver Inside Me* (diploma film)
2002   *Growing Up in a Day*
2001   *Family* (with Sami Saif)

Television:

2010   *Hjemmefronten – Fjenden bag hækken* (*The Home Front*, TV 2)

REDVALL: How did you end up becoming a documentary filmmaker?

AMBO: I'm not one of these people who always wanted to make films. I have a BA in Nordic Philology, but already during my years as a student I started to realize that I had a strong desire to tell stories based on reality. However, I wasn't at all interested in journalistic stories. I wanted my own voice to be included because I was really tired of not being allowed to say 'I' at university. I had a strong need to tell a story that was bloody well told by *me*! I was eager to put myself on the line, and to tell a story that didn't involve all sorts of references to the work of others. But the question was, 'Where could I do that?'

I'd spent some time in New York, where I'd worked in a restaurant so as to save up for a camera. And what happened when I got it was that I became fascinated by the process of looking through the lens of a camera, where you select the reality you want. You choose to include certain things in the frame, and to exclude others. It's a particular way of understanding the world around us. I've never been interested in fiction. What interests me is the chaos of reality. I used the camera to unlock a kind of code, and what I experienced was that what I excluded from the frame, what my gaze opted not to include, could actually be more important than what was in the frame. I became really fascinated by that, but I still hadn't figured out where I could go with these ideas, where I could develop them. But then someone suggested that I go and see the graduation films from the National Film School's Documentary & TV programme, and that's when I realized what it was I wanted to do. So I actually applied to the Film School without having made a single film.

REDVALL: Why do you think you got in without having made a single film?

AMBO: The head of the programme, Arne Bro, has an eye for quirkiness. He's good at seeing right through whatever it is you think you're projecting. Looking back, I now see that I applied on the basis of a very tough and confrontational piece of creative work, which was probably the sort of thing the School was looking for. What I sent along was an unedited ten-minute sequence documenting a conversation with my father about how he was dying. It was clearly handheld, there was no editing, and it was just on VHS. So what was clear was that I had a certain drive, but also that I didn't know anything about how to make a film. I remember thinking that, if I was going to spend four years of my life at that school, it had to be the sort of place that could accommodate all that. I was really tired of being moulded. And I wanted to be fully in the picture myself, so I really put everything I had into that application. Talking to someone who's dying is a pretty awful thing to do, but I just wasn't going to hold back. And then I got in, and it was such a relief to feel that someone had sensed that there was a kind of expressive form, an expressive language, somewhere in that rough and rather in-your-face material.

REDVALL: Arne Bro appears to be someone who's very important to you, but also to a lot of other documentary filmmakers from your generation. Why is that?

AMBO: Arne has absolutely no artistic scruples. He has no fixed ideas about what can and can't be art. So as a result he's very good at liberating a language. He's extremely psycho-dynamic in his approach, and that can be insanely exhausting. Sometimes it was really too much. I feel there was too much psychology and not enough technique, but the good thing is that you end up discovering what it is, deep inside you, that actually drives the storytelling. There's not a lot of emphasis on making films that look like films. Instead you're taught to focus on finding those films that are going to allow you to say what you want to say, and then the cinematic language just has to adapt. That's the most important thing you learn from his method. You learn to feel that the cinematic language can be adjusted because, after all, it's the language that has to match what you're trying to say, and not the other way around.

REDVALL: You made your first film, which turned out to be a very important one, while you were still in film school. What were your years at the National Film School like?

AMBO: It was hard being in film school. Initially you just feel happy and relieved because someone has faith in your abilities. But then I made *Family* after about one year at the School. And you're not really allowed to make films while you're at the School, so that in itself was a struggle because it all had to be a bit surreptitious. Looking back, it was very healthy afterwards to have those three remaining years to develop in; lots of time to make bad films that wouldn't have a lot of negative consequences. That's exactly what you should be doing while you're at the School. You should be experimenting as much and as intensely as possible, and investigating the limits of your expressive language, so that you take all that with you when you graduate. You need to make it a habit to think that every new film you embark on will require something new, and that having to innovate isn't something to be afraid of.

But of course it's difficult to make that transition from a 90-minute film to exercises with one character, one light, and in-camera editing. There was some pretty heavy energy involved in still being in school after having won a major award in Amsterdam, and after having had a theatrical release. *Family* was one of the films that initiated the new wave in Danish documentary film. It was a striking film too, because none of the journalists knew what to do with it. So they reviewed it as a form of journalism, which of course it isn't. I remember that *Politiken* claimed that the directors lacked a flair for journalism. And you just think, 'Good grief, there's still a long way to go.' But it was actually good to get those sorts of responses because that's when I realized that it made sense to talk to a much bigger world. If you just focus on the domestic market you end up seriously depressed. Things simply move far too slowly. It was good to be catapulted into a wider world, to discover a much bigger stage to play on.

REDVALL: *Family* appears to have been made with a theatrical release in mind, and this made it unique in the Danish context. There was that beautiful poster, and a lot of effort clearly went into generating interest in the film, which wasn't at all typical for documentary

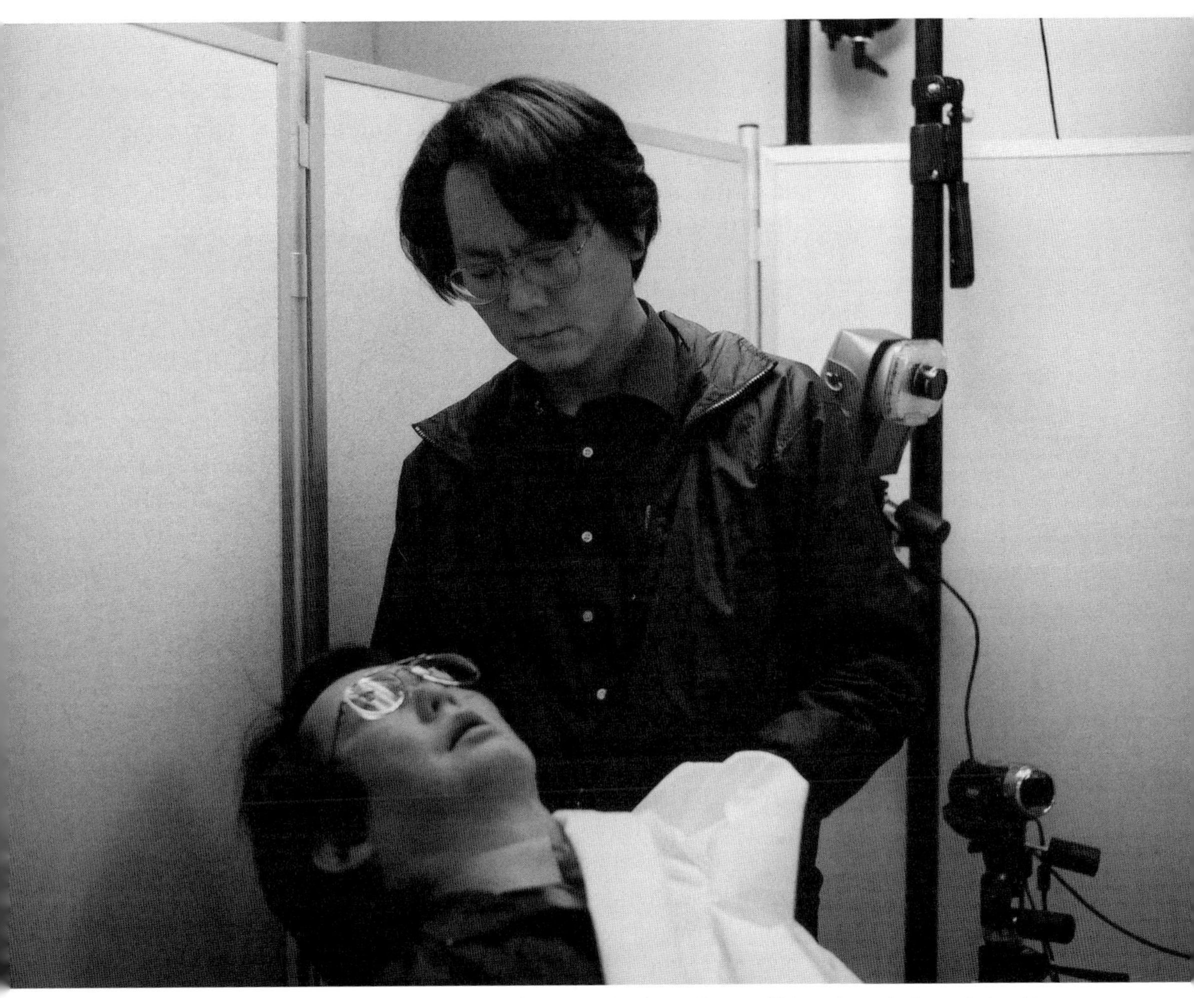

Japanese professor Hiroshi Ishiguro with his robot alter ego in *Mechanical Love*, which explores the interrelationship between robots and humans (photo: Phie Ambo. Courtesy of Danish Documentary).

films at the time. Were you thinking strategically about getting the film into the Danish cinemas from the very beginning?

AMBO: It was mostly our producer, Jonas Frederiksen, who thought a theatrical release would be amusing. He drummed up the money that was necessary to market the film, and he was really our torchbearer throughout that whole process. We were, of course, completely game, and it was all extra amusing because the film was actually a kind of crazy diary. It was great fun to shoot in CinemaScope and with the big screen in mind. That relation between something extremely intimate and its articulation for a broad audience was part of the concept from the outset. So that's why we also felt that it was appropriate to give the film a proper release. I have to say that the number of people who saw *Family* in the cinemas was really small, but all the things we put together – the poster and the packaging more generally – did end up going along with the film when it subsequently made its way around the world.

REDVALL: Did you travel a lot in connection with screenings of *Family*?

AMBO: Not really. I don't like that sort of thing much. When I've completed a film, I'm happy to be present at a few screenings, but I quickly tire of that because I think it's incredibly important to get on with the next film. If I keep talking about my old film, I can't get into my new film. I think I've attended all of two festivals, although I could have attended as many as 100. Some directors really benefit from traveling with their work, and from meeting various audiences and talking to them, but I'm just too restless. I really need to make sure I have time, peace of mind, and the conditions I generally need if I'm going to work on a new film. I like being constantly involved in the making of a new film; that sense of constantly being on the move. And I wouldn't have time for that if I were to travel all around the world. I make films because I'm curious about things. There's always something I want to figure out, and then I want to work on that constantly; that's part of the energy. It's like being a detective who's on the job. You can't let things that aren't related to the task at hand put that sort of energy on standby.

REDVALL: *Family* was in many ways a striking debut, perhaps because you and your then boyfriend, Sami Saif, were characters in it. What was the experience of being in your own film like?

AMBO: Well, Sami's the one who really gets stoked up. Our motivations for making that film were very different. He wanted to make a film, and he wanted to tell a good story, and he had a good story to offer. I, on the other hand, wanted to figure out how to make sense of him. For me, the film was a means of getting close to him. So, as a result, we were operating with two quite different approaches to the material. I'm not really that interested in intimacy for its own sake, and I very much doubt that I'll ever produce anything quite that intimate again. *Family* is the way it is because that's how I was best able to tell that story.

REDVALL: But you also figure in your diploma film, *The Diver Inside Me*. It's almost as though the Film School wants its directors to be in front of the camera at some point in their programme. Is that the case?

AMBO: Yes, it is. I suppose you could say that *Family* had taught me how to be on camera, how to be tough, and how to make use of myself as a fictional character. When you're in the editing room, you have to be able to look at yourself as though you were a different person. You just can't be vain; and the same is true for the main characters in your film. It's good to make films about yourself, and every film school student has done precisely that for that very reason. You get a sense of what hurts, and of what feels good, and you realize that it's good – at least as I see it – to make sure that people find themselves in situations where they lose their footing because that's when what they're all about as characters becomes really clear. But at the same time you have to make sure that there's a certain balance, so that they can actually live with it all afterwards. If you try to do this sort of thing with people you're close to, you find yourself protecting them in the process, even as you're pushing them on.

REDVALL: It seems like there's a lot of collaboration across the fiction/non-fiction divide in Danish film, and amongst practitioners with different specializations. How does that work and why do you think this is the case?

AMBO: We collaborate a lot, and I think this has everything to do with the Film School. You spend all that time sitting next to each other in the cinema, and you have to share what you've come up with in response to specific exercises. And you know that what you have to share is really intimate and really bad, but you have to put it up there on the screen nonetheless, so a lot of boundaries get pushed. But then you discover that nothing dreadful happens as a result of that. You realize that at some point you're going to have to screen the films you make for others, and that you might as well deal with any blows they're going to provoke in the company of friends.

You learn that there's protection to be had from the process of involving others in your work.

Family was really a great experience, partly because I felt lucky to have been able, so early on, to put something out there that was like a fist on a table. It wasn't this business of having placed some small film or other with a short film festival. Janus [Billeskov Jansen], who did the editing, is clearly an important part of the picture here. He wasn't afraid of big gestures, symphony orchestras – the works. That process of working very closely with Janus has been a cornerstone in my education. He means a lot to me because there's something raw about him. You can't lull Janus into some aesthetic stupor. He sees through that sort of thing straight away. He cuts right to the bone, and he's better than anyone I know at telling stories in a way that keeps them moving forward. Sitting next to him as we worked simply set the standard in terms of what I wanted to achieve in the future. I've used his expertise in every single film I've made since *Family*. Even if he isn't doing the editing, I still get him to take a look because he's not seduced by aesthetics, which other people sometimes are.

I've collaborated in similar ways with Jacob Thuesen on my most recent films. I bring him into the process when I can tell that something isn't quite working, and I can't precisely identify what's wrong. Jacob is capable of turning the entire film around, of suddenly making use of material from research I did five years ago, which I had no intention whatsoever of using. It's such an incredible gift to work alongside people who think about film in a completely free way.

REDVALL: Your first film after film school was *Gambler*, which looks at the challenges that Nicolas Winding Refn encountered when making *Pusher 2* and *Pusher 3*. It provides a complex picture of what's actually involved in creating a film. How did you end up making that film?

AMBO: After film school I had a real need to undertake a process of 'de-film-schoolification.' I wanted to do something that involved shooting from the hip. And it had to be fun, for film school had been pretty strenuous. There are so many opinions in play, and psychologically it's incredibly intense, so you reach a point where you have anxiety attacks just walking through the canteen. The Film School is an incredibly stressful place to make films, and after all that I had a real need to rediscover the very basic joy of telling stories. I had a strong desire to put aside all that learning I'd acquired, all those sophisticated ways of articulating things, so that I could just follow my instincts and go for what seemed like fun. When I look at the film now, I can easily identify all the things I'd learnt and that I'd started to do almost automatically without even being aware of it – the things that had become second nature. But *Gambler* was about a desire to get film to flow through me again instead of having constantly to stop the creative elevator for a bunch of obligatory consultations with consultant A, B, and C. It was a wonderful film to make because Jang [Nicolas Winding Refn] lived just next to me, and we were in complete agreement about the project. And he's insanely easy to film because he'll let you film anything. The more, the better. The process was really good, although it was hard to finance the film, and I ended up having to invest a fair amount of my own money in it. That film generated quite a loss, but at least it got made!

REDVALL: You shoot your films yourself, and with a good deal of intimacy in the case of *Gambler* or your film about enmity amongst neighbours, *The Home Front*. But you also take your camera into some pretty intimate contexts in your thematic films, where a particular issue rather than a personal project provides the focus. I'm thinking, for example, of *Mechanical Love*. Where do you find your stories?

AMBO: I like to alternate between stories that are part of a small, intimate world, and then those that can be opened up more. I'd already started preparing the ground for both *Mechanical Love* and *Free the Mind* with my diploma film, *The Diver Inside Me*, which deals with the connections between some pretty big issues. In that film, it was all about the connection between life and death; about the experience of watching someone die, while being pregnant. Thematically, the film has a powerful interest in the origins of life. It got me going with this approach that involves taking up a theme I'm interested in, and then gathering the various building blocks that match it. I find it very exciting to insert basic, human questions into a framework that has the effect of generating this multi-plot phenomenon. That's the area in which I see myself as working, and I'm just trying to come up with ever better solutions to the question, 'How do I get a big abstract story into something very intimate?' The films that don't rely on a single character should, in my view, be as intimate as they'd be if they did. I'm fascinated by those multi-plot stories that also have a powerful personal dimension, and I'm working hard to develop the best cinematic form for that sort of thing.

REDVALL: Is it important to you to have your films reach an international audience?

AMBO: Well, I sort of stumbled onto the international scene. I had no idea that *Family* would become an international success, but that film really opened my eyes and ears because it helped me understand that working internationally is precisely what's fun. If *Family* hadn't made its way internationally, it would have taken me longer to figure that out, and I probably wouldn't have become quite as insistent about getting my films out into a world beyond Denmark as I am now.

REDVALL: What does it take to get a Danish film into a wider world?

AMBO: Well, first of all you need a producer who's interested in doing all the hard work that's involved in financing a film internationally. You need to get a lot of TV stations involved – and that's a demanding process – and you constantly have to travel a lot. Also, you need a director who's on board for the idea of selling a film. And that means you've got to have a traveling salesman somewhere inside you. You've got to be able to be a circus horse. You've got to be able to find a seat at those pitching tables. At Sheffield Doc/Fest, for example, there's this 'meat market' where you meet twenty investors over the course of two days. It really is a meat market. They ring this cowbell every twenty minutes, and then you switch places. And then you sit there and blather about your film, and it's your job to project the idea that your film is the only film in the world worth supporting right now. For a lot of people, this is really tough. A lot of people have a hard time pitching in front of large audiences, or find it difficult to sell themselves. You have to be able to think about the film as being one thing, a space you'll enter once the financing is in place. And you have to think about the here and now of the pitching forum as involving a quite different space, one that doesn't really have anything to do with the film. It's just a question of getting the money for it. The balancing act has to do with making sure those two different things don't get conflated. It's important to be able to take off that cap the minute you start making your film because otherwise you'll produce a really shitty film. Because the point isn't to make a really long trailer or a promo. The idea is to make a film, and that film is definitely not going to be the same as the one you sold. That's simply a fact.

REDVALL: Film people often complain about the various application procedures that are involved in raising money. The claim is that

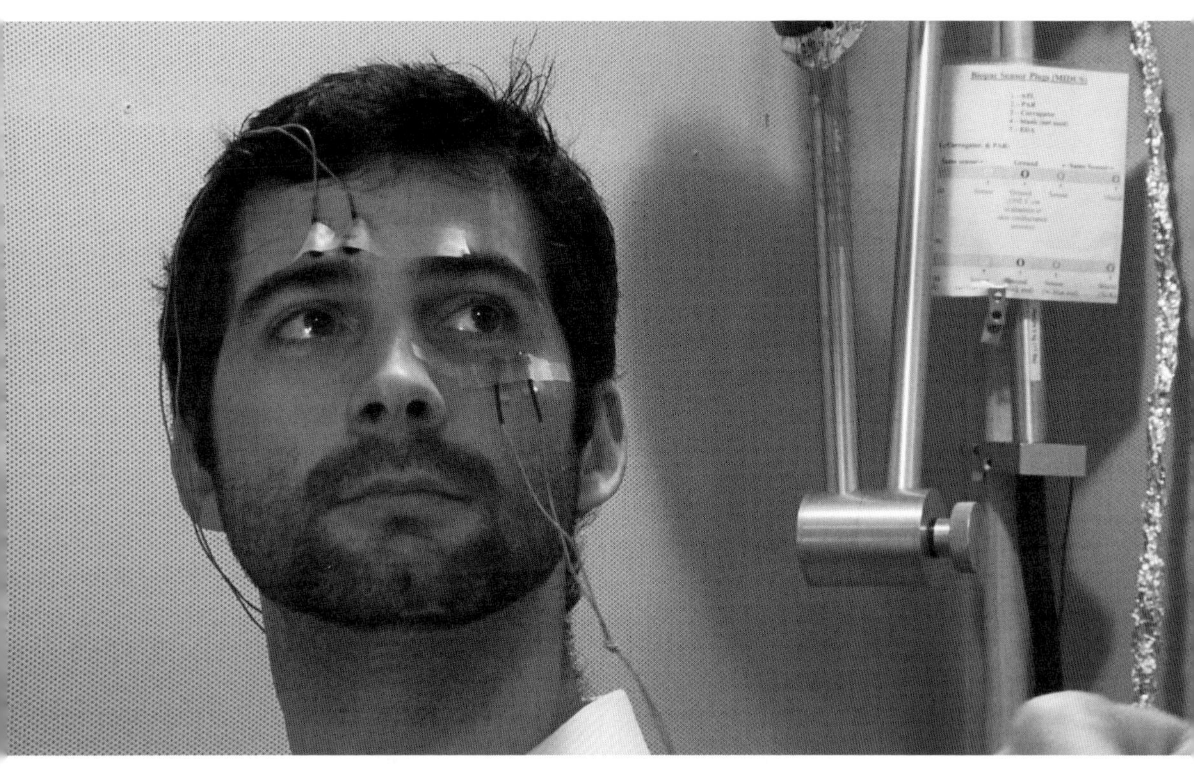

Recent research in neuro-science is explored in an effort to understand thoughts and their impact on the human body (*Free the Mind*, photo: Phie Ambo. Courtesy of Danish Documentary).

they're text-based, yet it seems that things like pitches and trailers play an important role these days. Is that your impression too?

AMBO: In my view, those processes have become a lot less text-based. I actually don't mind having to write things out, but it's a real problem if people think that what you've written is the film. What you provide is a piece of writing, and a text is not a film. They're not compatible. I don't mind writing about my film once I know I've fully shaped and defined it, but what that actually means is that I'd have to have shot the film before writing about it. That's the thing I dislike the most; that process of writing about something when you're really just guessing. It's a waste of my time, not to mention the commissioner's time. Why can't we just begin to explore things with the camera? After all, you can be sure that what you see in the camera's framings is true. I've worked really hard to reach the point where I don't have to write something that's not true. I'm willing to write down that I want to make a film about X, but I won't provide a step-by-step outline or pretend that I've shot such and such a scene. First of all, to do so would be to lie. And secondly, I know from experience that I'll end up standing there with some fiction or other in my head when I actually begin to do the shooting. And that means that all sorts of things will be going on, and I won't even begin to be able to see what they are because I'm too busy thinking about all the catching up I need to do. Chance may provide all sorts of possibilities, but there won't be room for any of that because I'll be busy thinking about having to get that scene I described on page five.

Being tied to a project description is really limiting, and it turns the making of a film into a process of mere execution, as opposed to discovery. And for me, the element of discovery is the core reason why I make films. I don't know what's going to happen tomorrow. If I did know what was going to happen, I'd be really bored, and there'd be no reason at all to film any of it. My film and my discovering something are integrally connected, and that's part of my method. A lot of other filmmakers make use of staged scenes, or they control the filmmaking process more. But what excites me is this idea of discovering something. And that's why this business of having to guess what the finished film will look like doesn't work for me. It's simply too limiting. So I've reached the point where I accept that I have to provide something on a page, because the filmmaker and the various investors need to have some sort of shared understanding. But I don't provide much.

	I'd much rather provide edited sequences. I'd rather do some research with my camera.
REDVALL:	What's your view on the system of public support for documentary filmmaking in Denmark?
AMBO:	That system is really excellent. I have nothing critical to say about it at all. We're extraordinarily privileged to be able to make these films without having to pay back the public monies that went into them. There's an incredible freedom in that. The only criticism I have concerns outsourcing, which is not a good practice. Too much money is being spent on that.
REDVALL:	What's the problem with outsourcing?
AMBO:	Outsourcing is basically an expression of the problem that film commissioners and TV editors are having with figuring out how to make films that are of interest to both parties. So they say things like: 'I'd like to see a film about poverty, or about the flow of money,' or some such. And then they hire some directors to execute their plans for that sort of film. But the thing is that making a documentary film is super complicated, so if your heart isn't really in it, you end up with hack work. And the films are never shown in serial formats anyway. So what's the point?

At the moment there's this outsourced project called something along the lines of 'This is Denmark,' and *The Home Front* would have been quite relevant in that context. I like making films about Danish realities, but I don't want to be part of some package deal, with film commissioners and film editors calling the shots. This is also why I've never made any films that were fully financed by TV, because then the TV people have all the power. The Danish Film Institute, on the other hand, is committed to making sure the director gets final cut. I've at any point been able to say, 'I just can't accept that, and it's fine with me if you want to withdraw your funding.' That's been really important in terms of my being able to hold on to my integrity.

I think it's important to tell stories that are aimed at a broad Danish audience. It's their tax monies we're spending. But I'd like to show that it's possible to engage that broad audience without all that outsourcing. One of the assumptions underwriting outsourcing protocols is the thought that if directors can be brought in line, then they can be made to make films for a general audience. But trying to control the directors merely produces boring films. I made *The Home Front* to prove that it's not hard to reach a broad audience. That film was seen by a very large number of people, and

I'm now working on a film about the bailiff's role, as I think it's important to draw attention to poverty in Denmark. But the more I get into that film, the more I realize that it's not so much about poverty as it's about our welfare system. Films develop along the way, and they have to be able to go in whatever direction I want, unconstrained by some political agenda. The film has become more and more poetic, rather than hard-hitting, and I have the freedom I need to allow for that shift because it's not some job that's been outsourced. It's my film. It's something I'm genuinely passionate about, yet it's also in the ballpark of what can be shown on TV at 8 p.m. It's fun making films for a broad audience. But I do want to be able to decide exactly how I'm going to do that myself.

REDVALL: Where do you find the inspiration to make films?

AMBO: The last documentary I've seen, which I found wildly inspiring, was *Exit Through the Gift Shop* (dir. Banksy, 2010). It's an amusing spoof documentary, where the elaborate process of making the film becomes the content of the film. But other than that I don't get a whole lot of inspiration from watching other films. It's more a matter of being puzzled by something. That could, for example, be something about how time works. I've always asked these somewhat anthropological questions about very basic issues. How does time get understood in a linear way? And then I focus my mind on that for a while. Actually, time is one of the issues that I'm dealing with in my next film, *Ripples at the Shore*. The convention-based underpinnings of reality interest me a lot. And that's why I make documentaries as opposed to fiction films. Reality is crazy enough for me, and it's always fascinated me. I get inspired by life as it's lived around me, by the people I meet, by what people say.

REDVALL: It's clear that being able to control the filmmaking process, and thus your own films, is very important to you. Is this why you and a number of other directors established the company Danish Documentary together?

AMBO: It all started with our wanting to release our films on DVD. We just didn't want them to end up in some vault. You don't normally make any money on documentaries, and so typically no-one other than the director is especially interested in promoting or distributing the films. If a company goes bankrupt – which of course happens all the time – then it won't continue to carry a given film. So our premise was that we wanted to get our films out there, and we then eventually established our own production company.

REDVALL: Do you collaborate on each other's films?

AMBO: Yes, there's a lot of really good synergy. When Sigrid [Dyekjær] heads off to a festival with a film by one director, she'll also pitch films by the rest of us, and that works really well. It's a lot cheaper to produce films that way, with this package approach. We also make good use of each other in creative terms. For example, on Monday I'll be screening my new film for the ladies in the company. I know them really well at this point, so if something strikes them as not being quite right, they'll definitely tell me.

REDVALL: It makes good sense to collaborate in the ways you describe, and yet directors rarely seem to establish companies together. Why do you think that is?

AMBO: I think it rarely happens because the process of establishing a company is quite complicated. You have to get clear on the sort of company it's going to be, and then there are all those meetings with accountants and lawyers, and so on. The process of establishing a company is hard work, and that work has nothing whatsoever to do with the work of being a director. I also think that a lot of directors see the responsibilities involved as being far too onerous. After all, you have to be willing to accept certain economic responsibilities. But, as I see it, there's just no way around that. As a director in Denmark, it just doesn't work to think of yourself as being on somebody else's payroll.

I've found having our own company really liberating. You can see exactly where the money is going, and you can actually see that money isn't being used to fund some enormous reception, or to cover costs that are vaguely related to some fiction film that has nothing whatsoever to do with our own documentary filmmaking. When I set off to do my shooting, I do so with one of those little trolleys that old-age pensioners often use. The trolley's got my camera and my sound equipment in it, and then I've got my tripod over my shoulder. And that's that. The organizational structure is incredibly simple, so it's very easy to keep it transparent. The economic picture is much better now, and that means we can do a better job of developing the films we want to make next. There's simply a much more steady flow of money.

REDVALL: Is it possible to make a living as a documentary filmmaker in Denmark?

AMBO: Yes, it is. But I wasn't able to make a living as a documentary filmmaker until I created my own company. Too much money was simply going in the wrong direction. For example, 10% of the budget is normally put aside as a so-called contingency, and if that money doesn't actually get spent, it ends up in the coffers of the production company. So the director's efforts, in terms of ensuring the contingency budget doesn't get touched, are not rewarded. In our company, unused contingency monies end up in our account. Whatever gets saved then gets used to develop subsequent films. A complicated film budget is full of small ticket items, and we now get that money, which we never did before.

REDVALL: There's a great deal of interest in Danish documentary filmmaking these days. Why do you think that is?

AMBO: My producer, Sigrid, has this theory that, in Denmark, documentary directors operate in surroundings that are very peaceful. There are no tsunamis, no earthquakes. The sense of peace that we enjoy here makes it possible to relate to the world and to be curious about it. It can, of course, be important to tell stories out of a sense of necessity, but that kind of process often involves an emotional deficit that can be very hard to deal with. We're very privileged in Denmark. We're able to take an open and critical approach to all sorts of things because we've grown up in a context that's essentially safe and secure. We don't have to put a lot of energy or time into trying to survive. We can put energy into really enjoying the process of telling stories the way we want to. To make a film like *Burma VJ* (dir. Anders Østergaard, 2008), for example, you've got to have a lot of emotional strength to draw on, and you've got that in a Danish context. A Burmese filmmaker might not have given the film the aesthetic form and structure that it now has. You need a certain perspicacity and energy to get the formal properties in question. We're privileged to live in a part of the world that has a well-functioning system of public support for film, and where there are no violent political conflicts.

I think another important factor is that, during our years at the Film School, we all learnt to work with the people who are making fiction films. Those relationships set a different standard for the storytelling, which then becomes more palatable. I have to admit that I don't go to a lot of film festivals, but when I do have the occasion to see documentary films from other countries, I often think: 'Why don't they make some cuts? Why did they hold that frame for 10 minutes?' You can't help but wonder how people can be so indifferent to their audiences. We can't be accused of having that failing in Denmark. We really do want to communicate what we have to say to an audience, and in that respect it's very helpful to work closely with practitioners from the world of fiction film because they're used to a different rhythm and to having to think in terms of the requirements of audience appeal.

REDVALL: With reference to this idea of a film finding its audience, there's been a lot of talk about the promise of new digital modes of distribution. The idea is that even a narrow documentary film stands a better chance these days of finding an audience. What's your take on the current situation, as far as the distribution of documentary films is concerned?

AMBO: It's simply wonderful that people can get hold of the films. We've created a set-up that allows people to download our films from our website. The thought that everything might end up being digitalized doesn't worry me at all. The alternative is that people just don't see the films. Unfortunately, the process often grinds to a halt because some producer or other worries about missing out on 25 cents. It's not a smooth process. But inasmuch as we own the rights to our films through our company, and given that we really want people to be able to see our films, we're definitely going to go for it.

Chapter 2

Dola Bonfils

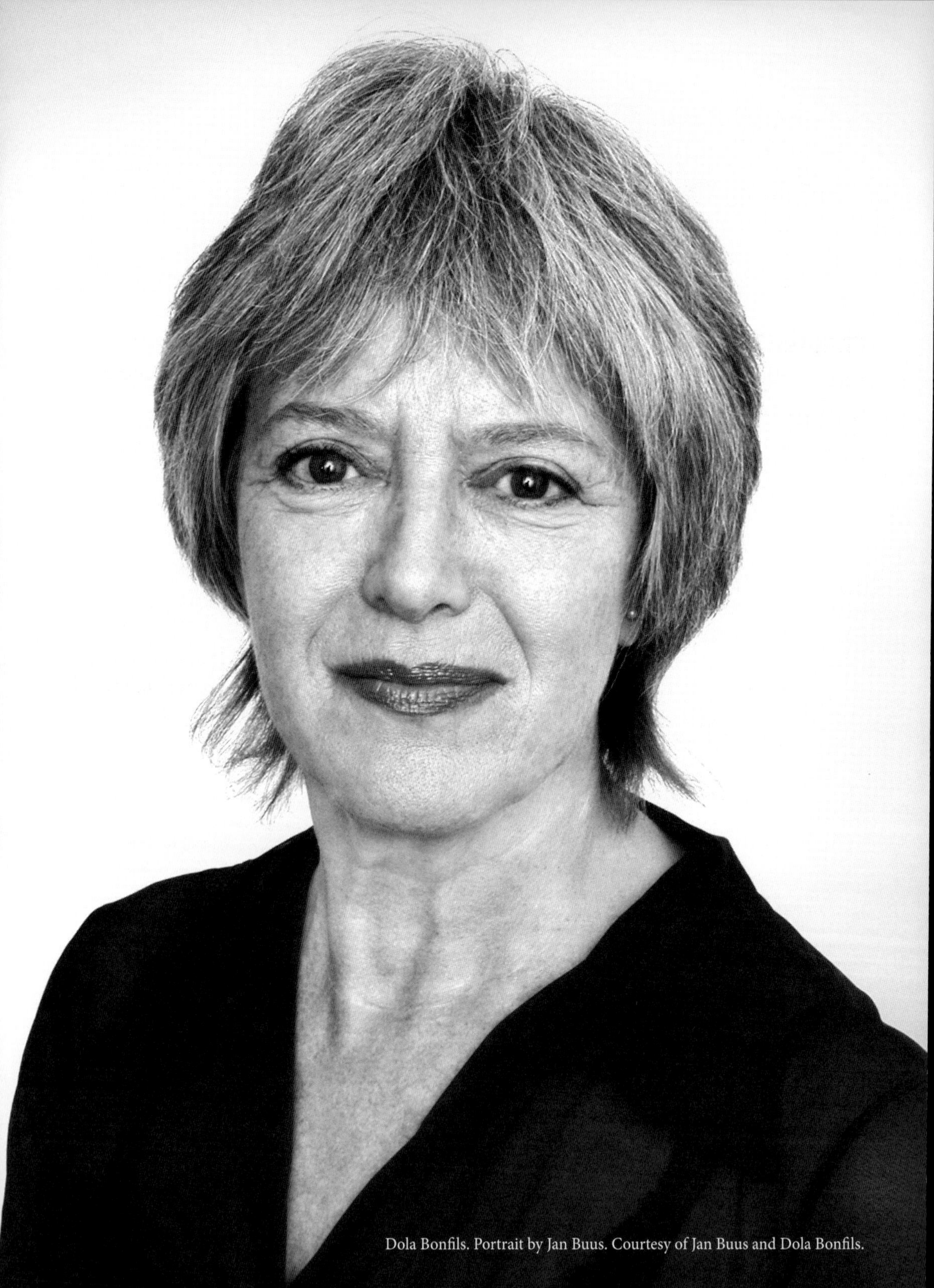

Dola Bonfils. Portrait by Jan Buus. Courtesy of Jan Buus and Dola Bonfils.

Born 1941. Dola Bonfils is a self-taught film director who became part of the Danish film milieu by working on specific projects, and as a result of her encounter with filmmaker Henning Carlsen in the late 1960s. She was involved in setting up a cinema dedicated to documentary films, Kino Valde, which was a Dagmar Cinema initiative. As a result of this work, Bonfils developed contacts with both the Danish and international documentary film milieus. Following her debut as a director in 1972, with the collectively authored, feminist film *Kvinderne og fællesmarkedet* ('Women and the Common Market'), Dola Bonfils went on to become one of Denmark's most noteworthy observational documentary filmmakers. She also had a decisive impact on the Danish film milieu through her work as a DFI film commissioner from 2004–09.

As a film director, Bonfils is clearly inspired by Direct Cinema, especially Frederick Wiseman. Many of her most significant films provide vivid insight into people's lives as these are shaped by the workings of specific institutions. Bonfils' interest in the institutional aspect of reality is evident in such classic works as *Gymnasiet – en skoleform* ('Secondary School: A Kind of School,' 1983), *Politiet i virkeligheden 1–3* ('The Police as They Are 1–3,' 1986), and the hospital film, *Med døden inde på livet* ('In the Shadow of Death,' 1989). Bonfils drew on and further developed these portraits of specific institutions in the science documentary *Tankens anatomi* ('The Anatomy of Thought,' 1997), in her portrait of a knowledge-intensive industry, *Drømme med deadlines* ('Dreams with Deadlines,' 2003), and in her very intimate and striking documentary about the military, *K-Notatet* (*C-Memorandum*, 2004), which was part of the large DFI/DR project known as 'Magtens billeder' ('Pictures of Power'). Bonfils' film is noteworthy for its penetrating exploration of an institution that cannot be said to have a reputation for openness or transparency.

Dola Bonfils' films are marked by a socially engaged perspective that at times reflects a global dimension. The film series entitled *Levende ord 1–3* ('Living Words 1–3,' 1996–2001) provides good examples of globally relevant films about the environment and democracy; of films that attempt to foster discussion on a global basis. Another striking film with a dialogic dimension is the dual portrait of the experienced left-wing activist Bente Hansen, and the much younger activist Helle Hansen, *Billeder til tiden* ('Images for the Times,' 1994). In this film, Bonfils successfully combines a poetic mode of expression with portraits of two politically engaged women from different generations.

Dola Bonfils' films also reflect her longstanding interest in all forms of visual art. Key titles in this connection are *To malere – to værksteder* ('Two Painters, Two Studios,' 1992), *Lydbilleder – 6 variationer over et tema* ('Sound Pictures: Six Variations on a Theme,' 1993) and *Billedkunstnerisk praksis 1–2* ('Visual Arts Practice 1–2,' 1999).

Documentary features:

2004   'Magtens billeder': *K-Notatet* ('Pictures of Power': *C-Memorandum*)
2003   *Drømme med deadlines – en genfortælling* ('Dreams with Deadlines')
1999   *Billedkunstnerisk praksis 1–2* ('Visual Arts Practice 1–2')
1997   *Tankens anatomi* ('The Anatomy of Thought')
1994   *Billeder til tiden* ('Images for the Times')
1989   *Med døden inde på livet* ('In the Shadow of Death')
1986   *Politiet i virkeligheden 1–3* ('The Police as They Are 1–3')
1983   *Gymnasiet – en skoleform* ('Secondary School: A Kind of School')
1982   *Fremtid søges* ('In Search of a Future')

Documentary shorts:

2001   *Levende ord 3: Mødet med det fremmede* ('Living Words 3: Encounters with the Other')
1997   *Levende ord 2: Miljø og udvikling* ('Living Words 2: The Environment and Development')
1996   *Levende ord 1: Fællesskab og demokrati* ('Living Words 1: Community and Democracy')
1993   *Lydbilleder – 6 variationer over et tema* ('Sound Pictures: Six Variations on a Theme')
1992   *To malere – to værksteder* ('Two Painters, Two Studios')
1990   *Gurps* ('GURPS'; acronym for Generic Universal Role Playing System)
1985   *Lutter lagkage?* ('Sheer Bliss?')
1984   *Kan man give æstetikken et køn?* ('Can an aesthetic be gendered?')
1972   *Kvinden og fællesmarkedet* ('Women and the Common Market', with Mette Bauer, Mette Knudsen, and Li Vilstrup)

BONDEBJERG: You belong to a generation that didn't have access to formal film training. Training to become a film director, especially a documentary filmmaker, is a relatively recent phenomenon in Denmark. So learning by doing was really the typical route into film. How did that work in your case?

BONFILS: Yes, I'm an autodidact. Having done the Danish equivalent of A-levels in 1958, I really wasn't sure what I wanted to do next. I wasn't especially motivated, but I did go to university for a bit because I was quite interested in art history. I also spent a couple of years in Amsterdam, where I did some more studying, and also matured quite a bit and came to understand myself better. What I got out of those years was a certain method, an understanding of the importance of investigating things. Around 1967 I started studying Film at the University of Copenhagen. But what really made a difference was that I ended up getting a job as a student helper on a film production; and that then led to more practical work. My second job involved being a runner and scripter for Ole Roos' feature debut *Kys til højre og venstre* (*Kisses Right and Left*, 1969). That job lasted the entire summer of 1968, a very eventful year! It was a decisive experience. Instead of going back to Film Studies, I started working for different people at Laterna Film. I met Christian Hartkopp [1939–1980], who'd edited Henning Carlsen's films, among others. That encounter was crucial because Hartkopp ended up really including me in his milieu. We worked in a room behind the Dagmar Theatre, and it was all very congenial. At the time, Henning Carlsen wanted to do more for documentary filmmaking, so he asked the film students whether they'd be willing to commit to a project along those lines. But back then the whole student milieu was extremely politicized, and the students were ambivalent. So Henning Carlsen asked me whether I would like to take on the task he had in mind. And that turned out to be Kino Valde. Kino Valde ended up, to a very significant extent, becoming my film school. I saw an incredible number of documentary films and must have organized about 70 screenings over a period of three years. There was a lot going on internationally in documentary film back then, not least in the area of political documentary filmmaking. There were a lot of festivals, and all sorts of alternative ways of doing things. Also, this was when the European documentary scene was beginning to discover Third Cinema. Being part of all that was an eye-opening experience. Dagmar provided a really great film milieu and a good film school, and so did Laterna Film. All the directors who mattered at the time were running around in the cellar of the place. It was learning-by-doing, and I learnt a lot by peering over the shoulders of others. What taught me the most, besides all those documentaries I saw, was sitting next to Hartkopp and trying to get a grip on Henning Carlsen's *Er I bange?* (*Are You Afraid?*, 1972).

BONDEBJERG:	The first film you co-directed, 'Women and the Common Market' is quite typical of its time. It's a feminist film and one that's very critically minded, both in terms of content and form. What do you think of that film today?

BONFILS: I suppose I don't really think of it as being my film. It was made by a group of very strong and very politically engaged women, and I was only involved from the sidelines. But it's true that it, in many ways, was very typical of its time. But at this point it's not a film that I'm able to see myself in.

BONDEBJERG: But if we look at your oeuvre as a whole, we do seem to find clear tendencies or preferences. First, there's a tendency to examine society critically. This tendency is clearly expressed in 'Women and the Common Market,' but also in several of the films that deal with global problems and social encounters. I'm thinking, for example, of 'Living Words 1–3,' or of your poetic and political film focusing on two portraits of the left-wing, 'Images for the Times.' Second, there's a strong interest in different forms of visual expression, in almost poetic visual experiments. 'Sound Pictures: Six Variations on a Theme' would be an example of this tendency. Third, there's what might be seen as the main tendency in your work: observational filmmaking about social institutions, apparently inspired by American documentary filmmaker Frederick Wiseman. Would you be inclined to agree with this description of your work?

BONFILS: Yes, that's probably a pretty good description of the main tendencies in my work. And it's true that Wiseman is my most important source of inspiration. His films really knocked me off my feet when I first saw them. The first film where his influence is really noticeable is also the first film I directed entirely on my own, *Fremtid søges* ('In Search of a Future,' 1982). This film looks at four unemployed young people and follows their daily lives. I started working on that film when I was working with Christian Hartkopp. But then he died and it ended up becoming very much my film. But 'Secondary School: A Kind of School' is clearly my 'diploma film' as a director. With that film I was really in charge of the whole process; from the beginning to the very end.

BONDEBJERG: 'Secondary School: A Kind of School' was produced by Høyberg Film and supported by The National Film Board of Denmark [SFC], the Ministry of Education, and the Egmont Fund. In that sense it was financed in quite a traditional way, through a mix of private and public monies. Several of your films have involved quite a complex mix of funding sources, as well as collaboration between the milieus of film and TV. 'The Police as They Are 1–3' was, for example, co-financed by SFC and the Danish Broadcasting Corporation [DR]. And 'In the Shadow of Death' drew on funding

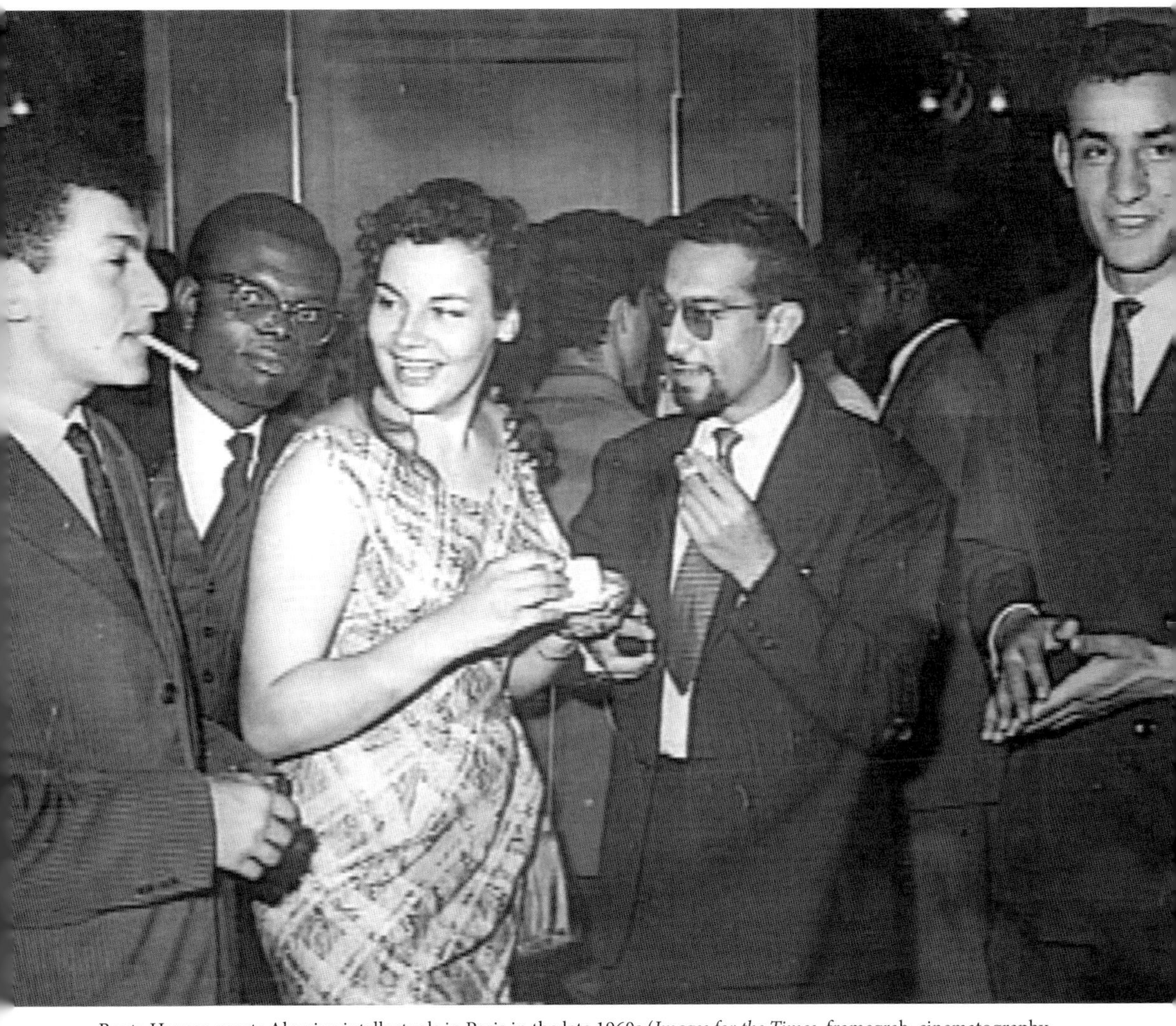

Bente Hansen meets Algerian intellectuals in Paris in the late 1960s (*Images for the Times,* framegrab, cinematography by Morten Bruus).

from all kinds of sources: SFC, Forsikringsselskaberne i Danmark [Insurance Denmark], the Gangsted Fund, Sundhedsstyrelsen [The Danish Health and Medicines Authority], Dansk Sygeplejeråd [Danish Nurses' Organization], and AIDS-Fondet. Has the process of financing your films been especially complicated or conflictual? Have you encountered any problems with respect to control as a result of the complexity of the financial arrangements?

BONFILS: I feel that I've very rarely been involved in conflicts having to do with the form and content of films. In some of the productions I've helped to initiate, both as a film commissioner and as a director, there have been discussions about the basic framework and concept, but the director's freedom was usually respected. But the process of financing a film – of persuading various organizations, and so on, to contribute money to it – can be exhausting and quite conflictual. Far too frequently the director also has to throw herself into this process, although the producer, of course, also does his or her bit. I experienced 'In the Shadow of Death' as an especially difficult production to get off the ground. I had to fight for my film and my ideas when dealing with various organizations and financiers, and I was met with a great deal of scepticism in terms of what I was trying to achieve with that film. It's about two vulnerable people who find themselves in a life threatening situation, and about people who fight to help them. Perhaps the scepticism had to do with whether it would be possible to get these people to open up and cooperate with the filmmaker. And then there were all these ethical considerations having to do with how close you could really get to people's private lives. But I finally managed to get the film financed and made.

BONDEBJERG: 'The Police as They Are' is the result of collaboration between film and TV. Those sorts of partnerships, which are absolutely crucial for Danish documentary film, have also generated some serious conflicts, at least from 1988 onwards, when the TV sector was opened up to commercial channels. But this film was made before 1988, when the state-funded channels still enjoyed a monopoly. So, perhaps the situation was different with this film.

BONFILS: There were no problems with that film, and the collaborative aspect was absolutely fine. The idea for the film actually came from SFC. They felt it would be a good idea for me to make a film about the police, and in the beginning I was frankly a bit afraid of the idea. I'd just made 'Secondary School: A Kind of School,' which had been an incredibly complicated and difficult film to make. I'd had to depict life at the school in a whole range of places: the classrooms, the teachers' lounge, schoolyard, and so on. But at a school, all the doors close when the bell rings, and it can be really difficult to figure out *where* you need to be *when* in order to capture the life of the place. So after all that, my inclination was to do something very different in my next film. But it was hard to say no to the challenge I was suddenly given, and it was certainly an interesting project. The collaboration with DR was very smooth during the production process itself, and the financing was entirely in place early on as a result of the monies from SFC and DR. But problems arose when the first episode was broadcast because suddenly there was a legal injunction to contend with. This was because a woman, whom we'd filmed while her boyfriend was being arrested, complained about having been exposed. But we managed to get a settlement. Other than that it was a smooth production, even though it was quite demanding. I had a meeting with senior police executives, and was guaranteed that I could make the film I wanted to make. They were very pleased with the type of film that I proposed – one that would describe the daily life of the police – and they liked the fact that I wasn't interested in a journalistic angle or in making a critical, investigative film. That was one of the first times I experienced the difference between being a journalist and being a documentary filmmaker in terms of the kind of responses I was met with.

BONDEBJERG: It might be interesting to contrast this very positive experience with 'The Police as They Are,' involving exemplary collaboration between film and TV professionals, and the much more conflictual and problematic collaborative process of making 'Pictures of Power.' You wore many different hats in connection with that ambitious project because you were one of the people who initiated it, and because you yourself directed one of the films in the series, *C-Memorandum*. How would you describe the conflicts and problems that this project generated?

BONFILS: Yes, I was certainly very much involved in all this because I was the one who suggested that the Danish Film Institute should get involved in this kind of project. The idea was based on a large research project called 'The Study of Power,' which was run by the now deceased Professor Lise Togeby at Aarhus University. I actually lured Henning Camre, who was the DFI's director back then, to Aarhus to discuss the idea. I felt it was a real pity that all those research findings were destined only for books aimed at a tiny group of experts, and I felt that in this regard film could make a real difference. Allan Berg Nielsen, then film commissioner at the DFI, was excited about the concept, and saw it as building on basic Griersonian principles. At a given moment he managed to get Henrik Grunnet at DR on-board, and so the tendering process started. And that's when the power struggles began, for DR and the DFI had to agree, quite concretely, on all the subsequent steps. Part of the disagreement had to do with the different parties' preferences concerning who, ideally, the directors were to be, and then there was the way in which all this was handled. Pitching the project idea was something that took place in front of an insanely large panel consisting of commissioning editors and other people from the Danish Broadcasting Corporation, and of all the DFI film commissioners. Part of the problem was that a procedure had been agreed to, whereby all of the Danish Broadcasting Corporation's people were to interview the people who had independent film projects to propose, while the DFI's film commissioners were to interview the people whose angle was closer to TV or journalism. This gave rise to a lot of tension because people simply didn't speak the same language at times. But there were also other conflicts in play, and these had to do with the Danish Broadcasting Corporation's desire to slot in programmes that had actually already been planned beneath the umbrella of the new project. At times it was quite hard to figure out what the power struggles were all about. For example, one problem that I ran into when presenting my ideas to the commissioning editor at the Danish Broadcasting Corporation was that he was completely unaware of observational documentaries as a distinct type. There was just no sympathy for the idea that something worthwhile could be produced by means of an observational approach; the view was that something far more direct and journalistic was called for. But it wasn't all negative, and some of the intentions behind 'Pictures of Power,' as the series was eventually called, were certainly good. When we got together through workshops and seminars to discuss the project and each other's ideas, it was exciting to try to figure out how we could complement each other and work together. The idea itself was not at all bad, but implementing it was difficult. And when the project was finally ready to be shown on TV, no effort at all was made to get it out to viewers.

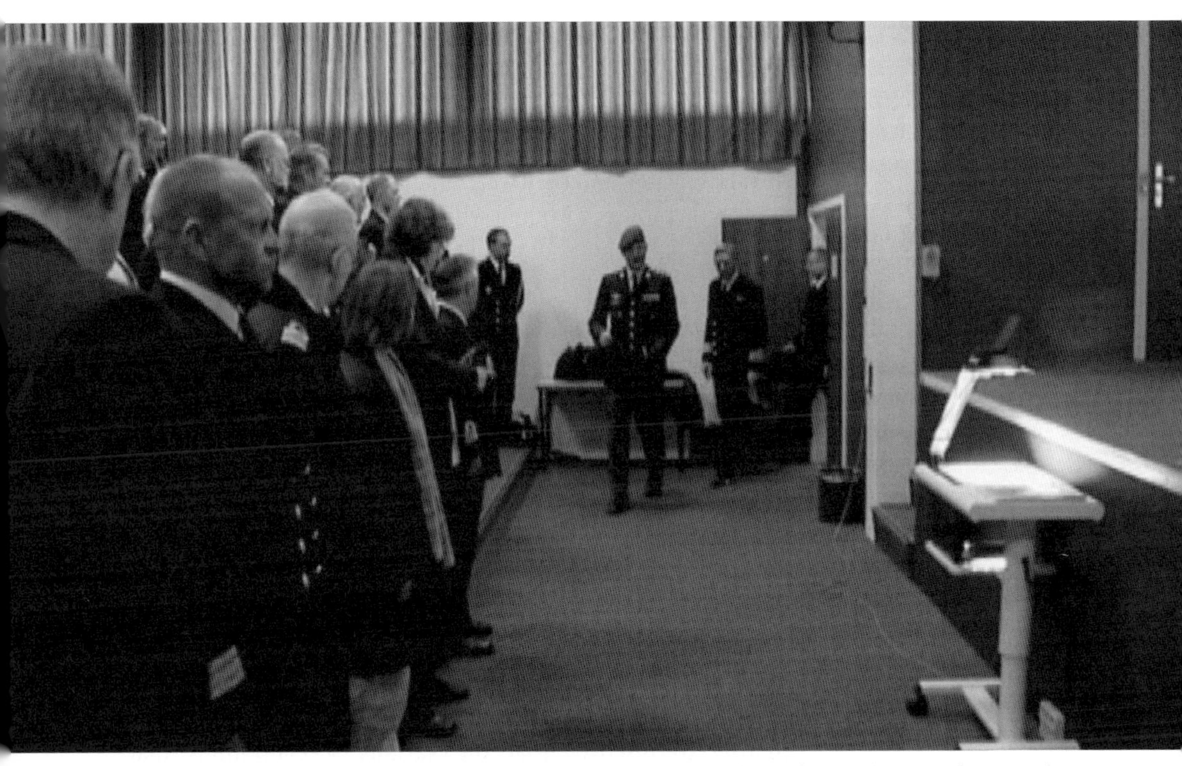

Danish military leaders are on their way to present the new strategy for the military after 9/11 (*Pictures of Power – The C-Memorandum*, framegrab, cinematography by Henrik Bohn Ipsen).

BONDEBJERG: Would you say that you had a good working relationship with the Danish military and Ministry of Defence while making *C-Memorandum*? As good as your relationship with the Danish police while making 'The Police as They Are'?

BONFILS: Yes, working together was actually wonderful, probably because I got on extremely well with the Chief of Defence, Jesper Helsøe. We immediately clicked and he was totally supportive; both of the idea for the film and of my approach. I made it clear to him from the very beginning that I knew nothing at all about the military, and that everyone close to me was opposed to it on principle. But he and his colleagues just found that amusing. They basically saw it all as an opportunity to educate me a bit, and to articulate a quite different perspective. The military consists mostly of very chivalrous men, and they were not, of course, left entirely cold by the fact that it was a woman who was going to be trying to depict their world. I'm good at dealing with tricky situations, and that aspect of my personality stood me in good stead. Also, they were beginning to explore a new strategy of openness – which the film could easily become part of because it was descriptive and suggestive, rather than critical and confrontational.

BONDEBJERG: Your two documentaries about the knowledge society and its jobs, 'The Anatomy of Thought' and 'Dreams with Deadlines,' also involved a lot of different funding sources. I imagine that it was quite helpful that the first one was made during the Year of the Brain. What was involved in getting those two films made?

BONFILS: Yes, that was indeed the context for the production of 'The Anatomy of Thought.' That film was greatly facilitated by the researcher Benny Lautrop, who put me in touch with very interesting people at Hvidovre Hospital, among other places, and with developments in the area of brain-scanning. I found it very exciting to discover that the various specializations that I previously had experienced as competing for resources – in connection with 'In the Shadow of Death' – were beginning to work together in connection with brain-scanning. 'The Anatomy of Thought' is a little different from my other observational films because it combines the depiction of a milieu with a structure informed by the sociology of knowledge. I didn't have to fight at all in order to make that film, and the process of collaborating with the DFI and the Danish Broadcasting Corporation was conflict-free. 'Dreams with Deadlines' took a lot more effort to get financed, but also to pull together in a form that actually worked.

At one point, my editor and I actually had to abandon the observational approach that I otherwise always adopt. The research processes and technological aspects that we describe – based on the two cases we followed at Novo Nordisk – are simply so difficult for ordinary people to understand, so we needed some kind of pedagogical, explanatory narration. So we ended up adding that after we'd given up on other solutions. The observational, anthropological depiction of a work environment is still there, but it's very much in the background, as compared with the elements of a more expository science documentary. But it's also a film with a lot of very dramatic stories, from a reality that involves a lot of competition in a global market.

BONDEBJERG: Up until now we've been talking about your observational documentaries, and about some variations on the observational approach that involved your moving in the direction of science documentaries. But you've also made a number of films in which you explore the world of art in different ways. How did you become interested in that world, and what was it like making those films?

BONFILS: 'Sound Pictures: Six Variations on a Theme,' to select just one title, is actually an example of basic research, carried out through film, and focusing on sound and images. I became interested in making that film because of the fascination that I, and other documentary filmmakers, experienced when watching video art and music videos, all of which were completely new at the time. It was incredible to see just how varied and creative the visual style of these people is, when you think about how complicated the process is that we have to go through to get just a little fade, or whatever. Video art and music videos played around with sound and the visual in a way that made it all seem like a breeze. That's why I divided that film into six variations, the intent having been to explore different boundaries in each of them. I feel that a couple of the variations were very successful, while others didn't work that well. I had a very talented technician helping me, and I'm very happy with the film and pleased to have learnt as much as I did by making it. Basically, the making of that film involved my researching aspects of film aesthetics that are rarely used in documentary filmmaking of a more observational type.

BONDEBJERG: 'Images for the Times' strikes me as being an important film in your oeuvre as a whole because it brings together two characteristic tendencies: on the one hand, it's a dual portrait of two people who stand for different generations of leftist women who are very politically active in society; on the other hand, you developed a much more poetic and symbol-laden visual style in that film than you did in previous films. In 'Images for the Times' your interest in visual arts and visual expression combines with your own, very political commitments to society.

BONFILS: Yes, that film is one of my absolute favourites, both on account of its topic and the two people [Bente Hansen and Helle Hansen] it depicts, and because its visual style is shaped by an interest in a female aesthetic. In that sense it also follows very directly from 'Sound Pictures: Six Variations on a Theme,' although topic-wise the two films are as different as films can be. Throughout my life as a filmmaker, I've been interested in praxis, in how people live and act, and I've also been fascinated by conversation as a form of communication and mediation. But that sense of fascination also encompasses how words and images can work together. My interest in a female aesthetic also finds expression in my film 'Two Painters, Two Studios,' which involves an encounter between two female painters – Nina Steen Knudsen and Ursula Reuter – who belong to different generations. First we visited one painter's studio together, and then the other's. In other words, they met each other in their respective artistic worlds, so to speak, and so the film was about what these women from different generations had to say to each other. The film was about how being both a woman and an artist allowed for some very special experiences, including being part of quite a unique community. Conversation was the central element in that film, which explored some really interesting issues.

The combination of conversation and visual imagery is really pronounced in 'Images for the Times.' The film is a portrait of, and an encounter between, two people: one of whom belongs to the Sixties generation [Bente Hansen]; the other to that of the young rebels who emerged in the Nineties [Helle Hansen]. Their mission is essentially the same, although their specific stories are very different. What was good about that film was that I was able to build on this dialogue between two articulate and politically engaged people, on their conversation about what it was that had been the driving force behind their political involvement. At the same time, both women had an enormous amount of cinematic material about their lives and their political work. Helle clearly did because she was working for TV Stop when we were shooting the film. But Bente also had a lot of material. As a result, we had a lot of options when it came to combining words and images. I worked on the film with Torben Skjødt Jensen, and together we created the montage and that layered style that characterises the film, and gives it a profound visual effect. We didn't create that visual aesthetic just for the sake of having effects in the film, but because the film was about history and memory, and was a dual portrait. Through the visual montage we were able to illustrate the interaction between the present and the past, and also the ways in which the two women were similar and different. The quite unusual, experimental approach that produced the film's characteristic style is also evident in its alternative mode of production. The film was made in collaboration with, among others, TV Stop and the Casablanca Society, the latter having been established in 1980, with the aim of supporting experimental and popular art.

BONDEBJERG: As a director, you've been involved in the Danish film milieu over a really long period of time. During this time there have been quite a number of changes, with clear implications for Danish documentary filmmaking. You've witnessed the artistic explosion of the Sixties and the emergence of TV; the introduction of an influential Film Act in 1972; and various new developments in the 1990s. In the last five years or so you've also been a commissioning editor at the DFI; the person charged with funding and otherwise supporting the documentary films of others. What's your take on the changes that have occurred over the years in terms of Danish documentary filmmaking? Has it become easier or harder to make documentary films?

BONFILS: I had a strong desire to become a documentary film commissioner while Henning Camre was still the head of the DFI. He had such clear views on documentary film, and was never afraid to make it clear where he stood. I don't personally feel that the decision to dismantle the SFC, and to slot documentary filmmaking into the structure of the new DFI, was problematic. The production of a lot of different types of documentary films continued to be a high priority. I think the biggest problem was the gradual disappearance of the truly excellent distribution system that the SFC was in charge of, and through which they got the documentaries out to all sorts of institutions. Nothing was really put in place as an alternative to that. Shortly after I assumed the position as commissioning editor in 2004, there was a meeting with members of DFI's Kontaktudvalg

[Stakeholders' Committee]. Anders Geertsen, who was the sector head for distribution, had prepared some statistics on DFI's involvement in the production of short films and documentaries over the last few years. It turned out that 40% of the productions ended up lying around on shelves and never found distributors. The point he made was a shattering, even paralyzing one because the thought was that such films *couldn't* be distributed. His position was that more effort should be put into supporting the kind of films that had a better chance of reaching an audience. Although the figures were really dreadful, it would have been perfectly coherent to say that the marketing process needed to change because the films were good and deserved to be seen. But instead the idea was that there was something wrong with the films, and that the film commissioners needed to think more carefully about the sorts of things they wanted to support. Films had to be of use in the context of education, and they had to be of interest to the TV stations. I felt the whole experience provided a very clear example of just how vulnerable the film commissioner system can be. I mean pressures are easily brought to bear on the commissioners if they're seen as supporting films that for some reason or other are too experimental. At the same time, I have to say that the idea that supporting documentary films is a matter of supporting art is perhaps a bit too elitist. I felt that all the rethinking and reorganizing that went on when the new DFI was established was really healthy. It was like a wake-up call for the industry; an invitation to rethink the place of documentary film in the context of a new media culture. DR and DR2 have helped to initiate a number of excellent projects. As far as the film commissioners are concerned, TV 2 has been a lot harder to deal with, although things have worked quite well in the context of New Danish Screen. But as a result of the 2007 Film Accord, TV was given far too much power. So, there was this dramatic shift from a perhaps somewhat 'out of touch' commitment to documentary films as art to a much too commercial emphasis on target audiences. The entire DFI subsidy system became so dependent on collaboration with the TV stations that experimental documentary filmmaking essentially ground to a halt. What emerged was a situation of mutual dependence, which was ultimately unacceptable to both the TV stations and to the DFI.

BONDEBJERG: New forms of digital distribution by means, for example, of the DFI's online film site, Filmstriben, seem quite promising. In many cases, directors and producers are free to explore their films' commercial potential. A few directors have created their own websites, where DVDs can be purchased. And then there are the video-on-demand sites that are actually working quite well. But all of this doesn't exactly amount to a digital revolution! Do you think that the film industry and the DFI are aware that there's a lot of still unexplored potential in the area of digital distribution?

BONFILS: Yes, there are a lot of discussions about all this in the film milieu, and plans have actually been developed with the aim of making documentaries in digital formats readily available to Danish viewers in the future. But none of this is really on the rails yet. Although everyone understands that the current economics of documentary film production just isn't viable in the long run, someone has yet to produce alternative models capable of commanding sufficient support from members of the film industry. We're simply going to have to keep updating our subsidy mechanisms in light of developments in the areas of marketing and distribution, so that we make sure our industry is sustainable.

Chapter 3

Dorte Høeg Brask

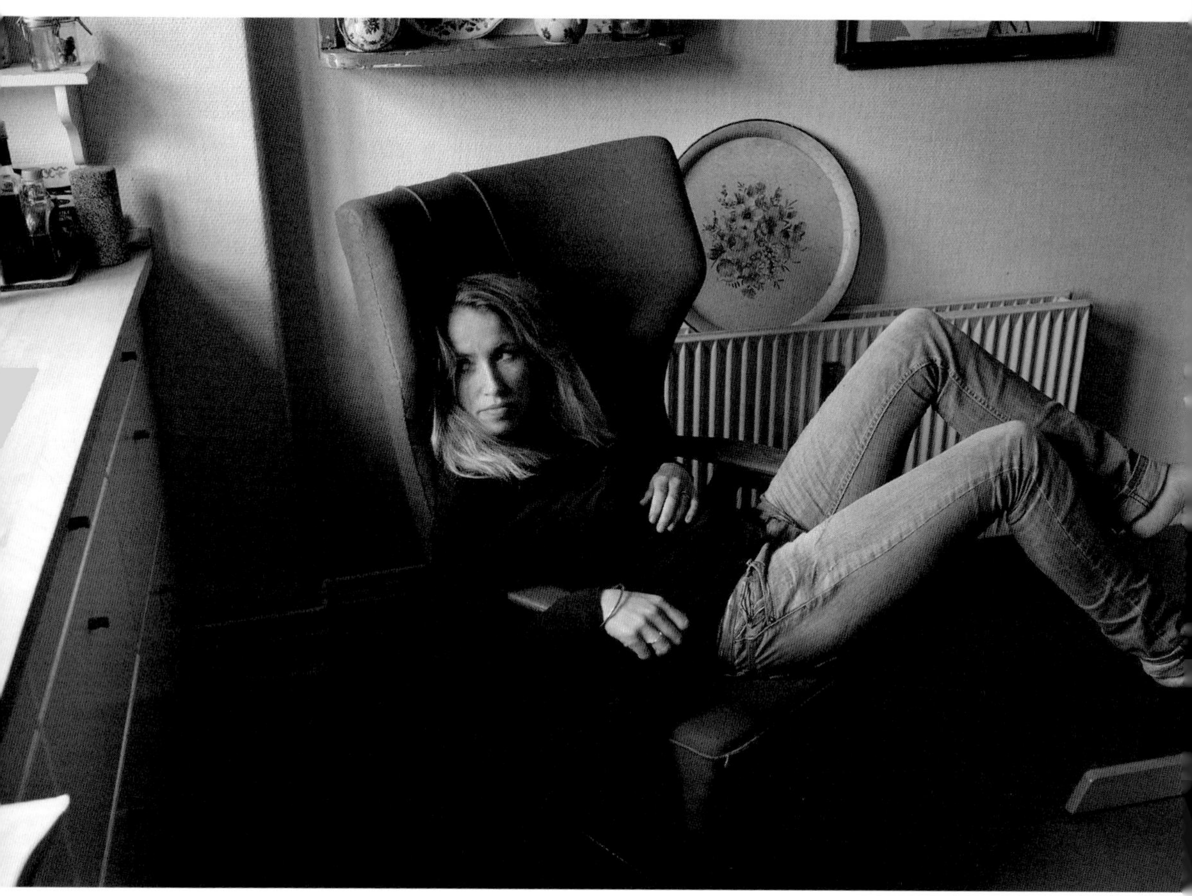

Dorte Høeg Brask. Portrait by Steven Achiam. Courtesy of Steven Achiam.

orn 1970. Høeg Brask received her training as a documentary filmmaker at the National Film School of Denmark, graduating in 2001. From 1994 up until her film school years, Høeg Brask worked as a TV host and filmmaker for the Danish Broadcasting Corporation (DR). Høeg Brask started out in the Children & Youth Department, and later became part of The Reportage Unit. One of her early productions for DR is *Mor kommer snart* (*Mum is Coming*, 1996), about two boys in a Danish children's home. Høeg Brask's diploma film, *Notater om tavshed* (*Notes on Silence*, 2001) provides a personal account of what it meant to lose her mother. In 2001, Høeg Brask also won the Danish film industry's Robert prize for best short documentary with *Radiofolket* (*Talk Radio*, 2001), a film that explores the sense of community enjoyed by a group of elderly radio enthusiasts as they communicate by radio. Høeg Brask's contribution to the collective film project entitled 'Min…' ('My…'), which encompasses films by six women, marked a return to personal themes. *Min elskede* (*My Love*, 2002) depicts a passionate, personal love, and the sorrow and self-questioning that occurs when her lover decides to end the relationship. *Duften af Beirut* (*The Scent of Beirut*, 2006) is similarly concerned with difficult love-related issues. In this film, Høeg Brask tells the fateful story of a 60-year-old woman called Brita, who worked in Beirut when she was young. As it turns out, when this woman fled Lebanon on account of the civil war, she also left behind the man she'd never be able to forget. Høeg Brask's most recent film, *Et hul i himlen – Når mor og far er i fængsel* (*Scattering Clouds: When Mom and Dad Have Wronged*, 2007), follows the lives of three children with either a mother or a father in prison. The film raises questions about both absence and betrayal, but also about how we as a society relate to crime and punishment. Høeg Brask chaired the Association of Danish Film Directors from 2008–10. In 2010, she was appointed as the Danish Film Institute's film commissioner for children's shorts and documentaries.

Documentary features:

2007   *Et hul i himlen – Når mor og far er i fængsel* (*Scattering Clouds: When Mom and Dad Have Wronged*)

2006   *Duften af Beirut* (*The Scent of Beirut*)

Documentary shorts:

2002   *Min elskede* (*My Love*, part of the TV series 'Min...' ['My...'])

2001   *Radiofolket* (*Talk Radio*)

2001   *Notater om tavshed* (*Notes on Silence*)

Television:

2000   *Erik og Karl* ('Erik and Karl')

1998   *Selskabsdamer* ('Society Ladies')

1997   *Smukke* ('Beauty')

1996   *Mor kommer snart* (*Mum is Coming*)

REDVALL: How did you end up deciding you wanted to work with moving images?

HØEG BRASK: I got into RUC [Roskilde University] when I was 20, and I just couldn't sit still. I remember we had this camera, and that I suggested we be allowed to produce children's TV instead of doing written project work. We produced some really juvenile stuff, but I liked being behind the camera, and I enjoyed the storytelling aspect. So I started playing around with the idea of working with TV. I got in touch with the Danish Broadcasting Corporation's Children & Youth Department, where I discovered that people were approaching children's realities in a very respectful and playful way. I then applied for a position as the host for a children's programme, and when I got it, I became the public face of a weekly programme dedicated to news for children. It was a live programme with music, and we'd discuss things like why there was a war going on in Chechnya, or why a bunch of bullies were angry on Nørrebro. We tried to discuss current sociopolitical agendas in a way that would make sense to children, and we put a lot of thought into trying to figure out how best to explain realities involving adults who are incapable of talking to each other.

That was a challenging, but also very instructive period of my life. I see myself as having basically received the training I needed during that period because it's all about being humble and about having a certain respect for the mass media, and for the many children who are watching and listening. If I were to identify the guiding thread in what I do, I'd say it has to do with being attentive to children and giving them a voice. At the same time, I'm driven by a sense of indignation, and by an awareness of wanting to change the world. I want to make the world a better place with my camera. In addition to making films, I've been involved in the political work that's part of my professional terrain. This has been in my capacity as chair of the Association of Danish Film Directors, and through my current role as the commissioner for children's shorts and documentaries. But my own work producing programmes and films for children has always been most important to me, and still is.

REDVALL: For how long did you work at the Danish Broadcasting Corporation's Children & Youth Department?

HØEG BRASK: I was there for a few years. Then I met Mariella Harpelunde Jensen, and we shared an understanding of childhood as a space where adults should leave children in peace. We wanted to tell stories in which children were depicted as enjoying autonomy in their own world. The next step was my first documentary film, which involved moving into a children's home with my camera. I think I was 25 at the time. Today, I don't quite understand how or why I did that, but at the time I felt it was important. I had read Peter Høeg's *De måske egnede* (*Borderliners*, 2006), and I'd been able to relate to that sense of only possibly being well suited for something or someone. The book's story partly takes place in a children's home, and in one especially powerful passage, Høeg describes how the children are waiting to be picked up. The scene captures the joy of anticipation, and what it feels like to watch other children being picked up, and it does this in a very evocative way. I felt that the scene in question simply had to exist in reality, and it did. I found it at a children's home in Roskilde, which is where I moved in with my camera.

My time at the children's home allowed me to make *Mum is Coming*. The film focuses on two boys, aged 7 and 9, who are waiting for their mother to pick them up. The film shows how the boys' use of imagination gets them through each day. One of the points made in the film is that you can cope with a lot if you're able to use your imagination. It was *their* story in spite of it all. They weren't victims, and there was room in their reality for humour and playfulness, even though the larger context of their lives was tough and involved serious problems. What I hadn't grasped was just how attached the boys would become to me. Of course I became the mother who asked how they were feeling, and who was there when it was time to go to sleep. And then I disappeared and they found themselves abandoned yet again. I had a hard time coping with that, also because there were all these really intense responses from grown-ups who wanted to adopt the boys after they'd seen the film on TV. I realized I'd exposed the children, although I hadn't meant to do that. And the question I grappled with was, 'Who's going to protect them if I can't?' That question has stayed with me throughout all my projects, and it's probably the reason why I've sometimes moved away from the camera and into a more political world. It's sometimes hard to live with what we do, with the power that TV and the camera have.

After having worked for the Children & Youth Department, I joined DR's Reportage Unit, where the established practice was that we filmed our stories ourselves. I was very concerned about our relationship to the people whose lives we were documenting, and about their vulnerability; and my application to the Film School was motivated, among other things, by those concerns. I was actually quite old by the time I applied; I was 27 and already fairly well established. I could simply have continued working for DR, but I missed being in a place where what we do gets vigorously discussed. What I missed was kindred spirits.

REDVALL: DR's Children & Youth Department is highly respected because it's seen as having produced a lot of very original programmes. It's also seen as having been a place where Danish film and TV talent was nurtured and developed, especially under the leadership of Mogens Vemmer. You yourself have said that you belong to the 'Mogens Vemmer school.' What was so unique about the Children & Youth Department's approach at the time?

HØEG BRASK: People were given a lot of space. Nobody asked questions. There was an enormous amount of trust, also at the senior management level. We were given the space we needed to develop, but at the same time there was always a set of core concerns or values. There are certain rules that have to be observed when you're telling stories aimed at children, and we were made to understand that right from the start. You have to be aware of what it is you're doing, and you have to approach the children with respect. What I learnt from that department is that children are our equals; that they're just as nuanced and complex as adults. Children have a need to engage with stories that are about them and their realities. Some of these stories have to be quite complex because they're about what it means to be lonely, or different, or to be looking for a friend. Vemmer was really important because he was good at hiring originals and giving them space. He hired people who were finely attuned to the dynamics of a situation; people who were driven by indignation or by their imagination; people who were deeply creative. In that sense he was a really good person to work for. I was at the Department during a period when it was all free play, and it was a lot of fun. We were one big family, with a unique sensibility.

REDVALL:

What was the transition from DR's Children & Youth Department to the National Film School of Denmark like?

HØEG BRASK:

It was a struggle being there. I had to learn how to be back in school again, and I have a lot of trouble with the premise that everyone has to agree; with the idea that there's only one way of doing things.

REDVALL:

Is there only one way of doing things at the Film School?

HØEG BRASK:

No, but it is after all a school. I found starting at the Film School difficult. I felt that I already knew a lot and had a lot of experience. There were two things that were especially difficult. First of all, I found that I suddenly had to be more self-aware. Our teacher, Arne Bro, sat us down in a circle on our third day, and asked us to talk about the most significant event of our lives. The only thoughts I had were, 'My mother died last year,' and 'What am I going to say?' I felt that I'd be unhappy if I spoke up about my mother in front of a bunch of strangers, but then Arne got us started with an extremely troubling story, so I thought, 'OK, we're supposed to talk about something that really hurts.' The others then told their stories and then I told mine. The room was completely quiet. Telling the story was a struggle, but I could feel that it was OK. The point is that the Film School was a place that reached into your personal space, and I just wasn't ready for that.

The other thing that was difficult was this business of being part of a tiny world for so many years. There wasn't a lot of room for difference – yet we *are* different, and our differences make us better. There can be this expectation that people will converge on the same language and culture as they go along, and I never really felt that I was fully part of the community. I felt like an outsider, and was probably more interested in realities outside the Film School, in politics and society. At the School we were interested in ourselves, in how we were changing and developing. That's why I had trouble adjusting to the School in the beginning, but I ended up being very happy there.

REDVALL: A lot of directors who graduated from the National Film School of Denmark talk about how overwhelming it was to have to be as focused on their inner selves as Arne Bro's teaching required them to be. But they also talk about how they eventually came to appreciate his approach. The films made by the School's students just before they graduate, or immediately after their film school years, are often very personal. Your diploma film is, for example, very personal. What was it that you came to appreciate about the School? Did you find that your way of expressing yourself changed as a result of what you were exposed to and taught?

HØEG BRASK: Arne is without a doubt a powerhouse in the context of Danish documentary filmmaking. And he still means a lot to me. He's able to identify the tone, the underlying narrative drive, and the expressive language of your films, and he's able to point out why your films work, although you couldn't do that yourself. In terms of what I learnt, I suppose it had to do with trying to understand the reasons why you do what you do, before you begin to direct your cinematic gaze at what others have done. It was hard, and while I really fought the School's approach in the beginning, I finally succumbed to it completely. As a result of those years, my diploma film ended up being this very personal, even inevitable film about leave-taking, *Notes on Silence*. I would never have made it had it not been for Arne and his stubborn and sensitive support. That's what a good mentor can provide. Indeed, a mentor shouldn't be doing more than that. But you do need some sort of post-graduate training after the Film School.

I returned to the Film School as a part-time teacher a few years after I'd graduated, and I basically taught the things I felt I hadn't been taught myself. I felt we hadn't really been told much about what it was like to step out into a larger reality. You have to be able to articulate your thoughts in a way that's comprehensible to others, and you have to understand that the stories are to be found in that larger world, and not within you. The bridge to that larger reality – to the Danish Film Institute, and to the film industry – is an important one for the Film School. I'm now working for the

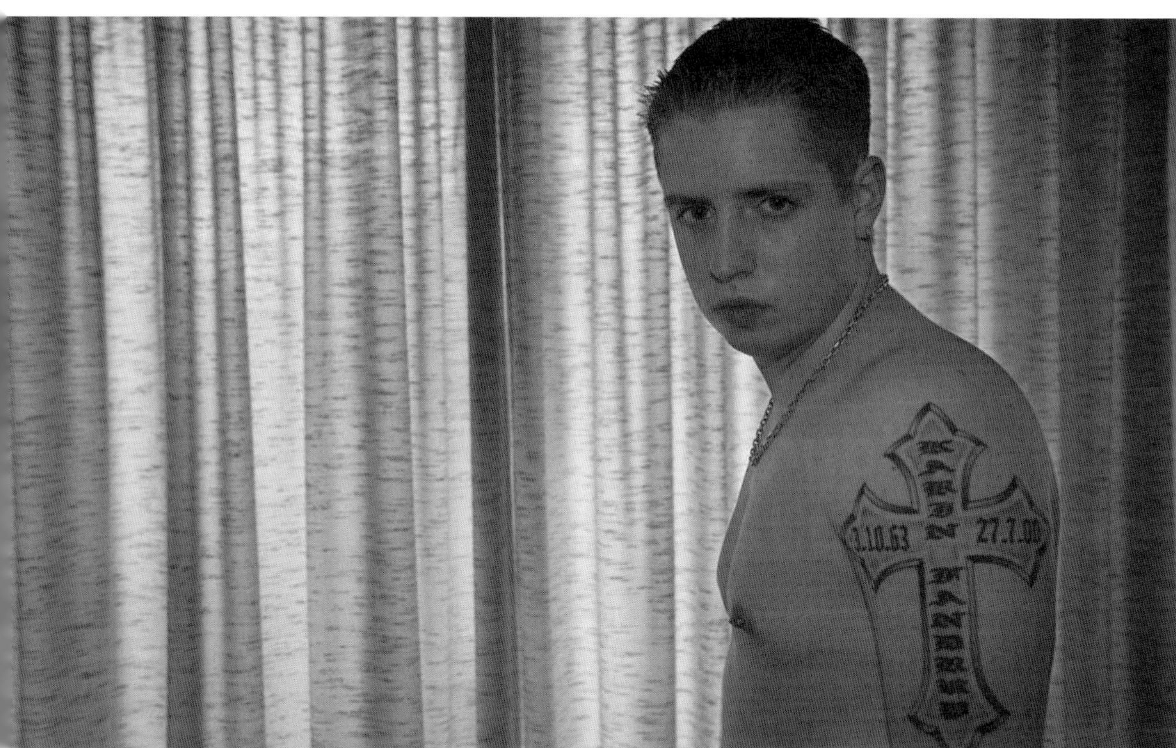

Alex, whose father is in prison for killing his mother (*Scattering Clouds – When Mom and Dad Have Wronged*, photo: Helga C. Theilgaard Courtesy of Dorte Høeg Brask).

DFI as a film commissioner, and I look at things from the other side. It's very clear to me that learning about that bridge is very important.

REDVALL: How did you establish yourself as a filmmaker after graduating from film school? You managed to make *Talk Radio* quite quickly, and the film won the Robert prize for best short documentary of the year.

HØEG BRASK: I was very lucky to be able to go straight into the milieu with *Talk Radio*, which I'd already started working on before I graduated. That film made things a lot easier because it became such a big success. It's basically a story about some people who, much like the children in the children's home, are sitting somewhere in the world and just waiting. These are people we don't normally see or hear, but one night I was lying there unable to sleep and I heard their voices on the local radio. I visited them with my camera and got to know them. They were elderly, lonely, and indignant people who sent messages to one another without ever having met face to face. What they had was a kind of community without strings attached. What they actually longed for was someone who'd simply listen to them. And beneath all that there's a story about what our society is like. There's a group of people in our society who don't feel that they can be seen or heard through the normal channels. Today we have the Internet and blogs and a lot more local radio stations, but things were very different back then. With that film I felt I was able to return to something important.

REDVALL: You also contributed to the collective film project 'My...' shortly after film school. That project involved six directors, all of them women. How did that project get off the ground and what was your experience of making *My Love* like?

HØEG BRASK: I really enjoyed the process. Initially, I didn't really expect to find it that interesting to be working together, as a group of six women, but it was. Not because we were women, but because it was interesting to be together. Being together was really nice, among other things, because you tend to work alone a lot as a documentary filmmaker. So suddenly we were able to assist one another, also with very practical tasks. We were able to look over each other's shoulders during the shoots, which was quite helpful, given how tight the production process was.

Yet I hardly remember making the film because I was so madly in love. I'd made the film about the loss of my mother. And then

I was to make this film with the title *My...* about someone I was close to, and I didn't have anyone to focus on. But I was really in love with Kasper, and so he just said, 'Why don't you just film me?' And, very naively, I just started filming him a lot, until he left me... At that point the film ground to a complete halt because I was so sad that I couldn't cope with the idea of finishing it. But I did sense that I was in the process of telling a story about myself. But was I ready for that?

In *My Love* you can clearly trace the impact of the Film School. It became a very intimate and personal film. The film deals with this great love I felt for someone, and it's quite strange seeing it today. The strangeness also has to do with my moving on and falling in love with someone else. But then there's this film I've made called *My Love*. And I can't make another film with that title because that's the way it is with titles. But I was actually quite happy with the film, and Kasper was too. He did the music and subsequently put out a record with songs, some of which are responses to the film. So we were working our way along this absurd little meta-love track. But I see the film as being about a particular phase in my life.

REDVALL: The film is interesting in relation to issues like having to take responsibility for the people you put in front of the camera. After all, that responsibility also has to encompass *you* if you're going to be as much of a presence as you are in *My Love*. The film deals with intimate family relationships, but you're also in the frame a lot. What are your thoughts about this issue of also having to take care of yourself?

HØEG BRASK: *My Love* is probably the film that's generated the most responses, although I put a lot less thought into it than the others. I suppose I just wanted to get rid of it when it was done, but I've received so many unsolicited letters from people whose love for someone is unrequited. Letters from people who are looking for advice, or who want to give me advice. My advice is that you have to think about what you're doing if you're going to follow that track. I'm glad I made the film. I think it's a good film about a certain state of mind. It helped me achieve a sense of closure, but at this point I do find myself laughing about it.

REDVALL: As I understand it, you spent a number of years producing various TV documentaries before making *The Scent of Beirut*, which once again tells a story about a family, albeit one with a striking difference. How did you end up making that film?

HØEG BRASK:

I did a number of different things before making *The Scent of Beirut*. For example, for a few years I was working on a project that involved collecting home movies made by Danes. I put ads in the local newspapers all along the western coast of Jutland, and ended up collecting more than 100 hours' worth of material, which I wanted to use in some sort of story about Denmark. But suddenly this other project came up. It's also based on home movies, and is entitled *Danskernes egen historie* ('The Personal History of the Danes'; prod. Mediehuset Substanz, 2004–). So I ended up dropping the project I was working on, although I was actually keen to examine the images that had been produced carefully, instead of merely using them as a means of illustrating what a certain period was like. That material is waiting for me in my attic, and it contains a lot of really fascinating lines of inquiry. For example, it's about how pictures of women are taken by men. It's the man who films the family, so it's his image of life, or of everyday existence, that's reproduced.

The Scent of Beirut was a difficult film. Basically, I was interested in how someone can make her life cohere if she refuses to do what everyone else does. Is it OK to opt not to have a family? Is it OK to live in the past and not to move on? Do I have the right to say that some life choices are better than others? Those were the sorts of questions that were driving me, and what I discovered was that I didn't have that right. I couldn't create a conception of the right life that was valid for others. The film is about a woman who's opted to live in the past. To me she was a goddess who walked into my life when I was a child. But when I grew up my image of her changed completely. I discovered that there was a dark side. She'd lost her lover and she lived in the past. She couldn't embrace what happened in the here and now. That surprised me a lot.

REDVALL:

In connection with your next film, *Scattering Clouds: When Mom and Dad Have Wronged*, you wrote an article about what's involved in making a life for oneself as a documentary filmmaker. One of the challenges of such a life, at least as you describe it, has to do with the amount of time that various processes take to unfold. How do you see all that today?

HØEG BRASK:

While I was making *Scent of Beirut* I started to think, 'I can't make a living doing this, but if I'm going to try to do precisely that, I have to *own* my films.' I became involved with the Association of Danish Film Directors, and then became the chair of the Association at one point. One of the issues I was interested in discussing had to do with the conditions we faced as directors. How do we get our working life to work? At the same time, I started working on a film project that grew out of my first film about the children in that children's home. It was basically about the children that we don't ever see. The premise of *Scattering Clouds* is that every time a father goes to jail, there's a child somewhere who loses his or her father for a certain period of time. Why don't we ever hear about those children? First, I got in touch with a prison priest, who told me about various conversations with the imprisoned fathers, and the shame that their imprisonment entailed. So I started to realize just how hard it would be to make a film about what I had in mind. But that's when I knew that the project was important and that I had to pursue it.

It took me three years to make the film on my own, as both its director and producer. First there was the idea, but then there was all the research, which included visiting just about every low- and high- security prison that exists in Denmark. I examined what it was like for a child to visit a mother or father in prison. I talked to a lot of fathers, and to some mothers. I spoke to social workers and grief support groups. And then one day I got a call from a boy called Alex, who had heard about the project. His father had killed his mother, and he said that he wanted to be part of my project if I could promise him that he wouldn't be seen as a victim. He wanted to tell his story, and he wanted to help determine the nature of his participation in the film, and I'm a strong supporter of precisely that. It's important to work out some solid agreements with the children because they have to live with the consequences. When we decide to be part of something, we do so as adults. But they're not adults, and you have to take that seriously.

So, in the end, I found these three children who told me their stories, and that project has meant the world to me. Both in terms of creating something that gave these children a voice, and in terms of breaking a taboo, and confronting the shame that weighs on children and families who have relatives in prison. The film was first shown on TV, and I knew, right from the start, that I wanted more than that. I wanted to travel with the film, so as to anchor it in schools, and in society more generally. So that's why I put together quite a substantial 'film & debate' tour together with the children, with stops in schools, prisons, trade schools, and churches. What we wanted to discuss was the relationship between crime and punishment. I established an interactive educational site where children could test their responses to different dilemmas, prompted by questions like, 'What would I do if someone took my bicycle?' The children had to think these dilemmas through in terms of ideas of vigilante-style responses, an eye for an eye, a tooth for a tooth, and so on. I also illustrated the various punishments we have in Denmark, and the children could have a go at responding to punishment-related questions such as, 'What sort of punishment do you get for stealing? Or for shooting someone?'

You put a lot of years into a project like that. And, as a director, the responsibility you have vis-à-vis those who are part of it is really huge. But then it's really fantastic when I get a Facebook message from Alex saying that he's really happy with the film, and feels that it's made a difference because he was able to talk about his life, and about things that can be difficult to put into words. I believe that a documentary film can help certain young people make their way, as long as the filmmaker takes good care of them. But if you're interested in working with children who are especially vulnerable – which is the case for me – then you have to make sure there's someone in the wings who's ready to step in and connect with them when the project comes to an end. There has to be a network around them. Alex had that.

REDVALL: There are some very powerful moments in *Scattering Clouds*. For example, we learn that when a child sees a parent being arrested, he may feel as though he has to go to prison himself. It's also thought-provoking to see Alex being told that it's a good thing that relatives aren't given the power to deliver verdicts because they're inclined to mete out the harshest of punishments. The film clearly captures the impact that this utterance has on the boy. As a viewer, one senses the considerable research that supports the film, but it's the children's voices and faces that are ultimately of central importance. Do you think there's a unique tradition of making documentary films about, and for, children in Denmark, or in Scandinavia more generally?

HØEG BRASK: In my mind, the process is very much about sorting in terms of age, about getting the adults out of the picture. It's about finding the children's level. In the good old days of the Children & Youth Department, we certainly had a tradition of listening to children, through children's radio and TV programmes, with and for children. I think it's incredibly important to listen to children; to their deliberations, their hesitations, and to the doubts they might

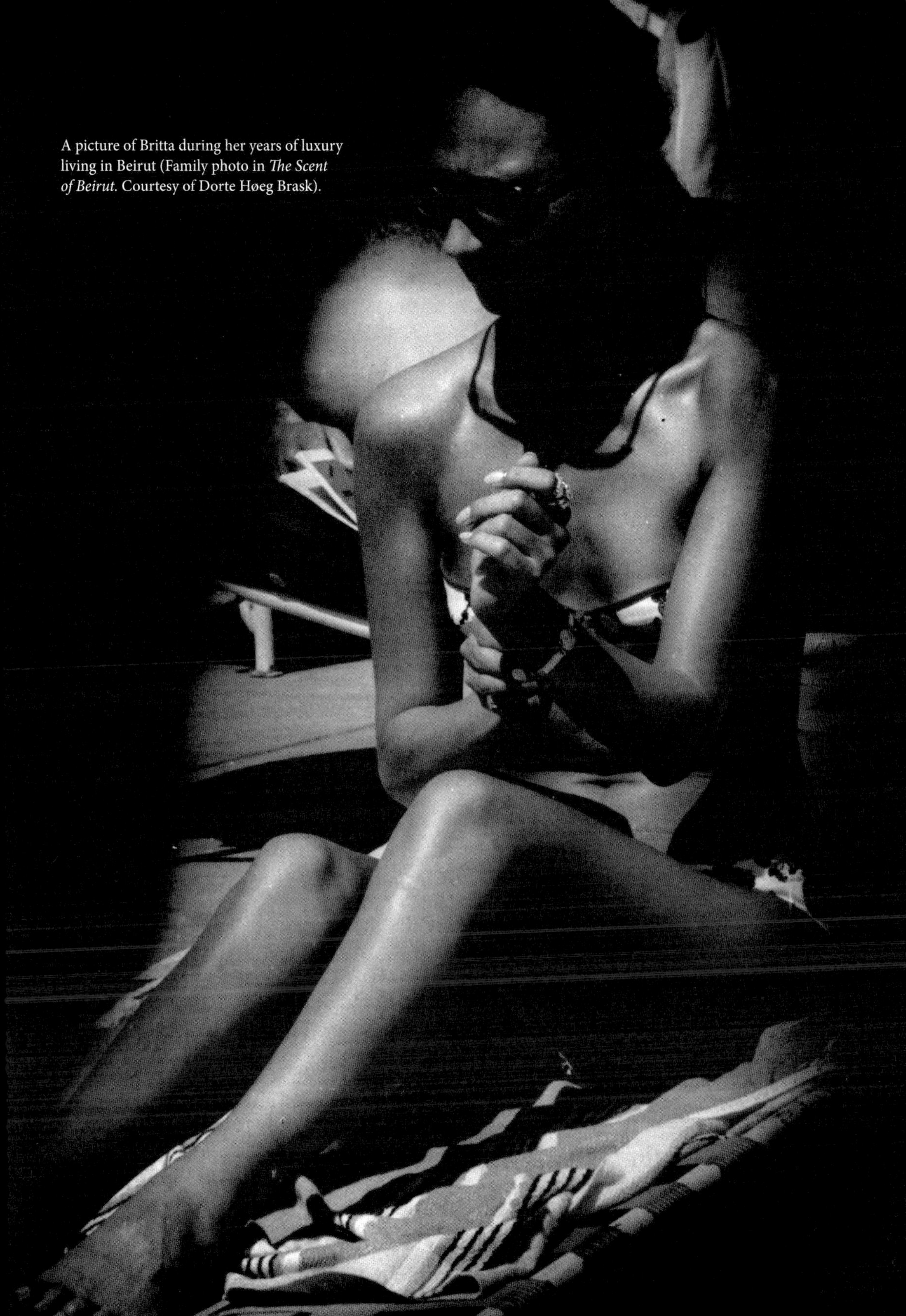

A picture of Britta during her years of luxury living in Beirut (Family photo in *The Scent of Beirut*. Courtesy of Dorte Høeg Brask).

have as they relate to things both small and large. I don't want to romanticize the past, but it's just not the same today. DR's new children's channel, Ramasjang, is fantastic, but the focus just isn't where it used to be.

I've taken on the job of being the film commissioner for shorts and documentaries for children because I think it's so incredibly important that we listen to them. Also, I felt there was a real lack of stories about children's lives seen through a documentary lens. There's no question that fiction can achieve something quite unique because it can camouflage reality and thereby make it possible to talk about feelings, major changes in children's lives, or situations that are difficult. But it's something quite different to have children experience the world of *real* children whose situations resemble theirs. That's enormously effective. From the child's perspective, that encounter may provide a fleeting sensation of not being completely alone. That's an important sort of experience to be able to give children.

Yet, in my experience, a lot of children feel that they're just not reflected in the world of TV. So, as a consultant, I want to draw attention to the existence of other sorts of children's lives, other sorts of children's stories. Stories about growing up far away from the city, about being adopted, or about having nine siblings or a lesbian mother. This isn't just about some peripheral or especially vulnerable group; it's about nuancing the images we have of children's lives, and about creating new images. That's what I see as my task.

We clearly do have certain strengths in Scandinavia, but at the same time there's been this tendency for directors to use children's film as a kind of practice area, and then they move on to making films for grown-ups, which they see as far more appealing. So the area lags behind in terms of talent development. DR's Children & Youth Department was a fantastic place to work with children's stories because of the emphasis on mentoring. But there's nothing like that anymore. The Film School doesn't offer anything like a child's perspective, and there are no supplementary training programmes focused on children's stories. I believe there should be enough money to allow for playful explorations and for mistakes, because mistakes are necessary. There's got to be a lot of space. Otherwise the desire to make these films disappears. If you look at children's stories from Denmark, including the animated films, you notice that these are edgy stories about serious issues, or that they have that Nordic melancholy. We're committed to telling stories that hurt, but there also has to be room for laughter. A lot of my work is about making room for difference, with reference to genre, perspective, and themes. And this is true of the conversations I have with both TV programmers and filmmakers.

REDVALL: What's the collaboration between film and TV like in the context of Danish documentary filmmaking, as you see it?

HØEG BRASK: If we're talking about children's films, then it's safe to say that the film industry still has this fairly conservative understanding of them as discrete works that are best seen at a film festival. But how does that fit with a children's TV channel? How do we go about giving some substance to stories for children, and how do we foster an interest in these stories? A large part of my job consists of translating the reality of TV into terms that people in the film industry can understand. They have to understand that it's important that the children actually see the films. If that means we have to develop series or whole worlds on the Net, then we'll just have to explore those areas. But the collaboration with TV is really very good, and in my experience we're often after the same thing: something that's edgy and of high quality for children.

REDVALL: In your capacity as a film commissioner, in what ways are you involved in the projects as they unfold?

HØEG BRASK: I'm very involved indeed, if that's what people want. But it's clear that you always have to tread carefully. When should you be offering help, and when should you be pulling back? You have to be sensitive to the projects' differences. What is it that's needed in a given case? Documentaries typically develop in a far more complicated way than fiction films. Since I'm the only commissioner in the area of children's film – and have to cover everything from the small child in a snowsuit to the person who's almost grown-up – I get a lot of very different material. It's a question of pushing without pointing. It's clear that there's a tricky balance in that I'm the person who can help develop a project, but also have the authority to shut it down. That dual role is quite difficult, but I can live with it because what I reject is a project, not you. You're always welcome to come back again. I know what it feels like to be on the other side, and how hard it is to get turned down and to be left thinking that one's future has been destroyed for the next three years. But it doesn't have to be that way. It's just that the particular project in question wasn't

REDVALL:

HØEG BRASK:

REDVALL:

HØEG BRASK:

strong enough. It's very important to signal that, but I'm not saying it's an easy job.

In your capacity as film commissioner you see most of the films that get made. You're also aware of the projects that don't ultimately get realized, and of the films that are on their way. How do you see Danish documentary filmmaking today?

It's fantastic. It's agenda setting. Danish films have a sophistication, in terms of their film language, that is far greater than that of most films. There may be a lot more, or a lot less, money available elsewhere in the world, but we have this unique attentiveness when it comes to how we tell stories. We have the cinematic tradition we need to lift the quality of the films so that they become distinctive cinematic works. Danish films have that dimension, but they're also shaped by a strong desire to say something, and there are some really important stories being created. Take a film like Mads Brügger's *Ambassadøren* (*The Ambassador*, 2011). Brügger places himself where few would dare to be and says: 'I'm not afraid to do this. You don't have to agree with me, but I'm going to give this a go.' It's an extremely courageous film that we can be really proud of. I certainly am, and the same is true for many other Danish documentaries. And what I don't understand is why there's a lot of general talk about how Danish film is in crisis, with Danish documentary films being mentioned as a mere afterthought.

Do you have any thoughts about why there's this sense that Danish fiction film is doing poorly, as compared with Danish documentary film, which is seen as thriving?

At the DFI, we're talking about this a lot these days. Personally I don't understand why so few fiction films engage with the world around us. There are very few films that raise questions about how we live our lives. And I'm not just thinking about the nature of our relationships here. We're at war. We're in the midst of a financial crisis. People are losing their houses and homes. These are tumultuous times, but none of that is reflected in the fiction films. And that's exactly what the documentary has to offer. It can grasp reality and relate to it. The fiction film has a much harder time doing that.

I think what's lacking is the courage to think outside the box. We have a Lars von Trier, and a film like *Melancholia* (2011) is clearly about that doomsday feeling. It asks questions like, 'What happens when the world falls apart?' The answer is complicated and difficult, and it takes a lot of courage to take up these issues. And I don't find a lot of the necessary courage on the fiction side of things. But it's also very challenging because it takes such a long time to learn how to make a feature-length fiction film. The Danish film industry doesn't make room for people who need to practice their skills. You're not allowed to make a whole lot of films that don't work. But some of the directors who've looked beyond Denmark *have* been given an opportunity to practice their skills, and perhaps that's why they've achieved as much as they have.

REDVALL: It's my impression that women have gravitated in far greater numbers toward documentary filmmaking than fiction filmmaking. Why do you think that's the case?

HØEG BRASK: It's true; there *are* a lot more women in documentary filmmaking. It's hard to say why, and I've often pointed out that we need to take a closer look at this. When I was chair of the Association of Danish Film Directors we did research on how directors support themselves. What we found was that women generally produced fewer commercials, and stopped pursuing their careers earlier than men. Men, on the other hand, seemed to get public funding more than once in the course of a career. Perhaps the ideas were simply better, yet it's clear that the conditions that Danish film offers differ, depending on whether you are a man or a woman. Most of the documentary filmmakers being trained these days are women, and I imagine that some of these excellent and very wise filmmakers will move up and start making feature fiction films. And that would somewhat rectify the imbalance. But it's important to discuss the reasons for that imbalance. Following on the research that we did through the Association of Danish Film Directors, we did talk about how women aren't good enough at selling themselves, or at competing. Yet sometimes that's exactly what's needed.

REDVALL: I take it that you're not making any films yourself, now that you're working as a film commissioner?

HØEG BRASK: No, I don't have time for anything else, and I also don't feel like it. I clearly get excited about certain areas, but right now my sense of involvement comes from being a film commissioner. I'm passionate about the projects I'm involved in, and I want to do everything I can to help them succeed. They'll never be mine, but when they do succeed, I feel that I've also succeeded. You just feel so proud. I love my job, but I'm also doing a degree programme at the

University of Copenhagen at the same time. I've got a natural drive. I'm so eager to make good use of my time. When I turned 40 and got divorced, I thought to myself, 'You've got to do what you've always dreamt of doing, namely study law.' Basically, I'm interested in the foundations on which our society rests, and in the question of how we should be treating each other. So I've started studying social law as a part-time student, the focus being on the rights of children and young people. I'm at university once a week. Nobody knows who I am. Nobody knows what the Danish Film Institute is, or that I'm a film commissioner. I take that cap off, and find my studies incredibly meaningful. They provide an outlet for a lot of my sociopolitical energy, and a context for discussions about children's conditions. Also, I'm very involved in the Children's Media Think Tank, an initiative that Mariella Harpelunde Jensen got off the ground. That's also provided a space where I can take all my indignation on behalf of children.

Chapter 4

Mads Brügger

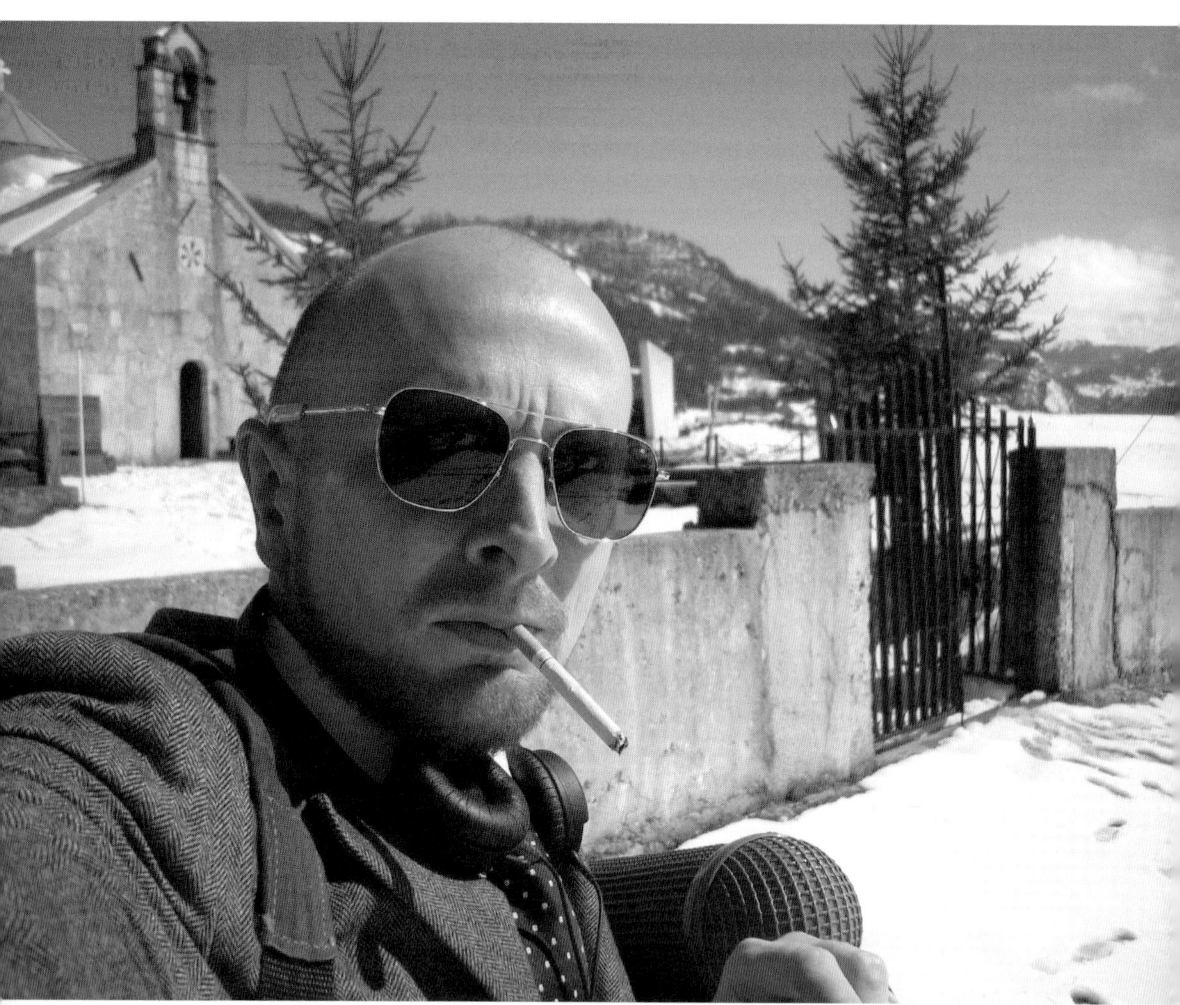

Mads Brügger. Self portrait. Courtesy of Mads Brügger and The Danish Film Institute Stills & Posters Archive.

Born 1972. Brügger holds a BA in Film Studies from the University of Copenhagen (2001), as well as a degree in Journalism from the Danish School of Media & Journalism (1998). In addition to his work as a documentary film director, Brügger has been active as a journalist for radio, TV, and various newspapers. As of 2011, Brügger has served as co-director, along with Mikael Bertelsen, for Denmark's most recent public service radio station, Radio24syv. In 1996, while still a journalism student, he was hired by the Danish Broadcasting Corporation (DR), where he contributed to such radio programmes as *Harddisken* (about computers and technology) and *U-land*, which targeted young listeners. In 1998, Brügger joined the Danish Broadcasting Corporation's Children & Youth Department, a department that is legendary for its experimental, boundary pushing programming. His role was to oversee the Department's documentary programmes. Brügger has worked with radio and TV, and with satirical as well as documentary genres. In 2002, he was awarded the Kryger prize for the radio documentary entitled *Skjoldhøjarkivet* ('The Skjoldhøj Archive', 2002). This documentary was made in collaboration with Mikael Bertelsen and Kim G. Hansen, and focuses on a suburban neighborhood in Aarhus. In 2001, he hosted DR's satirical talk show, *Kleinrocks kabinet* ('Kleinrock's Cabinet'). He later served as a co-host (with Mikael Bertelsen) for DR2's offbeat and surrealistic TV talk show, *Den 11. Time* ('The 11th Hour', 2007), as well as for DR2's innovative outreach programme focusing on literature and literacy, *Læsegruppe Sundholm* ('The Sundholm Reading Group', 2011).

Brügger's work as a journalist is characterized by its subjective, staged, and reflexive traits, and by an exploratory approach to reality and the roles that this offers. His documentaries for film and TV build on his journalism, both in terms of their formal properties and underlying method. Brügger first caught the public's attention with a staged documentary TV series produced by DR2, *Danes for Bush*. The series follows Brügger and Jakob Boeskov as they make their way in the American Republican millieu, having penetrated deeply into it by pretending to be strong Danish supporters of George W. Bush. Brügger made use of the same method in yet another documentary series for DR2, *Det røde kapel* (*The Red Chapel*, 2006). Here the focus was on a fictitious communist theatre group, of which he purported to be a member, and which he managed to take to North Korea. In 2009, the film based on the series won Nordic Panorama's best Nordic documentary award, as well as the Jury Prize for best documentary at the Sundance Film Festival. That same year, Brügger made his most recent documentary TV series for DR2, *Quatraro mysteriet* (*The Quatraro Mystery*, 2009), which is a kind of documentary thriller about a mysterious death in the European

Union. Brügger's most recent film is the performative documentary, *Ambassadøren* (*The Ambassador*, 2011), in which he assumes the identity of an honorary consul general in the Central African Republic, his aim being to expose the workings of corruption on the African continent.

Documentary features:

2011   *Ambassadøren* (*The Ambassador*)
2009   *Det røde kapel* (*The Red Chapel*)

Television:

2011   *Læsegruppe Sundholm* ('The Sundholm Reading Group,' TV literature programme, with Mikael Bertelsen)
2009   *Quatraro mysteriet* (*The Quatraro Mystery,*, TV series, based on an idea by Mads Brügger; directed by Jeppe Rønde in collaboration with Brügger and Mikael Bertelsen)
2007   *Den 11. Time* ('The 11th Hour,' TV talk show, with Mikael Bertelsen)
2006   *Det røde kapel* (*The Red Chapel*, TV series)
2004   *Danes for Bush* (TV series)
2001   *Kleinrocks kabinet* ('Kleinrock's Cabinet,' satirical TV show)

Radio documentary:

2002   *Skjoldhøjarkivet* ('The Skjoldhøj Archive')

BONDEBJERG: I'd like to get a sense of your background; of how you ended up pursuing filmmaking and journalism.

BRÜGGER: Well, I actually did a BA in Film Studies at the University of Copenhagen, and technically I'm still enrolled as an MA student. One of the courses I took was about the role of political ideology in film. Karsten Fledelius was teaching it, together with the Romanian ambassador. It was a pretty crazy course, but also really interesting. What happened was that I got a job at the Danish Broadcasting Corporation [DR] while I was still doing my BA. I got into the two-year programme that DR had established in collaboration with the Danish School of Media & Journalism. The programme was called 'Digital Radio,' and it was developed at a time when new expectations were emerging about what journalists were supposed to be able to do. They were expected to be far more technically proficient than previously; to be capable of doing all the technical work associated with the recording and editing of programmes. Having completed the programme, I found myself hired by DR, where I ended up doing radio programmes for P1 as a member of DR's Children & Youth Department. So radio was actually how I got into film and TV production. And I have, of course, started working with radio again more recently, in my capacity as co-director for Radio24syv. But given my Film Studies background, the leap from radio to TV and film wasn't actually that great. When I was doing Film Studies at the University of Copenhagen, I actually had a student job at Kanal2 Rapporten, which gave me some insight into how news is conveyed visually. The model being used was very much an American one, and although I had very little experience, I often found myself being thrown some pretty challenging tasks without much time at all to prepare. At one point, for example, I had to interview a woman who had been raped by someone who also torched her home. My coverage of that story ended up being really awful, but I did learn a lot from trying to do that kind of news reporting

BONDEBJERG: You've been a student of film as well as journalism, and you've worked as both a film director and as a journalist. How do you see these two types of training as playing out in the work that you've done as a documentary filmmaker?

BRÜGGER: In a way, journalism is my fate because both my mother and my father are journalists. So the choice of journalism was a very natural one for me, and that's essentially what I saw myself as pursuing. I'd actually tried, early on, to get into the Danish School of Media & Journalism, but I wasn't accepted. But I don't think I had a particularly clear conception of what it was that I wanted to do as a journalist, of the medium or media I wanted to work with. I figured that out later. It was really a coincidence that radio became my principal point of access to documentary work and journalism. But I was very lucky to end up working in DR's Children & Youth Department, and with radio documentaries and radio montages. The Department itself, but also radio as a medium, provided a lot of room for experimentation with form and genre. After all, in terms of genre, radio montage is a bit of a hybrid. In my own work, I've been very inspired by the Danish tradition of radio montage, which combines a journalistic depiction of reality with a pronounced personal vision, and with a properly creative mode of expression. My work with radio montage really helped me come to grips with narrative economy, with issues of time as they pertain to the process of gathering material, and with the nitty-gritty of actually telling stories. It's fair to say that by the time I was brought on-board, the Children & Youth Department, as well as radio documentary itself, were no longer what they had been. And structural changes to the Department were in fact introduced soon afterwards. So it wasn't always that easy to persuade people of the merit of one's ideas, or to make ends meet. As I said, you really had to do things yourself, to familiarize yourself thoroughly with the necessary technology. But I also learnt a lot from all that.

BONDEBJERG: You have, as you've suggested, been involved in making documentaries for radio. In fact, you received the prestigious Kryger prize for 'The Skjoldhøj Archive.' How would you characterize that documentary radio series? How do you see it as relating to the Danish tradition of radio montage that you mentioned, and to your work with film and TV?

BRÜGGER: 'The Skjoldhøj Archive' was a series of broadcasts about life in the largest of Aarhus' suburban neighborhoods. It provides an anthropological and very observational description of all sorts of lives – from the ordinary to the more absurd – in this particular part of Denmark. We simply rented a house, moved in, and started recording. The aim was simply to capture the specificity of the life forms that existed in the neighborhood. But, at the same time, the broadcasts provided a kind of portal to the decline of the welfare state because it was one of the first neighborhoods to witness an exodus in the 1960s. The broadcasts followed, among others, a

<table>
<tr><td></td><td>concierge who talked about how life in the neighborhood had changed, and about the strange and often telling things he found in garbage cans and the area itself – things that mirrored the changes and the process of decline.</td></tr>
<tr><td>BONDEBJERG:</td><td>Your style, both as a journalist and as a documentarist, seems to be inspired by new journalism, as well as by the tradition of performative documentary filmmaking. Your work also has a strong reflexive dimension, for you both reveal and comment on the process of production. Are there any documentarists who have been especially important to you?</td></tr>
<tr><td>BRÜGGER:</td><td>Yes, I'm happy to acknowledge my debt to those particular sources of inspiration. But my style is also marked by the development of the Internet, for that sort of pulled the rug out from underneath traditional journalism. If the ordinary person in the street in principle has access to the same sources and the same information as I do, then I, as a journalist, have to bring something unique to the documentary process. I feel I have to take certain risks myself, and that I have to take risks with the story. The proliferation of media has really sharpened people's capacity to recognize patterns, which is something that Marshall McLuhan was on to, I think. People nowadays are far more intimately aware of the patterns that define the media's ways of telling stories, and of conveying information. Because of this, it becomes really important to be able to break the moulds. You really have to push the boundaries. You have to create new patterns, new ways of telling stories.</td></tr>
<tr><td>BONDEBJERG:</td><td>Yet there are those who remain committed to a traditional conception of journalism and documentarism. In their eyes, your approach is likely to be seen as crossing a certain line, as being a matter of fiction and of staged realities.</td></tr>
<tr><td>BRÜGGER:</td><td>Yes, that's clearly true. And I have to say that if everyone were to work with journalism and documentary filmmaking the way I do, it would really be too much. At the same time, I think it's fair to say that in Denmark there aren't a lot of people doing the kind of 'modern' journalism that I emphasize, for new journalism remains a mostly American phenomenon. American journalism has a much wider range of topics to work with, and journalists have a lot more room to manoeuver in. In a Danish context, initiatives inspired by new journalism easily become awkward. In Denmark, the typical attitude towards that kind of thing is probably that new journalism is ultimately about self-staging rather than about depicting reality.</td></tr>
</table>

BONDEBJERG: The talk shows and satirical work that you've done for the Danish Broadcasting Corporation seem to build on some of the traditions associated with the Children & Youth Department that you were once part of. Do you see yourself as drawing inspiration from those traditions?

BRÜGGER: Yes, that's absolutely correct. The things that Poul [Nesgaard] and Nulle [Elith Jørgensen] produced have been a major source of inspiration. For example, their TV series, *I sandhedens tjeneste - En rejse i det ukendte Europa* ('In the Service of Truth: A Journey through the Unknown Europe,' 1991) was clearly ahead of its time, and incredibly sophisticated and thoughtful. But when you watch these programmes today, you also get a clear sense of just how much faster the rhythm of TV and film culture is today. Their whole approach to reality, and to the people they worked with, was to think in terms of a participatory stance being more effective than an oppositional one. And that's certainly something I've adopted in my own films and programmes. In my films and TV programmes, I often adopt the persona of someone who's on the side of the characters or participants, and included in their reality. I'm never the critically minded documentarist and journalist with an objective, external perspective on things. Instead I wait for my characters to reveal, perhaps inadvertently, what they and the reality they're part of are all about. The participatory approach is often a good way of getting at the characters' strategic manoeuvres, and at the way they communicate. Nesgaard and the people he worked with were proponents of an ironic, reflexive media culture and strategy, and in this sense they were all really far ahead of their time. Their way of telling stories about reality involved a lot of different levels, which they negotiated beautifully. I've always been really fascinated, but also inspired, by that aspect of their work.

BONDEBJERG: *Danes for Bush* introduces your now distinctive approach to performative documentarism. And we also meet you in this series, as the character Mr. Cortsen. How exactly did this TV series come about?

BRÜGGER: It's fair to say that this particular project was cheap and quick, and slightly out of control. The out of control bit refers to what happened when we had a special ballpoint pen produced, with an image of Mærsk ships transporting weapons to Iraq. The idea was to hand out these pens to Bush supporters in the US. They absolutely loved that pen, and what the image on the pen depicts

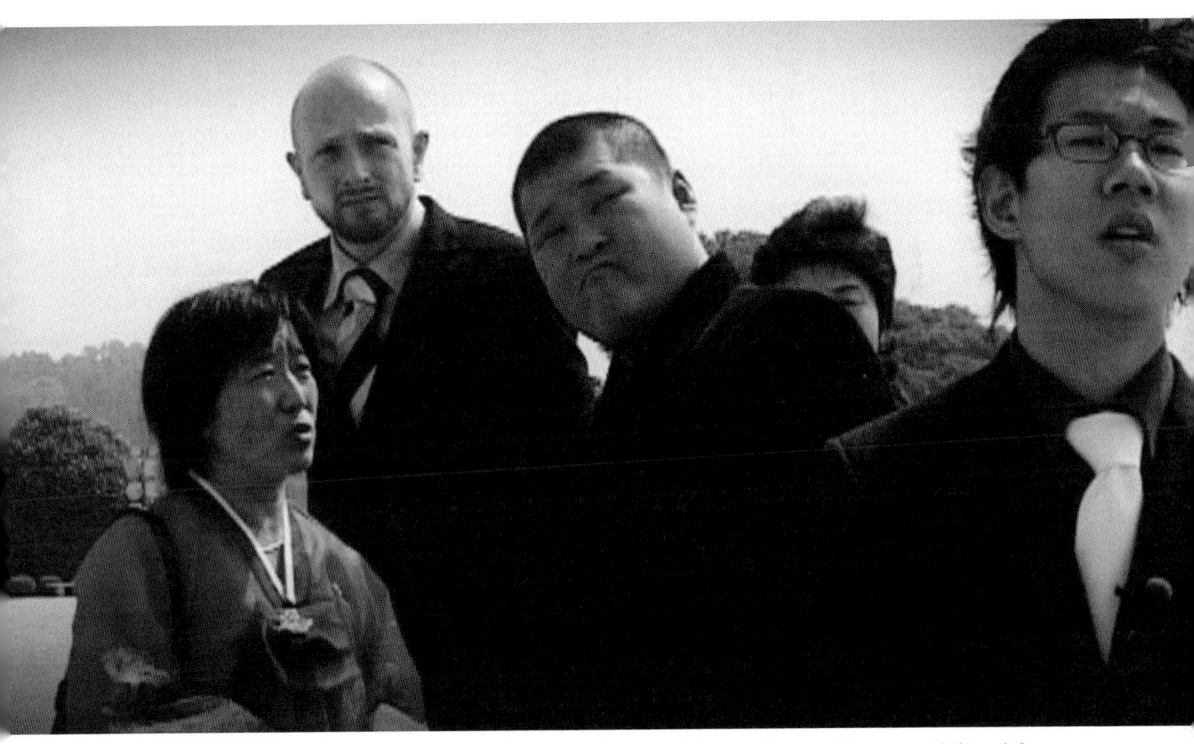

Mads Brügger, his Korean contact person and his two Danish-Korean followers Simon Jul Jørgensen (left) and the stand up comedian Jacob Nossel (right). (*The Red Chapel*, framegrab, cinematography by René Sascha Johannsen).

is, of course, completely consistent with reality. But when the Danish Broadcasting Corporation discovered that pen, they immediately intervened and put a stop to what we were doing. Mærsk and his company are virtually sacred in the Danish context, and not to be made fun of. We simply received instructions specifying that all remaining pens were to be destroyed. We also had to draw up a list in which we identified where and to whom we had distributed the offending pens. But the actual production process started with our website, Danes for Bush, which had our political manifesto, a programmatic statement, and a description of who we were. We chose to wear costumes, but not to disguise ourselves completely. And unlike some of my later films, we decided that we didn't want sequences in which we stepped out of our characters. In other words, we opted *not* to punctuate the story with commentaries that subjected both ourselves and the people we were depicting to intense critical scrutiny. We just stuck to our guns and behaved like utterly convinced Bush supporters throughout.

The narrative structure we came up with involved introducing our photographer to people as a Danish Broadcasting Corporation employee charged with making a documentary about Jakob and myself. That way people knew that they were being filmed, and thought they knew why they were being filmed. We drove from Los Angeles to New York and it quickly became clear that the Republican voters we met simply adored us. We were virtually the incarnation of their wettest dream! Here were these foreigners who agreed with them and were on their side! When they saw our bus, with the slogan 'Save us from the old Europe,' they were really touched. One of the things I was really struck by as we were shooting *Danes for Bush* was how willing people are to believe you're the person you say you are if that person fits neatly into a particular world view. People are persuaded by what fits into a context, even if it's not necessarily normal, expected, or standard. I felt that we played out our roles with a good deal of exaggeration, but that didn't prompt any negative reactions at all.

BONDEBJERG: What was the balance between planned scenes and improvisation like in the series? How much of what we see was actually planned, and even arranged, before you left for the US?

BRÜGGER: What we had was a general framework for it all, and then we developed the scenes, often in a fairly improvised way, as we went along. Our own characters and the general set-up were the project's cornerstone, and then we generated the specific scenes through improvisation along the way. What also happened was that we ended up with more and more contacts as the project unfolded because the jungle drums in the Republican camp were busy announcing that Danes for Bush were on the way. So we were inundated by invitations to all sorts of meetings, receptions, and parties. And of course we became better and better at playing our roles. What you discover is that if you're cheeky and daring enough to play along with reality, the most incredible things can happen, and you end up meeting the most extraordinary people. For example, we couldn't possibly have planned this: an encounter with a very rich woman, who's a Republican member of Congress, and decides to drive us through New York and serve us champagne in her limousine. And what happens is that we run into an anti-Bush demonstration. She decides to stop the car and to confront the demonstrators. And we decide to play along and be consistent with our roles, and so we almost get arrested by the NYPD for obstructing the demonstrators from conducting a legal protest.

BONDEBJERG: You managed to end up on the front page of the *New York Times*, and the social media also reflected a good deal of interest in the series. What's your view on its reception, both in Denmark and the US? Were people outraged by, resistant to, or generally critical of the approach you took in *Danes for Bush*?

BRÜGGER: Well, we received hate mail as well as very positive expressions of support from both ends of the political spectrum. Morten Messerschmidt, for example, the Danish People's Party's very young Member of Parliament, was really excited about the series. He saw it as a much needed antidote to the otherwise very critical stance typically taken by the Danish Broadcasting Corporation towards the US in its Republican incarnation. But some people did make it known, whether publicly or privately, that they felt we'd exploited the people we depicted, and perhaps even abused some of the openness and freedom that exist in the US, where it's possible to shoot everywhere you go without permissions. Some people felt that we'd made life too easy for ourselves by choosing Republicans as our target. They also had questions about how serious we were about our involvement with the Republicans we met, about whether we'd really risked anything at all ourselves. I think that's probably why I started to develop the idea for *The Red Chapel*; because it's simply impossible to claim that North Korean realities are easy to access or depict.

BONDEBJERG: Well, let's talk about that film then. *The Red Chapel* began as a TV series, and went on to become a film. As such, it gave you a bit of an international breakthrough. In *The Red Chapel* you make use of some of the very same strategies as in *Danes for Bush* because here too you manage to penetrate to the core of an otherwise very closed society, and again by means of a staged identity and secret purposes. When watching the film it can be hard to understand how the Koreans could possibly have been so accepting of your stories, and how you managed to get in. How did you go about developing the framework for this particular project, and how did you get the necessary contacts?

BRÜGGER: Well, the idea followed quite logically from this feeling that we had that we should try to do something that involved our taking greater risks ourselves. Somehow the kind of documentary filmmaking that we had gravitated towards seemed to require that. The choice of a dictatorship was a fairly obvious one. And where do you find the world's most closed dictatorship today? In North Korea. At that point in time I didn't know much about North Korea; but the more I thought about the idea, the more I realized that it just might be possible to penetrate the system if we used the concept of cultural exchange as a strategic device. Cultural exchange is one of the hardest things to be opposed to. As for genre and our general approach, we opted for humor because it masks the strategic side of things quite effectively. I then started to implement the basic concept by establishing a sort of avant-garde Laurel and Hardy double act with the Danish Korean Simon Jul Jørgensen, and the stand-up comedian Jacob Nossel who has cerebral palsy. At that point in time I didn't actually realize just how much this precise combination would touch our hosts, and appeal to their way of thinking, both ideologically and in terms of propaganda. But Koreans are very interested in race, and in a way North Korea just might be the most racist country in the world. So the thought of two people with a Korean background returning to their roots – and to North Korea rather than South Korea – was enormously appealing. In fact, my sense is that it was that very thought that got them to buy the whole project. Actually, there was a bit of extra honey on our bait because one of the comedians was a person with a serious disability. Our project seemed to make it possible to counter all those stories that appear in the international press from time to time about how North Korea doesn't treat people with disabilities properly.

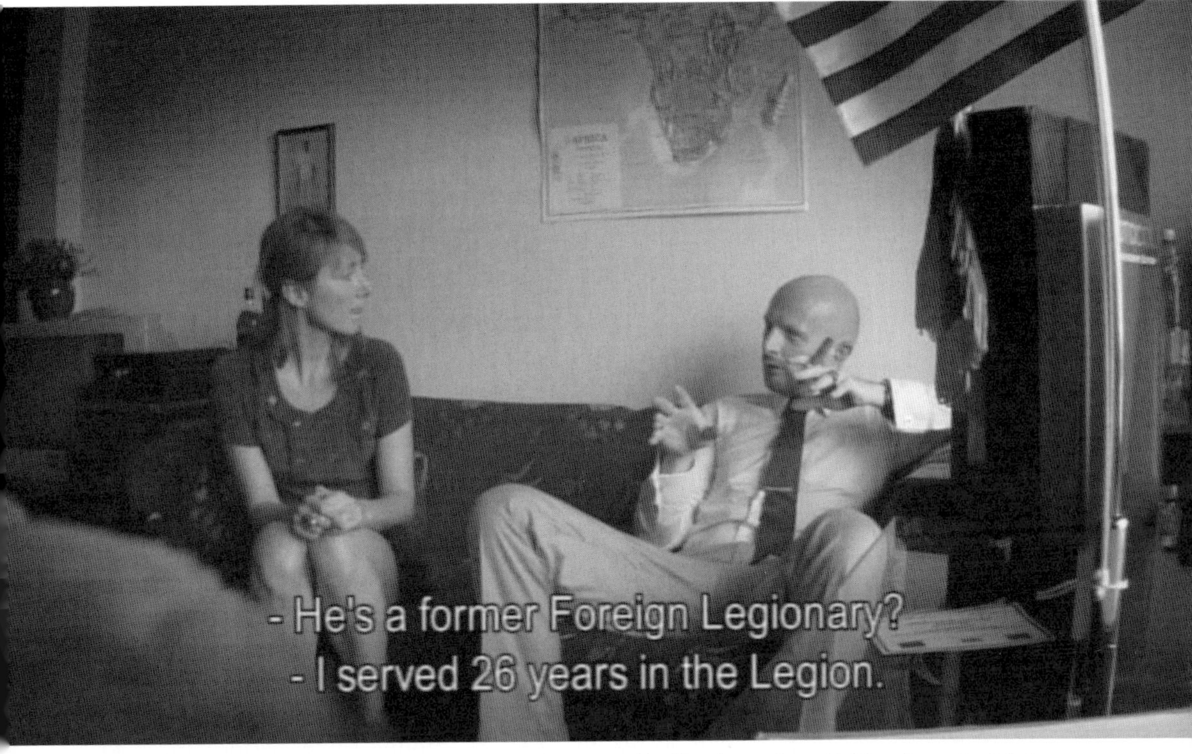

Brügger in his role as Liberian consul to the Central African Republic (CAR), together with his assistant, Eva Jakobsen (*The Ambassador*, framegrab, cinematography by Johan Stahl Winthereik).

BONDEBJERG: Who were you negotiating with during this phase of the project? Who had to approve your proposed plans?

BRÜGGER: I made a trip to North Korea myself, and negotiated with various officials over a period of almost two weeks. That involved a whole lot of drinking together. It was quite a surreal experience in that we kept going back to square one again, day after day. It was as though everything that had happened the day before, and about which I thought we'd reached some sort of agreement, had simply been effaced. The people I met with were a mix of diplomats, officials, and bureaucrats from the Ministry of Cultural Affairs. My role involved being a director, journalist, and theatre person. I also had a present, namely the Danish TV series *Matador*, to hand over on behalf of the Danish Broadcasting Corporation, for which I worked. A few days later I received a request for English translations of the 24 episode summaries. But then they suddenly decided to endorse the project, and we moved ahead the minute we had a green light. From that point onwards, everything was a lot easier, in the sense that we were really just dealing with a perfectly ordinary TV series about this theatre group that travels to North Korea in order to mount some performances for audiences in that country. But just beneath the surface of this quite straightforward production there was this experience of an utterly paranoid world. At the end of each day, we had to hand over all our takes to the officials, so that they could examine them. Also, everything we did was filmed and photographed, which gives you some insight into the atmosphere of the place. It was a pretty layered set-up. Who was performing for whom? Who was exploiting whom? What was it exactly that had happened when this new group of men showed up and suddenly started controlling everything?

BONDEBJERG: How was the series received?

BRÜGGER: Internally, in the context of the Danish Broadcasting Corporation, it was seen as an absolute fiasco. But it has to be said that it was broadcast at a really bad time in December, when just about everyone in Denmark was participating in some pre-Christmas lunch or other. Also, most Danes know very little about North Korea, and so it's not really a place they can relate to. I imagine that quite a few people also felt that it just wasn't right or appropriate to make fun of Asians who are being oppressed by a brutal regime. The TV series does, of course, expose a dictatorial system that nobody is likely to feel much sympathy for. At the same time, it's true that it can be difficult to distinguish between those who represent the system and then the 'ordinary' North Koreans with whom we also engage. Although some of the scenes suggest an element of intimacy, and appear to capture expressions of emotion on the part of certain North Koreans, the fact is that we were never allowed to meet an ordinary North Korean unsupervised. In North Korea, someone is always watching, and everyone is always watching everyone else. There are protocols for absolutely everything, and many, many levels of control. You can't depict what's really happening in the hearts and minds of North Koreans, because you just don't have access to the people themselves, let alone to what's going on inside them.

BONDEBJERG: Do you know whether your project had any consequences for the people who were somehow involved in it? Has anyone been sanctioned by the regime?

BRÜGGER: I talked to an English journalist who knows the regime and the country well. He told me that some relatively mild sanctions were imposed on certain people. Some of the officials who figure in the programme were required to be re-educated ideologically. But it appears that all of them have returned to their former positions at this point. Of course the problem is that I can't be sure that this is actually true, because you can't be sure of anything in North Korea. The thought of possibly having harmed someone does weigh on me. No matter who these people might be, I don't want to have been responsible for having put them in harm's way.

BONDEBJERG: Although the TV series did poorly, the film version that you produced with Zentropa actually established you internationally. How did you end up making a film based on the TV series? What are some of the key differences between the film and the series?

BRÜGGER: I'd wanted to edit the TV series into a tighter, more consistent, and better integrated documentary narrative for quite some time. But the Danish Broadcasting Corporation wasn't especially interested in this idea, and couldn't find a budget for it either. But Peter Engel, who had been my boss when I worked for the Children & Youth Department, and who had since moved to Zentropa, liked the idea a lot. So he persuaded the people at Zentropa to invest much of the money that was needed. But the overall budget was still really tight, and we only had two weeks to edit everything. The only reason this was even feasible was because René Sascha Johannsen, my editor, is a cinematographer too, and had actually shot everything for the TV series. So he knew the material really

BONDEBJERG: well. But sometimes a very tight budget and a tight deadline can help to release a lot of creative energy.

The film ended up winning the award for best Nordic documentary at the Nordic Panorama film festival, and went on to win the prestigious Jury Prize for best documentary at Sundance. Suddenly you found yourself in the international big league.

BRÜGGER: Although *The Red Chapel* won a Nordic award, I think the Sundance award suggests that the film is ultimately more American than European. The way it defines the issues appeals to Americans; at least the kind of Americans who believe that humanism and the inalienable dignity of the individual are important. In a way, that's what the film is all about because it exposes a reality and a regime where humanism is obliterated. I have to say that I was a bit stunned to find myself surrounded by deeply moved Americans immediately after the screening at Sundance. I'd never experienced anything like that anywhere else in the world. As a result of its American success, the film has enjoyed a long life on the international festival circuit. It's been released on DVD, and is selling well in the US. Actually, it's been quite widely distributed internationally.

BONDEBJERG: Towards the end of *The Quatraro Mystery*, Mikael Bertelsen, who was the other main character in this TV series, describes it as 'a jigsaw puzzle inside a mystery, wrapped in a riddle.' The series is ostensibly about an EU official's death as a result of a fall from a window in Brussels. But then it develops into a story about a possible plot involving the EU, the Freemasons, and the Italian mafia. Part of the inspiration here seems to come from 'In the Service of Truth: A Journey through the Unknown Europe,' which was produced by DR's Children & Youth Department. In that TV series, Poul Nesgaard adopts the persona of a cynical EU speculator. Hitchcock couldn't have done more with the story you tell, and as for the aesthetics of your series, with its dark lighting and many close-ups, well it simply exudes mystery. How much of this remarkable story is invented, and how much of it is actually true?

BRÜGGER: The way we've defined our roles – both mine and Mikael's – and the relationship between them, clearly involves a high level of fictionalization, and a good deal of staging. But the role differentiation and assumption of roles are based on something that's genuinely part of who we are as real persons. Mikael, for example, is far more careful than I am, whereas I tend to be far more willing to take risks. But the rest of the story is based on solid journalistic research. Although the dramaturgical aspects of the project draw on the conventions of crime dramas and thrillers, we actually researched every detail and every character very carefully indeed. I see *The Quatraro Mystery* as very much an example of public service programming. We take up an issue that none of the media really wants to touch – something that's simply been shelved – and then we make it more interesting by placing it within the crime genre context, with music by Ennio Morricone, and so on. Our current plan is actually to re-edit it all as a film, and we've actually done some additional research and filmed some more interviews with this in mind. Even though the final episodes have that envelope – which some of the key characters see and which supposedly contains the name of Quatraro's murderer – the murder mystery isn't actually solved by the end of the programme. We feel we need to follow the Italian trail a bit more in order to get to the bottom of it.

BONDEBJERG: Unlike *The Red Chapel*, *The Ambassador* didn't begin as a TV project. Zentropa is credited as the film's producer, but you also received a lot of financial support from many other sources: New Danish Screen, the Nordic Film and TV Fund, Cineworks, Potemkino, Film i Väst, The Finnish Film Foundation, and the EU Media programme. How did you come up with the idea for this film? How did you find the backing you needed?

BRÜGGER: *The Ambassador* was a project that was quite difficult to pitch to the people who had to buy the idea, and whom I needed to persuade to invest money in the film. For reasons that were unavoidable, the actual story had to be kept largely secret, so we could really only provide a very general outline of the basic idea. New Danish Screen provided the initial support we needed. Jakob Høgel, who runs New Danish Screen, comes from a family of diplomats, and he happens to know Africa quite well. At first he was really very sceptical about the whole idea. He didn't, for example, believe that diplomatic passports were being bought and sold. But we nonetheless managed to get the money we needed to begin developing the project. When it became clear, at the end of that development phase, that there was substance to our idea, we were given full support. The film's project is somewhat inspired by Michelangelo Antonioni's *Professione – reporter* (*The Passenger*, 1975), and by the dream of being able to change one's identity completely, and to penetrate deep into a quite different reality.

But it's also a classic documentary project, and one that follows quite naturally from *The Red Chapel*. Much like *The Red Chapel*, it relies on a journalistic strategy that provides access to a very closed world that would otherwise remain invisible.

BONDEBJERG: You used hidden cameras a lot, which makes perfect sense given that you were telling a story about abuses of power and corruption. The film also includes a number of very revealing scenes that appear to have been shot quite openly. I'm thinking, for example, of the various meetings with the mine owner, Dalkia Gilbert. It seems that some of the characters didn't have a problem with the camera, and were quite happy to have their corrupt behavior recorded. What sorts of principles were you working with in terms of this business of whether to hide the camera or to shoot openly?

BRÜGGER: A lot of people have seen the film at various festivals where I wasn't present, and thus I couldn't talk to them about how I made it. And it's pretty clear that a lot of them think the film is nothing but a mockumentary. That is, they think that absolutely everything has been staged and scripted, and that none of the characters or the realities they're caught up in are the least bit real. But that's not the case at all. In the scenes where we didn't make use of a hidden camera, we used a Canon E05, which might look like an ordinary still camera to a lot of people. The Africans whom we filmed with it could see the camera, but they seemed to be indifferent to its presence, probably because they didn't really think of it as being part of a *film* shoot. I'd told them that I'd brought along a photographer to document our conversations and the context in which they took place, and what they saw was just him doing his job. We used a hidden camera for all the scenes focusing on the process of getting a diplomatic passport, but did indeed shoot the scenes with the African miner Dakia Gilbert quite openly. Although these scenes clearly document corruption and bribery, he was completely unconcerned.

BONDEBJERG: The use of hidden cameras raises a lot of issues, and has often been debated by journalists. The Danish Broadcasting Corporation has very clear guidelines about the matter, for example. Do you feel that your use of a hidden camera is ethically defensible?

BRÜGGER: Yes, I don't think you can criticize the film on those grounds. The basic rule, after all, is that it has to be impossible to get the information any other way. Also, the information you're trying to get has to be of sufficient social significance to justify the means.

The issue in question has to be a matter of considerable public interest. I'm completely convinced that the film meets any and all of the relevant journalistic norms. The only critical response we received about a putative violation of norms came from a Dutch diplomat who, I have to say, is known to have a rather dubious profile. He tried to stop the film from being shown at IDFA. But as a result of his efforts, he himself ended up in the media spotlight. There's been some discussion of the film's use of comedy and irony as a means of dealing with a serious problem, and I did worry about what Africans would think of it. But most of the Africans who've seen it have liked it a lot. The film represents a departure of sorts, in that it does not see Africans as victims. It's also very different from the standard TV reports about the sufferings of Africans. What ordinary Africans notice is the attempt to cover the world of the rich and powerful, which is something that never happens through their own media. In a way, they really like my very direct approach, the fact that I don't wear kid gloves and am willing to risk being offensive. They're even able to see my comic stunt with the two pygmies as humorous.

Chapter 5

Pernille Rose Grønkjær

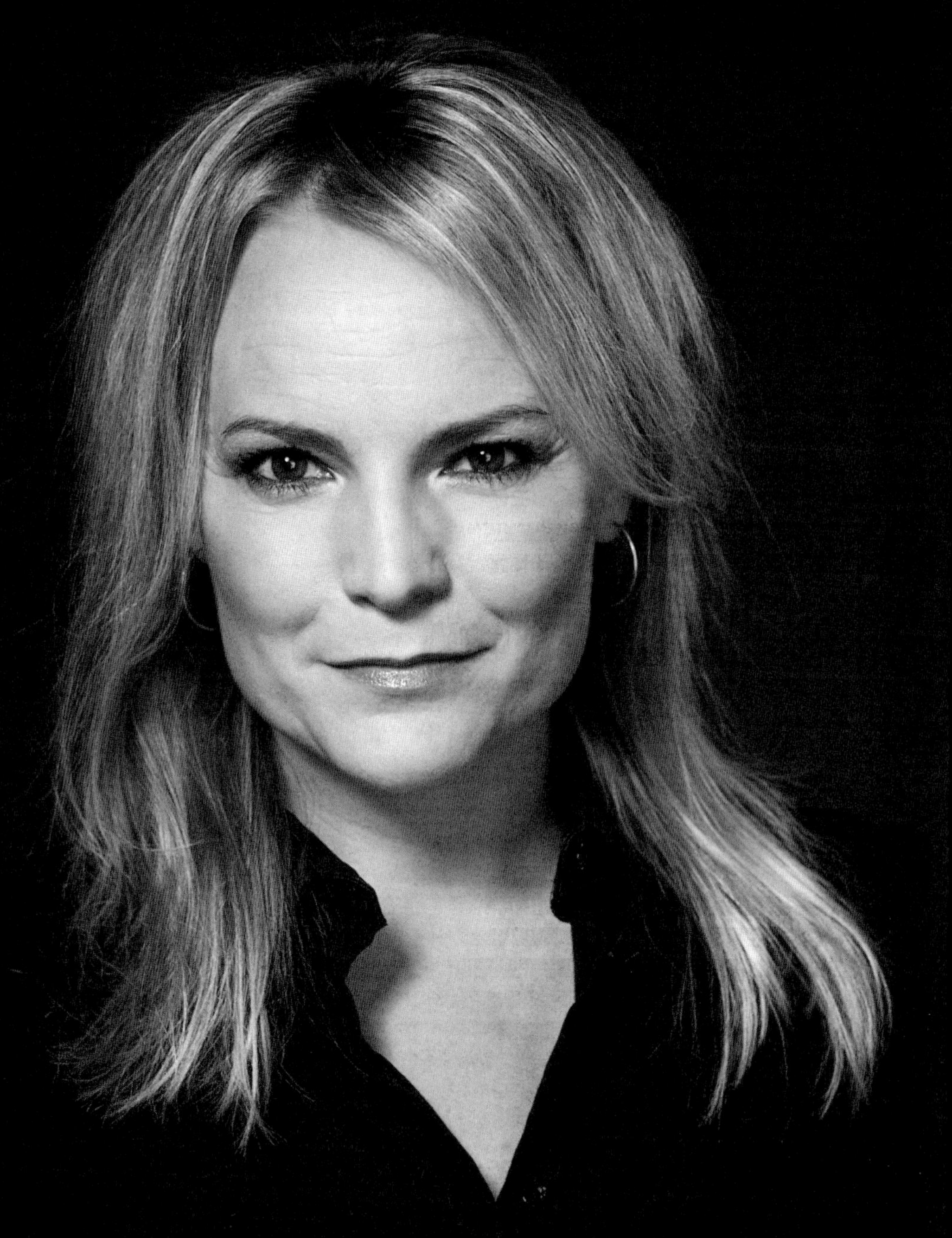

Pernille Rose Grønkjær. Portrait by Ty Stange. Courtesy of Danish Documentary.

Born 1973. Grønkjær trained as a documentary filmmaker at the National Film School of Denmark and graduated in 1997. In 2001, Pernille Rose Grønkjær garnered attention with the portrait film *Min morfar forfra* (*Repeating Grandpa*). The film documents Grønkjær's five-day car trip in Northern Jutland with her maternal grandfather. The filmed conversations in the intimacy of the car's space depict an encounter between two generations. The film was nominated for the annual Danish TV Festival's best documentary film award, but Grønkjær achieved her breakthrough, also internationally, with yet another very fine portrait film about an elderly man. In *The Monastery: Mr Vig and the Nun* (2006), Grønkjær provides a very cinematic, but also touching and humorous, depiction of the 82-year-old Mr Vig's stubborn attempts to realize his dream, which is to transform a derelict castle on Funen into a monastery for Russian orthodox nuns. The film won the prestigious Joris Ivens Award at the International Documentary Film Festival Amsterdam (IDFA) in 2006, and a Bodil award for best Danish documentary film in 2007. It went on to be shown widely on the film festival circuit, including at Sundance and at the Sydney Film Festival. In her next film, *Love Addict: Stories of Dreams, Obsession and Longing* (2011), Grønkjær explores the ways in which romantic love can become an all-consuming obsession. This exploration of obsessional thoughts about the 'one and only' is characterized by a fine sense of documentary realism and by a poetic sensibility, but also by the filmmaker's use of cinematic devices from the toolkit of fiction film. The film premiered at IDFA in 2011. 2011 also saw the release of the art film *The House Inside Her*, which Grønkjær co-directed with the artist Astrid Kruse Jensen for the exhibition 'Film/Kunst – Art Moves #1' ('Film/Art: Art Moves #1'). Grønkjær co-owns the production company Danish Documentary, together with directors Phie Ambo, Eva Mulvad, and Mikala Krogh, and producer Sigrid Dyekjær.

Documentary features:

2011   *Love Addict: Stories of Dreams, Obsession and Longing*
2006   *The Monastery: Mr Vig and the Nun*
1998   *Der var så mange glæder... (Those Were the Days)*

Documentary shorts:

2011   *The House Inside Her* (co-directed with Astrid Kruse Jensen for the art
        exhibition 'Film/Art: Art Moves #1')
2001   *Min morfar forfra* (*Repeating Grandpa*)

Television:

2005   *Familien* (*The Family*, DR TV, four episodes)
2004   *Det komplicerede familieliv* (*The Complicated Family Life*, DR2, two episodes)
2003   *TV-Glad* ('TV Happy,' eight episodes)
1999   *Modellerne* (*The Models*, six episodes)

REDVALL: You got into the National Film School of Denmark's programme in Documentary & TV at the age of 21. How did you become interested in documentary filmmaking?

GRØNKJÆR: I started out in radio. I find it very interesting to create soundscapes. So when I'd finished secondary school I began working with radio in a media house in my home town. It was a place that also worked with TV and commercials. At a certain point, people in the production company decided that I had the ability to do something that was more visually oriented, so I started working for TV Aalborg. That was an incredible laboratory for me. The budgets we worked with were small, but if you proved that you were committed, you were really given a free rein. That's something that really characterizes my entire training period: commitment. I'm good at working hard, and that's stood me in good stead on many an occasion in this business. Working really hard, I ended up becoming the TV editor for various programmes, but my mother, who's a school teacher, always felt that I should get myself 'a proper education.' She was the one who noticed the announcement when the National Film School launched its Documentary & TV programme, and she encouraged me to apply, as an alternative to my auto-didacticism. So I applied and suddenly found myself, at the age of 21, making that transition from the provinces in Northern Jutland to the high-profile film school in Copenhagen.

REDVALL: What was it like going from a TV production milieu to film school?

GRØNKJÆR: I experienced a huge cultural clash between the local hard-core milieu of TV production and the artistic world of the Film School, where it was all about finding a way into a sensitive inner self. At the Film School, we were given three weeks to edit a film. I was used to editing 15 minutes in just eight hours, so I did my editing really quickly and then made it known that I was done. But then the head of the programme, Arne Bro, came by the editing room I was working in and started taking everything I'd done apart. That's when I started to understand how time is an important factor in good storytelling. At the same time, I could still make use of being efficient. It was really good for me to be able to master both these things.

The Film School involved a very personal process. It was a place, for example, where people produced portraits of family members and friends. The personal approach took me pleasantly by surprise. I had prepared myself for the entrance exam by memorizing the answers to three earlier sets of exam questions from the Danish School of Media & Journalism – questions about political facts and figures; not because I loved doing that, but because I thought that that was what was expected of me. But the Film School's entrance test involved answering questions about how I felt about my grandmother. The professionalism in question was completely different and it really spoke to me. Learning something about what the person opposite you is actually like – about what sorts of stories she's able to tell – is actually far more interesting to me than facts and figures. I'm deeply interested in stories that have a very powerful human dimension. What excites me is the relationship between people, what we do to each other.

REDVALL: There's a lot of talk about ethics in the context of documentary filmmaking, and it's interesting to think about how best to teach documentary ethics, about how to instil the necessary awareness of ethical issues in aspiring filmmakers. My impression is that the Film School takes up these tasks in a very practical way; by letting the students taste their own medicine, so to speak, and by prompting reflection through practice. Does that seem right to you?

GRØNKJÆR:

It's basically crucial to understand what you're doing to a person when you put him or her in front of a camera. When you've been there yourself, when you've interviewed your father on camera or sat in a studio with your mother, you begin to sense the incredible vulnerability. You begin to understand just how careful you have to be as a filmmaker. You can tell stories about painful things, but there has to be an element of gentleness. That aspect of the programme was really important, but when I was actually at the Film School, I didn't realize that it was precisely this that I was learning. I realized all that later on. With reference to ethics, what you also learn from that kind of process is that there's no such thing as an *objective* truth. After all, there are lots of truths. As far as I'm concerned, it's what's subjective that's interesting. The personal truth is the interesting truth because that's where you find the element of actual experience. When I tell a story, it's very important to lay out the personal truths of the people in the film. They have to be able to recognize themselves. That's the final litmus test for me, and I came to understand that during my years at the Film School.

REDVALL:

Is it your impression that the teaching that takes place at the National Film School of Denmark differs from that of other film schools elsewhere in the world?

GRØNKJÆR:

What a film is like ultimately depends on the director and the same is true of film schools. What a programme is like has a lot to do with the mentor or teacher who defines the place. Arne Bro has a very particular world view. That has a decisive impact on the programme, which then ends up being very different from what's on offer elsewhere. The teachers one has at film school really do have an impact on one's experience of it, and I have to say that I was really glad to be taught by Arne. He just saw my most recent film and his response to it spoke clearly to my innermost and most basic narrative impulses. That response wasn't about dramatic climaxes or expected viewer numbers. He always speaks to my inner desire to tell stories. He creates this space where there's a sense of freedom, where desire becomes central, and that's incredibly important. You have to find your way to that tiny little kernel within you that's going to become everything because if that's not there, then nothing else is going to matter much.

REDVALL:

You created the company Danish Documentary, together with three other directors from the Film School. There's a lot of talk about how Danish film reflects a culture of collaboration, with

	people inviting each other into the editing room and discussing things as they go along. Are collaboration and sparring central to the way in which you work as a documentary filmmaker?
GRØNKJÆR:	Sparring is important to me, but you have to know when you're ready for it, and you have to be clear about whom it is you're inviting into the process. In that connection, the women in the Danish Documentary company are really utterly unique. The editing process is decisive. A lot of films are actually created during the editing phase, and that's when I'm incredibly eager to get some external input. In general, I depend a lot on a number of steady partnerships that have everything to do with my being able to produce my best work as a director. After all, it's about finding the people who are able to grasp what you're thinking and able to take the ideas further. Directors are control freaks and it's really important to feel completely comfortable with the people around you, and to feel that you're able to let down your guard with them. I trust my producer, Sigrid Dyekjær, completely. Her energy is utterly unique and she's the only producer I've ever met who never thinks something's impossible. Often, when you're trying to implement an idea, it's all about constraints. But, with Sigrid, nothing is impossible until she's given it a shot. So I have this sense of security with her because I can believe that I'm doing the right thing. I have another unique partnership with the editor Pernille Bech Christensen. It can be very hard to let go during the editing process because the material is so personal to me, but with her I can say 'Look at all my dirty laundry,' and then trust that she'll make the right decisions. Her knowledge and understanding of people are simply incredible, so she's able to find things in the material that even I hadn't noticed. It's really amazing to experience that. I also work a lot with Jens Arentzen. In fact, he's been a script consultant on all of my films. He's got a bit of the same romantic outlook that I have, and a very delicate and fine understanding of pain and its place in our existence. But he's also very tough minded and almost mathematical in his approach to dramaturgy, and I really like that. Being able to collaborate with him means a lot to me.
REDVALL:	What was the transition from film school to the film industry like for you?
GRØNKJÆR:	It was really overwhelming. I didn't have much of a network in Copenhagen, but I established a company with Sami Saif, who was at film school with me – he later went on to make *Family*

(dir. Sami Saif and Phie Ambo, 2001) – and producer Jonas Frederiksen. Having just emerged from the Film School, I was not even sure what I had learned yet, and it was perfectly terrifying to be facing the commercial world we suddenly found ourselves in. At that moment, I found myself needing to draw on my early TV Aalborg efficiency. It was important simply to start producing something.

First I made a film about a very sophisticated elderly lady who'd been an ambassador's wife and was moving into an old people's home, *Those Were the Days*. We managed to sell that film to the Danish Broadcasting Corporation. I tried to be involved with projects of a commercial nature, as well as with more artistic ones, such as *Repeating Grandpa*. You have to earn a living, and it's also really great to be in production because that's how you hone your technical skills. Our line of work is actually a kind of craft, and mastering the technical side of things is a source of enormous strength. It's important to take on a lot of projects. You have to have the kind of experience that's simply inscribed at the bodily level because, when you're in the middle of making a documentary film, you have to be ready in a split second, so you can't afford to let the technicalities of filmmaking become an obstacle or you might lose the moment. In that sense it's good to be very productive. For example, by the time I made *The Monastery*, I'd been involved in TV production for ten years.

REDVALL: *The Monastery*, which won the prestigious Joris Ivens award, became a major breakthrough for you. It took you a long time to make that film, and my impression is that it wasn't an easy process. How did you end up making that film?

GRØNKJÆR: I'd made that film about the ambassador's wife, and for a while I was especially fascinated by old people, which is, of course, what *Repeating Grandpa* is also about. I actually spent a year and a half driving around the country to visit old people's homes and assisted living facilities, in search of yet another old person to make a documentary portrait film about. I'd started shooting a film focusing on an elderly lady living on Lolland, and then one of my friends told me about this old man who had a castle on Funen. So I went there, to check this out, and as I'm speaking to Mr Vig in the castle's grandest room, just before his trip to Russia, I realize that there's something here that I'm not going to be able to let go of. So I promise him that I'll go with him to Russia, so that he'll know that I'm completely serious about making a film, and I then

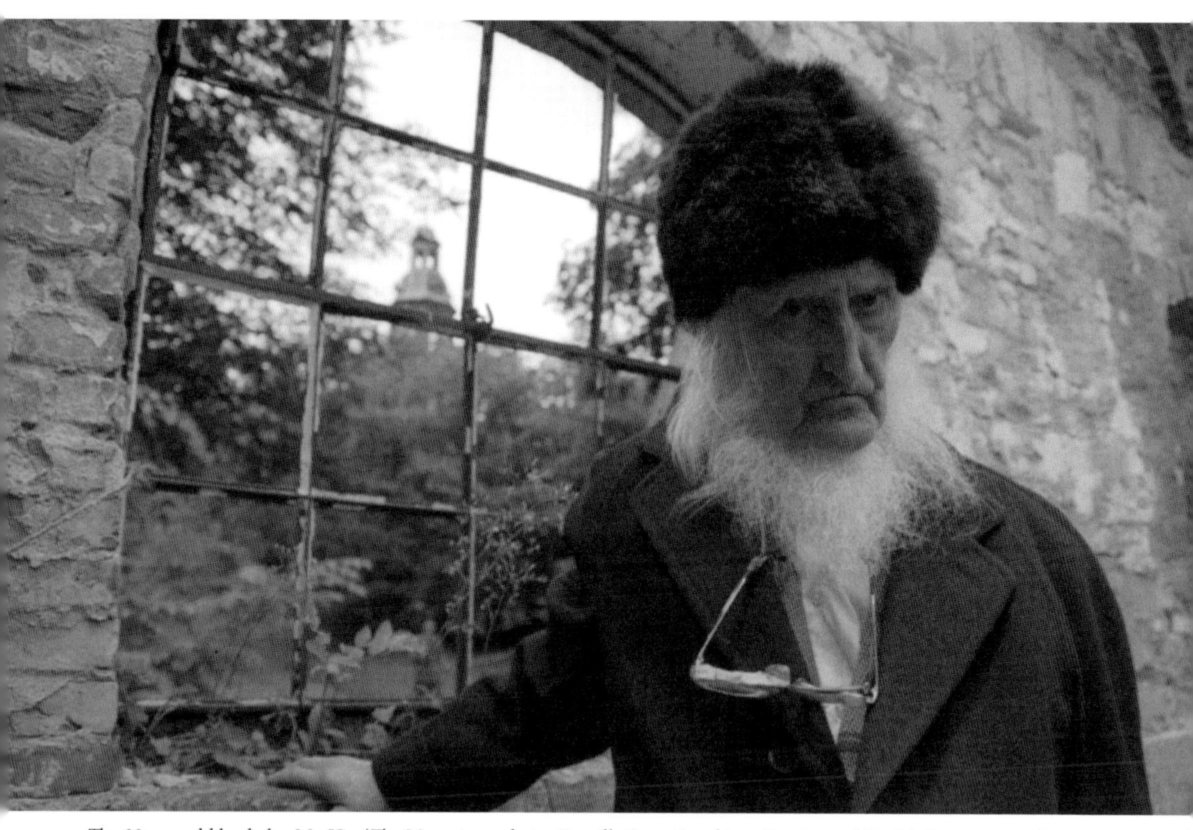

The 82 year old bachelor Mr. Vig (*The Monastery*, photo: Pernille Rose Grønkjær. Courtesy of Danish Documentary).

shut down the other film project. In connection with *The Monastery*, Zentropa's willingness to take risks – in terms of lending out equipment for projects that may or may not pan out – meant a lot. I was allowed to borrow what I needed so that I could get going immediately, and I then shot the film over a period of several years while doing all sorts of other things that were more commercial in nature. It took a while to figure out what was actually going to happen to the material I shot. Several companies took a quick look at the project, but none of them really made a commitment to the film. I even had a conversation with a company about making a documentary that would be just 40 minutes long. I came very close to accepting those terms, but in the end, although I had some doubts, I simply felt too strongly about what I'd shot. At some level I had a fair bit of professional pride caught up in that project, after having spent years shooting material for the film, and driving around with my cardboard box full of tapes. No matter where I ended up finding employment, I made sure a clause was added to the contract that allowed me to continue working on the film, and as it turned out, that was a wise move. At a workshop I attended with the aim of developing the project I then met Mikala Krogh and Sigrid Dyekjær, who were there with Mikala's film, *Alt er relativt* (*Everything is Relative*, 2008). They both felt the project I was working on was fantastic, and when the workshop was over and we'd all returned home, they contacted me to see whether I'd be interested in making the film together with them. And that became the start of the film as it exists today.

We attended a pitching session where I presented the film to potential investors. Initially, we'd planned just to bring along some slide-show stills, but before we set off, I figured I might as well put together a trailer. I love big, expensive American films – and certainly their trailers – and I wanted to produce a trailer for *The Monastery* that was inspired by all that. I was able to do just that because I have all the requisite editing skills. So the day before our departure, I edited this trailer, and having responded with only moderate enthusiasm to our slide show, members of the pitching group asked whether we'd got anything else to show them. So then we showed the trailer and that ended up really capturing their attention. And, to this day, that's the trailer we use for the film. If we hadn't had it with us, I'm not sure we would have been given the funds we got.

REDVALL: Some of the most gripping moments in *The Monastery* reflect your presence in the film, as you speak to Mr Vig. And you're similarly present in parts of *Love Addict*. What are your thoughts about this kind of directorial presence in documentary films?

GRØNKJÆR: We discussed this issue a lot in connection with *The Monastery*. In the beginning, I wanted to be edited out because my view is that the director should only be there if her presence actually brings something to the story. In the case of *The Monastery*, we ended up seeing the directorial presence as a good narrative device. Dramaturgically, it gave us a third character, and that provided a certain energy because we then had this triangular drama involving Mr Vig, the nun Ambrosia, and myself. My presence is designed to provide just the slightest jolt here and there, but it's nonetheless very important. I have this idea that any given space only has so much room. So the question is, 'Who takes what?' If the director takes up a certain amount of room, then there's simply less room left for the others. With film it's very much a question of figuring out who's going to take up space, and how.

With *Love Addict*, which is about a very complicated issue and about things that go on inside people's heads, it took us a long time to figure out where the story was. Eventually, we decided that the story was in the conversations, in that dynamic of my asking a question and something happening in response to it. So in that sense my presence in that film is different, but it remains a kind of motor, a device that prompts people's storytelling. It's never actually been my intention to include myself, but it happens. I actually think I'm incapable of not establishing that bond with the people I spend so much time with. I don't believe in all that 'fly on the wall' stuff – not at all. It's completely pointless. The minute someone walks into a room with a film camera, the room changes. That's why, as a director, it's much better to put your cards on the table. The director is present – although possibly in a minimized or condensed way – because the director shouldn't necessarily take up a lot of room. I do think there's a certain method to being able to think clearly about one's own presence in a given film.

REDVALL: In both *The Monastery* and *Love Addict* the viewer clearly senses that the bond you just mentioned is completely central. As a director, how do you manage to develop such a good relationship with the people you work with?

GRØNKJÆR: I have very little faith in staging, and a lot of faith in relationships. Filmmaking, for me, is very much about establishing relationships with people. If that bond isn't there, you'll feel its absence in the film. Film is an exchange, at least in relation to the people I work with. It's all professional, of course, but it's an exchange. When I made *Those Were the Days*, with the elderly ambassador's wife, we simply had these negotiations, along the lines of 'one walk in the park equals one interview.' Or 'I'll pick up your food if you let me film you while you're doing your hair.' It was all very direct. She was a lady with a good business mind, so that's how we did things. And this approach meant that I demonstrated respect for her, while she demonstrated respect for me. Respect is very important. It's offensive to think in terms of being a mere recipient, along the lines of 'Come on, come on, I want this and I want that.' Documentary filmmaking is also about *seeing* the other person. But in these 'time is money' days that other approach is often emphasized because there's an acceleration in terms of production modes, which means that there's less time for respect and reciprocity. There's a risk of things becoming impoverished and one-dimensional. When you're watching a film, you can tell whether the necessary relationships were actually established. In other words, you can tell whether the director did her job. The viewer has to have a point of access, and those relationships provide it.

REDVALL: *The Monastery* is a very personal portrait of one particular man with a fascinating project, whereas *Love Addict* is organized thematically and involves quite a number of central characters. What prompted you to make *Love Addict* after *The Monastery*?

GRØNKJÆR: After *The Monastery*, I looked at a lot of similar stories and was offered lots of stories about old men living in all sorts of places. But I could just feel that I was done with that. I just didn't have that sense of curiosity. Fortunately, my producer picked up on this, and she then helped me to move in a new direction. She kept saying, 'We're just going to try this. It doesn't matter if it ends up going nowhere.' I let curiosity be my guide, and started doing research on gambling. And that led me to different forms of addiction. One day I came cross a website for a rehab centre devoted to 'love addiction' in Arizona. I'd never heard of the concept before. Could it really be necessary to go into rehab because of love? Why does love end up becoming an addiction for some people? Why? I began to look for knowledge about this, and did so by contacting different therapists because it was important to me to find a professional approach to the addiction milieu.

Also, I didn't want to end up with a tabloid-like angle on it all, based on extreme cases. I also started talking to Jens Arentzen about how to achieve that sense of a single story being told in the context of a theme-based film with lots of people in front of the camera. It's been a very interesting research process, and it was also fascinating to explore the issue of what fictional devices can bring to a documentary.

REDVALL: There's a lot of poetry in the depiction of decay in *The Monastery*, and one of the things that's noteworthy about *Love Addict* is that you approach each of the milieus of the various participants in a visually distinctive way. At one point, for example, you make use of staged material that's quite romantic or poetic and that involves two children in a forest. What are your thoughts about documentary film aesthetics? How, quite concretely, did you manage to achieve the different moods that we find in *Love Addict*?

GRØNKJÆR: The fact is that I'm not actually that interested in reality. I'm interested in imagination. I'm not interested in transport systems and zebra crossings and all that sort of thing. I'm interested in taking a close look at things that are different, or at things I haven't seen before. *Love Addict* is a film with a lot of different people in it and a lot of different perspectives, and we spent a lot of time thinking about the issue of interview contexts. Where are people likely to talk about those sorts of experiences? Should we be filming them alone or together? How can we make their milieus articulate so that they help to tell the story? During the development phase, I put together a book about visual strategies with Adam Philp, who's a cinematographer, and Niels Sejer, who's a set designer. One of the things we were investigating was how to convey moods of loneliness or madness. We also talked about different ways of mixing reality and fiction. A lot of love addicts have traumas relating to their childhood, and it was important to me to be able to include a more poetic depiction of childhood as a point of contrast for a reality that was very bleak. But then in the staged layer, where the actress Eliza enacts love addict experiences, we make use of a thriller aesthetic that's inspired by *The Blair Witch Project* (dir. Daniel Myrick and Eduardo Sánchez, 1999). It was really wonderful to have time during the development phase to discuss image composition, texture, and colours in detail with really talented people. It's not often that a set designer is involved in a documentary film, but those conversations were really fruitful.

And I learnt a lot from the process of trying to combine the different voices into just one voice; from trying to tell an integrated story through many voices; from trying to create a sense of narrative development in a story where there was no real progression.

REDVALL: How do you see the conditions for documentary filmmaking in Denmark?

GRØNKJÆR: There's a huge difference between being a well-established figure and an unknown novice. If nobody knows you, you have to put in an enormous amount of work yourself if you want to be part of the game, and that's exactly what I did with *The Monastery*. It's incredibly hard work, and you have to be completely committed, in the sense of really wanting it. Desire is important, among other things, because you have to keep your own interest in keeping your story alive. It took me eight years to make *The Monastery*, and three years to make *Love Addict*. You really, really have to want this.

In Denmark, we are quite fortunate to be able to fund our films with public money through the Danish Film Institute. I like the collaborative dimension a lot because it provides a space for dialogue about the artistic aspects of your film. It's the DFI's aim to develop Danish film art, and what I also see is an interest in helping the director to develop, which is quite unique. I really notice this when I travel all around the world and meet colleagues who are constrained by all sorts of commercial or private interests, and by various dictates about what their films have to be able to deliver. It's not easy to finance documentary films, but fortunately I'm part of Danish Documentary, and we're all very stubborn women. If we're interested in something, we'll simply commit to doing it. And then we sort out how we're going to finance it all later.

REDVALL: My impression is that Danish Documentary works hard to sell its directors' ideas both prior to production and after they've been turned into films. For example, you produced that trailer for *The Monastery*, and there's been an emphasis on learning effective pitching skills. Many of the films that Danish Documentary produces have catchy English titles too, even when they're initially released in Denmark. Do you see Danish Documentary as being unique in this way, at least in the Danish context?

GRØNKJÆR: It's hard to know exactly what others are doing, but I do know that we take the sales side of things very seriously indeed. Documentary

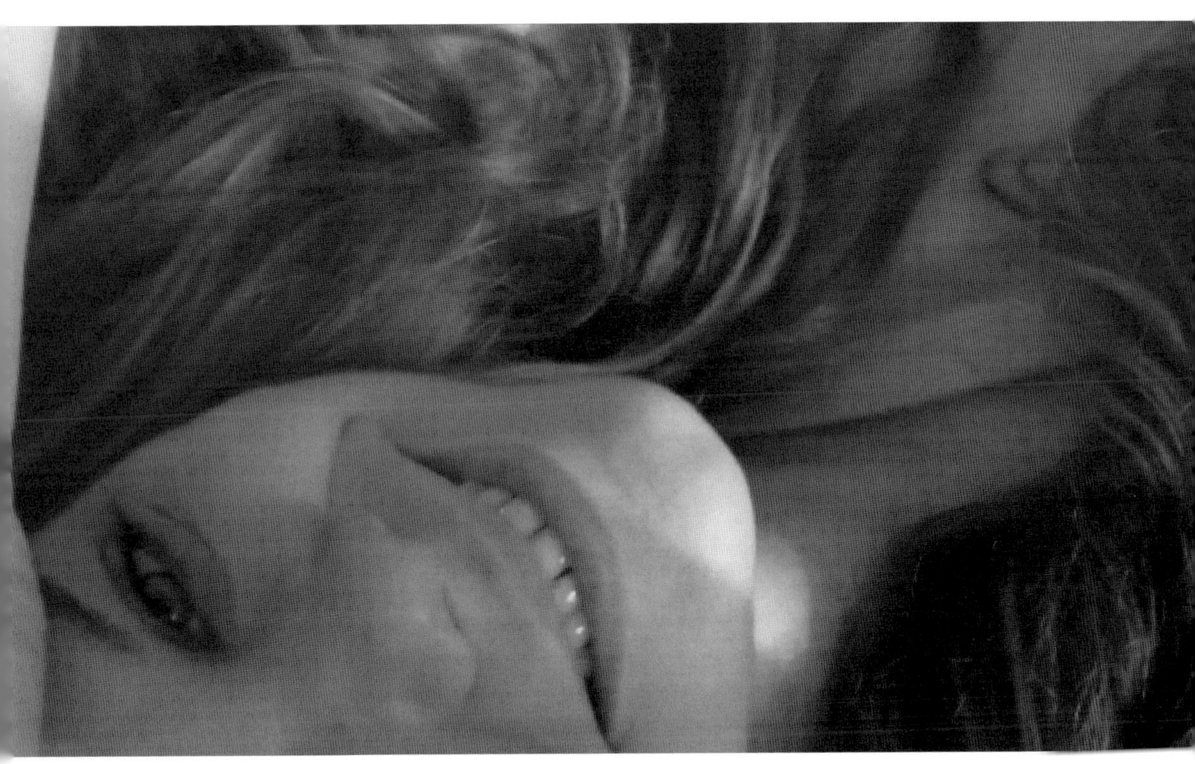

Dreaming about love (*Love Addict*, photo: Pernille Rose Grønkjær. Courtesy of Danish Documentary).

films have had a very dusty and unsexy reputation for a long time. We want to change that because we feel that our films are intriguing, engaging, and interesting. We really put a lot of effort into the story, and are genuinely interested in being entertaining. So we take the process of presenting our projects very seriously. If you're thinking about putting a million into something, you want to be able actually to hear what the people in question are saying. You also want some apparent clarity about the aims, in terms of what that million will be spent on. We try to make our projects appealing, and we've also discovered that the director is the film's central pillar when it comes to sales. I have to be able to explain my own film, and I shouldn't be afraid of explaining how and why it's going to be good. As for film titles, well, they're always tricky. A lot of people had a lot of ideas about what *The Monastery* should be called. Some felt that it should be called 'Mr Vig and the Nun,' for example. That's now the film's tagline, and that works well because it's got an element of humour and fun to it. But I remember having a conversation with Eva Mulvad about this issue, and she said, 'You've made a cinematic work of art, and you should give your film a title that reflects that. And you don't call a cinematic work of art "Mr Vig and the Nun." The right title is *The Monastery*.' That's also why *Love Addict* is called *Love Addict*. The title has to sound kind of monumental. And then the title needs to work in English because if we want to be able to finance our films, we have to see the entire world as our market. There are only about 5 million people in Denmark; that's not a big market for a small niche product, and documentary filmmaking is a bit of a niche. But I have to say that although we think carefully about how to sell our ideas, our projects never find a starting point in a commercial line of reasoning, but in the irrepressible desire that we each individually have to explore something. And, speaking from experience, I can say that the projects I've tried to conceptualize in commercial or economic terms just haven't succeeded to the same extent that my other films have. That's clearly true. The projects that have worked are the ones that have some real blood in them: a shot straight from the heart. So I've had very poor experiences with this idea that you can calculate or be strategic about it all. It has to be interesting to you, if you're to work at it and keep the energy going year in, year out. It's best to be motivated by thoughts that are a little more meaningful than 'Ok, I'm doing this for the sake of the money.'

REDVALL: Is it possible to make a living in Denmark as a documentary filmmaker once you've won prestigious prizes and enjoyed a good deal of success?

GRØNKJÆR: A lot of people thought my success meant wealth, but it didn't. All the prizes that *The Monastery* won actually cost me a lot of money. That's because I ended up traveling a lot and because I was spending money at a time when I wasn't earning any. Still, money can't buy the experiences I got out of all that. Our company is set up in a very frugal way now. We really live within our means. There are, of course, challenges given that it takes three years to make a film. Our hope with this company is that the money that might otherwise have gone to a production company will end up going to the directors because they own their own films. And that extra bit of income is then supposed to help the director keep the wolf at bay until the next film hopefully gets funded.

REDVALL: Danish documentaries have enjoyed considerable success in recent years, both in Denmark and on the international festival circuit. How do you explain this?

GRØNKJÆR: What we're good at in Denmark is working with stories. We're not afraid to tell stories and to use the material at hand. That's a very important part of the picture because if you think along the lines of having collected a chunk of reality, it's then your responsibility to make it come to life in a cinematic way. You have to take responsibility for having been there, or for having brought this piece of reality home with you. What are you going to do with it? What's the best way to give it a shape? What's the story and how do you make it as powerful as possible? All those sorts of questions have to be present to mind throughout the entire filmmaking process.

A lot of the Danish documentary filmmakers work with incredibly talented cinematographers, sound designers, and editors. When we make a documentary film, we put the same kind of time into it that others put into fiction films. I spend half a year editing each of my feature length films. Our way of working with sound is identical; we produce music, and so on; we work with the best possible people. The idea is to take storytelling seriously, and to be interested in making sure that the audience gets something out of that experience of watching the film. It's our task to mediate that reality, and we're not afraid to use everything we've learnt from fiction in order to achieve it. I'm sure that this is all closely connected to my generation of documentary filmmakers having been mostly trained at the National Film School of Denmark, where there's a unique tradition of storytelling. There's an interest in telling a good story and in coming to grips with the material. It's all about getting the best that you possibly can out of the material. So telling stories, that's what we're good at in Denmark, and that's a great thing because you have to take storytelling seriously. I once saw a film with a friend about suffering children in Africa. The film was very poorly told, and stripped of narration and direction. You could feel how the members of the audience were bored out of their minds. When it was over, my friend got up in a very aggressive way and said, 'If you want to save the world you should join the Red Cross, but if you want to make films you should do just that!' We're filmmakers and we make films. We don't make films in order to save the world, but then again, filmmaking actually is a way of saving the world. If you make a good film, it becomes a way of making a difference. And if, for example, you make a film about Africa, you should still take the storytelling dimension of it all seriously. It's really sad if the audience ends up feeling bored while watching a film about children who are hungry and miserable. That's a real problem. As a director, you owe it to those children to do a better job of telling their story.

Chapter 6

Jesper Jargil

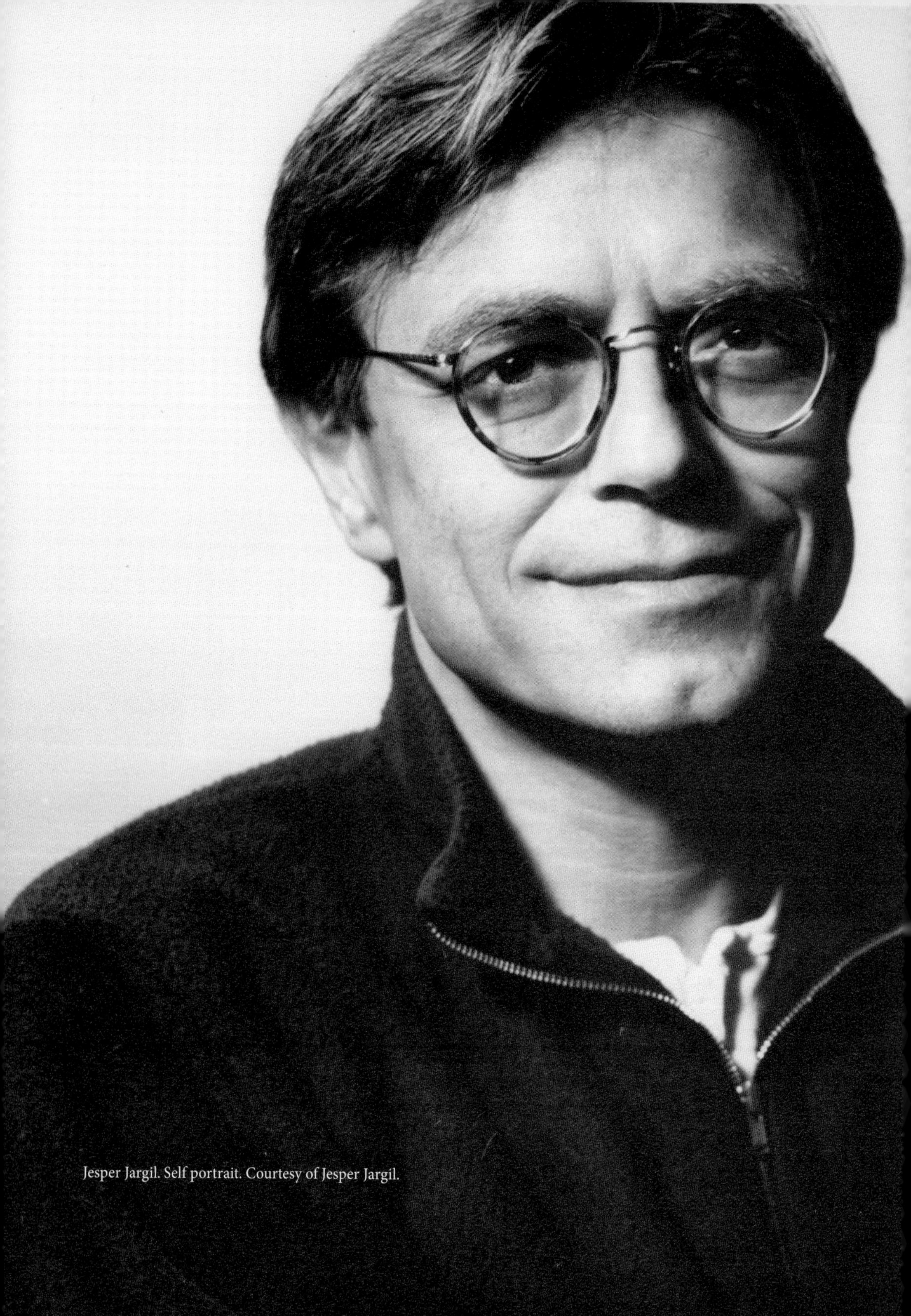

Jesper Jargil. Self portrait. Courtesy of Jesper Jargil.

B orn 1945. Jesper Jargil's path into filmmaking involved industry training as opposed to film school experience. His contributions to Danish film include a number of noteworthy documentaries, and he has also been active as a director of commercials. Jargil began his film career at Nordisk Film, where he served as an apprentice to such central figures as Erik Balling in the 1960s. Jargil's years at Nordisk Film led to key positions at Nordisk Reklamefilm, at a time when the legendary Erik Dibbern was at the company's helm. He subsequently worked for Per Holst's Petra Film and for the Bellevue Studio, before establishing his own company, Jesper Jargil Film, in 1974. In his capacity as an independent producer, director, and scriptwriter, Jargil has been responsible for the production of approximately 700 commercials, many of them prizewinners at the Cannes Advertising Film Festival. Jargil made his first documentary film in 1996. Entitled *Per Kirkeby – Vinterbillede* (*Per Kirkeby: Winter's Tale*), the film follows the Danish painter's creation of a large oil painting, from the first stroke of his brush to the last, as he talks about his thoughts and feelings regarding the creative process. The film won a Robert prize for best documentary film in 1996, as well as a number of international awards. It is the first of Jargil's many penetrating studies focusing on the process of artistic creation. Jargil subsequently made a documentary trilogy, 'Troværdighedens rige' ('The Kingdom of Credibility'), consisting of *De ydmygede* (*The Humiliated*, 1998), *De udstillede* (*The Exhibited*, 2000), and *De lutrede* (*The Purified*, 2002). *The Humiliated* focuses on Lars von Trier's production of his Dogma film *Idioterne* (*The Idiots*, 1998), while *The Exhibited* documents an experiment spanning the worlds of theatre and art by the same director, namely *Psykomobile #1 – Verdensuret* ('Psychomobile: The World Clock'). This experiment consisted of ants in New Mexico controlling the interaction of 53 actors located in exhibition rooms belonging to the art association at Gammel Strand, in Copenhagen. The third film in the trilogy, *The Purified*, documents exchanges between Dogma brethren Lars von Trier, Thomas Vinterberg, Søren Kragh-Jacobsen, and Kristian Levring as they reflect on their own Dogma films, while also taking stock of the Dogma movement as a whole. Jargil went on to make *Skitser til et portræt af en maler* ('Sketches for a Portrait of a Painter,' 2005), a film that is similarly focused on the process of artistic creation. Using twenty thematically organized sequences, Jargil provides a portrait of the painter Vibeke Tøjner, based on her creative activity in her studio. The film was made as an interactive DVD, but also exists in a definitively edited version. More recently, Jargil has followed with his camera such artists as Olafur Eliasson, Malene Landgreen, Lars Kræmmer, and, once again, Per Kirkeby, the intention being to produce a large, integrated work about creative processes across various art forms.

Documentary features:

2005   *Skitser til et portræt af en maler – En interaktiv film om Vibeke Tøjner* ('Sketches for a Portrait of a Painter: An Interactive Film about Vibeke Tøjner')
2003   *De lutrede* (*The Purified*)
2000   *De udstillede* (*The Exhibited*)
1999   *De ydmygede* (*The Humiliated*)
1996   *Per Kirkeby – Vinterbillede* (*Per Kirkeby: Winter's Tale*)

REDVALL: You worked with commercials for many years before you started making documentaries. How did you get into the film industry?

JARGIL: I attended the choir school, Sankt Annæ Gymnasium, and initially thought I was going to have a career as a singer. My teachers thought my voice had potential, and I sang in various choirs and was able somewhat to support myself by doing so. But while I was enrolled at the school, I ended up spending a year in the US, which was quite unusual back then. I'd been inspired by Anne-Lise Gabold, who later became an actor and a director. She'd been to the US and it sounded fantastic, so I managed to find a way of getting to spend 1962–63 over there. It was an incredible experience. I was a member of a theatre group during that year, and ended up becoming very interested in drama and film.

I returned to Denmark and completed secondary school, and then I knocked on all sorts of doors in an attempt to get my foot into the world of film, but it was completely impossible. So I made a living singing instead, and had a job as a singer at Copenhagen's Cathedral, among several other places. Because I'd become good at English, I also had a job as a tour guide for the DFDS Canal Tours, and that's actually how it suddenly happened. After one of the tours, this man stayed on in the boat and said that he'd spent the last three months looking for the lead player for his next film, and that he wanted me. I'd never seen myself as an actor, but I'd spent a year and a half offering to wash stairs or whatever in order to get into the film milieu, all to no avail, so this seemed like a real opportunity.

It turned out that the man in question was Knud Leif Thomsen, who in many ways was the Lars von Trier of his day and a very sharp-minded social commentator. And he wanted me, although I was completely unknown and not at all what the producer at Nordisk Film wanted. I was sent to Mallorca for a fortnight so that

I could get a tan and learn how to use contact lenses, which were completely new back then. And while I was gone, Knud Leif Thomsen did his best to persuade people that a new face – as compared with a well-known actor – was a good thing. It turned into a protracted tug of war, with discussions about what was more important: taking a chance on someone new, or sticking to a known face. In the end he lost the battle, and the role was given to a pop star instead.

Since I'd in many ways been drawn into the conflict as a hostage, Nordisk Film felt they owed me something, so I was told I could do odd jobs in connection with the film. I did that for three days, and then it turned out that Erik Balling needed an assistant director because the person he normally worked with had fallen ill. That opportunity came with one day's advance notice; so all of a sudden I found myself working as the assistant director for *Slå først, Frede* ('Strike First, Frede'; dir. Erik Balling, 1965). I made quite an idiot of myself the first day because I didn't have a clue what a clapperboard was. It was tough, but I stuck with it and learnt a lot.

REDVALL:

Many of the younger documentary filmmakers received their training at the National Film School, whereas you were trained on the job, in the context of the film industry. What was it like being apprenticed to a director like Erik Balling?

JARGIL:

Balling didn't put a lot of effort into training anyone, but you were included in a process and as a result you began to understand the routines. But mostly you just slaved like mad, often for 15 hours a day. I was just happy to be there, and I completed the tasks I was given. And once you got a foot in the door, you might get lucky and find that someone noticed what you were doing. I kept at it and I was happy to go the extra mile, and so I got a reputation for being someone who did what was needed. The executive producer, Bo Christensen, noticed that. And he subsequently recommended me to Erik Dibbern at Nordisk Reklamefilm, where I found myself in amusing hands. Erik Dibbern was effervescent, and I ended up working for him for three years. I learnt a lot and also started making commercials myself. I wasn't the least bit concerned by the thought that making commercials might be seen as uninteresting or as politically incorrect.

I actually applied to the Film School when it opened in 1966, but I only got as far as the first round in the admissions process and never reapplied. I was having a good time and was getting paid for what I was doing. When the Department of Film & Media Studies was established at the University of Copenhagen, I attended a number of lectures, and these were largely defined by problems with projectors and by the atmosphere of youth revolt that was very much a feature of the period. The idea was to get rid of the teacher, and a lot of the students were Leninists or Trotskyites. To be honest, it was a lot more fun making commercials, not least of all because there was money available for experimentation. I was allowed to try a lot of different things, to play around with new technologies. Those were really good years. But I started to get a lot of wind in my sails and came to be seen as a competitor by others in the company, so I was fired. An earlier employee, namely Per Holst, had warned me that this would happen. He'd been through the grinder himself, and he said that when it happened to me down the road, I'd be welcome in his company, Petra Film. So that's where I ended up and I just continued making commercials.

REDVALL: You made your first documentary film, *Per Kirkeby – Winter's Tale*, at a relatively late stage in your career. Had you been interested in becoming a documentary filmmaker all along? Or had you been involved in documentary projects that didn't ultimately work out?

JARGIL: Not really. I was so busy making commercials. But I've had this secret dream since the 1970s of making an adaptation of Johannes V. Jensen's novel *Kongens Fald* (*The Fall of the King*, 1900–01). I held onto the rights for 30 years, and I did a lot of research and put a lot of energy into looking into various possibilities, but I was never able to pull it off, because it would be a very expensive film to make. For example, just staging the bloodbath in Stockholm could easily cost a few million. I finally had to relinquish the rights, although I'd put a lot of energy into the project and had involved a lot of people in it in all sorts of ways. It was a passion of mine, and a very fine one I think, because quite a lot of good things came out of it. But I'd never thought about making a documentary film before I made the one about Per Kirkeby.

REDVALL: Do you see the Danish film milieu as being a divided one, with some filmmakers producing fiction films and others documentaries and commercials? Or do you see people as working across various boundaries?

JARGIL: This varies, I think. In the years when I was learning on the job, I felt the world of advertising was a very creative one. The small companies were thriving, the competitive element was based on creativity, and people cared about narrative form. In many ways this all changed when TV 2 was established and introduced TV commercials to Denmark for the first time. Before then, the commercials were being made for the cinema screen, and there was generally a sense of respect associated with the activity. At one point I was making about one third of all the Danish commercials that were being made in a given year. I was shooting on 35mm film, and I had large budgets to work with, and big crews. So I was able to get the best people from the world of feature filmmaking to work on these commercials. My experience is that the milieus in question are far more separate these days.

REDVALL: What prompted you to establish your own company?

JARGIL: After I'd worked for Petra Film for a few years, Bellevue Studio, which was owned by the advertising agency of Gutenberghus, hired me as a film director. I had a good contract with Bellevue Studio as a freelancer, and my salary was fine. But after three years I wanted to renegotiate the conditions of my contract, and my proposed changes did not meet with a favourable response. So I started my own company. But for the longest time this didn't amount to more than a registered name and some letterhead. It took me a while to get the shop up and running, but fortunately I managed to do so in the end.

REDVALL: Many of your earlier commercials are very cinematic and clearly designed to be seen in the cinema. Your more recent commercials have typically been made for TV and tend to be more like documentaries, both in terms of their form and content. I'm thinking, for example, of the commercials that you've made for the supermarket chain Netto. Can commercials be made as documentaries?

JARGIL: There's often a documentary element in commercials. For example, I've made a lot of what I call 'hurrah films.' 'Hurrah films' are like adaptations of annual reports, in the sense that the overall impression to be conveyed simply has to be positive. You're hired to shout 'hurrah.' You may have bad experiences making those sorts of films, but at the same time you're often out there filming in a real context, and trying to capture something central about the company.

I've made some slideshows for the Rheumatism Association that I'm still quite pleased with. I did the photography myself and was, of course, working with true stories. My experience was that you want the stories you choose to have an element of hope. I discovered real people whose fates were truly gripping, and I found that in many ways documentary techniques were needed to tell their stories in the best way possible.

I generally feel that right now there's a lot of formal experimentation going on in commercials. The Netto films are certainly documentary in nature. The idea for those films emerged from Netto's profile, which is all about how things should be cheap. It made sense that the company's commercials shouldn't look like they'd cost a fortune to make, so I simply set off with a cheap VHS camera and started shooting in the shops. It was very much a question of going out and capturing the moment. In that sense there's a lot that's real in those films, although the depicted moments clearly are chosen with a good deal of care, and shown from a particular perspective.

REDVALL: Could you talk about the context for your first documentary film, *Per Kirkeby – Winter's Tale*? That film is, of course, the first of a series of films that you've made about creative artistic processes.

JARGIL: I've always been interested in artistic processes, but I don't think it's very interesting to load all of an artist's triumphs onto the table so as to describe how great the person is. What's interesting is exploring the doubt that's part of the artistic process, being part of that process oneself, and hearing the artist say things he's never actually articulated before. Art, for me, is intuition that's found material expression. In these films, there's a will to unsettle the conventional or expected; in terms of my own creative process and through the challenge that my camera represents for the person who's in front of it, but also for the viewer. To depict those sorts of processes you need time, curiosity, human sensitivity, and a bit of luck, coupled with a whole lot of persistence and patience. Those are the elements that are needed if the ground is to be made fertile for that magical moment when the artist lets go, allowing us to witness how he's touched by or moved to respond to some source that, for him, is genuinely new.

The idea for *Per Kirkeby – Winter's Tale* occurred to me when I read this interview with Per Kirkeby in which he seemed to be furious about just about everything. He was bitching about there being art here, there, and everywhere, but his way of complaining was rather creative and quite fascinating. It occurred to me that it might be interesting to observe him while he worked on a huge painting, and he'd then be able to bitch and complain about life,

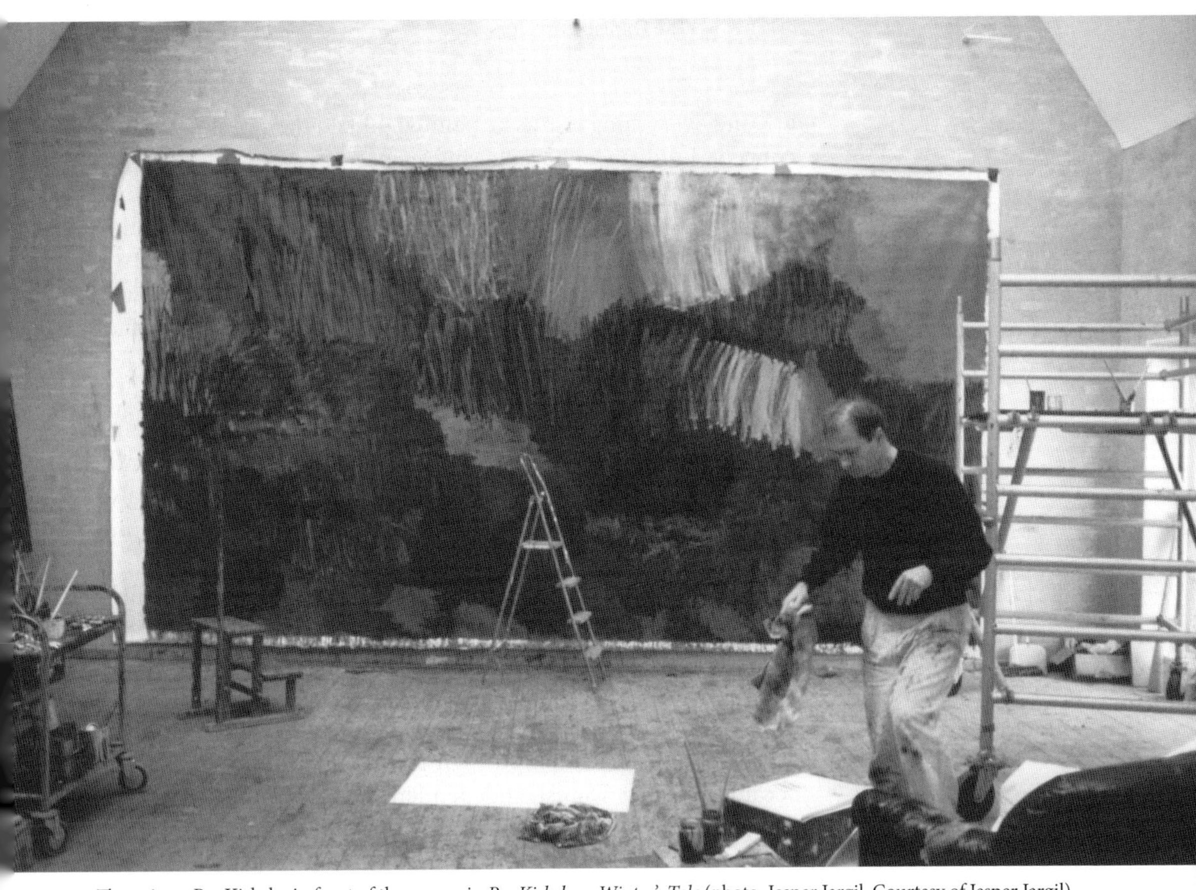

The painter Per Kirkeby in front of the canvas in *Per Kirkeby – Winter's Tale* (photo: Jesper Jargil. Courtesy of Jesper Jargil).

art, and everything else as he painted. I liked the simplicity of that concept. I didn't want even a single close-up.

I knew Per a bit from earlier, and so I called him and told him I had this idea for a film. What I got in response was: 'I hate films about artists.' But when I explained my idea more fully, he was seduced by its simplicity and decided to give it a go. I then wrote a page or so describing the concept and sent it to what was then called the National Film Board of Denmark. It was my first application for money, and I was rather surprised when I received a letter three days later indicating that I had half a million Danish Crowns at my disposal. I have to admit that for a split second I thought, 'Why have I been wasting my life making commercials?! This is a good deal easier.' But I'd applied at exactly the right time, because it's not normally that easy.

It then took me a few years to get ready to shoot the film, because I wanted to shoot in HD and first had to sort out the technology. I needed HD to realize what was essentially a simple compositional concept. What I was after was something like a continuous full shot that would also capture the rich details of the brushstrokes. That required high resolution video, and the film became the first Danish independent HD TV production. The technical side of things involved an enormous amount of work. And before we'd even started shooting, Per Kirkeby ended up regretting that he'd agreed to it all, so we also had to do a bit of arm-twisting before everything fell into place.

REDVALL: The application process you describe in connection with *Per Kirkeby* was clearly very smooth. What have your experiences in that regard been like since then?

JARGIL: I've been treated very well and can't complain, but it's my impression that the process has become a lot more formal and bureaucratic. Everything has to be thought through and pinned down in advance. That's just not appropriate when what drives you is curiosity or the desire to be able to follow up on things that are unanticipated and surprising. But the money that the DFI commissioners provide is really important. The DFI helps get the project off the ground, and then you have to find the rest of the financing yourself.

REDVALL: What's it been like, this business of having to find financing for your films?

JARGIL: The only reason it's worked is because I've made these commercials all along, which has helped to put money in the pot. For example,

I ended up getting some crucial financing for the Kirkeby film because I wrote a letter to the chief editor of *Jyllands-Posten*, Jørgen Ejbøl, whom I was making commercials for back then. I described the project, which I'd already shot, and explained that I lacked the money I needed to finish the film. He came over and saw a two-hour version of the film, and was very touched by what he saw, so he decided to put 300,000 Crowns into it.

REDVALL:
You've made this trilogy called 'The Kingdom of Credibility', which finds a starting point in projects or ideas by Lars von Trier. You were also one of the cinematographers for the Dogma brothers' real-time millennium experiment, *D-Dag* (*D Day*, 2001), which involved the shooting of four character-based trajectories in Copenhagen on New Year's Eve in 1999. This was all transmitted live on TV, and viewers were then able to zap between four different TV channels, each with its own trajectory, and thereby produce their own version of the story. How did you end up working with Lars von Trier?

JARGIL:
I've known Lars von Trier since his film school days. He started out working as an assistant on some of my commercials. He's a great person to talk through ideas with, or to have these 'tease meetings' with, where you test different ideas. We've done a number of things together because after his success at Cannes with *The Element of Crime* (dir. Lars von Trier, 1984) he became a household name, and suddenly found himself being asked to make commercials. When that happened, he asked me to be his producer and technical director, and he'd then be the concept person.

Peter Aalbæk and Lars actually met each other during the shooting of a commercial for PFA Pension, which I was producing. They fought vigorously the entire time! At a later stage, they then decided they wanted to establish a company together, and at one point I was considering joining them, but I finally realized it wasn't for me. They then created Zentropa, and that's worked out rather well. In some sort of warm way, Lars and I have known each other for a very long time, and so I'm able to sort of wade into his world the way those films of mine do. He knew me very well by the time I made those films, so they weren't that threatening.

REDVALL:
The first film in the trilogy, *The Humiliated*, which focuses on the production of *The Idiots*, provides an intimate and detailed account of the shooting of von Trier's film; you even had access to

the diary entries that he recorded on his Dictaphone during the shoots. These days 'behind the scenes' films are more common, and they're often what you would call 'hurrah films.' But *The Humiliated* involves a rather different approach in that it depicts some fairly turbulent processes. Was *The Humiliated* your idea?

JARGIL: Yes, it was. But I actually shot *The Exhibited* first. That film builds on the exhibition called 'The World Clock' which von Trier had mounted in collaboration with the Gammel Strand art association. And the exhibition space was just 100 metres from where my company was located. The film was very much motivated by my desire to play with my new little digital camera, and when I had a bit of time, I'd just visit the exhibition. In the beginning, I wasn't thinking in terms of making a film, and a lot of the material is quite random; but then again, in other ways it's not.

'The World Clock' was in many ways a precursor to Dogma. It has elements of the Dogma concept, especially, of course, the use of rules. Lars von Trier saw some of what I'd shot, and we also talked about some of the actors. When he found himself needing an extra cinematographer for *The Idiots*, he asked me. He'd already hired Kristoffer Nyholm, but he wanted an extra cinematographer, so there'd be an additional set of hands around just in case he went into a depression. That way work on the film would be able to proceed. I agreed, but on one condition: I wanted to be allowed to shoot my own material in a parallel process. I wanted him and his crew to trust me to the point where I was allowed always to be present with my camera. And I got what I asked for. The idea had always been to make a film with real intimacy, but there were certainly times when boundaries were transgressed. I wasn't a mere fly on the wall; I was also the elephant who blustered around in the middle of things, but eventually they got used to that.

REDVALL: *The Humiliated* gives the impression that Lars von Trier did a fair bit of the shooting for *The Idiots* himself.

JARGIL: Kristoffer is actually the person who did most of the shooting for the film itself. But Lars started grabbing the camera more and more, and I tried to help and encourage him. In many ways, I suppose, we were both going through the same process. I'd just experienced what it was like to work with this little DV camera, which I'd used for the 'World Clock' project, and I knew how fantastic it was as a director to be able simply to grab the camera. There was that feeling of, 'Bloody hell, can I actually do this myself?!' Ideally, as a director, you want to be able to control the

<table>
<tr><td></td><td>framing yourself. If you're working with a cinematographer, then of course you always hope that he's understood what you're after. You get that extra bit of precision if you're able to control the image from behind the camera yourself.</td></tr>
<tr><td>REDVALL:</td><td>The Dictaphone diary is a central element in the film, because it provides access to Lars von Trier's thoughts as we watch him struggle with the production and with the actors. How did that material end up becoming part of the film?</td></tr>
<tr><td>JARGIL:</td><td>Towards the end, Lars von Trier mentioned these diary recordings. He is, of course, this master manipulator! It was brilliant to get these recordings, and they had a decisive impact on the shape of the film. Up until then, I was having a hard time finding the right shape for the film, and there are still certain things that I'm not entirely satisfied with. For example, because of the diary, we get Lars von Trier's account of his relationship to the actress, Anne Louise Hassing. She never tells us her version of things, and I would have liked to have been able to include that. The way it is now, it's almost entirely his version of things. Had I known that he was recording this diary of his, I would have given her an opportunity to say something about that relationship as we were shooting. My agreement with everyone who was involved in the production was that they'd be allowed to see the film when I'd finished editing it, and that they'd have the right to raise any objections they might have. But nobody had any objections. Anne Louise Hassing was ambivalent about the film, but approved it. But I've later read that she has regrets about it.</td></tr>
<tr><td>REDVALL:</td><td>In The Purified, you bring together the four Dogma brethren in order to assess the impact of Dogma 95. Among other things, there are shots documenting the shooting of the films, and those scenes in von Trier's living room, which provide a kind of frame for it all and where we see the brethren discussing what it was like to work with the constraints. Along the way we get sequences with Mogens Rukov, who taught several of the Dogma brethren scriptwriting and dramaturgy at the Film School. Rukov, more specifically, chastises them on a TV screen as a means of getting the discussion going. How did you arrive at this particular form for the film?</td></tr>
<tr><td>JARGIL:</td><td>The Purified is the last film in the trilogy that I've called 'The Kingdom of Credibility.' Whether something is true or not is one thing; whether it's credible or not is something else entirely. I think credibility is a good word, and one that we film people</td></tr>
</table>

should be making reference to. I was involved in shooting *The Idiots*, and I also filmed material for *Festen* (*The Celebration*; dir. Thomas Vinterberg, 1998) and *Mifunes sidste sang* (*Mifune*; dir. Søren Kragh-Jacobsen, 1999). In the beginning I was just curious, but I knew the rules and could tell that they were cheating every now and then. Suddenly there are these towels in front of the windows on account of a light issue. This was the sort of transgression of the rules that I was noticing. I did a few brief interviews along the way, and after a while I started wanting to do something with the material I had. Doing something with rules is great fun, but the question, of course, is whether you're an honest player, or whether you have three aces up your sleeve.

The basic concept was that the film would investigate the extent to which they'd observed the rules. Initially the thought was that I myself would do the chastising, but somehow that seemed all wrong. There was a lack of solidarity in that approach, and my aim, after all, had not been to squeal on them. But I knew that I needed to get some kind of devil's advocate into the picture, and in that regard Mogens Rukov was perfect. We shot a few conversations about the rules, and he becomes the person who says what needs to be said. And since they all respect him, he becomes the catalyst for these conversations they have when I get them all together to talk about Dogma. And the gift in the story is that Lars, as the great visionary, refuses the lie and makes it clear that he has a bad conscience on account of the group sex scene in *The Idiots*, which was certainly a breach of the Dogma rules. The film ends with him stating that a real Dogma film has yet to be made.

REDVALL: You've experimented with new technology in a lot of your films. You made use of HD technology in *Per Kirkeby*; you were involved in the *D Day* experiment; your trilogy depends to a significant degree on your use of small DV cameras and the kind of access they afforded you; and your most recent film, about the painter Vibeke Tøjner, is an interactive work that allows viewers to choose the sequences they want to see. Is experimenting with new technology in your films an important dimension of your work?

JARGIL: It's fair to say that I've usually been quick to embrace technological developments, but I've never done this for the sake of the technology itself. It's always been a matter of finding a solution that takes the form and content to the highest level possible, while also posing some challenges. I think all the new things that are

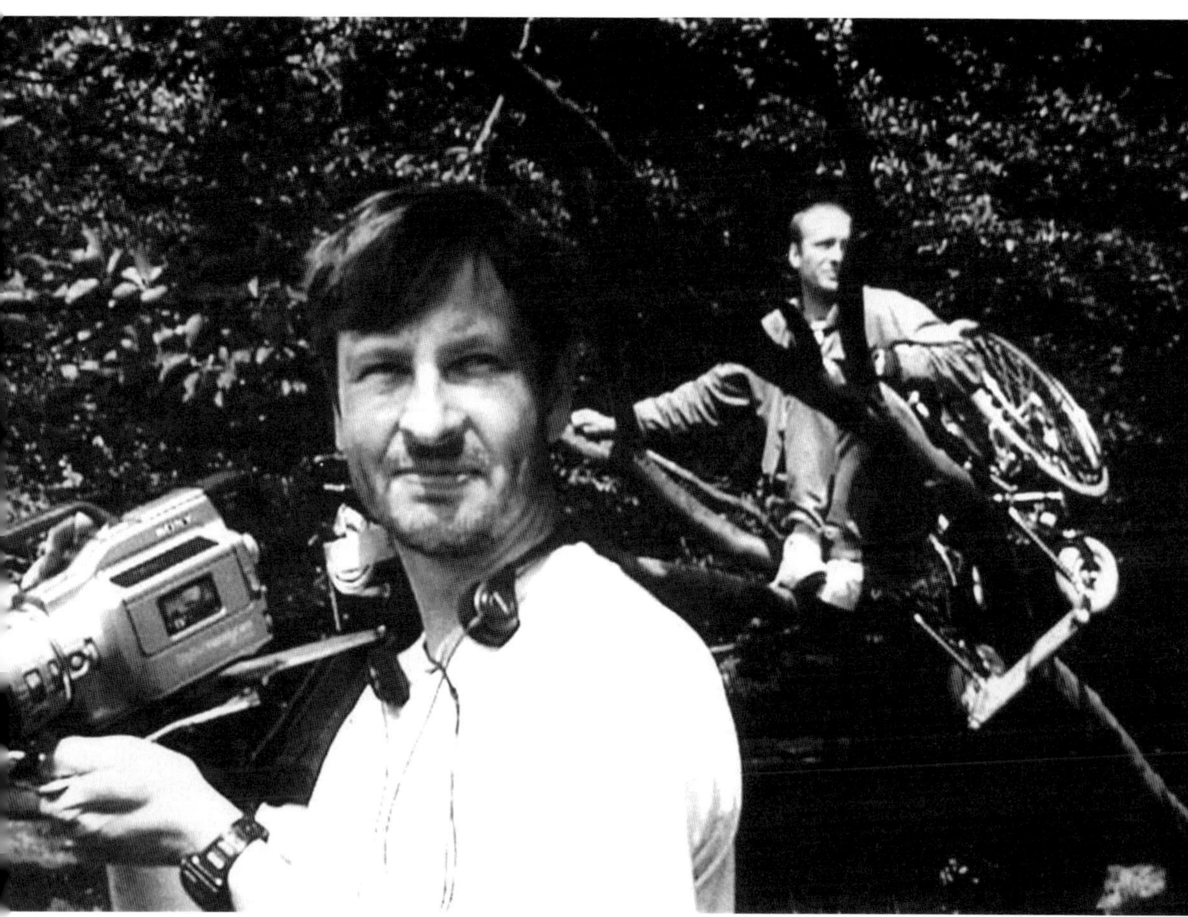

Lars von Trier with the camera during the shooting of *Idioterne* (*The Idiots*, 1998) (*The Humiliated*, photo: Jesper Jargil. Courtesy of Jesper Jargil).

going on are really exciting. The fact that everyone can make films today is, as I see it, not a threat, but a gift. I love stories and there's a lot of exciting work going on at the moment because stories can now be shaped in so many different ways. The rhythm of technological breakthroughs has been very intense in recent years. Today, anyone can use a mobile phone to shoot a film that's of higher quality than *The Celebration* and *The Idiots*. I'm certainly interested in making regular use of the new media technologies that are so readily available now.

I shot the film about Vibeke Tøjner with a cheap camera. As far as the technology is concerned, anyone could have made it. The idea was to structure the film in terms of twenty chapters, and to allow the viewer to play with the order in which they'd be seen. DVD was new back then, although this was just a few years ago. The Danish Film Institute was unsure about how to approach that new technology, and so the film became an example of what could be done with it. The film was shown at an art exhibition featuring Vibeke's work, and it offered people that opportunity I just mentioned, to select sequences. It's my impression that the people who started watching a given sequence ended up seeing all of them, but there were heated discussions about the order in which they were going to be seen, and about who was going to decide.

REDVALL: How do you see Danish documentary film today, and especially the terms one faces as a documentary filmmaker?

JARGIL: At the moment it's fantastic to experience how people are going to the cinemas to see documentaries. And how they're willing to pay for that. I just saw *Testamentet* (*The Will*; dir. Christian Sønderby Jepsen, 2011) in a completely full cinema. The film, after all, is about a group of social losers from the depths of Jutland. But it's a really good film, and that kind of documentary is now capable of competing with fiction films in the cinemas. It's really exciting, and what we're also seeing is this interesting area where there's a mix of documentary and fictional elements.

My sense is that that there's a lot of new talent, and that a lot of the directors, like my daughter Mira, for example, are having a lot of fun, in a deep and cool way, making films. But at the same time, the systems that surround that filmmaking activity seem to have become very bureaucratic, with film commissioners having to cover their backs and to be absolutely sure of their case. I was recently at a meeting of the Association of Danish Film Directors, and there were these film commissioners who'd been invited to talk to us about the process involved in their handling a given case. And I left thinking that I'd rather be a parking attendant!

But I say all this with a great sense of love for the system. The basic thought of having commissioners who have the power to say yes or no on the basis of their own subjective assessments is definitely the right premise. It's just my experience that the commissioners are hemmed in, and that's a pity because I think the original structures underwriting film support in Denmark are an important reason for the progress and success that Danish film as a whole has enjoyed. The fact that certain individuals are allowed to make choices and to take chances is the very nerve and heart of Danish film. There's something almost magically simple about that way of disbursing money for art or the production of films, and it would be stupid to somehow lose that.

Chapter 7

Torben Skjødt Jensen

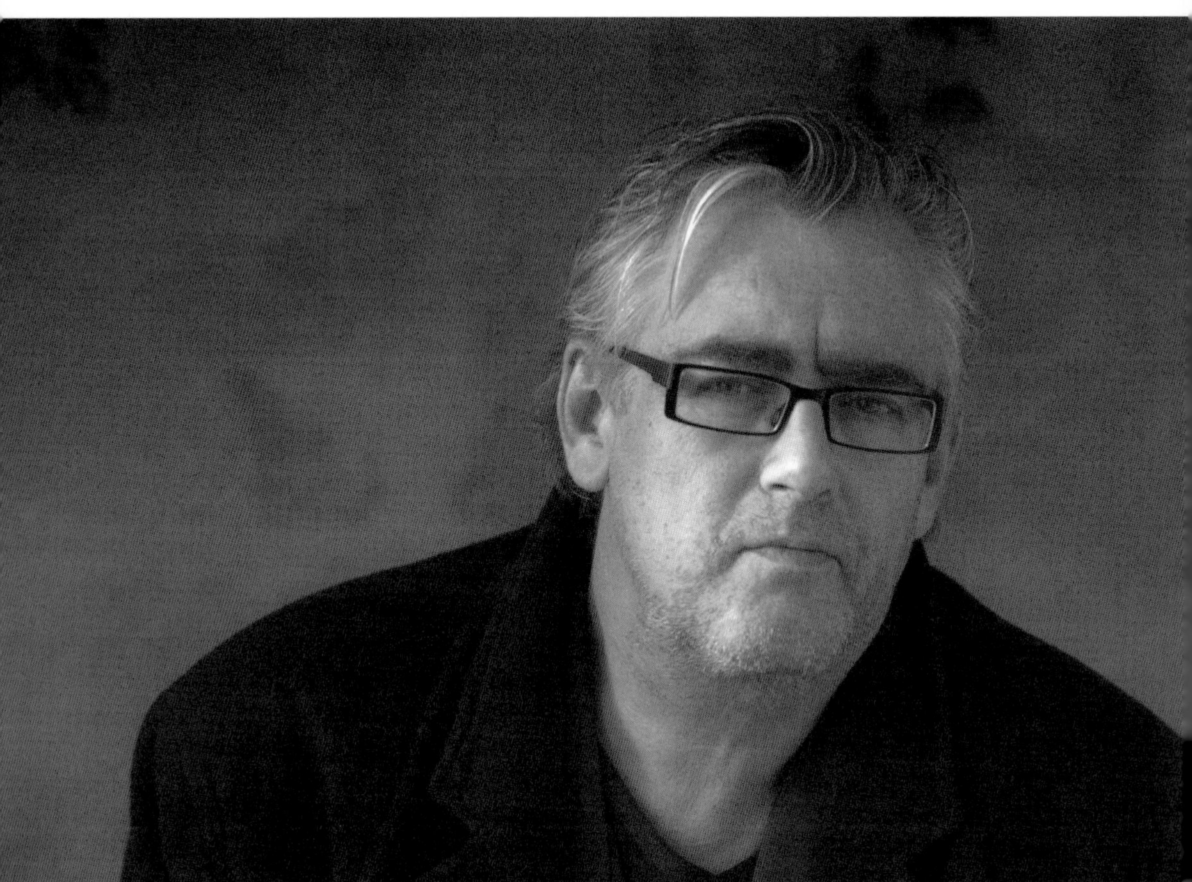

Torben Skjødt Jensen. Portrait by Niels Berg. Courtesy of Niels Berg and The Danish Film Institute Stills & Posters Archive.

B orn 1958, in Aalborg. Skjødt Jensen pursued Film Studies at the University of Copenhagen from 1978–81. Before embarking seriously on a career as a film director, Skjødt Jensen worked as a magazine and comic books editor for Interpresse and Runepress. He also worked in the area of graphic design, for such companies as Gutenberghus and Tegneværkstedet. Skjødt Jensen first began making films at the Video Workshop in Haderslev. During his time at the Workshop, Skjødt Jensen helped to establish the production company Englefilm, which produced programming for the regional TV station TVSyd. At that time, he was also part of the Danish music scene, through his production of music videos. Skjødt Jensen worked for the Aarhus-based production company ATC and also for the record company Genlyd.

Torben Skjødt Jensen's approach to filmmaking is experimental in nature. His films exhibit a striking visual style; one that combines an interest in people and the worlds in which they live with highly expressive aesthetic features. Skjødt Jensen has made both feature-length fiction films and documentary films, but the emphasis has clearly been on the latter. His preference for experimentation is already evident in his early music videos. With titles such as *First Annual Anti Anti Fashion Video Performance* (1983), these videos point to what would later become a clear tendency. Skjødt Jensen's early films have been released in an anthology of music videos entitled *Englefjæs* ('Angelface,' 1989), which includes both music videos and a short fiction film. Experimental, poetic, and reflexive elements are present throughout his work. Good examples of the style in question can be found in *Flaneur I-III* (1993–98), three films that deal with themes in European culture and literature through images of urban environments, texts, and portraits of particular persons.

Yet it is clear that Torben Skjødt Jensen's greatest contribution to Danish documentary film lies in his portrait films. In the first of these films, *It's a Blue World* (1990), which is about the painter Henrik Lerfeldt, he developed what would become his characteristic style: the combination of a documentary portrait with a staged and highly visual articulation of the artist's universe. The film for which he is best known internationally deals with an equally significant artist. In *Carl Th. Dreyer – min metier* (*Carl Th. Dreyer: My Metier*, 1995), there is an attempt to get to the artistic core of Dreyer's universe, but through a many facetted visual language that is very much Skjødt Jensen's. Skjødt Jensen has also made portrait films about controversial cultural figures. An example is *Den grimme dreng* (*The Naughty Boy*, 1996), which is about Ole Ege, who played a pioneering role in the context of pornographic films. This film is thematically related to his film about the history of sexuality, *Tugt & Utugt* (*More Sex Please, We're from Scandinavia*, 2001), as well as to his film about eccentricity and extreme wealth, *Simon Spies – Simons film* (*Simon Spies: Simon's Film*, 1999). In *Den talende muse* (*The Talking Muse*, 2003) he returns to the world of film, providing a sensational portrait of Asta Nielsen, one of the great stars of the silent era. Drawing on new archival material, Skjødt Jensen provides an account of Asta Nielsen that gets behind the protective reserve that has otherwise accompanied the star's image.

Documentary features:

2011   *City Slang Redux*
2009   *Vi skal jo hjælpe hinanden* ('We Need to Help Each Other')
2009   *Dr. Dante – Stjernernes legeplads* ('Dr Dante: Playground of the Stars')
2006   *Ud af grænselandet* ('Out of the Borderlands')
2006   *Erland Josephson – Spelar du i kväll* ('Erland Josephson: Are You Playing Tonight?')
2005   *Allan Hagedorf – En dansker i Hitlers Tyskland* ('Allan Hagedorf: A Dane in Hitler's Germany')
2004   *H.C. Andersen møder Carl Nielsen* ('H. C. Andersen meets Carl Nielsen')
2003   *Den talende muse – Samtaler med Asta Nielsen* (*The Talking Muse*)
2001   *Tugt & Utugt* (*More Sex Please, We're from Scandinavia*)
1999   *Simon Spies – Simons film* ('Simon Spies: Simon's Film')
1996   *Nyt dansk Danseteater* (*The Dancing Storytellers*)
1996   *Den grimme dreng* (*The Naughty Boy*; renamed in Danish *Ole Ege – Den uartige dreng*, 2010)
1995   *Carl Th. Dreyer – Min metier* (*Carl Th. Dreyer: My Metier*)
1993   *Som et strejf* ('Just a Touch')
1990   *Hans Henrik Lerfeldt – It's a Blue World*

Documentary shorts:

2007   *Den livgivende relation* ('The Life-giving Relation')
2004   *Surrational Cityscaping I: De Rerum Natura*
1998   *Flaneur III – Benjamins skygge* ('Flaneur III: Benjamin's Shadow')
1995   *Flaneur II – Dandy*
1994   *Wayfarer – 8900 Randers*
1993   *Flaneur*
1992   *Quatsiluni*
1983   *First Annual Anti Anti Fashion Video Performance*

Music videos:

1988   *Times Goes By*
1987   *Alt er dit* ('Everything is Yours')
1985   *Alt er som det plejer* ('Nothing has Changed')

Fiction films:

2003   *Afgrunden* (*The Abyss*)
1999   *Manden som ikke ville dø* (*The Man Who Would Live Forever*)
1996   *Hvileløse hjerte* (*Restless Heart*)
1996   *Freelancer*
1996   *To Be or Nothing to Eat*
1994   *Gensidig berøring* ('Mutual Involvement')
1993   *Le véritable homme dans la lune* ('The Real Man in the Moon')
1983   *Englefjæs* ('Angelface')

BONDEBJERG:	How did you end up becoming a filmmaker?
SKJØDT JENSEN:	I'm what is usually called an autodidact. That is, I never received any real training in filmmaking. But I have always been interested in film, and film has been an important part of my life. I was born in Jutland, but when I was about to start school, my parents moved to Roskilde, which was quite a culture shock for a boy from the provinces.

My mother had a job in the local cinema, so I saw and experienced films already as a child, and I also worked in that same cinema at one point. In fact, I was actually trained to run a cinema. So, it's really always been about film for me, both in practical terms and in terms of my interests. I think that meeting Peter Madsen (who later did the drawings for the Valhalla comic series) during the last years of secondary school at the Roskilde Cathedral School [HF] was also quite decisive. We became good friends, and in the mid-1970s we started doing things together. We were both part of the comic books milieu and were involved, for example, with Fantask. What this meant – quite concretely – was that, having graduated from secondary school, I got a job as an editor at Interpresse, which brought me into even closer contact with the comic books milieu in Copenhagen. At that time, I also moved to Copenhagen, where I began Film Studies at the

University of Copenhagen, a place where students were also allowed to try their hand at filmmaking. That was probably what interested me the most, although I'm also really glad to have seen the many films that I saw at the Danish Film Museum. I never completed my studies, but the courses I took with Martin Drouzy, Marguerite Engberg, and Peter Schepelern certainly provided a good basis for my subsequent work as a filmmaker. But what I discovered was that it was the actual *making* of films that interested me, not the academic study of them. One thing that was important was that I met Hans Bang, who ran the Video Workshop in Haderslev, at the Berlin International Film Festival. He introduced me to the Workshop milieu, which I hadn't known anything about at all. It was in that milieu that I really started to get serious about making my own films.

BONDEBJERG: How would you describe that workshop milieu in the early 1980s? What were some of the tendencies that found expression there? What sorts of things did you produce during the period in question?

SKJØDT JENSEN: It was a very open milieu, one in which all sorts of tendencies flourished. Following on that encounter at the Berlin Film Festival, I immediately sent in an application for support. And less than a year later I was able to show my three first short films at a festival in Silkeborg. Already then I was probably inclined towards the experimental, and I remember, among other things, meeting Nils Lomholt and Tom Elling, who were also part of that milieu. It's probably fair to say that the projects I was involved with during my first year at the Video Workshop weren't especially experimental. For example, 'Angelface' was one of the first things I made. It's a short fiction film and it's actually quite traditional, although it does have elements that tend toward the surreal. But at the time, I was mostly interested in producing video art, and since I'd also always been very interested in music, I ended up experimenting with music videos. Because of my job at the press, which also published music magazines, I ended up getting to know a lot of people in the music milieu. So it made a lot of sense to combine music with video production, and since I was quite good at editing, I ended up editing not only my own work, but also things produced by a lot of other people in the Workshop milieu. In the late 1980s, DR set up TVSyd, and that provided the impetus for the creation of the production company Englefilm, which I established with people I'd met at the Workshop.

<table>
<tr><td></td><td>We actually had a contract with TVSyd for the regular production of programmes, and that became an important part of my own practice-based 'film school.' A contract like that commits you to delivering programmes according to a precise schedule and on an ongoing basis. So, compared with a situation where you just pursue whatever you're interested in, it was all very new and different. Among other things, I had to learn how to communicate much more directly with a target audience. But I actually became quite interested in the local material we worked with, and in the stories that it encompassed. An example would be the migration process from rural, provincial areas to more urban environments.</td></tr>
</table>

BONDEBJERG: If we look at your activities up until 1986, which is when you moved back to Copenhagen, I suppose we could say that although you're known today as an experimental documentary filmmaker with a distinctive style, your early work is actually quite wide-ranging. You were involved in more traditional and commercial forms of cultural production, you produced mainstream TV programmes for a local TV station, and you did a lot of work on other people's productions.

SKJØDT JENSEN: That's right. And in a sense that continued, at least to a certain extent, even after 1986; I've always worked on other people's projects alongside my own. But part of my personal story is that when I moved back to Copenhagen, I met Dino Raymond Hansen, who was the head of the Film Workshop in Copenhagen back then.

He'd seen some of the things I'd made, and he suggested that I help with some of their productions. The Film Workshop had always had a bit of a reputation for being elitist and rather difficult to get into without connections. But the technical developments that were happening with video had the effect of somewhat sidelining film production, and Dino wanted to do more with video. So that became my point of entry to the Film Workshop. And while I was in that milieu I met an art director who introduced me to the painter Hans Henrik Lerfeldt, and to his work. And that became the start of my first portrait film, *It's a Blue World*. When I first met him I gave him some of my workshop videos, and after about a week he called me to say that he really liked my films. So I had the idea of making a film that would have a narrative, but also experimental work with images, based on the world of his paintings. The Film Workshop gave me financial support for that project, as a 16mm project. But while I was making that film, I was also working part-time on a whole lot of other workshop projects, and that was the case right up until 1993.

BONDEBJERG: Although the Lerfeldt film grew out of the Workshop milieu and brought together some of your different interests, it's fair to say that it also took you in a new direction. On your website you refer to it as your 'first real documentary film.' Also, having made that film, you began to distance yourself from the culture of the Film Workshop, and to integrate yourself into a more professional filmmaking milieu.

SKJØDT JENSEN: Yes, I suppose that's right, although it wasn't quite that straightforward.

The Film Workshop had actually provided support; not for an integrated film about Lerfeldt, but for a series of short films, each about two minutes long, all of them based on the idea of bringing his paintings to life through moving images. What then happened was that, in 1988, the National Film Board of Denmark [Statens Filmcentral, SF] was made responsible for including video productions in its catalogue. And Erik Thygesen, who became the relevant film commissioner, decided to buy a number of my earlier films, and these were then jointly released as *Angelface* (1989). Erik Thygesen then heard about my Lerfeldt project, and it was he who saw that it could be really interesting to make a more comprehensive and substantial film about Lerfeldt. The idea wasn't to produce a traditional 'portrait of the painter,' but to think of the film as a more artistic project about how art emerges and develops, and about how all of that connects with Lerfeldt as a person.

So that's the project I ended up pursuing, and the next two years of my life I was very close to Lerfeldt, and very involved in his life and with his world. But it was SF that made the more comprehensive project possible, and once a certain amount of the shooting had been done, TV 2 agreed to provide some funding too. And SF also came up with more money, so that the film could be more widely distributed, both theatrically and on the festival circuit. The film became a success, generated a lot of interest, and won a number of prizes. I remember being summoned to Gerd Roos' office at the SF, and her asking me what I wanted to do next. Inside I was still little Torben from the Film Workshop, who was just messing around with his own ideas. But Gerd Roos basically said that those days were over and I needed to find myself a professional producer. She had asked Thomas Gammeltoft from Film & Lyd to join us,

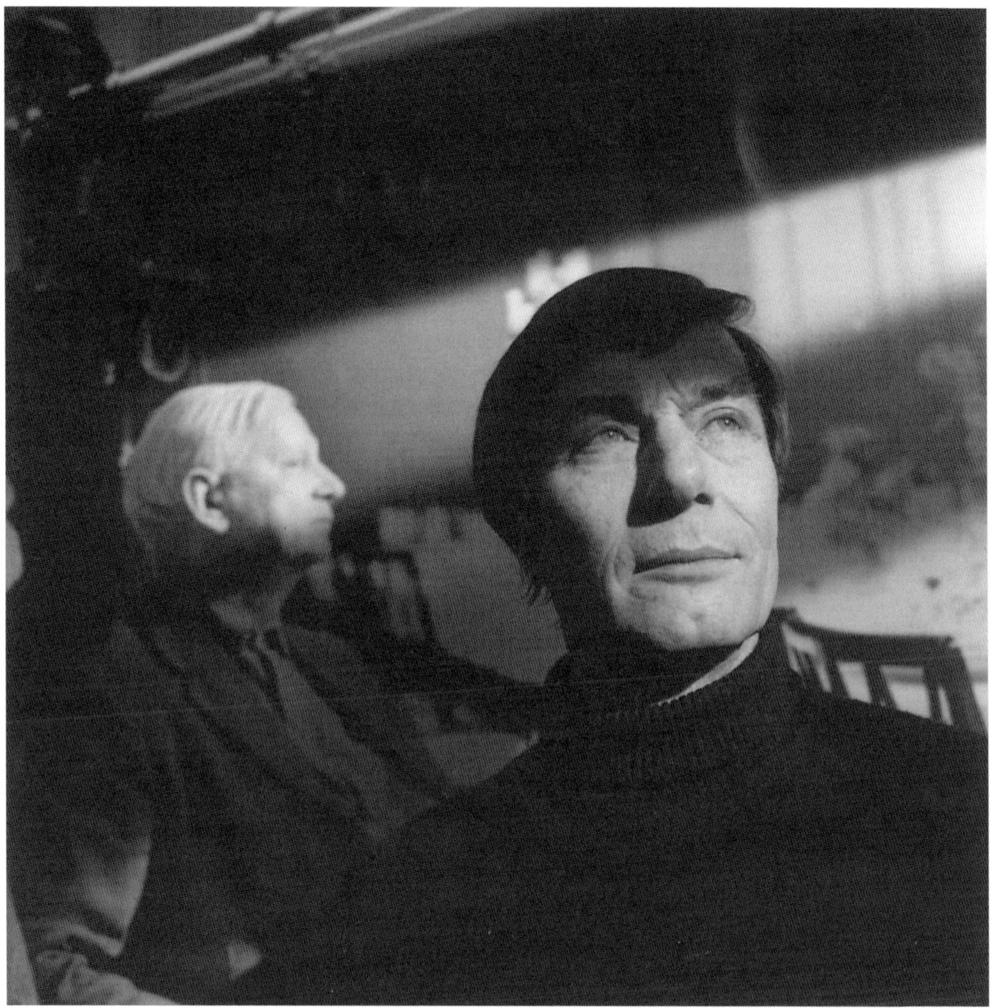

With archive images of Dreyer in the background, Danish actor Baard Owe, who played a lead role in Dreyer's *Gertrud*, is interviewed in the film (*Carl Th. Dreyer – My Metier*, framegrab, cinematography by Harald Gunnar Paalgard, Torben Skjødt Jensen and Prami Larsen).

and that became the beginning of a long and very fruitful partnership based on the films I'd go on to make between 1991 and 1996.

BONDEBJERG: You worked with Film & Lyd, as you point out, but also with other producers. And you also established your own production company, Point of No Return. But you also continued to explore smaller projects through the Film Workshop. Was that a conscious

	strategy, one aimed at maintaining a balance between the testing of more experimental ideas and the making of films for a wider audience?
SKJØDT JENSEN:	Yes, I suppose you could put it that way, although some of the less experimental work I did during those years also involved the Film Workshop, as in the case of *The Naughty Boy*, the portrait film focusing on Ole Ege. And some of my Film & Lyd productions are actually some of my most experimental films. I'm thinking, for example, of *Flaneur*. The people at Film & Lyd, but also Steen Herdel, with whom I've made quite a number of films, have always been very supportive of my experimental style. I've never had any problems with the different producers I've worked with. I've been able to work in a variety of milieus, and to go back and forth between them as I wished. My decision to establish my own production company in 1996 wasn't prompted by a sense of feeling constrained by certain producers. Having your own company can be an advantage when it comes to distribution rights, but it also makes access to equipment easier. New technologies have made it a lot easier to own one's own equipment. You don't always need to have access to large-scale, professional production facilities. Cameras and editing equipment didn't take up a lot of room any more, and you could keep it all in your home. In much the same way, it was simply practical in certain cases to have one's own production company. It also provided an opportunity to think more clearly about the issue of rights. If I'm going to invest my own salary in a given production, I might as well do so through my own company. Also, I've discovered that the rights to my own films are actually worth something. Thanks to the existence of my company, I've been able to take on the full rights to my films on those many occasions when my producer has ended up going bankrupt. That was possible because I'd co-produced the films.
BONDEBJERG:	Does this mean that you can activate these rights now that the digital revolution is underway? Currently there aren't a lot of documentary filmmakers who are able to do so.
SKJØDT JENSEN:	Yes and no. It's a difficult market. For example, *Carl Th. Dreyer: My Metier* is out there, all over the world. First it was on VHS, then in a DVD format, and now we're getting ready for Blu-ray. Of course that's also because the Criterion Collection bought it. It's provided a stable source of income for many years; not a huge amount, but a steady amount year after year. None of my other films have really achieved that; not even my film about Asta

Nielsen, *The Talking Muse*, although you'd think that a film about a silent film star would be of considerable international interest. A more narrow film like *Flaneur* has also made its way thanks to the festival circuit. I've digitalized almost all the films I've made, and I'm constantly working with different distributors, with the aim of getting my work out there.

BONDEBJERG: A portrait film can emphasize quite different things: a more personal dimension, an individual's professional life, or a larger context. And it can, of course, mix all of these things together. If you think about the six portrait films you've made, how would you describe your approach?

SKJØDT JENSEN: I think I've always been interested in telling stories about people, but in a way that isn't that direct or straightforward. I look for the contrasts, contradictions, and tensions. Ying and yang, black and white, and so on. For example, in the case of Lerfeldt I was intrigued, right from the start, by the contrast between this big, formless body, between this completely spaced out person living in messy and filthy circumstances, and then this very sophisticated artist. The huge hands attached to that big, clumsy body would pick up this tiny, little paintbrush and draw and paint with the most incredible precision and elegance. There was a massive contrast between Lerfeldt as an artist and Lerfeldt as a person; it was like beauty and the beast. I found something similar, although the nature of the contrast was quite different with Dreyer. On one level he seemed like an incredibly boring office worker, who just lived his life in an anonymous way and never spoke his mind, and wasn't very good at talking to people. But when he was behind a camera and planning his films, he became a different person and was completely in control. In the Simon Spies portrait, the contrast has to do with the drive to build an empire and the process of self-destruction. The Asta Nielsen film contrasts this global film star with the person who never really revealed her true private character behind the mask of the public film star, and never really spoke publicly after her career ended. What skeletons did she have in the closet? On the one hand I only make portrait films about people for whom I feel sympathy and love, and on the other hand I look for the contradictions in their being, for the secrets beneath the surface. That's where my portraits find their inner narrative and symbolic drive. In some cases audiences have rejected my films and the people they depict as a result. When *It's a Blue World* was shown at Nordisk Panorama, a number of women walked out, and by doing so they were explicitly protesting against what they saw as Lerfeldt's fascist attitudes towards women.

My depiction of Ole Ege – and for that matter Simon Spies – also provoked critical responses, perhaps because women saw them as horrible people on account of their views about gender and sexuality. When I was given a prize at the Odense Film Festival for *The Talking Muse*, the rationale for the jury's decision was that being able to make a good film about a thoroughly unsympathetic person was impressive. I do, of course, know that I've made portrait films about people who are often seen as strange or controversial.

BONDEBJERG: Let's talk a bit about the visual and narrative style of these films. Your films are very original in this respect. You tend to work on many different levels, and with powerful montage sequences, as well as complex sound/image relations. In *It's a Blue World* you have very realistic black-and-white images; and then there's Lerfeldt's artistic universe, which you capture through a mix of staged and more naturalistic sequences. The depiction of Lerfeldt's childhood brings a third style into play. And then there's the larger context of it all, but this is mostly suggested, rather than fully explored. How would you describe your documentary style?

SKJØDT JENSEN: My style does indeed rely on a number of strategies that cut across all of my films. But the weight that is given to these strategies, the use to which they're put in a given film, have everything to do with the person who's the focus of it, and with the story I'm trying to tell. For example, in the Lerfeldt film, the different layers in the story reflect the fact that he lives in what's almost a time capsule, without any relation whatsoever to a contemporary world or situation. That's why the thread having to do with the contemporary context is so thin. At the same time, his life and situation are clearly marked by his problematic childhood and youth. His paintings, which are completely surreal and very expressive, are an attempt to reconnect with that past. A lot of people see only a world of pornography in Lerfeldt's paintings, but that's just the surface of things, because they're really about something quite different. I can only get at that story through an expressive style because that's how I can connect the different levels or dimensions. Lerfeldt didn't really want to talk about his childhood again, and he kept saying that he'd already done that in a series of conversations with the author Christian Kampmann. And that's why he didn't want to 'blather' about it again, to me. But I was never able to find the tapes, and so that's why Lerfeldt's childhood is depicted in those reconstructed and almost symbolic scenes that are clearly related to the world of his paintings. But when the film was about to be re-released in a DVD format, I had the opportunity to improve its technical quality, which was welcome, as it was made using a variety of formats. But as I was doing this, I suddenly found Kampmann's tapes. Hearing them was a deeply moving experience, perhaps because these two men, whose lives had been so tragic, spoke so profoundly to each other. I was allowed to include these conversations in the film, and as a result, the parts having to do with Lerfeldt's childhood were given a lot more depth in the new version.

BONDEBJERG: In your next portrait film, *Carl Th. Dreyer: My Metier*, the visual style is also complex; perhaps even more so. The film's visual dimension is defined by layered images, with at least two layers in play at any given moment. Dreyer's intense accounts of his films are thus accompanied by images of your own, the result being a visually mediated commentary on his person, his persona as a filmmaker, and his films. Why and how did you develop this particular visual style?

SKJØDT JENSEN: This style, which relies on montage and dissolves, may not be fully developed yet in *It's a Blue World*, but that film does draw on the basic principles that end up cutting across all of my portrait films. This was when I was beginning to become more aware of what was involved in making documentary films, after a period of having essentially worked as an experimental video artist. But although I adopted an approach to reality that was documentary in nature and based on thorough research, I did want to infuse the depiction of reality with a sense of complexity and depth. I explored this approach to narrative in *Flaneur*, which is where I first used some of the stylistic devices that were to become characteristic of my portrait films. That film was a kind of laboratory for me, one in which I tried to combine a documentary account of reality with my more poetic visual style. In *Flaneur*, the point was to stage an encounter between a touristic view of the world and a more thoughtful, Benjaminian perspective on reality. In a sense, I work with a combination of reality-based images and dreamlike images, and I try, as the auteur tradition would have it, to use my camera as a pen. I want to leave my mark on the things I narrate, so that I'm recognizable in the narrative; not just for the purpose of subjective recognition, but in order to articulate a layer of experience above and beyond a more pure description of reality. In the Dreyer film, you could say that the world of the black-and-white images – the one in which he talks about his films in a very sober and precise way – ends up being infused with a more reflective, dreamlike dimension through the complex use of montage and dissolves. It's as though we're given a different point of entry to Dreyer's world, to the artistic space where he worked creatively with his cinematic universe. In the universe that my film creates, we get Dreyer's verbal account of the texts of his scripts, of the places where he filmed, and of the images he created, but fused with a dreamlike universe that's an attempt to visualize, but also interpret him, as a film artist. One of the people who were really supportive of the approach I took was the well-known documentary filmmaker Jørgen Roos, who of course is in the Dreyer film, and who also provided me with material for it. He was looking over my shoulder as I did the editing and really supported my narrative approach. He basically said something along the lines of, 'You may end up cutting yourself off from prime-time TV audiences with this narrative strategy, but this strategy brings something artistically significant to documentary filmmaking.'

BONDEBJERG: Your interest in the history of sexuality, and in the people who have somehow had a role to play in its development, provides a thematic thread in your work. *More Sex Please, We're from Scandinavia*, which you made with your wife, the film editor Ghita Beckendorff, provides an historical account of sexuality's diverse expressions and practices over time, and of its encounter with (changing) norms and moral standards. *The Naughty Boy* is a portrait of Ole Ege, who made pornographic films before pornography was legalized in Denmark, and who is one of the earliest directors of pornographic films. How did you come up with the ideas for these films?

SKJØDT JENSEN: The context for these films was my involvement with Museum Erotica, which was initially located in the Vesterbro area of Copenhagen, just opposite the Film Workshop. The people at the museum got in touch with me at a certain point because they wanted to put together an exhibition about Lerfeldt, and also wanted to screen films as part of their activities. This concrete experience of working together in connection with the exhibition had the effect of stimulating my curiosity about Ole Ege's own life and history because he was the person who had established the

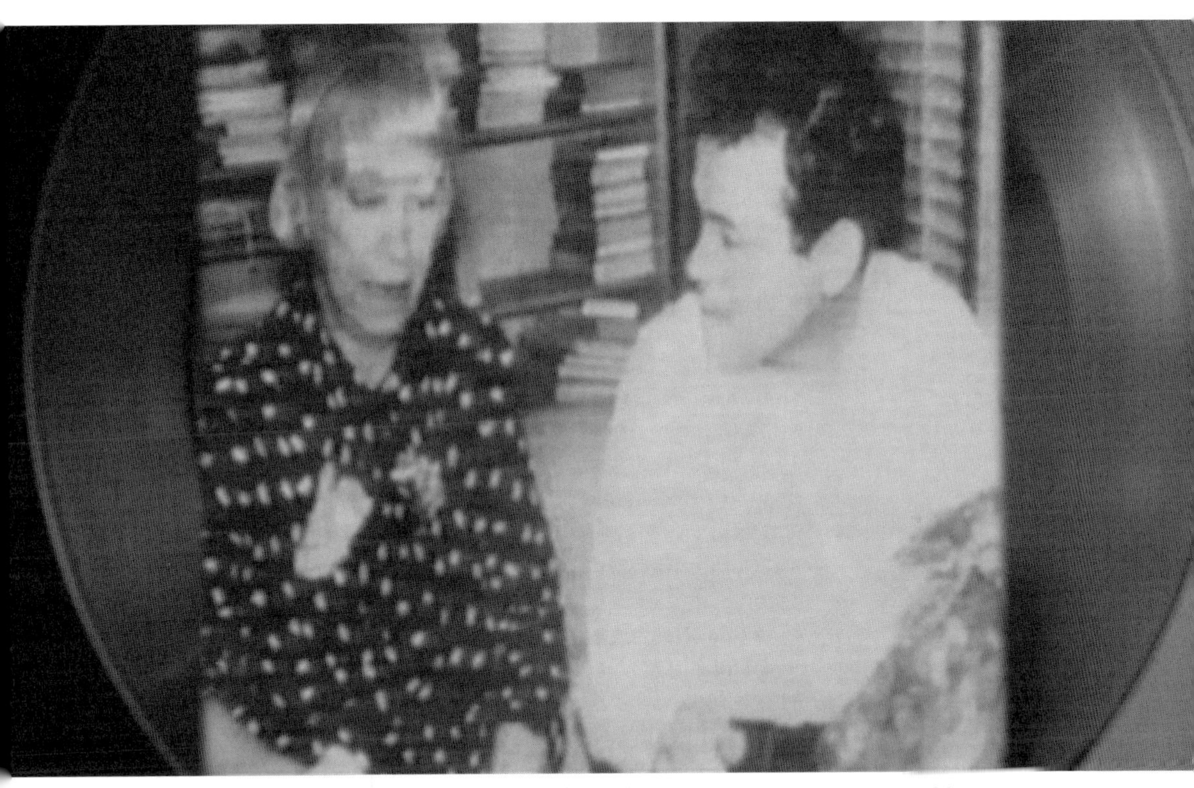

Asta Nielsen and book dealer Frede Smith, a close friend towards the end of her life, with the tapes of their conversations as background (*The Talking Muse*, framegrab, cinematography by Torben Skjødt Jensen).

museum. He was a very complex person. On the one hand he was the very incarnation of the libertine who was obsessed with women and sex. On the other hand he was someone who wasn't really able to capitalize on the commercial exploitation of pornography, probably because he, at some deep level, wasn't really interested in that side of things. What was interesting about him, above and beyond his complexity and his personal story, was his early involvement with the production of amateur porn films. There's a lot of very interesting source material, a lot of fascinating images, to be found there, and it's all very indicative of the times. I established a good relationship with him, and he was happy to talk about his life in great detail. I could tell that there was an interesting story to tell about personal fate; a story about a person who could have become a great porn impresario, but who also wasn't able to pursue that path, because he was ultimately too romantic and sensitive. He was certainly a libertine and obsessed with sex, but at the same time he wasn't motivated by a crass interest in profit, which was what ended up driving the industry in the wake of the legalization of visual pornography.

BONDEBJERG: The portrait of Ole Ege has a lot more about the context of the times in it than many of your other portrait films. And in the later film, *More Sex Please, We're from Scandinavia*, which explores sexuality historically, this aspect is really brought to the foreground. How did you end up making that film?

SKJØDT JENSEN: As is often the case, coincidence played an important role. I had become a member of the IDFA jury in Amsterdam because someone else had withdrawn. And there I met the renowned BBC editor of the *Storyville* series, Nick Fraser. I became good friends with him, and he became quite fond of me and ended up seeing some of my films, which, I have to admit, he did find a bit strange! But then I showed him my Ole Ege film, and he got really excited about it, and it was shown, with great success, on BBC Two. In terms of viewer numbers, that happens to be one of the BBC's most successful broadcasts ever. There were some problems with censorship just before the film was shown, and there was also a lot of sensational talk about it, but the reviewers nonetheless responded very positively to it. I suppose people had expected something quite different. But this portrait of a human being who wasn't actually a cynic, combined with a new angle on sexuality, really resonated with people. As a result of all this, the BBC got involved in the production of *More Sex Please, We're from Scandinavia*.

They wanted a broad cultural and historical perspective on the very story that the Ole Ege film tells in a much more abbreviated and personal way. Of all my films, this is the one that has been distributed most widely, especially in the English-language TV world. But it's DR that has been in charge of distributing it.

BONDEBJERG: With *Simon Spies: Simon's Film* and the film about Asta Nielsen, *The Talking Muse*, you appear to move towards the traditional portrait film, with its archive materials and many interviews with friends and experts about the persons whose lives and work are in focus. Although the films have your aesthetic and stylistic signature, they're a lot closer to mainstream film traditions than the Dreyer and Lerfeldt films are, or the *Flaneur* films. How do you see these two films?

SKJØDT JENSEN: It's true that the Simon Spies film was challenging in new ways. I felt that I'd already had quite a bit of success as a filmmaker. And yet, in the industry, I was often met with scepticism because I was self-taught and experimentally oriented. I was seen as someone who hadn't really learnt how to tell stories the way they were supposed to be told. So I think I was probably thinking 'I'll show you!' And Simon Spies provided the perfect focus because he was such a well-known figure, and everyone felt they had a stance or a take on him. And the thought, of course, was that the film would be shown during prime time. Making a film about Spies was originally Steen Herdel's idea, and the plan was to have Peter Larsen appear as Spies. In other words, the film was to have been made as a biopic. But then as we were researching the film, we found a lot of amateur footage, dating right back to the beginning of Spies' travel business, all of it produced by people who had themselves been on vacation with Spies. I transferred all of that material from the 16mm films, and then I edited it into five one-minute-long vignettes and added music by Philip Glass. And that material was then integrated with the screen tests that we'd done with Peter Larsen. But when we screened what we ended up with, it became clear to everyone that the Peter Larsen idea simply didn't work, whereas my vignettes were really spot on. So that material became the basis for the film, and at the same time, I managed to persuade everyone that the thing to do was to make a documentary film and not a biopic because, in this case, reality was far more interesting than fiction. Although we'd have to limit ourselves to archival material in the case of Spies himself, the fact was that a lot of the people who'd worked with Spies and who'd known him really well were still alive. So we just needed to get them to talk to the camera. So I suddenly became the person who was going to make a documentary portrait film about Simon Spies. But the task involved my making a film that could be shown on prime-time TV, at 8 p.m. on a Sunday. Even though this film was aimed at a broad audience, I used the very same set-up and techniques that you find in my other films, and to some extent, I even maintained aspects of the visual style that I'd developed. Once again, the focus is on a complex and controversial person who has spent his entire life searching for something, and who has tried hard to reconnect with his childhood. The focus is on someone who's pushed the boundaries to such an extent that there were times when those who were caught up with his activities feared that they were losing their grip on reality; as did he himself. That's why the film begins with that strange scene, where he's experimenting with a film, with the story developing backwards. But otherwise the film develops as a mostly chronological and quite classically structured story about someone who behaves as though the point is to conquer the world, but actually spends his entire life looking for himself. I show the person we all laughed with, or at, and it turns out that there really wasn't a whole lot to laugh about. The film was seen by more than 1 million viewers when DR broadcast it, so I must have managed to reach beyond the well-known, public figure to the human core that drove it all.

BONDEBJERG: *The Talking Muse* is also about a very well-known Dane, namely Asta Nielsen. As a person, this silent era film star was very private indeed, but here too you have managed to find unique material to work with, in the form of personally recorded conversations between her and Frede Smith, who was her friend and who ran a second-hand bookstore. The film is, of course, about a quite different person, yet the narrative strategies you use are pretty similar.

SKJØDT JENSEN: Once again we're dealing with someone who's developed an elaborate facade, and who has a very complicated personal history, including in relation to her daughter, whom she barely wanted to acknowledge. We're dealing with someone who was extremely introverted, although she was also a very public figure. I actually wanted to make a docudrama about her because I felt her life was a bit like a classical tragedy, and that this could be a basis for combining fiction and non-fiction. At that time, I was working for TV Drama at DR, and they gave me some financial support to write a script based on that concept. But when I came back with a script about a year later, Rumle Hammerich told me that he didn't think it worked. He said I needed to separate things, and so that's why I made two films about Asta Nielsen: the fiction film *Afgrunden* (*The Abyss*) and the documentary portrait film, *The Talking Muse* (both 2003). It was while I was doing the research for the documentary film and for an interview with Morten Grunwald that I suddenly came across the material that Frede Smith had recorded; more than 100 hours of it. That was really a decisive discovery because suddenly we could actually document aspects of her life that we otherwise would only have been able to speculate about. In a sense, those conversations enabled us to see a rather distant and somewhat forgotten icon as a real human being. But although the film engaged with material that was dramatic and even sensational, it was far less popular than my other portrait films were. It's as though she's a bit of a forgotten figure, both as a person and as a star. But the film has been well received by audiences at various festivals.

BONDEBJERG: Given that you've worked with both fiction and documentary filmmaking, it would be interesting to know what your views on these two approaches are, and how you see yourself as a director?

SKJØDT JENSEN: I've always been more interested in documentary filmmaking, but I've also had this desire to experiment with things, including with fiction filmmaking and drama for both TV and the stage. At the same time, I suppose you could say that everything I do is pretty experimental, whether it's a matter of fiction or non-fiction. This no doubt has something to do with my background as a self-taught filmmaker, and with my having been involved in so many different milieus. But it's the documentary side of things that has been the real magnet all along.

Chapter 8

Max Kestner

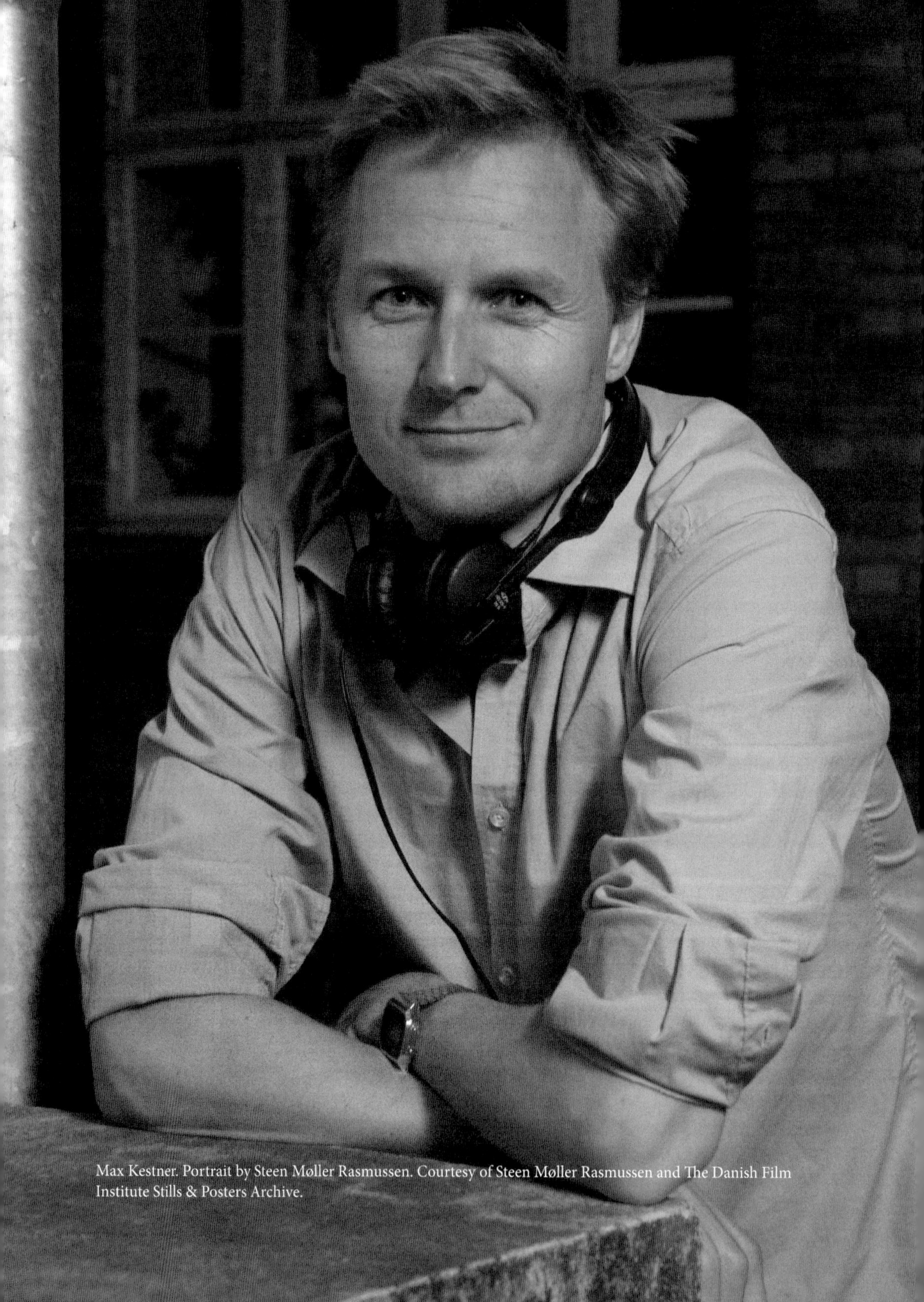

Max Kestner. Portrait by Steen Møller Rasmussen. Courtesy of Steen Møller Rasmussen and The Danish Film Institute Stills & Posters Archive.

Born 1969. Kestner was trained at the National Film School of Denmark's Department of Documentary & TV. His diploma film, *Clarks* (1997), is a documentary comedy about the battle for control of a football club. Having finished film school, Kestner worked for Danish Broadcasting Corporation's (DR) Children & Youth Department (B&U). During this period he also directed the documentary film *Atten Huller* ('Eighteen Holes', 2000). The experience that Kestner gained while working for an especially creative department at DR is reflected in his style as a documentary filmmaker. His films are characterized by humour, irony, and a playful approach to both reality and cinematic form. As a result, he is a central figure at the cutting edge of poetic and reflexive documentary filmmaking in Denmark, which is otherwise closely associated with Jørgen Leth. In an essay published in *Ekko* in 2005, Kestner defines his documentary strategy as follows: 'We don't recount reality. We tell stories about it. Reality isn't itself a story. It's endless, so a lot of choices about inclusion and especially exclusion have to be made in order to tell a story. And those choices require something as complicated and sophisticated as awareness.'[1] His style and method are already clearly evident in *Nede på jorden* (*Blue Collar White Christmas*, 2004), which he directed for DR, but with support from the Danish Confederation of Trade Unions (LO), among others. The film is about a workplace in Esbjerg, but goes beyond a mere depiction of that space and the everyday lives of those who work there to become a poetic film about people's dreams.

Kestner's films are at once matter-of-fact, probing, and factual, to the point of being parodic and absurd. In the both poetic and ironic *Rejsen på ophavet* (*Max by Chance*, 2004), family history becomes an expanding diagram accompanied by Kestner's rapid-fire commentary. In both *Verden i Danmark* (*The World in Denmark*, 2007) and *Drømme i København* (*Copenhagen Dreams*, 2010), the depiction of Denmark and Copenhagen respectively is defined by an almost surreal combination of details and statistical facts on the one hand, and powerful poetic moments and images on the other. Kestner represents everyday life in poetic and surreal ways, exploring the dreams and culture of Danes in films that encompass an enormous amount of documentation, as well as a deeply personal and poetic mode of cinematic expression. In addition to his work as a film director, Kestner has been active as a film editor and as a creative consultant for a large number of film and TV productions.

Documentary features:

2013   *Identitetstyveriet* (*I am Fiction*)
2010   *Drømme i København* (*Copenhagen Dreams*)
2004   *Nede på jorden* (*Blue Collar White Christmas*)

Documentary shorts:

2011   *Jennis storesøster* (*Jenny's Big Sister*)
2009   *Næste gang bliver vi fugle* ('Next Time We'll Be Birds')
2007   *De smås krig* ('The War of the Small')
2007   *Verden i Danmark* (*The World in Denmark*)
2006   *Mig og dig* ('Me and You')
2004   *Rejsen på ophavet* (*Max by Chance*)
2000   *Atten Huller* ('Eighteen Holes')
1997   *Clarks* (diploma film)

Television:

2002   *Nede på jorden* (*Blue Collar White Christmas*, six episodes)

BONDEBJERG: You graduated from the National Film School of Denmark in 1997, at a time when Danish film culture was changing a lot. What are your memories of that period like?

KESTNER: I actually started out at the Danish Broadcasting Corporation [DR], where I was involved in TV productions until around 2002, which was when I started to work my way into the Danish film milieu. I didn't really know the film milieu at all, and was barely aware of the existence of something called the Danish Film Institute [DFI]. I certainly hadn't had any dealings with it. The TV milieu is quite different from the film milieu because it offers employees permanent positions with regular monthly salaries. And then you just have to produce as many minutes of TV material as you can to earn your keep. The B&U Department that I got to know in 1997 was a place where people were given an enormous amount of freedom. You developed some ideas, got hold of a camera, and started shooting. Working there was in many ways a wonderful experience because of this freedom we had to experiment with things. But I have to say that I also would have liked to have been challenged a bit more, to have received some critical comments and feedback. In contrast, there's more than enough of that sort of thing in the film milieu, where you really have to fight for your ideas, and where it can take years to finance a project. The challenges involved can be quite considerable, so the film milieu takes you to the opposite extreme. Also, as a film director, you often have to pick up whatever work might come your way through other people's films and productions just to make ends meet.

BONDEBJERG: *Blue Collar White Christmas* was the first film you directed entirely on your own. In a way, this film exists somewhere between film and TV. It was financed by DR, but also received support from the DFI (and film commissioner Jakob Høgel), as well as from a series of private and public institutions (such as LO and The National Labour Market Authority). There's both a TV version of *Blue Collar White Christmas* and a film version. What's the story behind the making of *Blue Collar White Christmas*?

KESTNER: *Blue Collar White Christmas* was initially a TV series, but the intention was that the series should also be made into a film. *Koncern TV- og film produktion* and Lynx Media co-produced both the TV series and the film. The production processes for both were really difficult and painful. There were a lot of conflicts, especially with the producers, who insisted on all sorts of things that I didn't agree with. Also, because of this, there were a lot of financial problems. The DFI initially completely rejected the idea for the film. To begin with, the DFI people just couldn't see why they would want to pump money into a film that was based on TV material that had already been seen, and on a series that had even been on the verge of being aborted on several occasions. In the end, the DFI did come around though, providing money that made it possible to produce the film.

The TV series was a commissioned project. Producers from the two production companies basically asked me whether I'd be interested in shooting something about an industrial workplace in the provinces. The project was to focus on contemporary leadership styles and cultures of work, and I was told that a bit of humour would be welcome, too. As things got underway, my crew and I started to feel that the project didn't really have the producers' full support. The producers seemed very intent on meeting the demands that DR was making, whereas they seemed to have very little interest in listening to my ideas, as the director. In some ways

I suppose this was understandable enough, since this was one of my first productions and I was rather inexperienced. There was kind of a conflict between my perspective as a creative artist and the culture of the TV milieu. That conflict was only further aggravated by all the problems having to do with financing the project. It never really did receive full and proper financial support, and so the producers were mostly concerned with keeping the costs down. My problem, on the other hand, was that I was getting involved in my first big project as a director, so I was interested in thinking creatively, in developing new ideas, and, of course, in delivering what had been promised. None of this made for a harmonious set-up, and as a result there were conflicts from beginning to end.

BONDEBJERG: But how do you see your first major production today, in light of the reception it's enjoyed?

KESTNER: Well, the TV series wasn't especially successful, partly because DR initially broadcast it in a bad time slot. The film version wasn't commercially successful either, but it did receive a fair bit of recognition, and was sold to ARTE once it was finished. The 400,000 Danish Crowns that they paid for it helped to reduce the losses that had been incurred. The film's production history and financial aspects were and will always be unfortunate, and this in spite of the elements of artistic success and recognition.

BONDEBJERG: But what if you set aside the rather unfortunate production history and focus on the film itself? In my view, *Blue Collar White Christmas* allowed you to develop a certain approach to documentary filmmaking that you could build on subsequently. I'm thinking of the way in which you gave a story about actually existing realities a poetic dimension; one that finds expression in the film's cinematic style, but also in the story's intense focus on the dreariness of everyday life and on the dreams that it produces.

KESTNER: Yes, that's probably true. But at the same time the film grows out of a fascination for depicting reality and characters in a way that's intrigued me since my film school days. Already back then I was fascinated by how dialogues and spaces can be built up around characters. I was intrigued by what was comical and absurd, by forms of expression that are perhaps seen by some as belonging to the terrain of fiction, although it's just as legitimate to make use of them in stories about actuality.

But those sorts of stories also need to find a balance between the small things in life and something that's existentially much larger.

At that point in my career it was also very important for me to create a film with a language of its own, and not merely to reproduce reality. The film appears to be about what's banal and ordinary, but it actually creates a space around and above everyday life. This process is articulated in the film's construction of both cinematic space and its characters, and also, of course, in its visual language. The way one chooses to tell a story can bring a certain expressiveness, and even new dimensions, to the actual experience of reality. I remember that when I was at the film school in Copenhagen I was generally very inspired by the cinematic style of, for example, Peter Greenaway's *Inside Rooms: 26 Bathrooms* (1985).

BONDEBJERG: The way you tell your stories and organize your material suggests an approach that favours a very thoroughly prepared script rather than some loosely outlined idea.

KESTNER: Yes, it's true that I had a relatively detailed outline for both the film and the series, with descriptions of all the scenes. It wasn't really a matter of a completely developed script, for I hadn't spelled everything out, as is typically the case with feature-length fiction films. But I had what is called a 'full-step outline.' That is, I'd identified all the scenes in their order of appearance, and which characters and types of dialogue were needed for each of them. The people who were in the film didn't see this outline, but I told them that it existed and that they would become part of my story. It was very important to me to ensure that the people who were represented in the documentary series and film didn't feel that they were expected to play some already defined role. The outline wasn't meant to guide those who were in front of the camera, but me and my crew, so that we would always be clear about the kind of story we were after. I suppose it's fair to say that I didn't actually shape the reality I was filming to the point where it became fictional. But I did prepare the film very carefully; I researched my material very thoroughly. As a result, I could establish the film's structure in advance. I had a structure for the things, places, and people we filmed, as well as for the way in which we filmed them and finally edited everything together. But during the process of actually shooting the film, the characters and depicted realities developed in ways that were spontaneous within the constraints of the established framework.

BONDEBJERG: Your next film, *Max by Chance*, seems in all ways to be a very personal film. The film is shaped by your unique style and tone, and also provides a loving but ironic depiction of your own family and childhood. How did you come up with the basic idea for the film, and what was the production process like?

KESTNER: Well, there's a much happier story to be told about that film's production history. The impetus for the film came from the production company Barok Film, which had just been established back then, and had invited a number of directors to send along ideas and suggestions for documentary film projects. I sent in five different proposals, all of them very briefly described, and then they selected the idea that became the basis for the film. In many ways, this is an ideal way of getting involved in the making of a film. What could be better than having a production company be aware of your talent and then asking you to come up with an idea for a film yourself?

There's too little of this sort of thing in the documentary film industry, where people are typically hired to make films about very specific topics and aren't given enough freedom to explore their own ideas. That kind of freedom exists in some areas of the visual arts, and perhaps the film subsidy system should emphasize it more, although it's of course true that making films costs a lot more money than painting paintings does.

But the process of financing this film, which was supported by the DFI, DR2, and the Nordic Film and TV Fund, among others, was smooth. Also, there weren't any difficult conflicts about the film itself. DR2 is generally more responsive to the idea of film as art than the other TV stations are, although it's clear that all TV stations – DR2 included – are very concerned about viewer ratings these days. I'm talking here about a general, structural problem in the Danish film industry these days, although our system in many ways remains a good one. Our system does have a lot of 'doors,' so to speak; there are a lot of different kinds of subsidies. But there's a pervasive fear of failure in the system these days. The film commissioners have sometimes been almost afraid of supporting films, and the TV people are also afraid of committing themselves to film financing. Nobody has the courage to get a production process going in the absence of some kind of thorough analysis that ends up promising large numbers of TV viewers. In a way, the TV stations' commissioning editors, with the support of the DFI, are now the people who decide which films get made in Denmark. In other words, the decisions about which films to produce are not being made by people who are knowledgeable about film. Our industry – which is supposed to be committed to the concept of

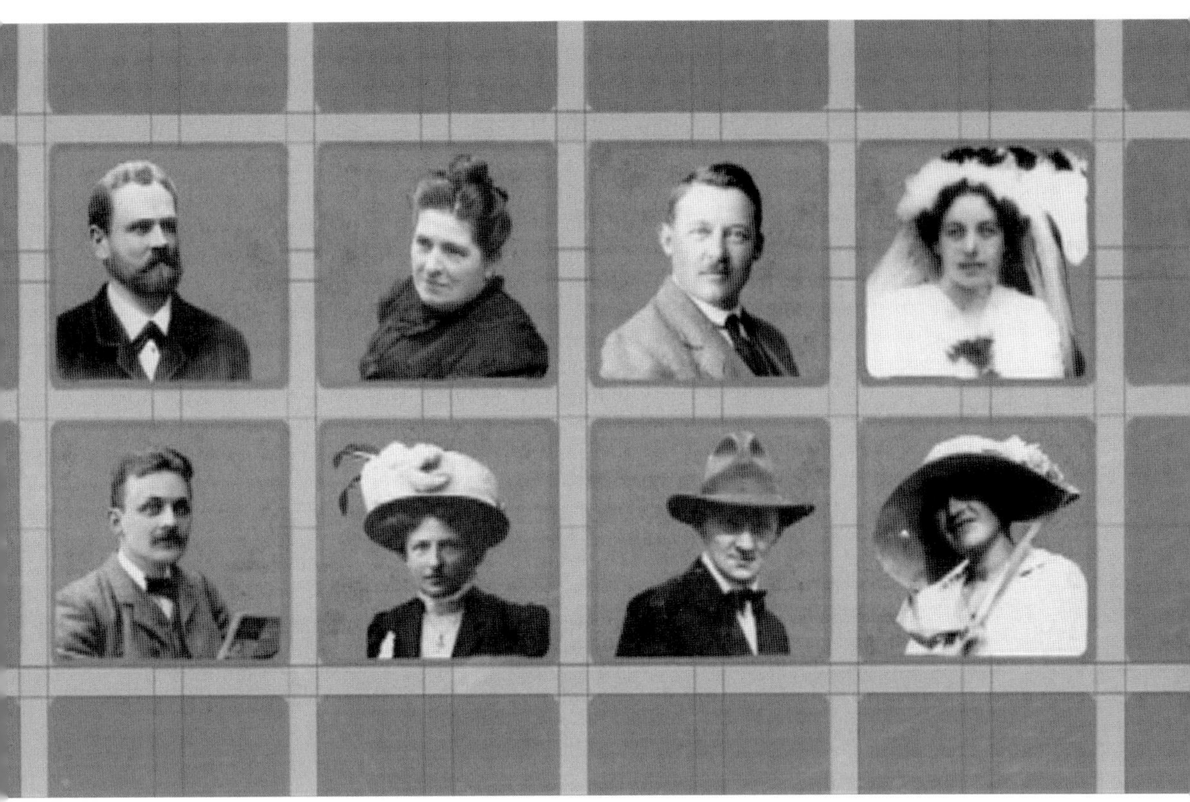

Picture board with ancestors used throughout *Max by Chance* (framegrab, cinematography by Max Kestner, Mårten Nilsson and Erik Molberg Hansen).

film as art – is in fact being managed by a quite different industry.

BONDEBJERG: Perhaps you remember the production of *Max by Chance* as having been quite a joyful process because it's a film that tells your own story. Also, this is the film in which you develop a style that you'll later return to, albeit with a number of variations: there's that very rapid pace that you establish; your unique manner of delivering commentaries; the use of spreadsheets; and that very creative mix of imagery, ranging from the most private to the most universal of images.

KESTNER: It's certainly true that the very personal story I tell in that film has implications for the production process, which I really was able to control. But here too I'd want to point out that the film's visual style was inspired, in very direct ways, by a number of other films. Jorge Furtado's Brazilian documentary entitled *Ilha das Flores* (*Island of Flowers*, 1989) has the same cumulative style as *Max by Chance*. My producer also showed me Nanette Burstein's *The Kid Stays in the Picture* (2002), which offers a very creative solution to the problem of how to use a lot of photographs and pictures in a documentary. These two sources of inspiration suggest just how often we filmmakers 'steal' ideas from one another. But compared with *Blue Collar White Christmas*, *Max by Chance* is definitely a film that is fuelled by my personal desire to tell a story, by the simple joy of telling it. So it really didn't take a lot of time to come up with the key scenes. I quite quickly wrote up about 150 scenes, and these were then reduced to about 80 in the actual film. I didn't need to do a lot of research, and I wasn't looking for truth with a capital 'T'. It was my film and my story, as seen from my perspective.

BONDEBJERG: The voice-over narration is characteristically yours in every way. There's that almost absurd fascination with facts that get stacked up, and then there's that ironic tone and the sense of distance.

KESTNER: Yes, it's probably fair to say that I'm fascinated by facts – at least by the types of facts that can give you a somewhat quirky and different perspective on reality. After all, when they're used in that way, facts become almost poetic. *Max by Chance* was initially described as a 'pseudo-scientific' film about my family and childhood. Hence the use of spreadsheets as the film's background. They provide the graphic material; the visual elements that are needed to underscore the pseudo-scientific dimensions of the film.

BONDEBJERG: *Mig og dig* ('Me and You'), which was supported by just two funding sources [DFI and DR2], also seems to have been an unproblematic film to make. Do you have similarly positive memories of making this film?

KESTNER: I do remember it fondly, although every film involves problems and challenges. In the case of 'Me and You,' I actually did most of the shooting before the financing was in place. I just headed off with Rasmus Nøhr and shot almost all of the scenes in exactly the way I wanted to. Financing for the film was secured later, so it was after I'd actually finished the shooting that Barok Film stepped in and covered my salary fully.

BONDEBJERG: The film can be described as a musical portrait film and as a comic road movie. It has a light, humorous, and off-beat tone, which matches Nøhr very nicely, both in terms of his personality and his style as a musician. But at the same time, of all your films, 'Me and You' is also the film that is the closest to the classic observational documentary tradition, at least in terms of its formal properties. There's a lot less of the characteristic Kestner style in this film than there is in your other films. What's your take on this?

KESTNER: It was very much a film I just sort of made during my time off, *con amore*. I hadn't really thought through how I was going to make it, so I just improvised as I went along. The real shape of the film only became clear the day I finished shooting it. I made the film without any kind of clear concept for it, based quite simply on my strong interest in certain characters. I had to make a number of choices (with Nanna Franck) during the editing process, because I had material about Nøhr's love life, which is related to the themes of his songs, and material focusing on his musical career and his relationship with his friends and his manager. I finally chose to prioritize that second part of his story, and so the tone, irony, and self-reflections of those people ended up defining the tone of the film.

BONDEBJERG: Your next film, *The World in Denmark*, took you to a new level of achievement. In this film you engage with an especially well-established genre of Danish documentary filmmaking, one that goes all the way back to the 1930s: the so-called *Danmarksfilm*. How did this film come about?

KESTNER: It was actually quite an easy film to make, in that it was a commissioned project for which money had been set aside. As soon as I won DR2's tender for a new *Danmarksfilm*, the money was simply there. DR2 and the DFI each came up with the same amount, and then the Bikuben Fund [BG Fonden] provided some additional monies. Bastard Film produced the film and they'd also encouraged me to submit a proposal in response to DR2's call.

BONDEBJERG:

My proposal was about three pages long, and it basically described how I wanted to make the film and all the elements that would be part of it. DR2 didn't interfere much once the project was approved, but I did develop a shooting list together with the writer Dunja Gry Jensen. I found working with Bastard Film completely unproblematic, maybe because the film was fully financed before we started making it.

When I look at your take on the *Danmarksfilm* genre, it seems to me that you innovate in relation to the existing tradition by insisting on your own cinematic style. Poul Henningsen's famous *Danmark* (*Denmark*, 1935) features the swinging rhythms of modern jazz and dynamic editing, as well as a matter-of-fact, even ironic tone that refuses to indulge a sense of national pathos. Klaus Rifbjerg, Lars Brydesen, and Claus Ørsteds' *Danske Billeder* ('Danish Images', 1970) has quite a special poetic dimension on account of the way in which Rifbjerg's poems and music are used throughout. But it's not just a poetic film, for 'Danish Images' also has an element of social critique. As I see it, Jørgen Leth's *Livet i Danmark* (*Life in Denmark*, 1972) provides yet another approach, with human beings and objects being depicted in a manner that recalls pop art. Were you inspired by any of these films – or any others – when you made *The World in Denmark*?

KESTNER:

Those titles were in fact mentioned in DR2's call, so I watched them and thought about them carefully. I was very aware of taking up a particular national genre with this film of mine, and of the likelihood of its being measured against a whole tradition. But it was really only Leth's film that spoke to me. The others didn't touch me at all or inspire me in any way. Rifbjerg, Ørsted, and Brydesen's film left me completely cold, and much like Poul Henningsen's film, it seems very much a product of its time. You need to know something about its context to be able to relate to it. Leth's film seems much more straightforward and timeless, although everything represented in it ultimately produces an extremely precise image of what we Danes were like in 1972. This mix of a timeless cinematic form and mode of expression with a very precise representation of the lives of Danes at the time when the film was made was something I also wanted to achieve. I was after something at once contemporary and future-oriented, in the sense that I wanted people at some future point to be able to see what things were like back then. So essentially, my film is a remake of Leth's, although it's also quite different, both in terms of form and content.

BONDEBJERG: Although the similarities with Leth's film are striking, the differences are also quite marked. Leth's film is highly stylized, representing its objects and characters in a very abstract way. You, on the other hand, chose to explore Danish realities by means of some very concrete stories. The viewer easily identifies different types of sequences in your film, each of them with their own specific angle on life in Denmark. There are sequences, for example, focusing on different workplaces, on modes of communication, and on places and landscapes in Denmark. I take it that the choices you made are informed by a kind of sociological reasoning about how to represent something larger through specific examples. What was your principle of selection? What kind of image of Denmark were you trying to evoke as you chose the elements representing larger categories?

KESTNER: You're right. I did end up going in a quite different direction from Leth, both stylistically and in terms of content. And what's genuinely different is the approach I take to the depiction of people and to storytelling. Those mini stories – in which the lives of different people are traced back from a current situation to the moment when they were born – have the effect of giving the characters in my film a more personal and concrete dimension, which is something the characters in Leth's film don't have at all. I also wanted to get at people's inner thoughts, which is why, for example, I filmed people speaking on mobile phones in public places. My take on documentary filmmaking is quite simply different from Leth's, although the style and form of his films have been a clear source of inspiration. He is looking for what's perfect, while I am looking for what's imperfect. I take my camera into different social spaces in order to capture how people speak and act in these actually existing spaces, whereas Leth places people in an entirely abstract space where they then adopt certain poses and perform for the camera.

BONDEBJERG: The cinematic style of your *Danmarksfilm* is both striking and varied. We have a number of observational sequences; those mini life stories that are characterized by rapid editing, and the somewhat ironic narration that accompanies the still images. And then there are those often very poetic images of Danish sites and places, where we get a bird's-eye perspective and an emphasis on music. How would you describe the aesthetic and stylistic choices that you made in *The World in Denmark*?

KESTNER: I actually adopted a very matter-of-fact approach. In a way, the film is meant to suggest the effect of something like a copying device being rolled across Denmark, capturing places, landscapes, social spaces and situations, and people along the way. But I also needed to include landscape sequences, and I suppose I have a rather ambivalent relationship to landscape cinematography; that is, to those beautiful, highly conventionalized images of landscapes with a distant horizon. Also, I don't actually like the Danish landscape very much. It really doesn't do much for me. So I was very aware of needing to find an alternative to what I saw as the conventional approach to depicting landscapes cinematically. So I ended up with landscapes as seen from above and with a spinning perspective; a perspective which could be said to underline the film's anthropological look at Denmark and Danes. It was my editor, Nanna Frank Møller, who suggested that we accompany these sequences with music by Carl Nielsen.

BONDEBJERG: Although your aim was to produce something that was very matter-of-fact, I'm pretty sure that most spectators end up feeling deeply moved by the film, and especially by those sequences with Danish landscapes and music by a very famous Danish composer.

KESTNER: Of course. I certainly wouldn't dispute the idea that the images and music in those sequences have a real emotional charge.

BONDEBJERG: Did you aspire to make a film that represents much of what needs to be understood about Denmark as it is today? If so, how did you go about trying to achieve this goal?

KESTNER: My guiding thought in this connection was really quite banal. My principle was simply the sociological one that whatever takes up a lot of room, so to speak, in Denmark today should also be given a lot of attention in the film. But of course, it's impossible to include everything that's essential. I am, for example, a bit sorry that there's not more about pigs in the film, because pigs are a big thing in Denmark. And then I've included Pia Kjærsgård, who represents politics in Denmark. She's not the leader of the biggest political party, but she does take up a lot of space in terms of public debate. Those mini life stories also encompass different types of Danes, including an immigrant. Basically, I emphasized the idea of evoking a larger reality by depicting representative instances of it, as well as the thought that whatever takes up a lot of space in Denmark today should be included.

BONDEBJERG: *Copenhagen Dreams* seems like an even bigger, more complicated, and thus far more costly film than *The World in Denmark*.

KESTNER: Yes, it is my most costly and most complicated film to date, and it was very difficult to get it fully financed. But the reason

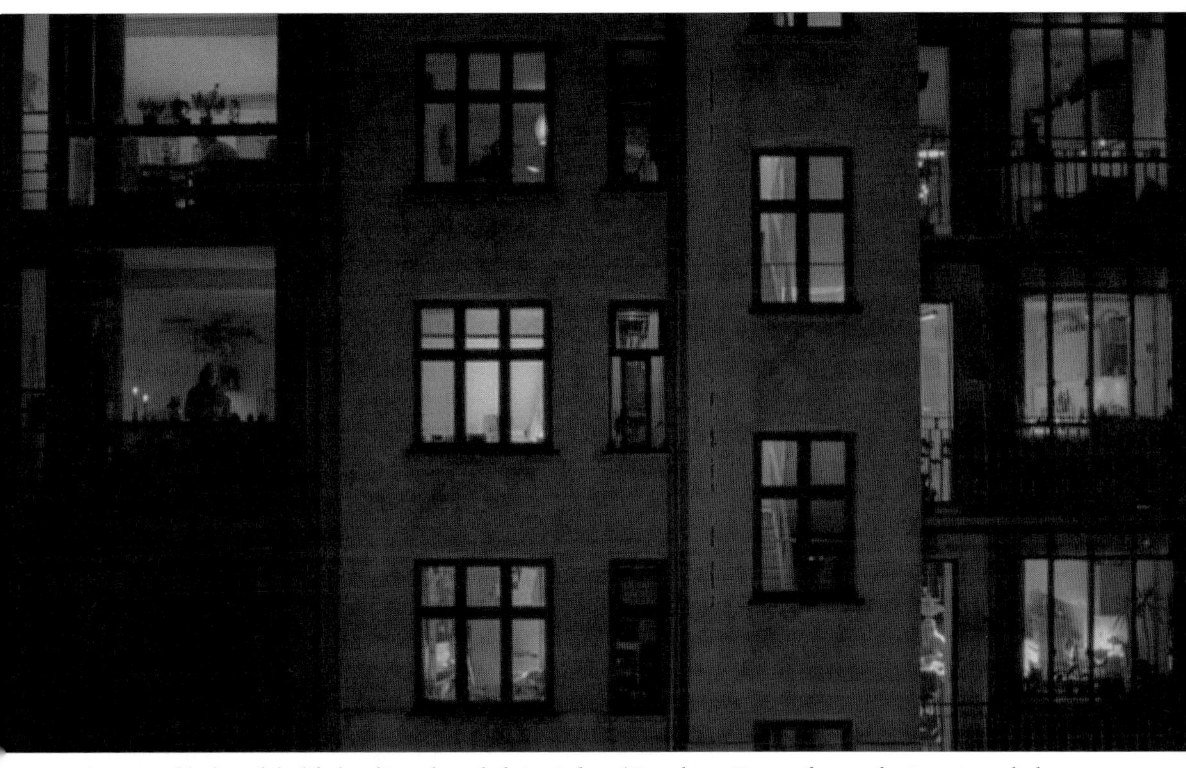

Apartment blocks and the life that shines through their windows (*Copenhagen Dreams*, framegrab, cinematography by Henrik Bohn Ipsen).

Copenhagen Dreams cost a lot more than *The World in Denmark* is that it's a much longer film. I was thinking very ambitiously about that film, and didn't want in any way to compromise on quality or to fall short of professional standards. The initial budget was 7 million Danish Crowns, and when we couldn't raise the full amount, we reduced our costs to 6 million, which was as low as we could go if we were going to make the film I wanted to make. But we only got 5.5 million from the DFI, DR, and the Realdania Foundation, and so the producer and I had to come up with 250,000 Crowns each.

But the fact of the matter is that the budget for this film remains comparable to that of a low-budget feature film involving shooting in only *one* location and with a very small number of actors. Yet, *Copenhagen Dreams* was a complicated film to make and required a large crew. We needed 300 extras for *Copenhagen Dreams*, and we had over 100 locations. So given the type of film it is, the budget was actually rather modest. Because of the budgetary constraints, we had to shoot three scenes per day in entirely different locations, and that sort of thing is simply exhausting for the crew. What is more, during the production process, we were working with a ratio of 1:10. In other words, we had ten minutes to shoot what would become one minute of screen time. That's a really challenging ratio to be working with, and I think most feature film directors would refuse to have anything to do with it because you're making the film with the odds stacked against you. There are clear reasons – other than the duration of the film – why *Copenhagen Dreams* cost almost three times as much as *The World in Denmark*. We were working with a much larger crew, and we needed to spend a lot more time preparing and researching our locations and characters. The number of scenes, shooting locations, and people involved are in some ways similar to a feature film production, although the budget was much smaller. But in the context of documentary filmmaking, it was a lot of money, and it took almost five years to sort out the funding. And the film almost bankrupted Upfront Film and me personally. In addition to financial difficulties, we also had problems with DR. In fact, the day we were supposed to start shooting, the people at DR suddenly decided to withdraw from the project, although they finally ended up supporting the film after all.

BONDEBJERG: There are clear stylistic and formal continuities between *The World in Denmark* and *Copenhagen Dreams*, however different the films might be in terms of their histories of production. How do you see the relationship between these two films?

KESTNER: Speaking about histories of production, I should point out that I developed the idea and project description for *Copenhagen Dreams* before making *The World in Denmark*. I ended up making *The World in Denmark* first because it took such a long time to get *Copenhagen Dreams* financed. But the stylistic influences actually go from *Copenhagen Dreams* to *The World in Denmark*, rather than the other way around. But there are also decisive differences between the films. The most important difference is probably that *Copenhagen Dreams* has a kind of multi-plot structure, with the stories of different people being developed throughout the film. The stories that are told in the film are longer and more cohesive, and each individual's story is developed in greater detail. This narrative structure and approach to character development is completely absent from *The World in Denmark*.

BONDEBJERG: The title *Copenhagen Dreams* refers to at least two ways of dreaming in and about Copenhagen: on the one hand, we have ordinary people with their everyday hopes and dreams, and on the other hand we have all the architects, town planners, bureaucrats, and administrators who are supposed to develop the city, and who have all sorts of ideas about how it should develop and change. What's the point of this kind of contrast?

KESTNER: I don't really see the film as pointing to a contrast, conflict, or contradiction, but as evoking a kind of synergy. We decided to include three categories of Copenhageners, all of whom are involved in the creation and development of the city.

First we have the people who just live in and make use of the city, but who as a result of doing that also, in a very basic way, are involved in its creation. Second, we have the people who maintain and actually build the city: the construction workers, the janitors, and so on. And finally we have the people who in a very professional sense have made the city their project – the bureaucrats, the architects, the urban planners – all of whom are involved in developing new ideas about the city. I suspect the last group is somewhat overrepresented, but I did try to include a broad spectrum of other kinds of Copenhageners. One of the points made in the film is that the city is the result of the interaction of millions of people's actions over a long period of time. The film tries to evoke the teeming life of the city through the use of the multi-plot format, and through synergies between different social processes and persons. I find cities incredibly interesting, and a fascinating phenomenon, and I love Copenhagen. My sense of self has a lot more to do with the city of Copenhagen than it does with the country of Denmark.

Note

1   Max Kestner, 'Jeg er en af dem, der tror, at sandheden er min,' *Ekko* 28 (2005); http://www.ekkofilm.dk/artikler/jeg-er-en-af-dem-der-tror-at-sandheden-er-min/.

Chapter 9

Mikala Krogh

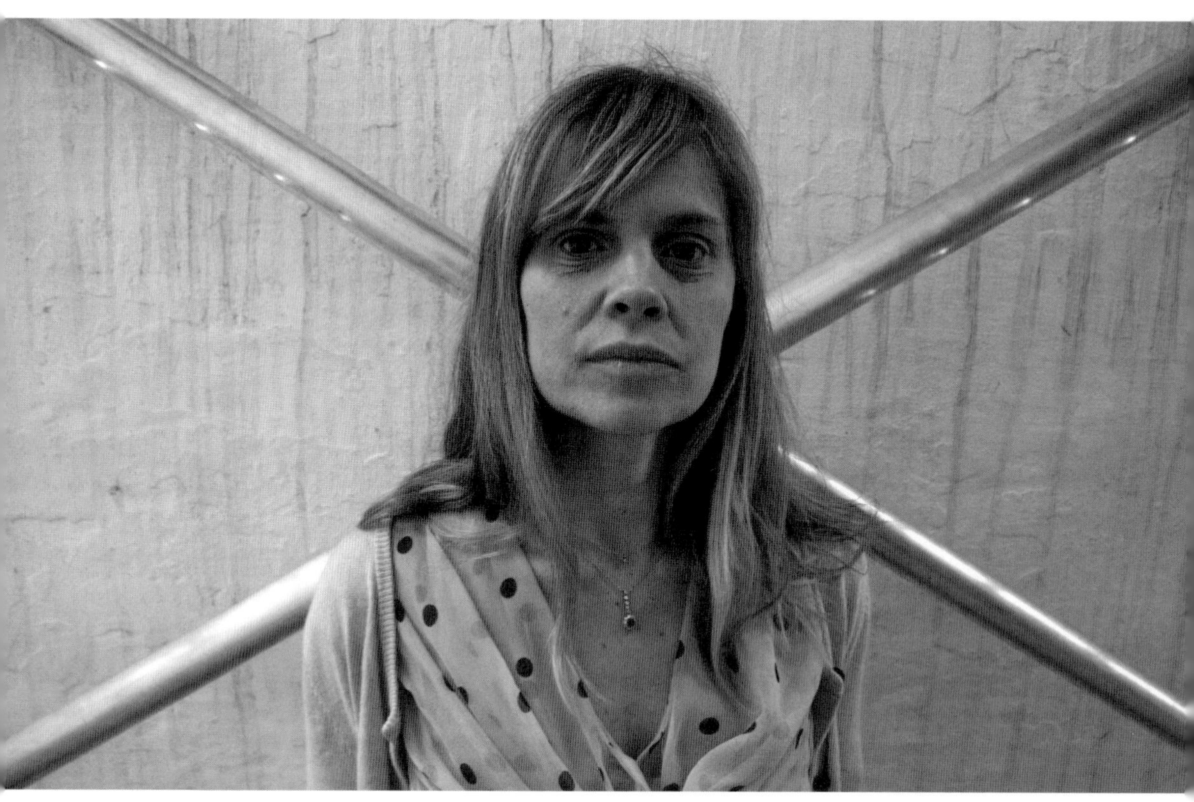

Mikala Krogh. Portrait by Minna Kirstine Katz. Courtesy of Minna Kirstine Katz and Danish Documentary.

Born 1973. Mikala Krogh graduated from the Department of Documentary & TV at the National Film School of Denmark in 2001. Krogh worked in radio from her early teens, and went on to establish herself fully in the field before making the transition to film school and documentary filmmaking in 1997. She made her first documentary short, entitled *Epilog* (*Epilogue*), with Sara Bro in 1992, and a second documentary short, *Ungdomsgarantien* ('The Youth Guarantee'), in 1996, following a period of intense collaboration in Haiti with filmmakers Jørgen Leth and Tómas Gislason. Made within the context of an innovative collaborative initiative involving the National Film School and the Danish International Development Agency (Danida), Krogh's short film about mixed marriages, *Fisk uden vand* (*Fish out of Water*, 2000), won the Jury's Special Award at See Docs in Dubrovnik in 2001. With her much praised kaleidoscopic diploma film, *MK* (2001), Krogh expressed a clear interest in situating her work in documentary film within artistic and experimental frameworks and traditions. Krogh's first feature-length documentary, *Omveje til frihed* (*Detour to Freedom*, 2001; with Sidse Stausholm), focusing on A'a'me Nameth following her release from a Thai prison, was selected for the main IDFA competition. *Min morfars morder* (*My Grandfather's Murderer*; co-directed with Søren Fauli, 2004) won the top prize at the Seville International Film Festival in 2005, and was awarded the Fipa d'or Grand Prize in Biarritz, also in 2005. In the film, which is very much a therapeutic project, Fauli and Krogh track down the Danish Nazi Søren Kam, who shot Fauli's grandfather, the journalist Carl Henrik Clemmensen.

Krogh has collaborated frequently with Manuel Alberto Claro, winner of the Carlo di Palma European cinematography award. Their teamwork encompasses key films such as *MK* and *Alt er relativt* (*Everything is Relative*, 2008), but also collaborative teaching at the National Film School of Denmark. A visually complex film about the lasting effects of parental abuse, *Beths dagbog* (*Beth's Diary*; co-directed with Kent Klich, 2006) builds on Krogh's art film, *Kvartermesteren* ('The Quartermaster,' 2003), which was part of an exhibition at the Nikolaj Church in Copenhagen. A powerful film that raises difficult questions about the ethics of documentary filmmaking, *Beth's Diary* won the 'Guldok' prize at CPH:DOX in 2006. Krogh has produced a number of films for The Danish Broadcasting Corporation, including *Cairo – Garbage* (2009), which was part of the innovative four-film project 'Cities on Speed.' The film was the first to be produced by Danish Documentary Production and brought Krogh a truly global audience. In *Mig og min tvilling* (*Me and My Twin*, 2011) and *A Normal Life* (2012), Krogh returns to a theme that is present in much of her work, namely the human capacity to cope with adversity. *A Normal Life* premiered at CPH:DOX in 2012, winning *Politiken's* Audience Award. Krogh is currently shooting *Avisredaktionen* (*The Tabloid Newsroom*; working title), a film that looks closely at the working practices of the Danish tabloid *Ekstra Bladet*, and at the challenges it faces in a digital era. Krogh is a former co-owner of Tju-Bang Film, and since 2007 a co-owner of Danish Documentary Production (with directors Phie Ambo, Pernille Rose Grønkjær, and Eva Mulvad, and producer Sigrid Dyekjær). She is the daughter of art historian Leila Krogh and journalist Torben Krogh.

Documentary features:

2014   *Avisredaktionen* (*The Tabloid Newsroom*, working title)
2012   *A Normal Life*
2008   *Alt er relativt* (*Everything is Relative*)
2004   *Min morfars morder* (*My Grandfather's Murderer*, with Søren Fauli)
2001   *Omveje til frihed* (*Detour to Freedom*, with Sidse Stausholm)

Documentary shorts:

2011   *Mig og min tvilling* (*Me and My Twin*)
2006   *Beths dagbog* (*Beth's Diary*, with Kent Klich)
2001   *MK* (diploma film)
2000   *Fisk uden vand* (*Fish Out of Water*)
1996   *Ungdomsgarantien* ('The Youth Guarantee')
1992   *Epilog* (*Epilogue*, with Sara Bro)

Television:

2009   *Cairo – Garbage* (part of 'Cities on Speed')
2004   *Behind the Scenes: Accused*
2004   *Har vi travlt mor?* ('Are We in a Hurry, Mum?', with Vibeke Heide-Jørgensen)
2002   *Min fars valg* (*My Father's Choice*, part of the TV series 'Min...' ['My...'])
1999   *Vi fik livet tilbage* ('We Got our Lives Back')

Art films:

2003   *Kvartermesteren* ('The Quartermaster')
2002   *Indretninger i hukommelsen* ('The Ways of Memory', with Kaspar Bonnén)

HJORT: You worked in radio for a number of years before applying to the National Film School of Denmark. During those years, you did, however, make the documentary short entitled *Epilogue* with Sara Bro, as well as 'The Youth Guarantee.' How would you describe the path that led you to the National Film School of Denmark?

KROGH: I got into radio at a very young age. I was the host for a children's programme on P3 when I was 13, and the host for a TV programme, Klub 12 [DR1], when I was 15. We featured children's journalism about politics, current affairs, and social problems, like the exploitation of children. I became very interested in journalism, and discovered that I loved telling these stories and had a talent for doing confrontational interviews. I listened to a lot of the programmes on P1 and P4 during my teens, and I always felt that it would be fantastic to be involved in producing them.

At the age of 17 I went to one of these special boarding schools that Danish secondary school students can opt to attend if they want to pursue specific interests of theirs. I met Sara Bro at Rantzausminde Efterskole, and we decided that it would be interesting to make a film about this boarding school phenomenon, which was mostly associated with the provinces and not actually that well understood. We got a lot of excellent support for this project because my father was an established journalist and Sara's father is Arne Bro, who's at the Film School. They put us in touch with Henrik Ruben Genz, who became our consultant. He was very much involved with the Video Workshop in Haderslev, and recommended that we look to the people there for support. There was also the Workshop in Copenhagen, but that milieu was much more focused on experimental approaches to film and video, and we had this story to tell that was very much about life in the provinces; so the Video Workshop in Haderslev was perfect and did in fact give us a grant.

I later started freelancing for P1 and P4, and went on to become a full-time producer with responsibility for all aspects of the programming. And then one day, Tómas Gislason called and asked whether I'd like to go to Haiti with him. Jørgen Leth was having some trouble making *Haiti – Uden titel* (*Haiti: Untitled*, 1996), and had asked Tómas to join him so that he could provide some input. At the same time, Tómas was making his documentary portrait of Leth, *Fra hjertet til hånden* (*Heart and Soul*, 1994), and needed a personal assistant. Tómas knew I'd recently been to Cuba, where I'd done some reportage work, and he'd heard that I'd be up to the task. Haiti was a tough place. So I spent three weeks in Haiti with Jørgen and Tómas. I had no idea how lucky I was when I was first asked to go. Listening to Jørgen and Tómas talk about their work made me realize that what I really wanted to do was make films. They're both extremely generous people, so I was simply immersed in this cauldron of artistic creativity. I was 21 at the time, but still felt that I wasn't quite ready to apply to the Film School. Also I wasn't really through with radio and P4 yet. And then DR developed a documentary initiative – inspired by various BBC programmes – that had made good use of small digital cameras, which had just been invented. DR invited ten people to direct a documentary short for them, and I made that ten-minute film you mentioned, 'The Youth Guarantee.' The film is about what it's like to be somehow on hold, and I shot it in the waiting room of the Social Security Youth Office. That film became a key element in my film school application.

HJORT: *My Father's Choice*, about your well-known father, the journalist Torben Krogh, is at once investigative and deeply personal. It provides a lot of insight into your family background, giving viewers a sense, for example, of your mother, Leila Krogh, who is depicted as a very capable and thoughtful woman. Do you see continuities between your parents' professional lives and your own?

KROGH: Yes, I do. My mother is an art historian, and was for many years director of the Villumsen Museum in Frederikssund. She's also served as chair of the Danish Arts Agency. So I also grew up in an art world. And I do think it's fair to say that documentary filmmaking is a combination of art and journalism. So in that sense I've drawn on both their worlds. I use modern art a lot in my work as a source of inspiration. *Family of Man* was, for example, a very important point of departure for *Everything is Relative*. Bill Viola's work has had a huge impact on me. Walter de Maria's land art is also something I'm fascinated by. Artists like Jane and Louise Wilson, who work with film, video installations, and photography, have meant a lot to me, as has the whole Young British Artists scene.

HJORT: What was it like making the transition from the professional world of radio, in which you'd established yourself, to the Film School?

KROGH: Having been accepted into the documentary programme, one of the first things I was told was that I wasn't allowed to make use of interviews any more. What I had to learn was how to tell my stories using images and scenes. That was, of course, completely true, but at the same time I really felt as though I'd suddenly been deprived of a language I knew well. I was good at delivering the goods, and came from a world where the production flow, at least compared with the world of film, was really efficient. So when I was given an assignment, I completed it in a day. I was able to identify a story quickly, and I'd immediately go out and shoot it, and then edit it together at the end of the day. In a film school context, what I produced wasn't especially good, and the feedback I got was quite critical and negative. The idea, clearly, was to get me to develop skills that were very different from the ones I already had. So I found the first couple of years at the Film School very hard.

HJORT: Documentary film training is one of the great strengths of the National Film School of Denmark. Indeed the school has played a major role in fostering the enormous success that Denmark is currently enjoying in the area of documentary filmmaking. What, for you, were the strengths of the training you received?

KROGH: The Film School has a very clear philosophy, and one of the key principles is that documentary filmmakers should be able to defend their main characters. That is, the students aren't being trained to produce journalistic work that aims to expose people. We were taught to look for main characters with a good deal of complexity, and, just as importantly, we were also taught that we had to be able to defend them at any point. After all, they give their lives to the film. A second guiding principle is that the students are supposed to figure out what they, quite personally, have to offer. We were taught to ask questions like, 'What are some of the basic stories that I, personally, have to tell and that I can build on?'

During the initial period at the School, you work alone a lot. Only later do you become part of one of those director/editor/cinematographer teams that we associate with the School. So I was supposed to explore one of those stories that came very much from within me, and I was to do this within the context of my own personal circle. My first assignment was to produce a portrait of my lover. And if I didn't have a lover, I had to produce a portrait of an ex-lover, or of someone I wanted to become involved with. To be honest, that first assignment really pushed against some boundaries. Our next assignment involved identifying a story about our family and then developing it into a documentary portrait. I got my mother to write me a letter in which she talked about what it was like being my mother. As you can see, we were really operating within a very intimate, private sphere. What was really instructive was discovering that a portrait of a mother or lover is of no interest to anyone if it glosses over everything to the point where everything is positive. You need to depict what's ugly or less appealing, as well as what's beautiful about the person. That sort of insight is really helpful because it's just as relevant in the context of a full-length documentary film about people you aren't close to. I remember feeling really angry when we were making our so-called 'lover portraits,' because it wasn't clear to me whether the point was to analyse our relationships or to make some films. During the discussions, people were saying things like, 'Oh, that relationship clearly isn't going to last.' But I learnt a lot from that because that's precisely how audiences relate to our work. They don't relate to a film in terms of its craftsmanship. What they do instead is assess, or take a stance on, the people whom they see in it. It was healthy to begin to understand the kinds of mechanisms that are at work once we send our films into the world. Looking back now, I certainly see the method in the madness, but at the time I found it all very heavy.

Once we were in our second year, we started to go further afield, and to work with cinematographers and editors. That's when I started to have some really incredible experiences. There was that sense of seeing work that you were doing being lifted to a higher level. I realized that, as a documentary filmmaker, even if you're able to do a lot of things yourself – and often do – a cinematographer or an editor can make all the difference. You really learn to collaborate during those four years at the School. You learn to work independently, but also as part of a team. The graduates from the School end up sharing a certain approach or method. The courses in film history and dramaturgy or narrative are also important because they provide these shared reference points. Let me give you an example. Over the years, I've worked a lot with the cinematographer Manuel Alberto Claro, but when I was getting ready to go to Texas to shoot some important scenes with American soldiers for *Everything is Relative* (2008), he wasn't able to come along. So I asked Erik Molberg [Hansen] to come along instead. He was one year ahead of me at the Film School, but we speak exactly the same language. We were in sync right from the start, and didn't need to adjust to each other at all. I think that's a very common experience in the Danish film milieu.

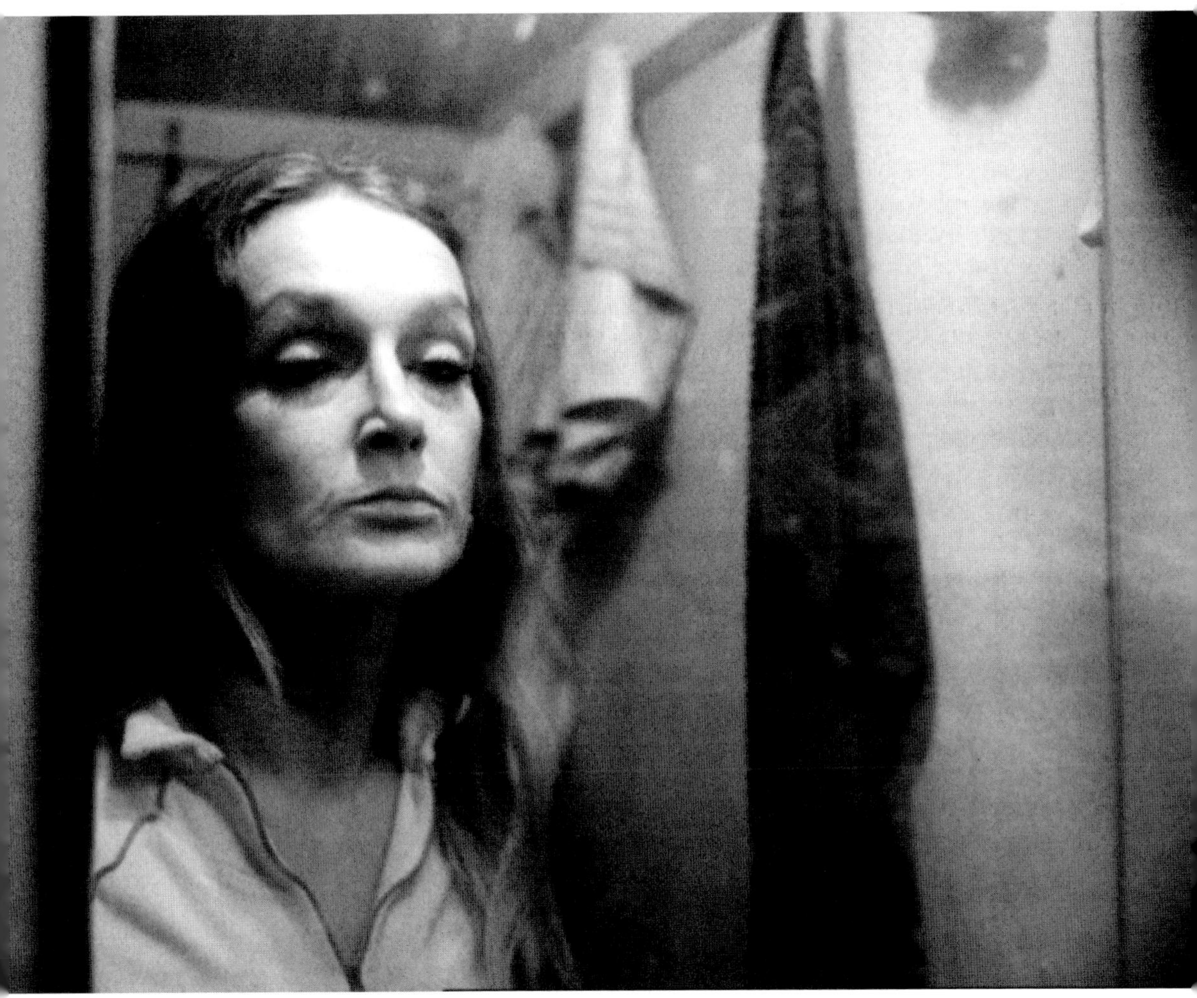

One of many still photographs of Beth by the artist Kent Klich (*Beth's Diary*, framegrab, cinematography by Kent Klich and Beth).

During our third year, we went even further afield because the School had set up this collaborative project with Danida, the point being to give us all an opportunity to make a film on something like a contract basis. So each of the students was sent to one of the countries in Danida's portfolio, and then we were supposed to make a documentary film there. We were supposed to select the theme of our film in consultation with the Danish ambassador to the country in question. So the idea was to have the ambassador decide whether there was a need, for example, to focus on water rather than, say, street children in that particular country. And I was sent to Bangladesh for a month, alone. And just before I left I was told that I'd proven that I was able to make films, so it was alright for me to go back to interviews if I wanted to do that. That was such a gift. I wasn't even sure I wanted to use interviews, but it felt just wonderful knowing that they were now allowed. And then I made this film, *Fish Out of Water*, in which I did in fact use interviews.

HJORT: Being sent abroad, to a country that one isn't familiar with, alone, and with the task of making a film, could be quite a challenging experience. Was there any kind of safety net in place?

KROGH: No, not really. We discussed all that quite intensely. We were the first cohort to be part of this kind of collaborative project involving the School and a partner organization with projects in the developing world. We really felt that this idea of sending us to a third world country on our own was incredibly challenging, and at times we even wondered whether the School knew what it was doing. There were cases of people having to see counsellors, and getting sent off after the rest of us had left. That assignment was really a very big deal. I'd lived in Chile and know Spanish, and I felt that it was important to know the language that's spoken where you're making your film. So I suggested that we divide up the nine countries we had along the lines of who spoke what. I'd also spent time in Bolivia, and Bolivia was one of the countries on the list. I also knew exactly what story I'd want to tell if I ended up there. But we couldn't make it work, and everyone was afraid of Bangladesh. Then my father said, 'Look, you'll never go to Bangladesh on your own, and it's a wonderful place. This is a gift. Go to Bangladesh.' And I ended up being really glad I did. But in the beginning I had images of myself, all alone in an Islamic country that's dealing with all sorts of problems, including overpopulation. Once I'd decided to go to Bangladesh, I quickly became committed to the idea of telling a very different kind of story about the place. I absolutely didn't want to tell a story about overpopulation, or about floods, and so on.

I ended up making a film about two Danish women who'd married Bengali men and had decided to live in Bangladesh permanently; and about a Bengali man who'd lived in Denmark, where he has four children, and who, at a given point, had returned to Bangladesh. It's a film about not really belonging anywhere, about being caught between cultures. I was involved with a Chilean man when I lived in Chile, and had met a number of people who'd moved there. So I was really interested in the issues, and as I was researching all this, before leaving for Bangladesh, I found the children who'd been left behind by this Bangladeshi man. They'd been in touch with him sporadically, but didn't really know him. So my thought was, 'Here we have these children, who've basically lost a father, and I'm going to see if I can find him.' The ambassador (who was charged with approving my project on behalf of Danida) thought this was a great idea because he's married to a woman from Trinidad and thinks mixed marriages are important. Danida's mission, of course, is to help with poverty, engineering work, and so on, so my proposal for this film about mixed marriages didn't connect that closely with what they normally do. But the ambassador supported my project, which made all the difference. I have to say that making *Fish Out of Water* was a really good experience.

HJORT: I'd like to go back to the short film about your father, *My Father's Choice*, which you made just after you graduated from the Film School. How did you approach the very personal aspects of that project?

KROGH: In a sense that film was part of a whole wave in Denmark, one that got started because the Film School had encouraged its students to make personal films. There'd been a lot of discussion about what was personal as compared with what was private. The idea, all along, had been that it was fine to make films that were personal, but not films that focused on what was private. At the same time, personal films were gaining ground at film festivals, and someone like Alan Berliner, who makes films about himself, was generating a lot of interest in certain Danish circles. Shortly after I'd finished film school, DR2 asked a number of filmmakers to come up with a concept for a series of short films. There were six of us: Pernille Rose Grønkjær, Mariella Harpelunde Jensen, Kathrine Windfeld,

Ida Holten Jeppesen, Dorte Høeg Brask, and myself. And what we came up with was the idea of investigating what happens when the filmmaker knows her main character really well. Some of us were working with main characters who were quite well-known, and others with people who weren't well known at all. Our films then became part of this series called 'Min ...' ('My ...', 2002).

I happened to be making *Detour to Freedom* at the same time. Sidse Stausholm, with whom I was making the film, was best friends with the main character, A'a'me Nameth, who'd spent four and a half years in a Thai prison on drug charges. Instead of trying to hide this friendship, as filmmakers might have done ten years earlier, we chose to make it one of the premises of the film. That decision actually had funding implications because the Danish Film Institute thought the personal dimension was very interesting. Films that were personal in this way were seen as being quite a new thing at the time, and then *My Father's Choice* and *Detour to Freedom* ended up becoming part of a wave of similar films. This was also around the time when Phie Ambo and Sami Saif made *Family* (2001).

Making *My Father's Choice* taught me a lot about the ethics of documentary filmmaking, especially in relation to the film's main character. I didn't want to make a film that was all about how fantastic my father was, because it wasn't his 60th birthday or anything like that. But at the same time, I also had to take good care of him, and I was very aware of that. My father had to be able to live with the film. The way I treat my father in that film is how I should be treating all the main characters in my films. Later on, I found that it was very helpful to be able to show the film to people I wanted to work with in front of the camera. I was able to say: 'Look, I've made a film about my father. So I really do know what's involved in giving your life to a film.' My father ended up being very happy with the film. And a lot of people appreciated seeing a completely different side to him. He's had this image as a very tough, brusque, and cynical man, whereas my film shows him as very sensitive and fine. So in that sense it was a great experience, although the actual process was a bit hard at times because he had so many questions about what I was doing and kept interrupting me.

HJORT: Several of your films were made in collaboration with Tju-Bang Film (*Detour to Freedom*; *My Grandfather's Murderer*; *Beth's Diary*; *Everything is Relative*). How did this collaboration get started, and what has the company meant to you?

KROGH: It all started with *Detour to Freedom*, which goes back to my days in radio. That is, when A'a'me was put in prison in Thailand, I was working for P4 and went to Thailand with Sidse, where we worked on getting her story out. When it became clear, some four years later, that A'a'me was going to be moved to the US, and that she'd probably be released soon afterwards, Sidse and I decided we wanted to be there with a camera, and to make a film about this. We flew to Thailand, where we talked to A'a'me, who was happy to be part of what we were trying to do. I was still affiliated with DR, so we got some financing from their Children & Youth Department, and started shooting the film. Having spent three years in film school, I put everything I'd learnt into that process, and then realized that I wanted to be making more than just another TV programme. We were dealing with a lovely woman at DR who agreed to continue to support our film, but also allowed us to look elsewhere for the financing and expertise we needed to take what we had to a higher level. We contacted Jakob Høgel, who'd just joined the Danish Film Institute and was very supportive of young film directors. He was the one who recommended that we get in touch with Tju-Bang Film. Jakob was new and perhaps a bit insecure, and we were young. Tju-Bang was known as a place with very high standards, and I think Jakob thought that they'd provide some quality control. The key people at Tju-Bang Film were Jacob Thuesen, Per K. Kierkegaard, Søren Fauli, Niels Graabøl, and Sigrid Dyekjær. They also liked our project a lot, so that's how I ended up at Tju-Bang. Søren Fauli then asked me whether I'd be interested in making *My Grandfather's Murderer* with him, and that led to my becoming a co-owner of the company. Theis Schmidt, who edited *My Grandfather's Murderer*, also became a co-owner, so then there were seven of us, which was great.

Tju-Bang Film was a highly creative collective, and that made it quite unique. We had our own cinema and lots of films. We also had plenty of time, and we spent a lot of it talking about what made a film really good, or why a given approach to editing worked. We also had this rule, which was that a film wasn't allowed out of the editing room until we felt it was completely finished. That meant that we continued editing our films well beyond the time frame that was actually financed. It was a really good place to learn a whole lot more about what's involved in making films. At a certain point, some of the filmmakers decided they wanted to make feature films, which wasn't something we could handle ourselves because of the expense involved. So we sold Tju-Bang Film to SF Film Production APS, which is the Danish production arm of Svensk Filmindustri AB. That didn't turn out particularly well, because Tju-Bang Film pretty much dissolved immediately afterwards. In perfect hindsight, I suppose that was foreseeable.

HJORT: As you said earlier, you've collaborated a lot with the award-winning cinematographer Manuel Alberto Claro. You first worked together on your diploma film, *MK*, and later on *Detour to Freedom* and *Everything is Relative*. Through Danish Documentary Production, which you're a co-owner of, you and Claro offer a lecture focusing on the visual language of documentary film. What impact has this collaborative relationship with Claro had on the cinematic style or styles of your own films?

KROGH: Manuel and I have this shared interest in art and the art world. Before *MK* we collaborated on 'We Got our Lives Back,' which is an archive-based film about AIDS that we made for DR's TV series called *Århundredets vidner* ('Witnesses of a Century,' 1998–99). *MK* is this kaleidoscopic film about a physicist, a monk, and an artist; that is, about three different ways of finding meaning in life. We developed a very tight visual concept for the film, one that was very much inspired by Roy Andersson's *Sånger från andra våningen* (*Songs from the Second Floor*, 2000). We agreed that there would be no cutting within a scene, so each scene would be one take, and that the film as a whole would consist of these tableaux. Our rule was that we could only turn on the camera when we noticed something unusual. It wasn't enough to see beautiful chimneys with smoke coming out of them. There had to be something surprising about the scene, something we couldn't have anticipated. So Manuel was never in doubt as to when he should be turning the camera on or off. And that's very much what it's all about.

Every time we make a film, we first make a visual mood board so that we know what the mood of the film is going to be. In the case of *Everything is Relative*, we even produced an entire booklet that described the film's visual style in images. We used that booklet to help the people we approached about participating in the film to understand what sort of project they'd be involved with. We select a number of photos and paintings that describe the film's mood, light, and colours. And then we devise rules for three kinds of framings that Manuel is allowed to use when we're shooting. And this is the sort of thing we teach our students how

<table>
<tr><td>HJORT:</td><td>to do. We've taught three different cohorts at the Film School, and the focus is always on this business of developing a very clear visual concept for their film projects.</td></tr>
</table>

HJORT: Two of your films – *Beth's Diary* and *Detour to Freedom* – focus on parental neglect and abuse. What were your aims with these films? Do you see documentary filmmaking as potentially having a therapeutic dimension?

KROGH: You can't use the therapeutic dimension as an argument for making a given film. It's not a good idea to tell people they should agree to be in your film because it will make them feel better. But that therapeutic aspect is there, there's no doubt about it. That's also very much the case with the film I'm making right now, *A Normal Life*. That film is about a pair of identical twins – who are 12 now – one of whom was diagnosed with leukaemia at the age of 2. I followed the family for two years, focusing on the mother, as the main character, who has to find some way of balancing the needs of a healthy child at home and a sick child in the hospital. The mother is in many ways a very special woman, and she's managed to persist with this idea that the girls have to live as normal a life as possible. I know that the fact that I was there with my camera over a period of years really made a difference.

The therapeutic aspect has to do with being seen. You simply can't underestimate the power of that element of recognition. For Beth, the camera ended up becoming a kind of friend, in much the same way that it did for Sara Bro, whom we see coping with cancer in *Everything is Relative*. The experience of cancer begins to make some sort of sense to Sara because someone's listening to her story about it. Why does A'a'me agree to be part of *Detour to Freedom*? If you've been through something as difficult as being imprisoned in a Thai jail, you want to find a way of making sense of what you've experienced. A'a'me said that all of the foreign women she was with in that Thai prison wanted to write books when they got out. Writing becomes a way of surviving, and the camera can play a similar role.

Kent Klich, whom I made *Beth's Diary* with, had been following Beth with a still camera for 25 years. He'd published a book about her, and had plans for an exhibition about her in the Nikolaj Church and in a museum in Stockholm. He then approached me about doing some video work with him for that exhibition. I was very interested in the project, and suggested that we give Beth her own camera, since Kent had already documented her life a lot.

In the beginning she'd do things like take the camera to the pub, where she and her drinking buddies would fool around with it. But by giving her some assignments, we got her to see what she could really do with the camera. She then started to see it as an intimate friend whom she could share her life with, and from that point on, she started producing really extraordinary material. I have to say, though, that she did end up having a somewhat ambivalent relationship to the film. On the one hand, she was incredibly proud of it, and really enjoyed the whole experience of being at various film festivals and receiving prizes. On the other hand, she also felt a bit overlooked at times, and then she'd want the film to be destroyed, so nobody could see it. But we're dealing with an addict, and addicts are complicated people because they're often in the grip of quite violent moods, which can shift dramatically from one moment to the next.

HJORT: With shooting in Dubai, Mozambique, the US, Japan, Thailand, and Denmark, *Everything is Relative* is a hugely ambitious undertaking. You credit Miriam Nielsen for research assistance, and Vinca Wiedemann for artistic supervision, in connection with support from New Danish Screen. Mogens Rukov also played an important role, inasmuch as he provides six monologues that help to structure the film. What was your basic concept for this film, and what role did Nielsen, Wiedemann, and Rukov play in developing it?

KROGH: I'd received a lot of praise for my diploma film, *MK*, which was this kaleidoscopic work, so I was interested in working with a similar concept again. I'd been intrigued for a long time by people's capacity to create new realities for themselves in response to their particular circumstances. So I decided that survival strategies would be the theme of the film, also because that theme was so universal. I then wrote this idea up as a proposal, together with Theis Schmidt, who edited the film, and we sent it to the regular film commissioner at the DFI. We received all sorts of critical feedback, and I could just feel that things were being taken in a direction that wasn't going to work for me. I then met Vinca, who'd praised *MK* a lot on various occasions, and I started to think about approaching her. Before doing that, we used our own pennies to pay Mogens Rukov to help us articulate the shape of the project a bit better. He wrote this absolutely fantastic treatment, which was quite abstract, and we then sent that to Vinca. And she was wonderful because she was actually happy to get something

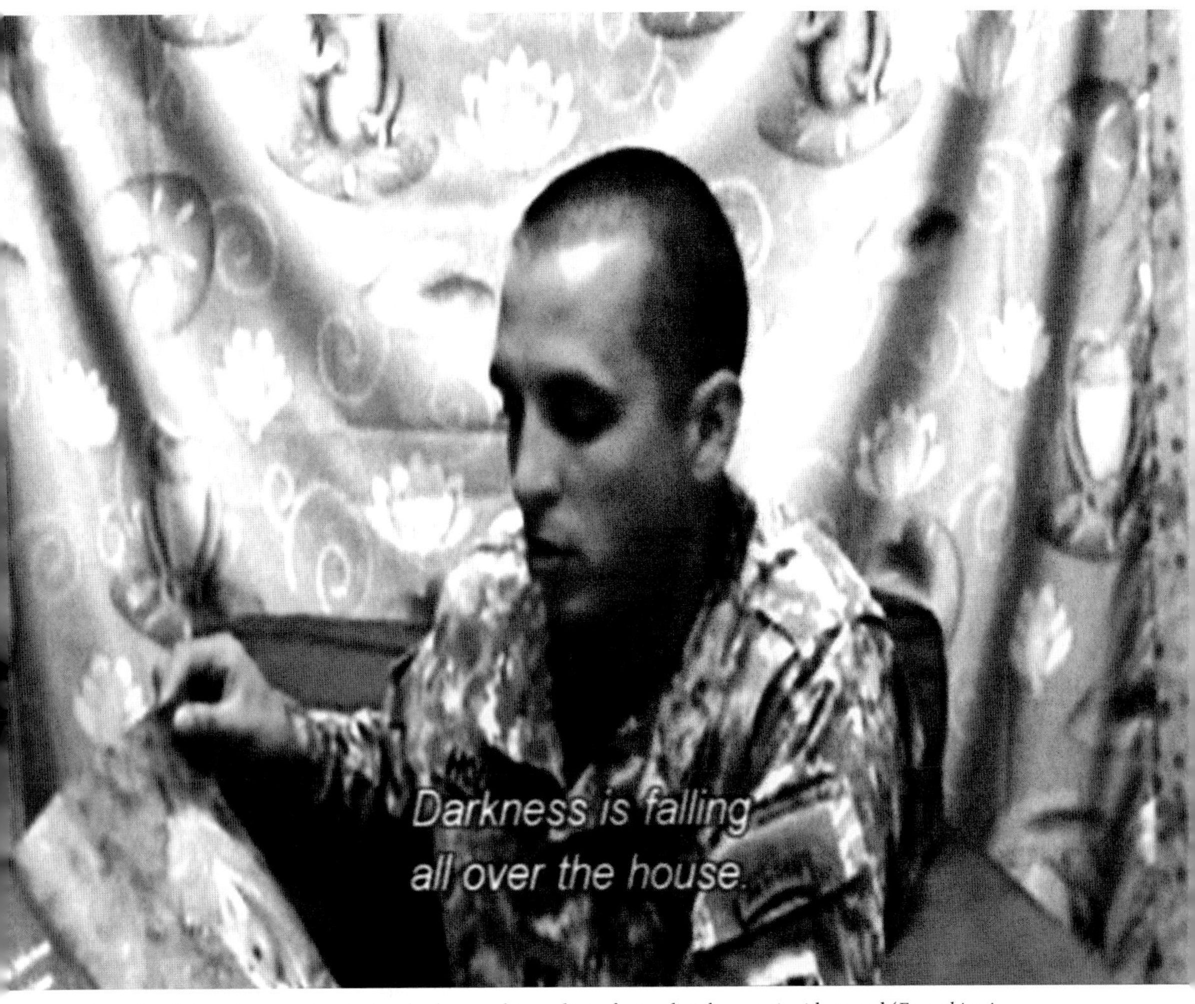

A soldier, father of a two year old, breaks down as his reading of a good night story is videotaped (*Everything is Relative*, framegrab, cinematography by Manuel Alberto Claro; this scene by Erik Molberg Hansen).

that didn't just describe a film, but provided the basis for a kind of investigative process. She immediately said, 'This is a film that has to be made. And I'm going to give you all the money right from the start, so you won't have to keep justifying yourselves along the way.' Normally you get money for the research, then you get money to develop the film, and so on. Vinca was amazing throughout the whole process. I've never experienced sparring at such a high level from a DFI film commissioner. She'd been to see what was supposed to have been our final edit of the film, and the next evening she called me to say that she was completely convinced that a cut we'd discussed at length just didn't work. We'd kept insisting that it was our most important cut. Initially, we'd cut from the flood in Mozambique, where people had lost absolutely everything they had, to Sara complaining about how she's put on weight because of the chemo she was receiving. We felt the contrast was brilliant because it really underscored this idea of everything being relative. But Vinca said that the point had already been made, and that we didn't need that contrast, which actually cast a pretty harsh light on Sara. She was absolutely right.

HJORT:	Rukov's monologues are a crucial part of the film. Were these planned from the start?
KROGH:	No, they weren't. We knew we wanted some kind of narrator, and perhaps even a voice-over, to tie everything together because it was all so fragmentary. I had the idea of drawing on an actor, and we produced some pretty good scenes with David Dencik. But Mogens, who'd written the lines, felt that they sort of came out of nowhere. We then made David an actor in the film, and had him deliver the lines on the old stage at the Royal Danish Theatre. But it still didn't work. And finally Vinca said, 'But who wrote the lines?' and we said, 'Mogens did.' 'Well,' she said, 'then Mogens is the one who should be saying them.' So that's how he ended up in the film. He's there because we kept doing all these tests. That's really something I've learnt over the years. You have to keep testing things to make sure they actually work.
HJORT:	Your contribution to the 'Cities on Speed' project, with *Cairo – Garbage*, further underscored your interest in working well beyond the borders of Denmark, and in developing a perspective that is in some sense global. How did you become involved in this project?
KROGH:	Michael Glawogger, who's one of my big heroes, has made this film called *Megacities* (1998), which is one of my favourite films.

Suddenly I noticed that DR and the DFI had put out this call for a project called 'Megacities,' and my first thought was that they couldn't do that, because the title was already taken. I'd been to Dubai in connection with *Everything is Relative*, and while I was there this woman called Laila Muhammad did some interpreting for me. She told me about the research she'd done on the women in these garbage towns, and I immediately felt there was a film there. I contacted Laila, did some more research, sent in an application, and was invited in for an interview. I was then told that DR and the DFI would be happy with a film about garbage in Cairo, but that I couldn't focus just on those communities, because there were already plenty of films about garbage dumps. So I explained that these were actually garbage *towns*, not just garbage dumps, but they just couldn't imagine what I was talking about. So, I just said 'fine' and then I headed off to Cairo to do my research.

Initially, I was thinking in terms of a kaleidoscopic film involving the whole structure of the city, so that it wouldn't be just another story about poverty, but something a lot of people would be able to identify with. I wanted to tell a bigger story that would also be about changing how we do things, about how hard it is for all of us to make the necessary adjustments, and about what needs to be done if we're going to save the environment. My reference point, as I was thinking about all this, was this wonderful Brazilian short film called *Ilha das Flores* (dir. Jorge Furtado, 1989). It's about the journey of a tomato, from the moment when it's plucked from a field to the moment it ends in a garbage dump. Incidentally, Max Kestner's *Rejsen på ophavet* (*Max by Chance*, 2004) is also very inspired by this film. It tells a story about the whole world, and does this with the help of graphics, still photographs, animation, moving images, the lot, and we just keep coming back to that tomato. I quickly realized, though, that the conditions I was working under in Cairo were far too complicated and difficult for me to be able to do something along those lines. So I decided I'd just have to focus my efforts on shooting scenes that were useable.

I worked with an Egyptian cinematographer called Sherief Elkatsha, who had a lot of connections in Cairo, and with Laila. This was before the Arab Spring, and we needed permission to shoot in Cairo, especially since we were planning on doing interviews. So we wrote up a list of the places where we wanted permission to shoot, and sent it to the authorities. I was then told that we could shoot in some places, but not in others. I then showed up in Cairo just as Ramadan was beginning, and informed the relevant officials that I was now there, and that the plan was to begin shooting nine days later. They weren't that interested in dealing with us because of Ramadan, and basically said 'fine.' We then knew that we had nine days to get everything done that we weren't officially allowed to do. We didn't use a production car, and just relied on taxis, so that it would be hard to follow us. There's a lot of traffic in Cairo, so it's easy to lose someone. People at the Danish embassy had said that we should go ahead with our plans to shoot in the garbage towns, so we knew that if we got in trouble we could count on their support. We also looked into what the worst that could happen would be, and as far as we could tell, it was a matter of having our material confiscated, but not jail. I had a nifty camera that was able to record what we shot on both a tape and a memory card, so I also knew that I could always hand over the tape without losing everything. We had the tapes, and then I'd put the material on three different hard drives, which were then sent out of the country in three different ways. But I also needed to make sure that the people I was working with wouldn't get in trouble later. The film has been seen all over the world, and was shown by Al Jazeera, so it was definitely important to be aware of whatever consequences it might have. Sherief Elkatsha's aunt was a member of parliament, and she assured us that there would be no repercussions, and that the permissions we were required to get had to do with officials wanting to ensure that Cairo was represented in a certain way. Another complicating factor in all this was my Danish citizenship. The 'Cartoon Crisis' was anything but a distant memory. Sherief was Egyptian and Laila was Palestinian, but I was Danish and I was working for a Danish TV station. Everyone said 'Just say you're Swedish,' but I just felt it would be unethical to do that, when I was producing the film for a Danish TV station.

It was an amazing experience being part of the 'Cities on Speed' project. The synergy effect that you get when you bring films together like that is extraordinary. The film was shown all over the world, ended up getting financial support from a lot of TV stations, and has also sold really well. But I have to say that at some level I don't quite recognize myself in the film. I just can't quite see the film's visual language as mine. It's extremely difficult to make a film in a place where you don't understand the language at all. Without the local language, it's almost impossible to connect properly with the people in front of the camera. Also, Sherief and I just didn't have the time we needed to develop a shared cinematic language. But compared with *Everything is Relative*, which does have those formal features that I recognize as mine, *Cairo – Garbage* was nonetheless a very gratifying project, because the film ended up being seen by so many people.

HJORT: The Danish documentary milieu is thriving these days. Why do you think that's the case?

KROGH: There are a lot of factors here. First of all, we really do have the best system of state support for film. And then there's the Film School and what it's been able to accomplish. The Film School's Documentary & TV Department does, of course, train a lot of really good documentary filmmakers, but that's just part of the picture, because the School also trains a lot of excellent editors, cinematographers, and sound designers. Half of the excellent documentaries that get made are directed by people who may not have gone to the Film School themselves, but have worked with cinematographers, editors, and sound designers who did. It's easy to forget that, when we reach, often rather quickly, for the label 'self-taught filmmaker.' Janus Metz may not have attended the Film School, but a film like *Armadillo* (2010) was edited by K [Per K. Kierkegaard] and shot by Lars Skree, who did. Their contributions are clearly crucial, so the Film School plays a very important role.

When I travel and see documentaries from other parts of the world, what I see is lots of good stories, many of them told in a way that suggests that the filmmakers had the patience needed to make a really good documentary film. But often the directors have done the editing themselves, and I think that's a real pity. An editor can help to tighten the string on the dramaturgical bow. Danish documentary filmmakers work with professional editors, and that's clearly one of the reasons their films are doing so well. We have truly excellent editors and cinematographers in Denmark. They're very much in demand internationally, which is quite telling, I think.

HJORT: You are now co-owner of Danish Documentary Production, which was created by Phie Ambo, Pernille Rose Grønkjær, and Eva Mulvad in 2007, and also involves producer Sigrid Dyekjær, who produced *Beth's Diary*, *Detour to Freedom*, and *My*

Grandfather's Murderer. She was also the driving force behind *Everything is Relative*. What, for you, are the strengths of Danish Documentary Production?

KROGH: The company consists of one producer and four directors. Sigrid is in many ways the reason why we all ended up in this company together. As I mentioned, we'd been co-owners of Tju-Bang Film. At a certain point, she and I were taking this course called 'Twelve For the Future,' which the European Documentary Network was offering. It was all about international financing, and through that process – which also involved DocPoint in Helsinki – we met Pernille, who didn't yet have a producer for *The Monastery: Mr Vig and the Nun* (2006). Sigrid and I, who were still at Tju-Bang Film, said we'd be glad to produce it for her. So then Sigrid and Pernille started working together. Eva and I were part of the same cohort at the Film School, and have had a strong sense of connection ever since.

The idea behind this company is to spend as much of the money as possible on actually making films. We have these two small rooms, which cost next to nothing. We don't employ anyone on a full-time basis. We only get a salary in those cases where we've pulled in a project ourselves. We own the rights to the films we make, and we decide what's going to happen with them when they're finished. So it's quite simple really because it's all about giving the power back to the directors. It's about spending money on the films themselves, instead of on overhead. It's also about being part of an artistic community.

HJORT: Is the company doing well?

KROGH: Yes, it is. *Cairo – Garbage* was the first film we produced, and that was quite an important project because it sort of gave the company a jump start in terms of our balance sheet. At this point we're making two or three films a year. We just produced Andreas Koefoed and Christian Bonke's *Ballroom Dancer* (2011), so we're beginning to produce other people's films too. Things are going well, and that's incredibly gratifying.

HJORT: You've mentioned *A Normal Life*, a film that builds on *Me and My Twin*, which the Aarhus-based production company Radiator Film produced for DR Ramasjang and the DFI. Are you currently working on any other film projects?

KROGH: I've always dreamt of making a film about a newspaper's newsroom. I grew up with a father who was a journalist, and that whole discussion about the role of the press in society has been a very big part of my life. I've always read five print newspapers every single day, and I'm fascinated by how news gets prioritized. I was always told that, in terms of making a film, it would be impossible to get genuine access to a newsroom, since journalists guard their methods carefully. But, having seen *Page One: Inside the New York Times* (2011), by Andrew Rossi, I started to think that it had to be possible to make a nuanced film about a Danish newspaper. I began by doing some research on different newspapers, but I quickly realized that *Esktra Bladet* provided the most interesting space for the kind of project I had in mind. *Ekstra Bladet* is a tabloid that relies on casual sales rather than subscriptions, and so there's this constant chasing of unique, sensational stories for the front page. *Ekstra Bladet* employs some of Denmark's most gifted journalists, and they dig up the stories, defining themselves in the process as the voice of the little guy and as critical of those in power. Everyone has a position on *Ekstra Bladet,* and the view that's taken isn't always positive. That's why I thought it would be really interesting to get behind the scenes, to see how it all happens. Also, they're facing a historic crisis because the demand for print news is in free fall, and there's a race against time to find new revenue streams through various digital platforms if they're going to survive. I think it's interesting to examine what impact this shift to the Internet is going to have on in-depth, investigative journalism.

I was allowed to observe *Ekstra Bladet*'s editorial team at work, and we then reached an agreement allowing me to do some research shooting over a period of four months. The idea was that I'd edit the material and produce a dummy that would provide the editor-in-chief with a clear sense of the kind of film I wanted to make. I also had to demonstrate that it was possible to make an interesting and engaging film while respecting the team's sources. On the basis of the material I provided, I've been authorized to make a film about the tabloid, and to follow what goes on in its newsroom throughout all of 2013. The film's working titles are *Avisredaktionen* in Danish and *The Tabloid Newsroom* in English, and I expect to finish it in the autumn of 2014.

Chapter 10

Simone Aaberg Kærn

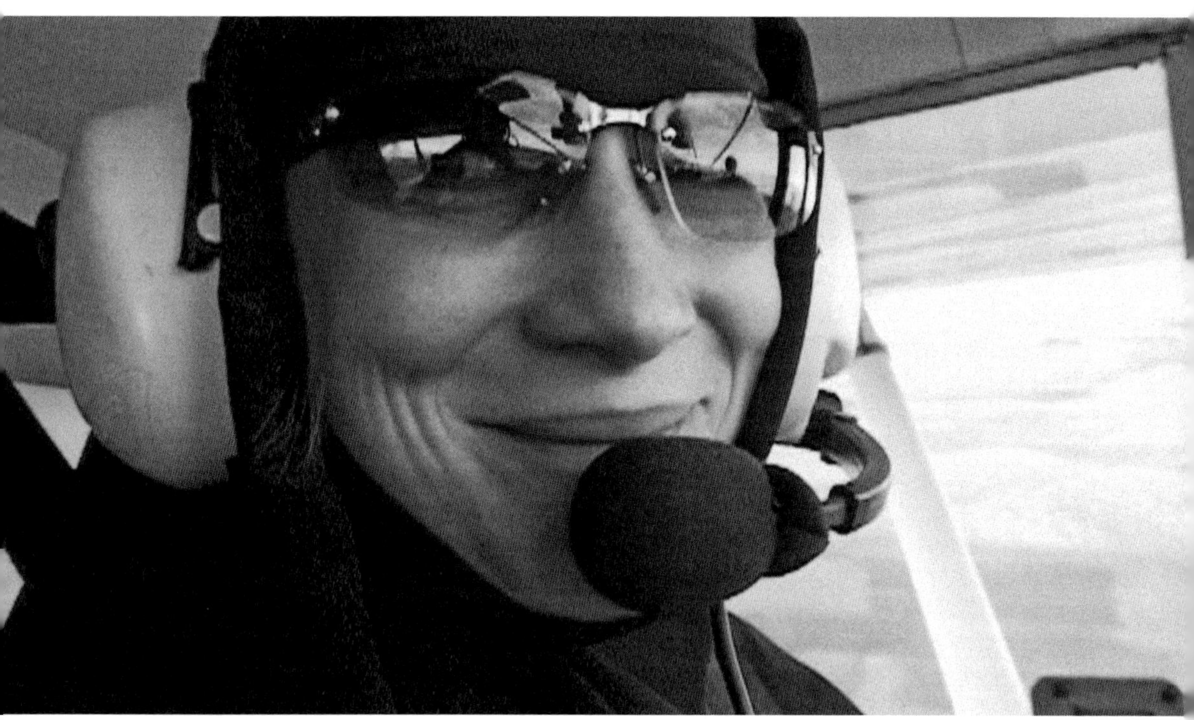

Simone Aaberg Kærn. Portrait by Magnus Bejmar. Courtesy of Simone Aaberg Kærn.

Born 1969. Kærn studied at the Royal Danish Academy of Fine Arts (1993–98), during which time she also pursued Fine Arts at Goldsmiths College in London. Her early installations focused on surveillance and control, but in 1996 Kærn became a licensed pilot, and since then her artistic work has dealt with themes related to flying. She has articulated a concept of 'aero-feminism' as the basis for an aero-feminist sisterhood spanning cultural and generational divides. Several of Kærn's works have been attempts to investigate the skies as a space of freedom. Examples include video works such as *Air* (1994–95), *Wanna Fly* (1995) and *Royal Greenland* (1996). In 1997, Kærn was selected as Artist of the Year in Denmark. That same year, her portrait series and sound installation entitled 'Sisters in the Sky' (about female fighter pilots from the USA, USSR, and Great Britain during WWII) was exhibited at the Louisiana Museum of Modern Art, North of Copenhagen, and two years later it was shown at the Venice Biennale. Collaborating with Stine Kirstein, Kærn turned 'Sisters in the Sky' into a TV series (1997, four episodes) for the Danish Broadcasting Corporation. In 2002, a newspaper article became the impetus for yet another noteworthy performance work and exhibition by Kærn. The artistic project included a documentary film, which Kærn made together with Magnus Bejmar. The article described a 16-year-old girl called Farial, who was living in Kabul, Afghanistan, where she dreamt of becoming a fighter pilot. Kærn developed what she calls a 'micro-global' performance work in response to the article. The work in question involved the artist flying her old one-motor propeller plane from Copenhagen to Kabul – a distance of some 6000 kilometres – in order to help the girl realize her dreams. Entitled *Smiling in a Warzone* (2005), the film forges connections between issues having to do with who controls or owns the skies, the plight of women, and traditional conceptions of heroes and the heroic. Kærn's performance role includes flying her Piper Colt into airspace controlled by the US army, without the requisite authorizations. The film went on to become part of a big solo exhibition in the Malmö Konsthall, 'Open Sky,' which was also presented at Thun in Switzerland and at the AROS Museum in Aarhus, Denmark. Kærn hopes to make a children's film entitled *Min gule flyver* ('My Yellow Airplane'). To date, a version of the material has been shown as an art film, and as an element in the eponymous exhibition at the Asbæk Gallery in 2012. Her most recent exhibition, 'Krig i Kunsten' ('War in Art'), was featured at the Museum of National History in Hillerød. Kærn is currently working on a painting depicting the war in Libya, based on sketches she made at the front in September 2011.

Documentary features:

2005   *Smiling in a Warzone: The Art of Flying to Kabul*

Television:

1997   *Sisters in the Sky – en roadmovie fra luften* ('Sisters in the Sky: A Road Movie from the Air,' with Stine Kirstein, DR2, four episodes)

Selected video works:

2008   *Spider Sisters*
2002   *Taraneh heading for the Stars* (video documentary and dual screen)
1996   *Royal Greenland* (single-channel video installation with sound)
1995   *Wanna Fly* (five-channel video installation)
1994–95   *Air* (video installation with sound)

Selected exhibitions:

2012   'Den lille gule flyver' ('The Little Yellow Airplane,' Martin Asbæk Gallery, Copenhagen)
2012   'Krig i kunsten' ('War in Art,' Museum of National History, Hillerød, Denmark)
2010   'Seize the Sky' (University Art Gallery, San Diego State University, USA)
2008   'Open Sky' (Malmö Konsthall, Sweden, 2006; Kunstmuseum Thun, Switzerland)
1999   'Sisters in the Sky' (Louisiana Museum of Modern Art, Denmark, 1997; Venice Biennale, Italy)

REDVALL: As a filmmaker, you're self-taught, but you studied art at the Royal Danish Academy of Fine Arts, and you were also trained as an artist at Goldsmiths in London. What was your experience of these studio art programmes like? Were you encouraged to work with film as a medium? Was there any collaboration with the film milieu?

KÆRN: Yes, there was collaboration with filmmakers. During my time at Goldsmiths I was taught by a teacher whose area was painting, but the Department of Fine Arts was very flexible, so it was easy to work across the media. The emphasis was on theory and ideas. Conceptual art was really in. If you actually managed to implement your ideas, people would start to look at you with a somewhat sceptical eye! The approach was very much that of a university, but it was also a collaborative one, and it was seen as perfectly normal to work with specialists from other disciplines or areas. In England, it was quite normal to think in terms of film. But this sort of thing also happened at the Academy of Fine Arts in Copenhagen. Gitte Villesen, for example, made a number of small documentary films quite early on, but I think she quite consciously steered clear of the film milieu because she didn't want her work with film to become over-aestheticized. When an artist becomes part of the film milieu, the expectation on the part of the film people tends to be something like this: 'Now we're going to produce lots and lots of *art*, and it's going to be *really different*.' And then every possible device is thrown into the mix: slow-motion images, reversed music, and so on. But the results, at least in terms of content, are typically pretty impoverished. The content ends up disappearing in this cloying aesthetic that is completely unmotivated. I think a lot of artists have pulled back, quite consciously so, from that kind of aesthetic excess. Also, people in the film industry have very firm ideas about what a story actually is, and about narrative more generally. You have a different take on that sort of thing if you come from the art world. And there seem to be some very strange ideas about what art is in the film world.

REDVALL: Did the Academy offer a sequence of courses focusing on video art? Or training of some sort in the area of moving images?

KÆRN: There was a video workshop linked to both the foundation programme and to the School of Media Art. A lot of video artists, especially women, acquired a medium there, without having to contend with exhausting male-dominated stories. Initially, a lot of them produced performance videos, or non-narrative video works with minimal expressive content. But during my time at the Academy, more and more of these women started to work with video in more narrative ways. I remember a lot of discussions about narrative and stories and so on. I think that one of the differences between the art world and the film world is that, as an artist, you're just not as focused on the message or on the product. At least during my time at the Academy the thinking just wasn't that product-oriented. The film industry is a completely different world. It's all about function, and the product, and target groups, and ticket sales. You have to have sorted all these things out before you can even get to the artistic project, and especially the artistic process. It's very hard to find the space you need to feel your way into a given area.

For example, if you think about those little narratives that Gitte Villesen developed with the DJ called Willy, who is passionate about records, you realize she felt her way into the work in a way that was more process- than result-oriented. When you're pitching a film, you virtually have to have worked out what it will look like before you've even started making it. That sort of expectation has a deadly effect on the creative process, and it's one of the reasons that I haven't really been able to make much progress on 'My Yellow Airplane,' which is a children's film that I'm working on at the moment. This time I simply refuse to work that way. We got some seed monies from DR, and there were strings attached in the form of expectations about what the process of making the film would be like. And I'm just not interested. I'm too old for that sort of thing. I'm going to make a really wonderful children's film, but not under those conditions, because I don't think it's the right way to go about it. At least it's not right for me.

REDVALL: What has the response from the Danish Broadcasting Corporation been like?

KÆRN: The whole situation is of course a bit difficult, so for now we've dropped the idea of collaborating. I've indicated that we'll get back to them once we're on the same page they're on. But it's all a bit difficult because we've got a fair bit of money invested in all this. I needed to have new wings sewn for my airplane this last winter, and I've kept the project alive for two years now. There's an awful lot of money involved, so it's quite a big problem really. But I have to say that I'd rather deal with all this uncertainty than proceed on their terms, with a kind of creative dry run. The film may end up taking five years longer than I'd initially hoped, and I may have to be very strident about my ideas, but so be it. You have to try to hold on to the basic tone of your film throughout. When I made *Smiling in a Warzone*, people were perfectly friendly and quite well meaning, but most of the input just wasn't that helpful. Most of the energy focused on getting Magnus and myself to conform to some predefined framework. If you're a soldier or a general, you know that you lose the war by holding onto the old way of doing things.

REDVALL: Do you feel the film industry is holding onto old ways of doing things?

KÆRN: There seems to be a bit of wave phenomenon in that regard. When things are going really well, it's difficult for innovative thinkers to make inroads because everyone's just discovered how things need

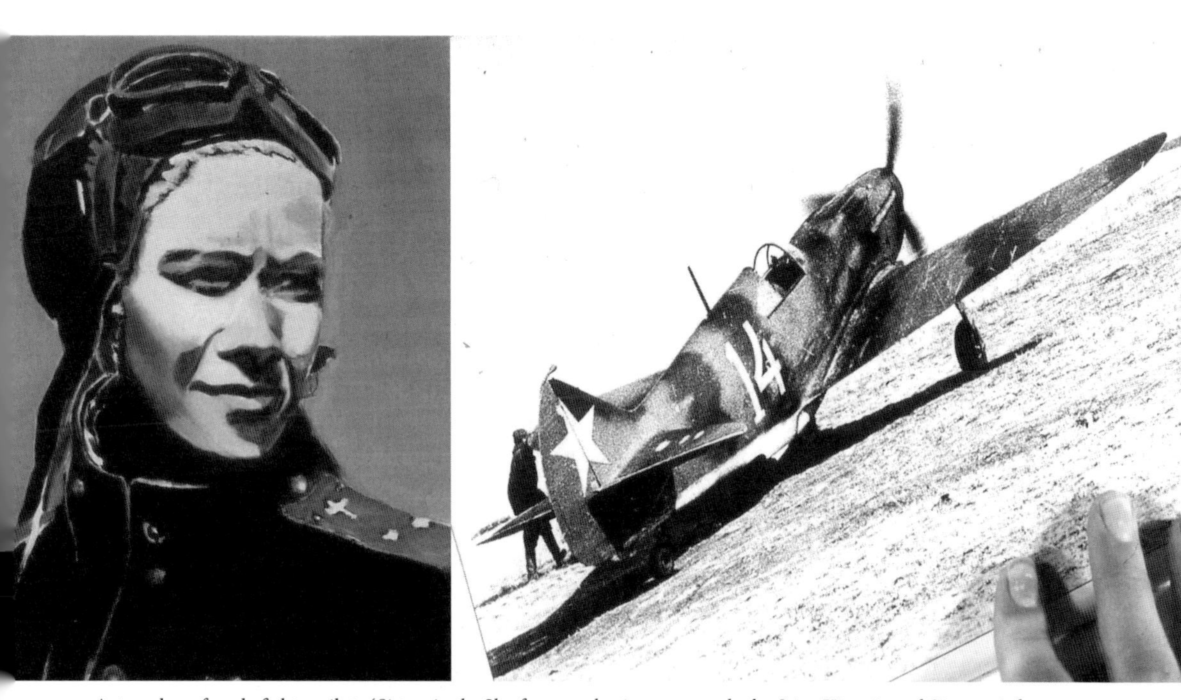

Art work on female fighter pilots (*Sisters in the Sky,* framegrab, cinematography by Stine Kirstein and Simone Aaberg Kærn. Courtesy of Simone Aaberg Kærn).

to be done. It's only when there's a bit of a slowdown that you get the conditions for a new wave. Suddenly the people who are associated with what's not working are seen as being 'out.' And that makes room for a new wave. But these enormous dips aren't at all necessary. All it takes to avoid them is the courage to focus on artists' creative potential, which would also yield a lot more diversity.

REDVALL: Do you see the process of financing documentary films as being very different from that of financing art projects or exhibitions?

KÆRN: Well, in the art world, it's all very simple because we just don't get any money! No, seriously, there are, of course, various grants, and it's the artist as an individual who gets them. I think that's a good principle. As far as documentary filmmaking is concerned, I just don't understand why it's so hard to grasp that it's the director running around with her silly camera who does all the most important work. That's where the gold lies. In the Danish film world, it's the editor who's God. In a way, that's wonderful because the editors do really know what they're doing, and so Danish documentaries are really good. At the same time, the producers and TV stations have a lot of power, and what you end up with is a very 'correct' situation, with everyone being given a say in this drawn out democratic process that's designed to be an equalizer and to put everyone on the same level. As I see it, this is profoundly unartistic. As far as the Danish film world is concerned, it's a pity that there's this emphasis on the National Film School of Denmark as providing the only real path into film. There's this sense of the School's way of doing things as being the only way of doing things. The School's students are required – through the teaching and so on – to fit into a mould that's also a great equalizer. At this point I know quite a few artists who've stuck their heads into that milieu, and who've produced a thing or two while there. And they really ended up getting some hard knocks. It's not like they got nothing out of the experience, but they all ended up leaving the milieu shaking their heads. Lars von Trier is one of the people who's been able to survive in that milieu, but you really have to have a hefty bag of Cipramil on you to do that, and I'm just not sure that Cipramil necessarily produces the coolest art. In that sense, the Danish film milieu is very provincial; but then so is the Danish art world. In the case of the art world, it's The Royal Danish Academy of Fine Arts that has that monopoly on quality.

REDVALL: When did you start working with the medium of film? Why were you drawn to moving images, rather than, say, painting?

KÆRN:

I started producing art back in 1990. Initially, I was making sculptures, but then I discovered video art and Nam June Paik. I went all the way back to early video artists like the Icelandic Steina Vasulka; all the way back to the good old days. I was also really intrigued by theoreticians like Bill Viola. For example, I found the way he described surveillance cameras, as both shining a light on us and as enabling us to shine, quite fascinating.

When I was little, I used to roller-skate in the evenings. We didn't have a TV, and in the evening I knew that everyone else was sitting in front of the TV watching children's TV or something else. And in that blue light coming from the windows, I sensed that community feeling that connected them all. I saw the TV as a kind of umbilical cord. I was really fascinated by surveillance. I remember my grandmother as having one of those old TVs, which was usually turned off. And when it was turned off, it was like an eye with a cataract looking dimly into the living room. In my first works, I had nothing on the screen. There were just these two TV screens encased in white cement, and then there were two of those big old TVs on display stands. I'd placed them in a round room, opposite each other, so that they were sort of looking at each other. And there was a small bulb between them, so that each of the screens reflected the other screen. In the beginning, I was involved in these very basic kinds of explorations, but gradually I started to collaborate with other video artists. At the same time, I was sort of a pirate student at the Academy.

REDVALL:

A pirate student?

KÆRN:

My view was that you can't learn how to be an artist at a school. So my approach was simply to go out and acquire the things I felt I needed to have in my backpack to be able to produce art. For example, I studied anatomy at the Panum Institute, at the University of Copenhagen. Back then you could get in anywhere. There were no iris scanners or electronic codes. The University of Copenhagen offered Art History, which was a good thing to know something about. But the approach was very old-fashioned, and I didn't feel there was anything innovative going on in the programme. There was a lot of innovative thinking going on at the Academy of Fine Arts, however, which was where I met Joakim Koester. And he said it would be fine for me just to show up 'because nobody will notice that you're not actually enrolled.' Claus Carstensen was a guest professor during that period, and I ended up having an incredibly exciting year at the Academy.

He brought in Jutta Koether and all sorts of other people, and it was all very dynamic, but also very theoretical, in a really productive way.

I subsequently got into the Academy on the basis of an artwork I'd produced that made use of surveillance cameras and motion sensors. There was also a machine gun, but that's a long story. And after that I produced a lot of work about that blue light, or about intimacy and screens and reflection. A lot of people were working with similar material, but in a Big Brother sort of way that suggested that these developments were just awful. My angle was quite different because I basically said, 'If God is dead, then this is what brings us to life. The camera sees us.' I was working with intuitions about something like tele-consciousness. It was a lot of fun. And then I was involved in setting up a gallery that was called SAGA Basement, where we showed a lot of video art.

REDVALL: Was there any interaction between the video art milieu and the film industry?

KÆRN: There were some connections at the time. We were a motley assortment of artists and musicians, and people from the youth club milieu, but I don't remember anyone who was really a filmmaker. Filmmakers are a bit like theatre people. They're interested in aesthetics, big lights, and huge cars. And if something doesn't cost a lot, they're too snobbish to be interested.

REDVALL: I imagine that the take on narrative also differs?

KÆRN: Yes, possibly. That said, there were plenty of authors and dramatists in the milieu. On the whole, I'd say that the art and film milieus were two separate worlds. At the time, I think we were divided by our take on aesthetics, but also by the issue of narrative. And by this business of films having to have a goal and a clear message. Where I come from, clearly articulated goals and messages are forbidden. It seems like the opposite is true of the world of film.

REDVALL: It sounds as though you feel the film industry lacks a sense of complexity.

KÆRN: Yes. I grew up in a time when complexity was seen as positive, and art is, of course, able to provide precisely this experience of complexity. It can, for example, provide a basis for multiple interpretations. In art there's been an attempt to refuse manipulation in favour of a more minimalistic approach to things. So that's a really major difference. But in recent years, there's been a blurring of the boundary.

Quite some time has passed since I first started working on *Smiling in a Warzone*. And before that I'd made *Sisters in the Sky* for DR, which was good because I got all the knocks I needed. I learnt that you have to decide either to fight for your ideas or simply to go with the flow. In the case of *Smiling in a Warzone*, I knew I simply had to be persistent to get my vision through. The underlying tone of that film is very pronounced, and so it didn't really matter that much that I ended up having to manipulate things a bit around the edges, or to take out something here or there. It could have been better, but basically I think it's OK. We wanted to make a film that would end up in the mainstream. It was quite interesting to try to retain the complexity of art in a context where everyone would be inclined to look for a message, but then wouldn't immediately be able to find it in the material itself. I feel like we pulled it off. I still travel a fair bit with that film, and give talks about it. And it's wild to see what people are able to pull out of it. It really does touch people. People resign from their jobs, change the way they live, and sit down together to discuss the film and its implications.

REDVALL: I'd like to go back to *Sisters in the Sky*. Was that your first attempt at telling a mainstream story with moving images? How did you put that project together?

KÆRN: Yes, that was my first attempt at working with narrative in that way, although the film wasn't the primary focus, since it was part of a larger artwork. By the time I came up with the idea for the project, I'd already done most of my research and met a lot of the women who were pilots during WWII. I'd also become a pilot myself, and people were very touched by the project. I'd put together an exhibition with portraits of female pilots at the Louisiana Museum in Humlebaek. Back then I was thinking about making a film, but I felt that sound was actually a better medium for evoking images than film was. That's why we created a soundscape for the exhibition. The idea was to evoke these visual memories about WWII in people's minds, and that work had quite an impact.

My thinking about that project was in terms of a critical, feminist work focusing on war, and questions of femininity, and good and evil. But Denmark wasn't at all ready for that. The response was more along the lines of 'Wow! Look at what women can do!' So I felt that I couldn't just keep my encounters with the female pilots to myself. I wanted to share all that. So when I was given an art prize worth 50,000 Danish Crowns, I announced that I now wanted to make a film, since I had a whole lot of money! I met Stine Kirstein at the awards ceremony. She was working for the Danish Broadcasting Corporation at the time, and ended up becoming part of the project.

I called the producer Vibeke Windeløv because she and her then husband, Per Kirkeby, had sent me a sweet letter saying that they thought the images at Louisiana were fantastic. So I asked her for some tips about how to go about making a film, and she invited me to Zentropa the next day. Ålen [Peter Aalbæk Jensen] was there, and Vibeke, who presented herself as our producer. And so we were off. Later, we drove a Nimbus motorbike into the lobby of the Danish Broadcasting Corporation and got them on board too, turning the project into a TV series. We were simply on the cusp of making this series, and the message was 'either you're with us or you're passé.' And then we simply took off. We rented the airplane and off we went.

Looking back it was probably good that Stine was a real workaholic. Before we really got going she'd mapped out the whole project using DR's scripting tools. It was all a bit overwhelming, but it was also really helpful to have everything spelt out very clearly, especially given the inexperienced nature of our team. Stine had done radio programming and I'd made video art, and now we had this contract to produce a TV series consisting of six episodes.

REDVALL: You ended up making four episodes, right?

KÆRN: Yes, we made four episodes, and I think they're quite good. They really work, and I think it's a pity they're not accessible. If I could renegotiate the rights I'd love to get them onto a DVD together with *Smiling in a Warzone*. Together, the TV series and the film tell this fine story about various developments having to do with the lives of women. You have the two 20-year-old women who embark on a journey and end up becoming inspired by these old female pilots, and then there's the moment when the baton is passed on to a teenager who isn't actually able to accept it. During WWII, women made use of the chaos that war brings to carve out a space for themselves. With *Smiling in a Warzone*, I thought it would be possible to use the war in a similar way. The idea was to help Farial in Kabul to carve out a space for herself, but I was so focused on the goal that the patient ended up dying. That sort of thing is probably quite common in Danish film because we're simply too goal-oriented. Fortunately, we're still attuned to the possibility of something interesting happening during the editing process. But just imagine what it would be like if the creative process leading up to the editing phase were to be seen as inherently valuable.

REDVALL: As an artist, you enjoy a great deal of control in terms of the design and execution of your artistic projects. How much control do you see yourself as having as a filmmaker?

KÆRN: The issue of control is clearly a lot more complicated in the context of film, and it's quite hard to have to relinquish a certain amount of control to others. The problem of control is apparent in *Sisters in the Sky*. That I desperately wanted to be in charge is clearly evident throughout the entire film. Stine will also tell you that it was hell to work with me. When I mount an exhibition, I'm an absolute fascist about details. That kind of fascistic attitude helps you to see things through to the end, but it's not very helpful when you're working as a team, because it has a pretty devastating effect on the people around you. Stine found it irritating to be working with this chaotic artist who constantly felt that something else was far more important than what was actually in the production plan. She was very good at a lot of things that I didn't know how to do. For example, she knew how to get the whole production onto the page, in the way that's expected and required. I find it hard to relate to those requirements. I find this idea that everything has to be spelt out in advance really problematic. What's great about film people though, is that they know how to collaborate. A lot of film people are quite happy to talk through their ideas in detail, and then to leave the actual writing to someone else.

When I'm making a film, I need the input of others and I respect the people I'm working with a lot, but it's also important to make sure that the material you're working with can unfold and develop. Also, I've never claimed that the work I do is objective. After all, when you make a film, you create or invent something on the basis of something that's real. You manipulate reality, but you're not really allowed to say this in the documentary filmmaking milieu. It can be hard to get people to accept that you see yourself as someone who creates a world, rather than simply recording or reproducing some reality. Another thing that's hard about film is that the various processes are so incredibly time-consuming. For example, I was really fed up with just how long it took to complete *Sisters in the Sky*. Towards the end I sort of said, 'You guys just wrap this up, because mother needs a new adventure.' And then I just flew off into the skies above the American desert and did things that I saw as meaningful.

REDVALL: It sounds like you weren't that interested in working with film again by the time you were through with *Sisters in the Sky*. But fortunately, you ended up making *Smiling in a Warzone*. My sense is that the film grew out of an art project. You've described the film as a 'docutale,' a kind of documentary fairy tale. Was the film an integral part of the art project from the very outset?

KÆRN: When it comes to film, I feel the same way each time: 'Never again!' It's hard when the creative process dies and it becomes a question of simply executing or completing something. I'm clearly someone who likes to initiate things. I have a lot of respect for people who complete things, and for those who become nerdishly engaged with the material. But that's not where my own strengths lie.

I actually had quite a good time making *Smiling in a Warzone* because I was clear about the constraints that come with the terrain of filmmaking and was willing to accept them. Right from the start, I thought of the film as an integral part of the 'Open Sky' exhibition in Malmö. I've done this with other projects as well, but just haven't been able to complete the films in question. I've mostly dropped this approach now because filmmaking is just such a clunky process. So I've gone back to drawing things instead. But it's quite interesting to produce an insanely elitist performance work that targets only exactly the people who happen to experience it, and then to go on to extend this to a much larger audience. It's actually possible to turn art that's quite elitist into something far more popular. It's not necessary to communicate only with your own subculture. The managers who move in the corridors of power tend to underestimate just how bright people actually are. People are quite eager to be challenged, and it's perfectly possible to present complex philosophical issues in ways that are neither tangled nor obscure. I find it very interesting to work in a space where popular and elitist elements are brought together, but I have a real problem with what's purely mainstream. There's a lot of talk these days about 'mainstreaming,' and that's exactly what we shouldn't be looking to do. We should be cultivating diversity because people get such a charge from experiencing something that ends up taking them in unexpected directions. Things that are very palatable get forgotten within about two seconds. We need things that are a bit more spicy than what our palates are used to, to stick with the culinary metaphor.

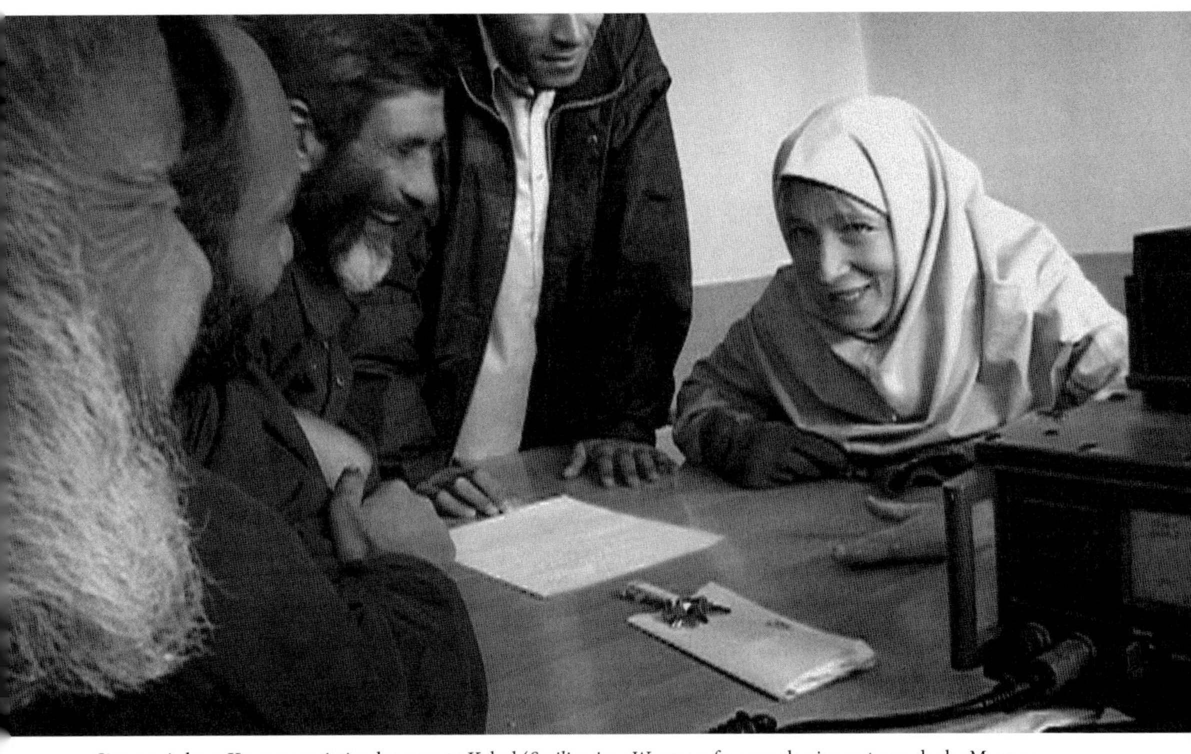

Simone Aaberg Kærn negotiating her way to Kabul (*Smiling in a Warzone*, framegrab, cinematography by Magnus Bejmar. Courtesy of Simone Aaberg Kærn).

REDVALL:

You've been a central figure in your own films, but there's a big difference between the way in which you include yourself in *Sisters in the Sky* as compared with *Smiling in a Warzone*. With reference to the latter, you've talked about how you worked with a performance role. What exactly did that involve?

KÆRN:

Sisters in the Sky is actually reality TV, although the concept of reality TV didn't exist at the time. In *Smiling in a Warzone*, the performative aspect is developed more systematically. My performance role brings together Leni Riefenstahl, Charlie Chaplin, and the Little Prince from the work of Saint-Exupéry, and I have something genuinely at stake in it. Those three figures are important to me. A performance role can make things both more and less interesting. It's easier to focus on the philosophical parts of the film when you deviate from the trend that's been quite dominant in Denmark, which is all about identification and deep feelings. There's a risk, however, because if the performance figure becomes uninteresting, we lose interest in the work more generally. I'm constantly struggling to achieve the right balance in each and every one of my projects, and when I first saw the 200 hours' worth of material for the *Smiling in a Warzone* film I had a lot of trouble finding Simone in it because Magnus had really shot a performance film. In that sense it was incredibly helpful to work with Molly Malene Stensgaard, who is a very gifted and experienced editor. So she was able to dig around and find a bit more Simone here and there. It was a long process, and there were a lot of people involved in it, but it was good fun.

I'm still very pleased with the film, and I'd like to make more films, but I do wish that the actual process of making a film wasn't so clunky. It's all too fiddly, and I'll never understand why films have to be so incredibly expensive. I don't, for example, understand why you can't just do the editing yourself with an editing programme. In the beginning, I had a lot of trouble with the collective dimension of filmmaking, but I've come to enjoy that collaborative aspect. After years in the desert in connection with *Sisters in the Sky*, I was more open to collaboration, I think. I'd gotten certain things out of my system and I'd received my medals. These days I really enjoy working with talented people, the whole process of sharing ideas. I'm very comfortable with the idea that things emerge here, at the table where we're all sitting together. I like this business of sitting there and pushing things back and forth as we develop them. I've got a clear sense of my own tastes, and once I've thought through the basic style of a work, I'm quite happy to let others develop it within the context of that space. But I'm not interested in bosses who want to make decisions about everything in terms of viewer numbers. That's when I get off the bus; you just can't calculate these things.

REDVALL: Why are you so fascinated by war? War is an important element in both *Sisters in the Sky* and *Smiling in a Warzone*, and it figures centrally in the exhibition you're working on now.

KÆRN: Yes, war is a constant. That's because I'm a born fighter, and as an artist I see war as the hotspot where the structures begin to collapse, the masks begin to come off, and our humanity starts to dissolve. It's where we truly show ourselves. War is like the scientists' petri dish – but with love, war, birth, and death in it. All the elements of conflict.

REDVALL: And you look at the conflicts from the perspective of women?

KÆRN: Yes, and that's exactly what hasn't happened a lot. And on those rare occasions when we have seen things through the eyes of women, the emphasis has been on victimhood. I'm interested in looking at what happens when women are actively engaged in war. Women have always sent their sons off to war, and they've always supported their husbands, but they've also often been the first to go out and demonstrate. Women were the first to demonstrate against Hitler. The first demonstration against the Taleban was mounted by women. There's incredible strength in us, and it's interesting to explore both the lighter and the darker sides of that energy.

REDVALL: What about the relationship between fiction and reality in *Smiling in a Warzone*? You've described the film as fiction, and yet non-fiction is very clearly part of the set-up. What was your thinking about all this?

KÆRN: Before we took off for Kabul, we'd clearly decided that we weren't going to be making a documentary film. Magnus had developed this docutale concept, and the idea was to insert me, in my performance role, into certain real-world contexts. And then we'd film what happened as a result of these different provocations. But we had a guiding concept that we'd keep making reference to as we shot the material. We had a clear sense of what it was about; a given situation that we wanted to make salient. We didn't pin down every scene on the page, but we talked about different scenarios. When you're embarking on a trip with a plane, there's a lot of very boring stuff having to do with take-offs and landings, so we knew we needed to find some sort of narrative progression. That was part of the concept from the outset. But we did have a lot of lively discussions about our approach with quite a number of people. My producer, Helle Ulsteen, was very supportive throughout, and clearly understood what we were trying to do. She's worked with a lot of artists over a period of many years. But otherwise, there was a clear sense of our being artists working in a film industry that we didn't necessarily understand, and who thus needed to be carefully monitored. A lot more artists would happily join the world of film if that attitude were dropped. It's hard enough to be creative under the best of circumstances, and it's simply exhausting to have to put so much energy into arguing with a bunch of people who keep saying 'no.'

REDVALL: How well has the film been distributed? My impression is that you've travelled a fair bit with the film, and that you're still doing just that.

KÆRN: The film is constantly being shown all over the world. It's doing extremely well. What I don't understand, however, is that none of the money is coming my way. I just don't understand that at all. I was given an obscenely small amount for making the film. We didn't come anywhere near recuperating our own investment in the film, and the producer who was imposed on us won't let us release the film on DVD. I find that really strange. At the moment, I'm thinking a lot about micro-financing. I think that could be the way to go. That would also involve a lot of work, and you'd have to have more control over the process. But given a really lively team to work with, I'd much rather do things on a small scale as opposed to an elaborate and grandiose one. Also, it's relatively easy to distribute smaller productions through the new channels of distribution.

REDVALL: Part of the challenge, I suppose, is that there's traditionally been an emphasis on the cinema as the preferred viewing space. What's your view on the cinema, as compared with the other screens that are now on offer?

KÆRN: The cinema provides a fantastic space, and it's wonderful to be there. I was at the True/False Film Festival in Memphis, where they have this enormous, quite derelict cinema. It was raining through the ceiling, but there was this massive screen and the whole town was there. Everyone was talking about the films, and it was just amazing. I think we have to try to hold on to the cinemas, but perhaps to transform them so that they become spaces where filmmakers show *and* discuss their films. I do these tours where I talk about my films, and I've actually just recently stopped working together with my former gallery. Ting isn't very good at selling itself any more, whereas, to be honest, I'm really very good indeed at talking about my projects. So I've just started doing this under my own steam so that I can pull all the things I've done together into a single package.

I think that, in the long run, directors will survive to the extent that they figure out how to tell stories about the process of filmmaking. I think I've pretty much recouped my investments, but only because I've engaged in all these activities that aren't intrinsic to the films and artworks themselves. The situation is a bit like that of the many authors who find it difficult to earn enough from book sales, and so give readings, tours based on their books, and so on. The problem is that even then it's only barely enough to live on. At the end of the day, there's not enough left over to initiate new projects, and it's also really exhausting to have to put so much energy into earning money in those ways. I for one find it impossible to work creatively two days after I've been out there talking about my work. You have to be a real extrovert while you're doing these things, and in my experience that just doesn't fit well with being deeply involved with an artistic project.

It takes a lot of energy to produce art, and you have to be willing to take risks. I'm not saying that you necessarily have to walk into a minefield when you make art, but you do have to stake your life somehow if the results are to be the least bit credible. You have to be willing to risk farting out loud on the Tivoli concert hall stage, in front of the queen mother, as a violin teacher once memorably put it, otherwise there's no point. If the various institutional bodies – the Film Institute, the TV stations, and so on – don't have the courage to support the necessary creative risk-taking, then let's just ignore them. Let's just leap over them. They're so yesterday anyway.

Chapter 11

Asger Leth

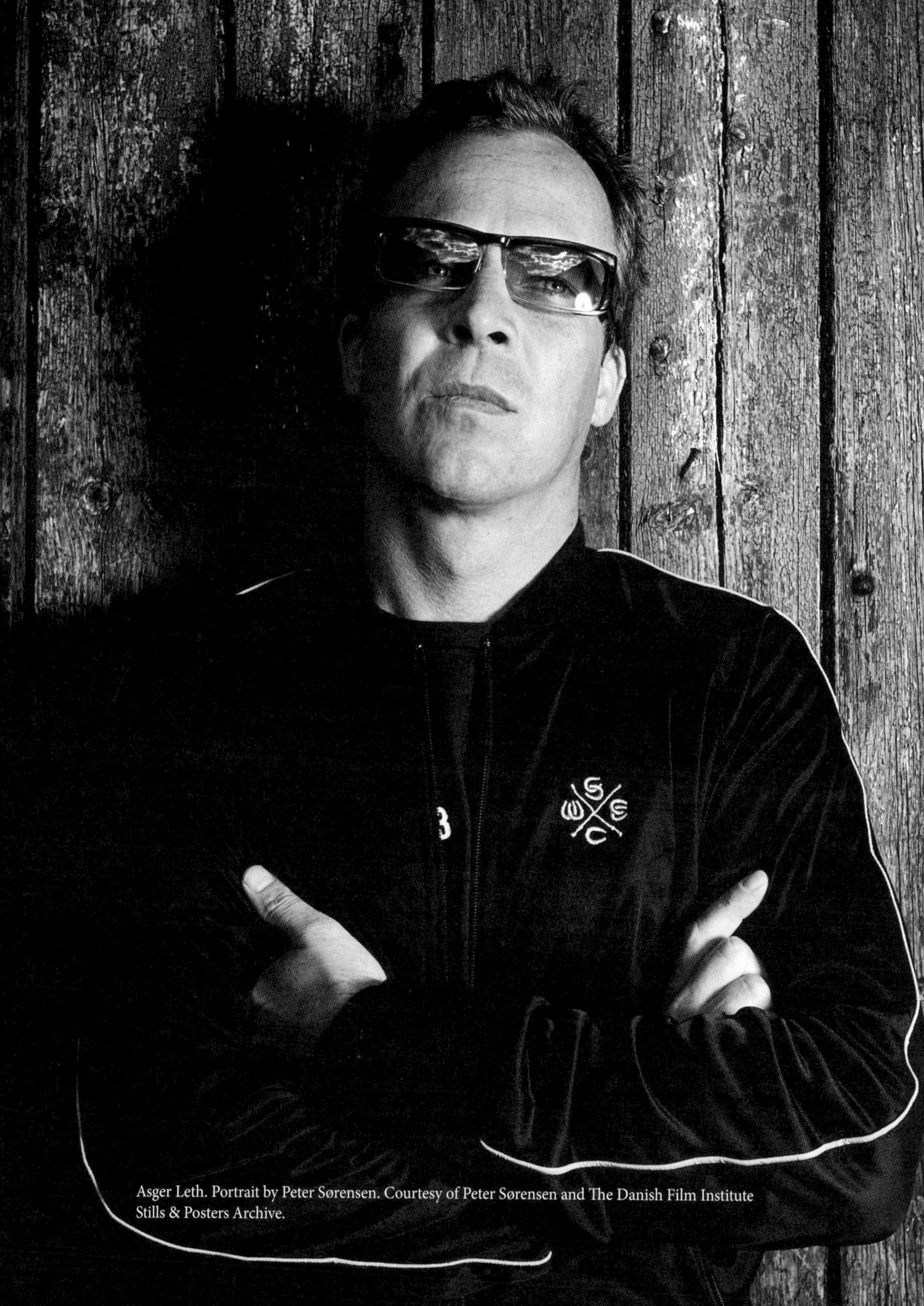

Asger Leth. Portrait by Peter Sørensen. Courtesy of Peter Sørensen and The Danish Film Institute Stills & Posters Archive.

B orn 1970. Asger Leth became involved in the production of music videos and commercials while pursuing a law degree at the University of Copenhagen. He went on to teach at a film and media school in Copenhagen called Rampen, before moving to New York. New York became Asger Leth's base for collaborative work on *Nye scener fra Amerika* (*New Scenes from America*; dir. Jørgen Leth, 2003) and *De fem benspænd* (*The Five Obstructions*; dir. Jørgen Leth and Lars von Trier, 2003). His role in the production of the latter, much acclaimed film – in which von Trier spars with his mentor and former teacher, Jørgen Leth – was significant, and encompassed writing, shooting, and second-unit directing. *Ghosts of Cité Soleil* (2006) was Asger Leth's debut as a documentary filmmaker and won the prestigious Outstanding Directorial Achievement prize from the Directors Guild of America. Shot in Haiti during the politically turbulent period leading up to Jean-Bertrand Aristide's ousting in 2004, *Ghosts of Cité Soleil* provides a personal angle on an intensely political story by focusing on two brothers who were gang leaders and supporters of the then Haitian leader. Asger Leth went on to make *Man on a Ledge* (2012), a big-budget thriller produced by Lorenzo di Bonaventura and Mark Vahradian, starring Sam Worthington, Elizabeth Banks, Anthony Mackie, Jamie Bell, and Ed Harris, among others. Asger Leth is the son of director Jørgen Leth, and film editor and news producer Ann Bierlich. Musician and author Kristian Leth and producer Karoline Leth are his siblings.

Feature films:

2012   *Man on a Ledge*

Documentaries:

2006   *Ghosts of Cité Soleil*

Assistant Director:

2003   *Nye scener fra Amerika* (*New Scenes from America*; dir. Jørgen Leth)
2003   *De fem benspænd* (*The Five Obstructions*; dir. Jørgen Leth and Lars von Trier)

HJORT:

You grew up with film, but you didn't initially see yourself as a filmmaker. The turn to film came via your involvement with the production of commercials, but also, among other things, through collaboration with your father, Jørgen Leth. How would you describe the path that led to your becoming a director?

LETH:

Obviously my father is a big dog in the Danish documentary film world, and in some sense I grew up with documentaries, but in their freest form. There were no boundaries. Something in a notebook could become a documentary. A documentary could be poetry. I mean, the sky was the limit. I guess I never knew that I was going to make any documentaries at all, but my father's understanding of how truly free the genre is has been unloaded on me since early childhood. I always felt that everybody else seemed to have such fixed ideas about what documentaries are. It was usually talking heads and issues – all that stuff – and that actually seemed a bit boring to me. I was never really in love with documentaries. It's like the baker's son who doesn't bake bread. Documentary filmmaking was something I just grew up with. It was part of my daily intake. I was living it, breathing it.

Growing up, I was actually in love with fiction. My best friend when I was growing up was Nicolas Winding Refn, who's also a director now. And his father is Anders Refn, who's a director too. Our parents were all extremely busy; too busy, really, to have kids around all the time. So he would stay at my place while his father was away doing something or other, and I would often stay with him too. And his uncle had the best cinema in all of Denmark, the Grand Cinema. Our parents would just park us in the theatre and we basically spent our childhood watching films non-stop. That was how we grew up. And what we saw was all fiction.

When I was a child, we had a production company, and in the basement we had editing suites. We also had our own cinema. And my father had all these projects on the wall; scenes and ideas on sheets of paper. And when I looked at that wall, as a kid, and at how he'd move the scenes around, it looked like fiction to me. And I had great fun moving things around when he wasn't looking, which he actually never even noticed. He always said that a structure was just an excuse to hang scenes on, so given that context, I suppose, it was fine to move scenes around. For me it became like some fictionalized card game. Also, as a child I'd travel all over the world with my father, to these places where he was doing his shooting. I'd watch him articulate his ideas, and how he'd produce these scenes together with his cameraman. Once again, it all looked like fiction to me. There wasn't anything especially 'real' about it as far as I could tell.

HJORT: It sounds like a pretty fascinating childhood in many ways.

LETH: Yes, I always knew that I loved the life. I loved the freedom, especially the creative freedom. I was fascinated by this business of having an idea and then developing it into something. Also, as a filmmaker you seemed to be able to carve out a life that was anything but ordinary. But then at the same time, you'd work to translate all those experiences into something that could be communicated to people who were living more ordinary lives. That seemed like a weird sort of thing to do, but it was also really fascinating to me.

HJORT: Being the son of one of Denmark's most revered living filmmakers must have been a bit of a mixed blessing at times.

LETH: It's difficult growing up as the son of a prominent filmmaker, especially when you're in your teens or your early twenties, and very vulnerable. As a young child, that relationship had been this great gift, but it became a really heavy burden later on. Also, I felt very conflicted, almost schizophrenic, because I was drawn to both documentaries and fiction films. It was all quite confusing, and at a certain point I just thought, 'To hell with it, I'm going to study law. I'll just do something completely different.' I really doubted my own abilities, and I just wasn't sure whether I had the psychological stamina needed to pursue the burden that it also is to follow in your father's footsteps. Secretly, though, I always thought that I'd find my way back to film. After all, I'd read that all those Hollywood producers were lawyers.

During law school I started helping out with commercials, as well as with some smaller film productions. I worked in all sorts of capacities: as a runner, production assistant, line producer, and so on. Basically, I started making a living doing all this, and it was a lot of fun. So I studied less and less, and worked more and more. I also started working for the Danish TV news – for TV 2 – which was where my mother worked. She was an editor and went on to become head of news production at TV 2. So I was basically having a kind of 'learning by doing' film school experience. But all this work also gave me a convenient excuse for not studying. About one month before by Bachelor's exams, I dropped out of law school. I figured it was time to be true to what I really wanted to do. I finally decided to apply to the National Film School of

Denmark, as an aspiring director, but I didn't get in. Again, sometimes it's not a good thing to be the son of someone prominent. I didn't apply to film school because I felt I needed a lot of teaching. After all, I'd been in a kind of lifelong film school with my very own professor. And the people who would come over for dinner might as well have been guest professors. I applied to the Film School because I realized that, mentally, I needed those four years. What I was attracted to was the free zone that the School represented; a space where you're actually allowed to make mistakes. As the son of a big-name director in Denmark, I didn't feel I'd be allowed to make mistakes unless I had that space to work in.

Within a month of getting rejected, I got a job teaching film instead, at this small film school called Rampen. I was hired to run their film department, which was surreal and really wonderful. It was a fantastic experience. As a teacher, you realize you have a responsibility because you're standing in front of a whole classroom full of students, who are so incredibly eager to learn. And I felt that to be a good teacher I also had to have an opinion about things. During my childhood years, I'd been overloaded with documentaries and fiction films, but I hadn't really started to develop anything like specific tastes, and now I felt compelled to figure out what sorts of films I really loved and why.

HJORT: Is that when you started collaborating with your father?

LETH: Yes. I was in charge of the teaching schedule, so I could work in a few extracurricular things, so to speak. So I worked with my father on *New Scenes from America*, and then there was the creative sparring during the early stages of our thinking about *The Five Obstructions*. During the shooting of *New Scenes from America*, in the summer of 2001, I met this woman in New York. And I was living with her in her apartment in Tribeca, when September 11 happened. It was a very, very heavy experience. And when you've gone through something that heavy together, there's a kind of fateful connection. We seemed bound together, and we ended up getting married, although we didn't actually know each other that well. So I moved to New York and this was when *The Five Obstructions* was really getting underway. I wasn't allowed to work in the States at that point in time, so I was living in New York, but travelling out to work on *The Five Obstructions* together with Jørgen. We collaborated a lot, and it was really great. I did some of the writing, a lot of the shooting, and the second-unit directing.

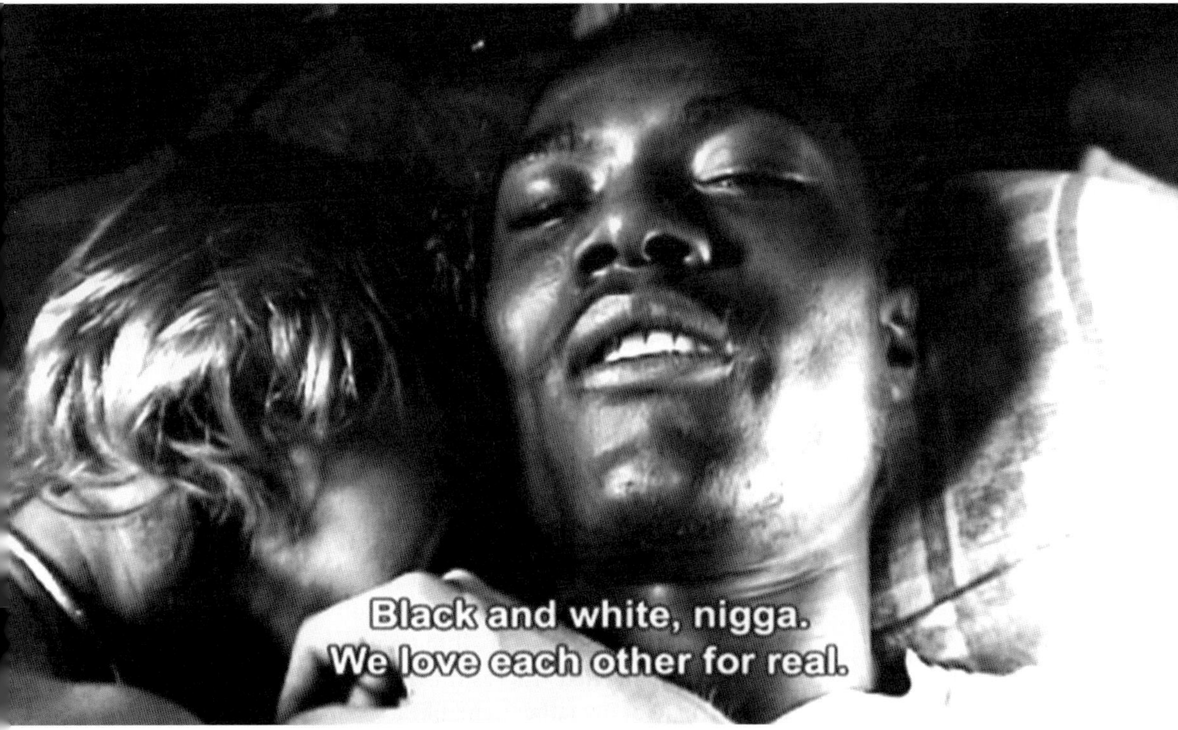

Lele Senlis, a French aid worker in Cité Soleil, becomes involved with 2Pac (*Ghosts of Cité Soleil,* framegrab, cinematography by Miloš Lončarević, Frederik Jacobi and Asger Leth).

We had a lot of fun. By then I was starting to feel a lot more confident about myself as a director, and also about working with my father. I felt we were dancing this dance together, and solving the problems as they came along. And I felt that I could match my father and that I could hold my own. I also realized that *The Five Obstructions* would be the last film I worked on that wasn't my own.

HJORT: So how did you get from *The Five Obstructions* to *Ghosts of Cité Soleil*?

LETH: There was a project I'd been working on for a few years. It was a fiction film that I wanted to shoot in Haiti, where I've spent a lot of time with my father over the years. I had this idea of taking a bunch of actors and virtually dumping them in the middle of the rainforest, and then shooting the film with a documentary size crew. I won't tell you the story, as I might still do it some day. It was becoming more and more difficult to do the necessary research in Haiti because of all these gangs. And then this freak connection happened. There's this French woman in Haiti, who's a good friend of my father's and like a second mother to me. She'd met this other French woman, Lele Senlis, who was an aid worker working in Cité Soleil, and it was clear that she had access to the gangs. I thought, 'There's a fantastic story here.'

There's a cyclical aspect to the politics of Haiti, and if you know the place well, you know that once a political uprising starts, whoever is in power will eventually get ousted. Whatever the nature of the uprising, it gets additional fuel from this shared knowledge that people have about where things are headed. I realized that there were these gang leaders in Cité Soleil who were doing their own thing, but also working for this president, Aristide, who wasn't going to be there any more in a matter of months. That was an epiphanic moment for me. The idea of documentary film as essentially free in terms of its form suddenly collided beautifully with that powerful structure that I knew from fiction films. Here was this unique story. It was unfolding in Haiti before my eyes. And I knew the structure, the time frame, and the ending. It was truly incredible and there was no way I was going to let it go. I'd been searching all my life, and I'd had so much trouble finding a way to break through, a way of following in my father's footsteps, and then suddenly I felt like I'd found the key to it all. I actually felt like I'd found the key to my life. I realized I could marry my passion for the hard-driven structure of fiction movies with the passion I had for reality and real characters, and that I could also make all this a unique opportunity for myself. Psychologically, I knew that making a film like that in Haiti, on my father's turf so to speak, was equivalent to my putting all of my father's work up against my own, and with one stroke of the pen, saying, 'Yes, I can make my own movies, and no, I am not my father.' I was going to make that film on his territory, and it was going to be unlike anything he'd ever made or ever would make. That was very important to me psychologically.

I eventually flew back to Denmark, to talk to my bank and to get the equipment together. I financed the film myself initially, and then got some money from other sources later on. So it was all very low-budget. I brought along a 16mm camera and several DV cameras. I'd never shot 16mm before. So before leaving Denmark, I had this friend of mine, Frederik Jacobi, over to my apartment. He's a cinematographer and he taught me how to use a 16mm camera in one night. So I was running around in the middle of these violent demonstrations in Haiti, shooting with this 16mm camera. I had no idea whether there was anything on the film. Meanwhile, the French woman, Lele, had this Serbian boyfriend, Miloš Lončarević, and I taught him how to shoot, and then Frederik Jacobi came over, so we had three people with cameras. Lele introduced me to the two gang leaders, and I wrote a synopsis after I'd talked to them and had gotten some sense of who they were. The outline I wrote basically matched what happened. The only thing that was completely unexpected was that love affair in the middle between Lele and 2Pac. I had no idea that was going to happen.

HJORT: *Ghosts of Cité Soleil* has won any number of awards, including a prestigious Outstanding Directorial Achievement prize from the Directors Guild of America. Werner Herzog is said to have praised the film because he saw a new 'grammar of film' in it.[1] The film's formal qualities no doubt provide reasons for its success, but it seems clear that the many awards also pay tribute to something else entirely: the risks that you and your two other cinematographers, Miloš Lončarević and Frederik Jacobi, were willing to take in order to tell a remarkable story. What did your deliberations about risk look like during the shooting of *Ghosts of Cité Soleil*?

LETH: I'm not an Indiana Jones kind of guy. But that film was like finding the key to my life, so I had to do it no matter what. Also, I didn't give a shit about my life at the time. I'd just been through a divorce, and I was seeing a shrink because I was extremely depressed. I was basically having a break down when the idea for the film occurred to me. So my thinking was basically, guns swinging and I don't care if I die. I hoped I wouldn't die. Or, to be honest, I'm not even sure that's true. The thing is that the brothers really wanted to tell their story. They were in their early twenties, they knew they were probably going to die, and they wanted to tell their story almost more than I wanted to tell it. So they were instantly on, and that's what made the film possible. Yes, it was dangerous, but we were shooting from day one. In some ways it was easy because they were desperate to tell their story and I was desperate to tell it. And the attitude I had about the physical risks basically carried over to the financial side of things too. I borrowed as much money as I could from my own bank, and I basically wagered everything I personally had on the film. In terms of the money, I just thought, 'Well, if I don't end up with a film, I'll just move to Jamaica and become a bartender.' So I was really willing to risk everything.

But I felt like a hustler. I hustled the bank, and I also had to do a lot of hustling in Haiti, or at least that's what it felt like, because so many of the situations I found myself in were so ambiguous. And that ambiguity had to do with the escalating violence. For example, I was living in this hotel where all the journalists and foreign correspondents were. These were war reporters who suddenly found themselves caught up in a story that had become far more violent than they'd ever expected. They thought they were going to Haiti to cover some demonstrations, not the ousting of Aristide. And we were all stuck there because the airport was next to Cité Soleil, and the gangs would shoot at the planes. The gangs would beat people up, chop them to pieces with machetes – and they also went after journalists. Meanwhile, I was living with all these reporters, and at the same time I was driving down the mountain to go into Cité Soleil every day. I knew the gangs, and I knew the gang leaders, so I was playing a bit of a double game because I was pretending I didn't know them. And that was all quite difficult.

HJORT: You were interacting with the gang leaders, with 2Pac and Bily. Both were killers and their relationship to each other was highly unstable. That must have brought further complexity to the situation.

LETH: Yes, while shooting the film I found myself stuck in the middle of something as old school as a brotherly quarrel. These guys were killers, but they were also so different and so unique that in their disputes and in their differences, willingly or unwillingly, I started to see them as people. We almost became friends, although I had to try to maintain a certain distance. In fact, I had to maintain that distance, but there were also moments when I had to take sides. Or, at the very least, there were times when I thought, 'If this were another world, I'd probably be friends with him, but not that guy.' 2Pac was probably the more brutal of the two brothers. He'd killed a lot of people, but he felt remorse and stopped killing, and then his brother took over. I always knew that 2Pac had the potential to be a real animal, and I was forced to be in the same room with him knowing he was a murderer. But he'd stopped killing; he was full of remorse and he'd started making music. So I found myself focusing on the remorse, and that made him very human. He also had a good sense of humour, and I actually quite liked him. I did not like his younger brother, Bily, as much, because he was ice cold. He was the real killer. The difference between 2Pac and his brother was that Bily enjoyed it. He liked it. And that's the danger with ideology: it provides such an excuse for killing. There are a lot of cold killers to be found in the history of ideology. Bily is one of them. I did take sides, and it was difficult not to, but at the same time it was important to push those personal inclinations away, and not to let them interfere with the work we were doing. It was quite difficult.

HJORT: A lot of what you've been saying, both about your interaction with journalists at the hotel and with the brothers, raises some pretty difficult ethical issues. It seems like *Ghosts of Cité Soleil* was a project fraught with all sorts of ethical conundrums.

LETH: Yes, definitely. In fact, there are so many levels to the ethical discussion about documentary filmmaking in this case that it's hard to know where to begin. But let's just start with my own aspirations as a documentary filmmaker. I want to make a film, and that's already a problem. I go to Haiti, and I want to make this film because I see it as somehow providing the key to my life. So I'm willing to go very far, and I definitely want something. A lot of documentary filmmakers have a tendency to think in terms of truth, history, freedom, issues, and so on, but that way of looking at things isn't entirely accurate. We have to acknowledge our own ambition. A documentary isn't driven by some straightforward desire to tell the truth. I think that sort of reasoning is bullshit. The world needs films that tell stories about reality, where there's an aspiration towards truth. Those sorts of films are really important. But I don't buy this idea of the documentary filmmaker as someone who's nailed to the holy cross, and busy sacrificing himself for the greater good. If you're a documentary filmmaker and you're making these films for a living, you're basically roaming the world and scouring the surface of continents in search of stories that you can tell. And the search for those stories is also about feeding yourself, paying your rent or mortgage, buying clothes, and so on. So let's not pretend that those things aren't part of the picture. It's not like these filmmakers make a documentary when the next story jumps out at them, and then they wait until another story jumps out at them. The filmmakers are like parasites, jumping from one subject to the next. And I'm glad they do precisely that because otherwise we'd never see those stories. And they're good stories. But let's be honest about what's going on.

As someone who grew up with documentary filmmaking, I felt that I knew the rules of what to do and what not to do very well. Those rules were part of the grammar of a kind of mother tongue that I felt I spoke. I had this powerful realization that if you're dealing with a story that's actually about real life, if you're making a documentary, then truth is your most important weapon or tool. That's the bottom line, and if you start meddling with that in any way, shape or form *while* you're shooting – and I underline 'while' – then you end up with nothing. As a director, you're really lost if you do that. And if the director is lost, then everything falls apart, because you won't be able to tell what's right or wrong any more. That means the people in front of the lens won't know what's right or wrong either. You just can't start interfering with people's lives. I know that some directors do exactly that, but I think it's really dangerous, and I would never do it.

Let me give you an example. 2Pac was making music as a way of distancing himself from Aristide, and the gangs, and all the violence. His dream was to get in contact with Wyclef Jean. I could have given him what he wanted because I knew people who knew Wyclef, but I didn't. In fact, I didn't even tell him I had those contacts, because if I had, I would have been interfering with life. Fortunately, what happened was that 2Pac was recording his music in this studio where he met another rapper, who happened to know Wyclef. So thank goodness 2Pac found Wyclef himself. After 2Pac had spoken to Wyclef on the phone, I felt that *I* could contact Wyclef myself. I didn't know him, but I knew people who did.

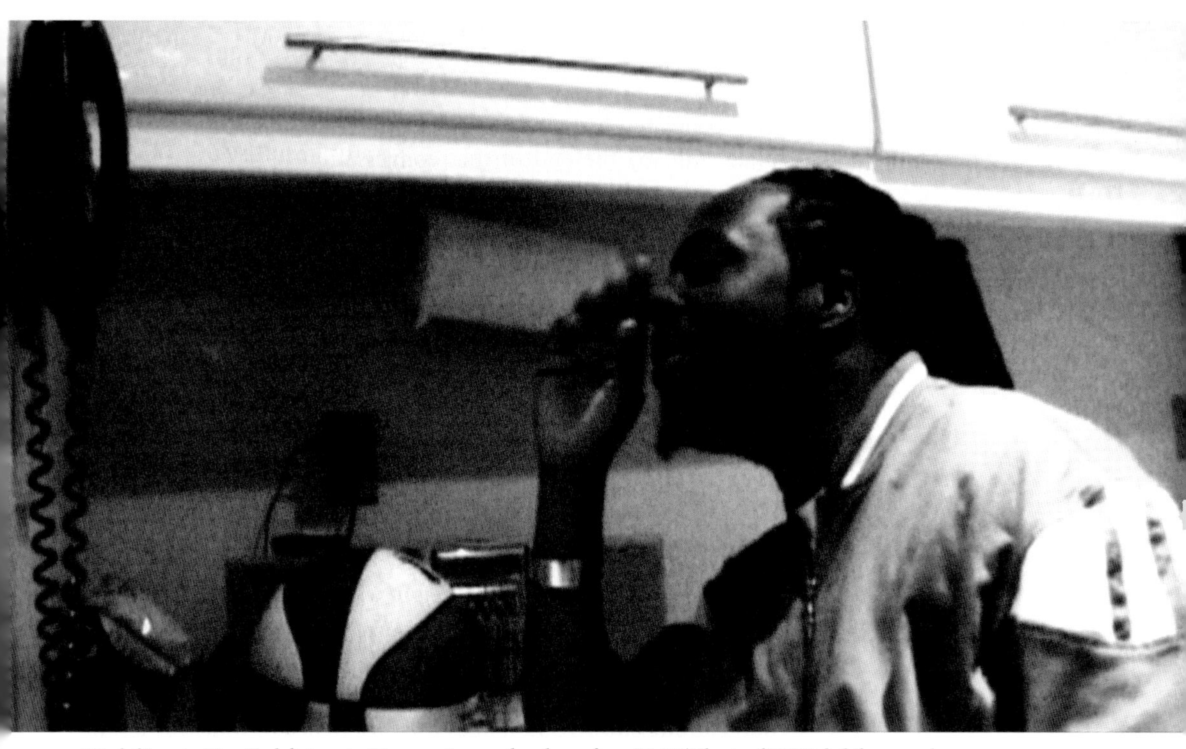

Wyclef Jean in New York listens to 2Pac rapping on the phone from Haiti (*Ghosts of Cité Soleil*, framegrab, cinematography by Miloš Lončarević, Frederik Jacobi and Asger Leth).

So I contacted him and talked about that phone call and about 2Pac. And by the end of that conversation he was saying, 'I'm coming to Haiti tomorrow. I want to meet that guy.' So they met, and it was great. They were jamming and talking music, and Wyclef was going to try to help 2Pac. And I tagged along and shot all that.

For me, there has to be truth during the shooting. But afterwards, I'm willing to cut corners here and there to make the story better. For example, there were actually two phone calls between Wyclef and 2Pac, but I realized that I couldn't include both in the film. And when we did the editing, we ended up with just one conversation, so there was clearly an ethical dilemma because the editing wasn't entirely truthful. But in the grand march of 2Pac's life, what's depicted in the film *is* what happened. As I see it, my most important task as a director is to work ethically and truthfully to deliver a film that's the closest version of the truth as we felt and experienced it. Because we have to capture that truth on camera and with microphones and so on, there's always a filter, and that waters things down and makes the experience of watching a film less than the actual lived experience. I'm willing to go quite far in my films to try and push things back towards what the actual experience *felt* like when we were standing there because that's what's true. That feeling is what's true.

HJORT: *Ghosts of Cité Soleil* appears to have been an intensely collaborative project, with roles being defined in response to changing circumstances. Jerry 'Wonda' Duplessis and Wyclef Jean are credited for the film's original music and original score. Wyclef Jean's company, Sak Pase Films, Inc., is one of the film's producers. One of the most moving scenes in the film is the one you just referred to, which shows 2Pac on the phone with Jean, singing a song that the aspiring rapper wrote himself ('The Life of Our Youth'). The film concludes with images of Wyclef Jean singing about Cité Soleil in a way that questions the established view of it as one of the most dangerous places on earth. Why was it important for you to involve Wyclef Jean more fully in your film?

LETH: After his trip to Haiti, Wyclef returned to New York, but kept in touch with 2Pac. The shooting was done, so I returned to Denmark to work on the editing, and meanwhile 2Pac went to the Dominican Republic, and then back to Haiti when Bily got in trouble. All along, Wyclef was trying to get 2Pac to the States. People think that because you're a big time whatever, you can just do whatever you want, but you can't. If you're dealing with someone from gangland, good luck. So 2Pac, who'd been stranded in the Dominican Republic, ended up going back to Haiti, where he was shot and died. That had a huge impact on Wyclef, who then decided to put money into the film, and who also decided he wanted to provide music for it. I felt that his music would bring a lot to the film. Among other things, it would give it a chance at a wider audience. So Wyclef and I agreed that he would be involved in scoring the film and in financing it. But I have to say that our agreement brought a whole new set of problems with it.

HJORT: What sorts of problems?

LETH: It's difficult with a production process like that because you're bringing together two very different filmmaking traditions. In our world, there's government support for film. I'd put my own money into *Ghosts of Cité Soleil*, but at a later stage I'd also received some government support through the Film Institute. The Danish system is basically one that gives the director a lot of freedom and control. Suddenly there was this American company in the picture, and it had a pretty powerful sense of ownership, I have to say. We got into a lot of fights. We worked it out, but it was tough.

HJORT: Could you give one example of something contentious?

LETH: We fought a lot about the music. For example, how much music was there going to be in the film? For Wyclef, music is an obsession. He *loves* his music. I also love his music, and he actually happens to be one of my favourite musicians. But in this particular case, I was making a film and I was interested in getting the emotions right. There's a huge difference between a film score and a series of hits. And however much I love the man and respect him, as a musician he didn't always get that difference. The first thing he showed up with was a compilation of five of his hits. These were hits, not a film score, and so I was like, 'We can't do that. This is not an MTV thing, this is a film.' He slowly came around, but it wasn't easy.

HJORT: As a documentary filmmaker, what's your take on the audience issue?

LETH: There's an inherent problem in documentary filmmaking. 99 per cent of the time documentaries are seen by the already initiated, by people who are already aware of the issues. So whom are you really making the film for? I don't want to make films for people who already know much of what there is to know about something. In the case of *Ghosts of Cité Soleil*, I wanted to make a documentary about a news topic, about this rebellion that would eventually lead to the ousting of a political leader. But I wanted to provide a personal angle on this topic, and that's where the story of these two brothers came in. The personal angle allowed me to get under the skin of the political problem, so that the political story got exposed, but in a way that also downplayed it. The political story is there because it's part of the real story about 2Pac and Bily. But the news story is subordinated to their more personal story. And if you go about making your documentary in this way, you just might end up drawing an audience that wouldn't normally see a documentary about the news story in question. At least that's how I see it. And, for me, that's what it's all about. If you're interested in documentaries as a means of fostering awareness, then you have to try to reach the people who aren't already in the know.

Sometimes, I feel there are two separate universes: one inhabited by directors who make fiction features, and one by directors who make documentaries. And these directors could actually learn a lot from each other. One thing documentary filmmakers could learn from that other world – where films have to sell tickets – is that it's actually a very good idea to think and care about your audience while you're making the film. A lot of documentaries are, for example, simply too long, which is ultimately a form of self-indulgence. And that's a real pity because excessive length can really weaken an otherwise strong and important film.

HJORT: *Ghosts of Cité Soleil* opened a lot of doors for you. Your second film, *Man on a Ledge*, is a big-budget thriller. What was it about this particular project that appealed to you?

LETH: I have to say that I went to Hollywood to make another film called *Cartel*, which was about the drug cartels in Mexico. I was supposed to shoot it in Mexico, and Sean Penn was to have been in it. It was a pretty gritty story, so in that sense there was more of a direct connection between *Ghosts of Cité Soleil* and the film that was supposed to have been my first production with a major Hollywood studio. But over the course of the two and a half years that it took to get ready to start shooting, things became more and more dangerous in Mexico, more and more explosive. So five weeks before we were supposed to start shooting, the film was cut and I found myself stuck in a hotel in Hollywood. I'd sacrificed a lot in order to be there. I'd been away from Denmark, where my family and friends were, much longer than expected. And I'd invested every cent I'd earned making commercials. But when the film fell apart I simply decided to double down the money, so to speak. I wasn't going to give up, because there was too much water under the bridge, and I felt I had to have something to show for it all. So I kept plugging away and I read a lot of scripts. When I read the script for *Man on a Ledge*, I felt that in someone else's hands it might become a glossy or slick film, but that I just might be able to bring some real life to it. As a director, it's important always to ask yourself what *you* specifically can give the material that nobody else can bring to the film. I'm a big fan of films like *Dog Day Afternoon* (dir. Sidney Lumet, 1975), and I miss those films. With the script for *Man on a Ledge*, I felt there was something there, and that it had the potential to become a New York event.

HJORT: How do you see your future?

LETH: The process of making *Man on a Ledge* was great, although it was also overwhelming and scary at times. I was basically telling the whole world that I could just go to Hollywood and make a giant movie. I know that a lot of people didn't believe it. Denmark is a very small country, and you know how we like to pick at each other here. And then there's this snobbism when it comes to American film. I love a lot of European cinema, but when American cinema works, I love that more. I just do. I'm more entertained, and I'm not afraid to say that. So that's where I want to go with my filmmaking because I think the possibilities are quite simply thicker. I'm not interested in making some small Dogma film about something that takes place in a basement somewhere here.

I'm going to make another film in the States, for sure. Perhaps several. Right now, I see myself as focusing mainly on fiction, but I'm not burying documentaries, because I love documentaries. But I don't want to become one of those filmmakers who makes a living that way. I'm not putting down those who do, but it's just not for me. I have to let the story find me, and when that happens I'll make another documentary. And I can't wait, but it has to hit me. I can imagine hoping to make two or three fiction features and then a documentary, and then two or three features and then a documentary. But right now I'm definitely going to make another feature film.

HJORT: A lot of Danish filmmakers have had real problems making the transition to Hollywood. How do you explain the ease with which you were able to make that move?

LETH: I've been going to the States with my father ever since I was a kid because he's shot a lot of his films there. I think I understand

Americans a lot better than most Danes do. So, for one thing, I'm less afraid of them. But there's another factor, and that is that there's a cramp in how Danish filmmakers approach American film traditions. There's a lot of snobbism, and this sense that working within the American film industry means losing your artistic integrity. And I think that's bullshit. I also think you can become obsessed with artistic integrity. I'd rather take a more relaxed approach and trust my artistic integrity. I think a lot of Danish directors have problems trusting their artistic integrity in that other context, and so they push back, and then the people on the other end do the same. It becomes a struggle, and you'll never get a happy marriage. Danish directors tend to focus on the disputes before they even get to them. The thing is precisely *not* to go into the trenches ready to fight for your artistic integrity. You need to drop the fists, to go in there with your head held high, and to trust that your artistic integrity is going to be visible in the final film. If you don't create the fight, there just might never be one. Because at the end of the day, the people you're working with in the States actually want something from you too, otherwise they would have hired someone out of Kansas City.

Note

1   Jørgen Leth, 'En umulig film,' *Information* (25 July 2007). www.information.dk/132063.

Chapter 12

Janus Metz

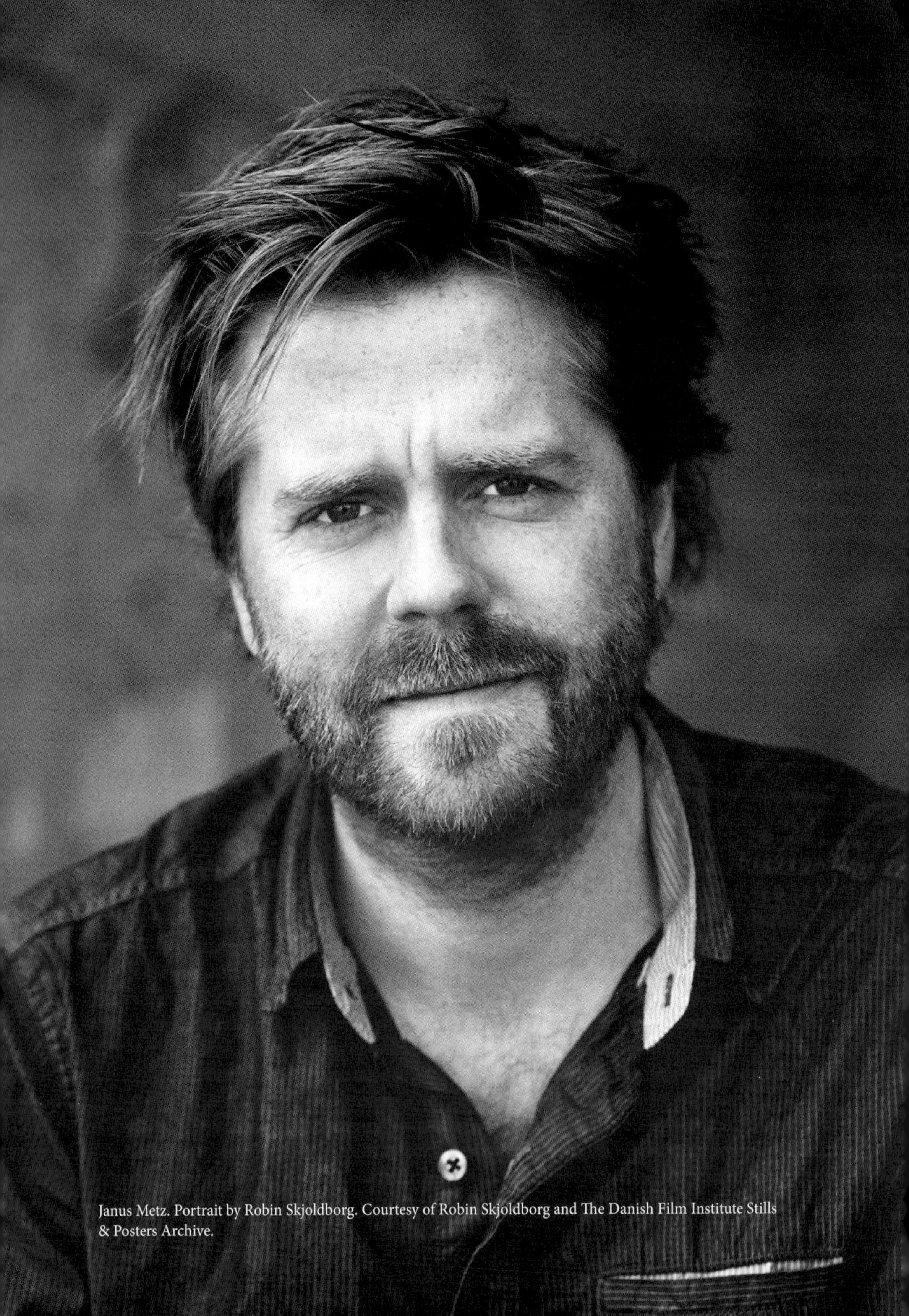

Janus Metz. Portrait by Robin Skjoldborg. Courtesy of Robin Skjoldborg and The Danish Film Institute Stills & Posters Archive.

Born 1974. Metz holds a Master's degree in Communications (with a minor in International Development Studies) from Roskilde University (RUC). As part of his degree programme, he spent a year in South Africa (2002–03). With his academic background, Janus Metz has managed to establish himself as one of the most promising members of a younger generation of Danish documentary filmmakers within a very short period of time. To date, all of his films have been defined by a clear interest in global problems. This interest in global issues is a constant feature of Metz's filmmaking, whether it finds expression in explorations of the relation between national space and globalization, or in clearly developed international themes. His first film, *Township Boys* (2006), grew out of his experiences in South Africa, and depicts the lives of a group of young people living in one of the townships. His next film, *Eventyrerne* (*Clandestine*, 2007), about the dangerous journeys undertaken through Africa by Africans who are eventually classified as illegal immigrants in Europe, explores themes and subject matters with a clear global dimension. Metz achieved a major breakthrough with the two interrelated films entitled *Fra Thailand til Thy* (*Love on Delivery*, 2008) and *Fra Thy til Thailand* (*Ticket to Paradise*, 2008), where a global theme is linked to specific national contexts. The films are about the relationship between men living in the northernmost part of rural Jutland in Denmark, and Thai women. With its anthropological, observational approach, these films offer an insightful account of a reality that has typically been grasped through stereotypes. The two films have been shown on TV on a number of occasions, and also drew large numbers to the cinemas. *Love on Delivery* won two GuldDoks at CPH:DOX. Metz greatly consolidated his status as a major contemporary documentary filmmaker with *Armadillo* (2010), which was seen by 150,000 cinemagoers, the second highest number for a documentary film since 1960. When shown on Danish TV, this film – about the deployment of Danish troops in Afghanistan – was seen by almost 1 million viewers. The film won the Grand Prix at the 'Semaine de la Critique' at the Cannes Film Festival in 2010, and went on to win a lot of international prizes, and to enjoy wide international distribution. As a documentary filmmaker Metz favours an observational style, and consistently demonstrates an exceptional ability to offer viewers an intimate experience of the realities he depicts. Metz also pays considerable attention to the aesthetic and dramaturgical aspects of his films. As a result, his films offer both a rich visual and narrative style, and great documentary authenticity.

Documentary features:

2010   *Armadillo* (as well as a shorter, 58-minute version for TV 2)
2008   *Fra Thy til Thailand* (*Ticket to Paradise*)
2008   *Fra Thailand til Thy* (*Love on Delivery*)

Documentary shorts:

2006   *Township Boys*

Short fiction:

2011   *Rupture* (with Christina Hamre)

Television:

2007   *Eventyrerne* (*Clandestine*)

BONDEBJERG: You have an academic background, which is somewhat unusual for a film director. Yet, your degree in Communications and International Development Studies has no doubt played a role in your filmmaking, in the sense that global issues are central to your work. How do you see the relationship between your academic background and your path as a filmmaker?

METZ: In Denmark, a filmmaker with a university background may be unusual, in part because we have such an excellent film school. But elsewhere in the world, my kind of background wouldn't seem unusual at all. In Denmark, there's almost a tendency, at least in the creative art milieus, to see academic training as a potential threat to creativity. But my university studies gave me an incredibly strong foundation, even though I found the actual experience of being at university frustrating, and certainly couldn't see myself as working in public relations or as a communications officer. My father is a painter and I've always had a creative side, which I was intent on developing, even when I was pursuing a more academic path. In terms of film, a lot of that development took place at the Film Workshop towards the end of my studies, and in the context of practical projects at RUC. I was intrigued by social themes because I could bring analytic skills from my university background to bear on them, and because they offered a way of connecting with this capacity I have for articulating things through images. The two dimensions of my identity somehow came together and became mutually enriching. Because of my academic training I find that I'm able to outline the broad strokes of the stories I want to tell very quickly and clearly, whereas other directors may initially have to work on the basis of a gut feeling or just an interest that they have in a particular character. My first films found a starting point in social themes and analysis, whereas my more recent films focus more on the psychological or mythological issues that help to explain social and global themes. I've engaged with big global themes in just about every project I've undertaken, but usually in a way that involves looking at how people deal with them and interpret them in a specific regional or local context.

BONDEBJERG:	You didn't go to film school, but as you've already suggested, you did acquire some film training in other ways. How exactly did you start making films?
METZ:	During my studies I did an internship with an organization in South Africa called Soul City that produces TV series in a social realistic vein. Before then, I made a small documentary film about integration issues for a Communications project at RUC. But the internship in South Africa in 2002–03 was my first really substantial experience of film and TV production. I remember my time in Johannesburg as an encounter with a country and a city with enormous political and creative resources, but also enormous social conflicts. There were the more affluent neighbourhoods on the one hand, and then there were the poor, crime-ridden neighbourhoods on the other hand. The series that I was involved in was the first South African series to deal with social issues in the townships that was targeted at and seen from the perspective of township audiences.

It inspired my first film, *Township Boys*, which took me to some very violent places that in every way were very distant from the university world I'd known. It was really learning by doing as far as the technical aspects of filmmaking were concerned. I got the equipment I needed from the Film Workshop. But the experience of making that film was also an incredible eye-opener because it introduced me to a completely different reality. The film was very much a low-budget film, with a budget of about 50,000 Danish Crowns for absolutely everything. Sisyphuz Film, which was owned by an Englishman called Arun Sharma, who lived in

Denmark, was to help with the actual shooting, as was my good friend Rasmus Steen, who was doing radio productions for the Danish Broadcasting Corporation [DR] at the time. It took four years to make that film. It was a deeply personal project and I learnt a lot from it. In a way, it was a kind of film school project because it taught me absolutely everything, starting with the basics. Among other things, it took me eight months to edit the film because I didn't have the experience I needed, or the concepts for what I was trying to do. During that period I also spent a bit of time at Haslund Film, and as an intern with Cosmo Doc. That all became a kind of extended apprenticeship for me because I was given the opportunity to work as an assistant for Max Kestner and Anders Østergaard, among others. When I think about *Township Boys* today, I see it as an authentic and very classic observational documentary film that actually has a lot of fine qualities, especially considering the circumstances under which it was made. Unfortunately, it hasn't really been screened much, and it wasn't purchased by any of the TV stations. CPH:DOX has screened it, and the Danish Film Institute [DFI] has been involved in trying to distribute it. It's been shown at a handful of film festivals, but that's pretty much it.

BONDEBJERG: Your next film also has Africa as both its context and theme. *Clandestine*, which you made for DR, tells a very violent story about illegal immigrants. How did you end up making that film?

METZ: One thing that happened as a result of my first film was that I decided to become a director. Jakob Høgel's encouragement also played a role. Høgel played an important role in the founding of the production company Cosmo Doc in 2003, and the whole environment at Cosmo Doc was an absolute powerhouse of talent. Anders Østergaard, Max Kestner, Jeppe Rønde, Christoffer Guldbrandsen, and many others were all involved in that milieu, so it was an incredibly inspiring place. *Clandestine* built on my experiences in Africa, and was motivated by my interest in these illegal immigrants, who risked absolutely everything to get to Europe. I got a grant from Danida to support my research, and I also took some scriptwriting courses. The concept was that these people call themselves adventurers, whereas we call them illegal immigrants. I was interested in the conflict between those two conceptions, which is also a cultural conflict. And then, of course, there was the film's very basic drama of life and death. I managed, along with a friend called Christian Vium, who was helping me

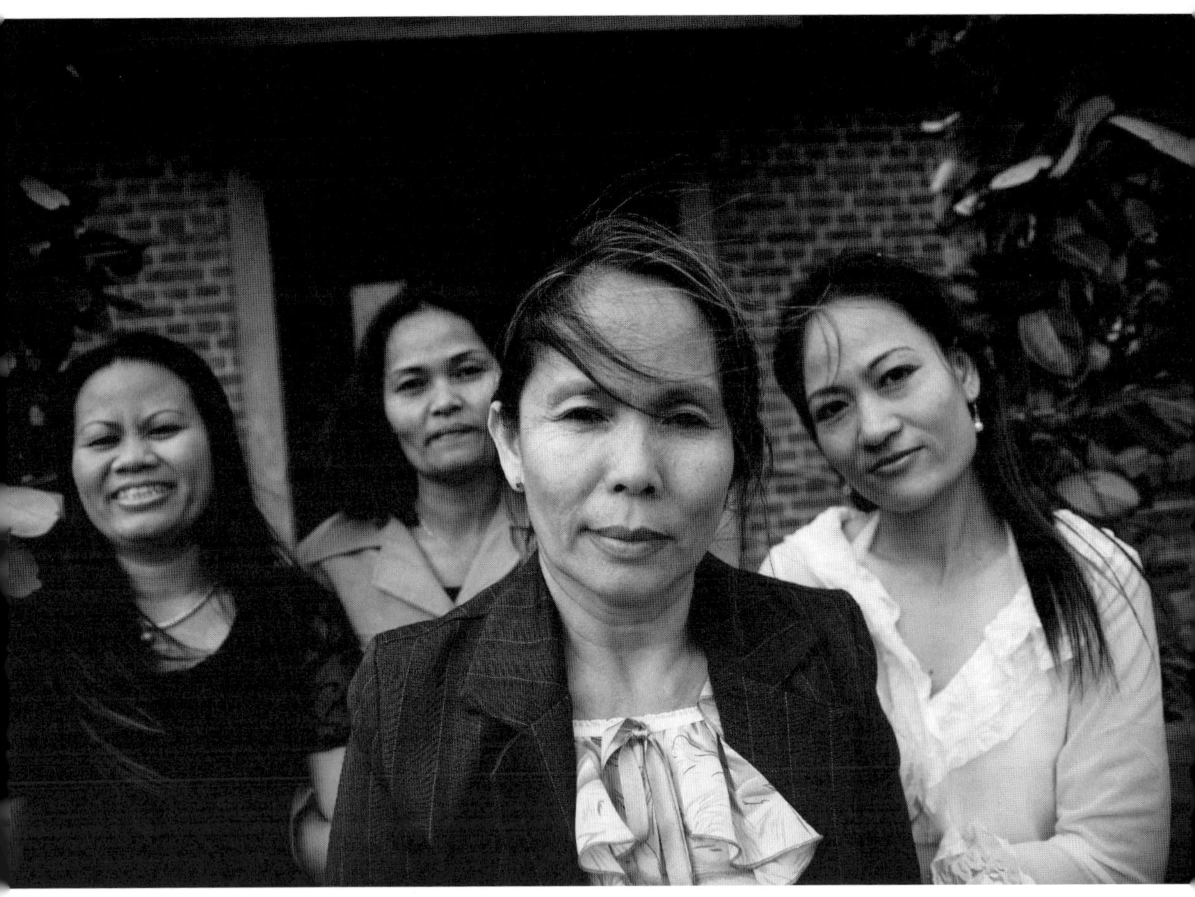

Strong Thai women with a problematic background find a new life in Denmark (*Love on Delivery*, photo: Henrik Bohn Ipsen. Courtesy of Janus Metz and Henrik Bohn Ipsen).

shoot the film, to get included in a human trafficking operation. We were actually captured and had a Kalashnikov rifle shoved into our faces. It was actually very dangerous, and we ended up having to escape under the cover of a sandstorm. I actually think that one of the reasons I was able to cope with what was involved in shooting *Armadillo* in Afghanistan was that I'd experienced all that, and had somehow miraculously survived it. When we got home and looked at what we'd shot, we realized that it was going to be too difficult and dangerous to go back and shoot the full-length film that we had initially set out to do research for. We showed Kim Bildsø at DR the material we had, and *Clandestine* then ended up being broadcast as a 28-minute documentary short and as a special edition of DR's *Horisont*.

BONDEBJERG: You achieved a major breakthrough with your next two films, *Love on Delivery* and *Ticket to Paradise*. These films are closely related, and essentially the result of one integrated project. *Love on Delivery* won two GuldDok awards at the CPH:DOX festival, the films were shown on TV and seen by several million viewers, and they went on to be seen by many more viewers at film festivals all around the world. Both films are also available on DVD. In a sense these two related films bridge the worlds of TV and film in a way that people in both milieus have been able to affirm. They are powerful, probing works, in part because they show how certain global and sub-national perspectives are inextricably linked. Where did the idea for these two films come from?

METZ: I met my current partner, Sine Plambech, when I was making *Clandestine*. Sine is an anthropologist, and a lot of her work has focused on Thai immigrants in Denmark, especially women. She was a huge source of inspiration for both of these films. The work that she'd done with the Thai community in Jutland, and the contacts she had with that milieu, were absolutely crucial. I simply couldn't have made the films without her work and her networks. The films are based on her anthropological fieldwork and are, in a sense, adaptations of it. The story told in these films isn't actually that different from the one in *Clandestine*, except for the Danish angle on things. It was that angle that made the project description so interesting to the people at DR, who saw prime-time material in it. The project involved a lot more money and a lot more oversight than anything I'd ever done before. Also, if we were going to pay everyone what we owed them, we'd have only about a week left for the research, and about 25 days for the actual shooting. So that was quite demanding. Fortunately though, Sine had worked in the milieu for three years, which meant that she knew absolutely everyone, and also knew a lot about the people's lives. I found that I ended up developing a much more professional cinematic language as a result of working within a new institutional framework and context of production. I really had to make sure that the different scenes worked and had a structure. This is also why I ended up with a much more professional team. I had two cinematographers: first Lars Skree, and then later Henrik Ipsen as well. And I worked closely with the producers, Jesper Jack and Henrik Veileborg. With the help of Sine's research and knowledge, and with support from Jesper Jack, I was able to develop a manuscript centred on the story of a wedding involving clearly defined characters and certain relationships. Lars and I then worked together to define the look of the film and the cinematographic aspect of the scenes. All this preparatory work, combined with Sine's thorough research, produced a very rapid response to our request for money, both from the DFI and DR. So we basically went straight into production. We were given a lot of freedom and people at both the DFI and at DR had a lot of confidence in us.

The people at Cosmo Doc, on the other hand, were perhaps a little worried about whether we'd be able to deliver prime-time material with a relatively untested director driving things. That's probably why we developed a really detailed script for our story. We were quite inspired by the way Max Kestner had worked on *Nede på jorden* (*Blue Collar White Christmas*, 2004). We came up with clearly defined characters and plot lines, but we also had a very thorough, analytic understanding of the reality we wanted to depict. As a result, we were able to tell a very universal story, but also to provide a very concrete and intimate description of a reality about which there's a lot of prejudice. There's a tendency to see these women as victims and the men as villains, but the truth is of course far more complicated than that. So we saw ourselves as demythologizing something that feminists in the West and people from the middle-class, among others, have a lot of trouble understanding and accepting. The films show globalization at work in a very concrete, human, and everyday life setting. They show us the face of globalization in a kind of close-up, framed on an intimate stage, and without prejudice or moral preconceptions.

BONDEBJERG: Your films feature very clearly developed characters and scenes, but are also characterized by a very expressive visual style. You really do a lot with the visual environments of your films, moving back and forth between very panoramic shots and indoor scenes, with extreme close-ups focusing on your characters. How would you describe the visual style you've developed in partnership with Lars Skree, among others?

METZ:
I am of course interested in depicting places as geographic – both physical and social spaces – but cinematic spaces are often interesting because they embody meanings and a certain symbolic dimension. In the films focusing on Thy, place is depicted in a way that evokes vast expanses, emptiness, and longing; the point being to suggest that, as human beings, we will always be insignificant in relation to the big existential questions. The idea of people dwarfed by a vast sky and horizon provides a kind of mental and existential landscape. The cinematographic approach that I adopt with the cinematographers I work with is actually inspired by fiction films, much more than by documentary films. The use of space and visual style is often very precise in fiction films. For example, the concluding scene in *Love on Delivery*, in which they drive off after the wedding, is pretty much directly lifted from the last moments of *The Graduate* (dir. Mike Nichols, 1967), where the characters escape into a vast expanse and to a new life.

BONDEBJERG:
Music, indeed sound more generally, also plays a very important role in your films. Your interest in exploring the expressive dimensions of the visual is matched by your interest in making good use of music and sound when the reality your story explores warrants it. What's your position on music and sound in the documentary film?

METZ:
What I really like to do in my depiction of reality is to get beneath the surface of an apparent reality to a deeper psychological level. Sound and music have a precision in that regard because they encompass mood and feeling. Music and visual style can help to articulate the underlying story, so that you begin to get at psychological space, and at the much more universal and human dimensions of things. *Love on Delivery* tells a very concrete documentary story, but the way in which that story is told encompasses elements of both comedy and a love story.

BONDEBJERG:
In the other film, *Ticket to Paradise*, the story is more about life in Thailand, where the women are from. How do you see the relation between *Ticket to Paradise* and *Love on Delivery*?

METZ:
In *Ticket to Paradise*, I switch genres to a certain extent, for the film draws on socially realistic dramas. It's a story about

prostitution, and the very difficult social circumstances under which the women and their families live. But it's also a home-away-from-home story – much like *Love on Delivery* and many of my other films; a tale about the desire to be elsewhere and to start a new life. There was a lot less interest at DR in *Ticket to Paradise*. It didn't have as clear a Danish angle as the first film. It's more a film about Thailand. But I felt that it was absolutely necessary to tell that story because it completes the picture and shows the other side of the story. Both films did very well internationally. The fact that they were both chosen to be in competition at the documentary film festival IDFA, which is the world's largest documentary film festival, played a really important role in that regard. I think both films have helped to nuance the image we have of globalization, and have helped to give globalization a more human face. The films' success with the general public seems to support this idea.

BONDEBJERG: The success of *Love on Delivery* and *Ticket to Paradise* paved the way for your next film, *Armadillo*, about Denmark's involvement in the war in Afghanistan. *Armadillo* was very well received indeed, and further cemented your reputation as a gifted documentary filmmaker. Through your Thailand films you'd clearly demonstrated your ability to work with the demanding constraints of prime-time TV, and to produce films of interest to both the TV and film milieus. But how, more precisely, did the idea for *Armadillo* arise, and how did the project materialize?

METZ: At IDFA I made contact with some pretty important people in the documentary film industry. My Thailand films were seen as representing an approach to documentary filmmaking that somehow delivered a certain kind of experience. Because of this perception, the commissioning editor at the Finnish TV station YLE, Iikka Vehkalahti, decided to support *Armadillo*. And his support meant that all the Scandinavian financing suddenly fell into place, including from the Nordic Film and TV Fund. That commitment on the part of YLE was really decisive in terms of our ability to raise all the money we needed because the film was simply too expensive to make with only Danish funding.

The trailer we used when pitching *Armadillo* really challenged the norms of traditional TV journalism. But that's precisely what the YLE commissioning editor liked. Iikka Vehkalahti is quite unusual in that he thinks in terms of a given film's qualities instead of in terms of the TV station's needs. But the premise for the film was actually that Fridthjof Film was to produce a series of six films for TV 2 about Afghanistan and our involvement there. The film was to be made within the parameters of the Public Service Agreement. The aim was to put Afghanistan back on the agenda because the sense was that the general public didn't really know what was going on, or, worse still, didn't really care. Although the war marks a dramatic shift in Danish politics – inasmuch as we've become a nation that is actively engaged in warfare, with soldiers being returned to us in coffins – the issue just isn't being taken up in the media. The idea was to have storytellers from the world of film make the films, rather than journalists. The narratives were to be character-driven, so as to facilitate a lot of emotional involvement and identification. I actually became part of the project at a fairly late stage. I had, however, quite independently, thought about making a film about Danish soldiers in Afghanistan. But then I met the film director Kasper Torsting, who'd come up with the idea for the Fridthjof film series, at the Roskilde Festival. He was the anchor person for the documentary series 'Love and War' on TV 2 made by Fridthjof Film, and he told me that they were looking for a director who would want to go to Afghanistan to shoot a film, and that they were especially interested in a story that was intimately involved with the lives of the soldiers on the front line. I ended up writing a proposal – actually two – for Torsting, based on my exchanges with him. The other proposal was about a field hospital, but the winning proposal was the one about a group of soldiers on the front line. That was clearly the stronger of the two. There was a bit of a conflict with TV 2, because they wanted the right to the final cut, which we couldn't accept. What we ended up with was an agreement whereby Kasper Torsting had the final cut privilege on the series, on all of our behalves. At a later stage, when *Armadillo* was taken out of the Public Service framework and thus financially out of the series, the final cut privilege was transferred to me, as the film's director, which is of course exactly as it should be. The budget was initially very modest considering that the film focused on 'history in the making,' and told a unique story that really hadn't been told before – whether in Denmark or internationally. But the budget changed when the film was made the flagship for the TV 2 series and was envisaged as having a documentary feature format. Suddenly monies from sources other than the Public Service budget became available. We used the material we'd shot with money from the initial subsidies to raise more money. As a result, both TV 2 and the DFI were able to put more money into the film,

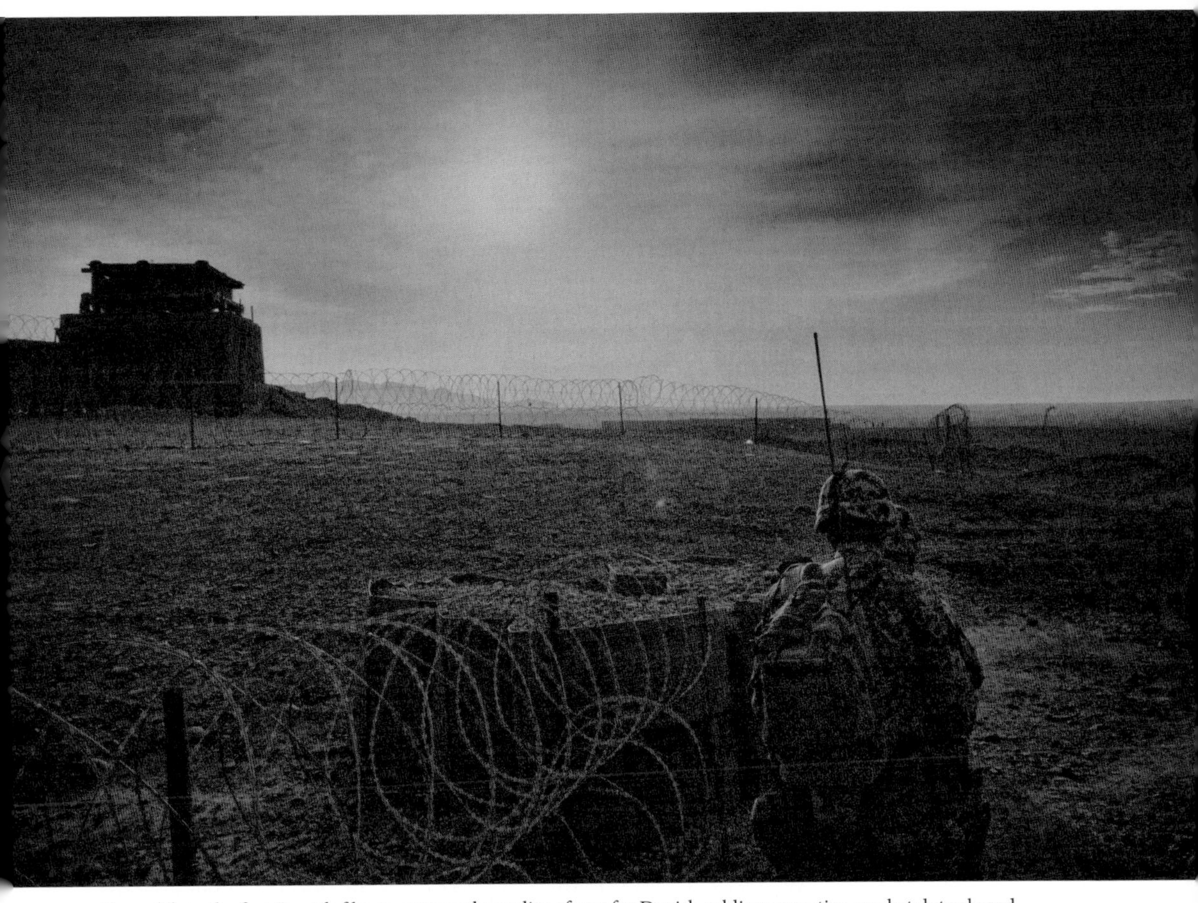

Camp life in the first Danish film to capture the reality of war for Danish soldiers on active combat duty abroad (*Armadillo*, photo: Lars Skree. Courtesy of Janus Metz and Lars Skree).

and at a later stage the budget was further supplemented by Scandinavian and international financing.

BONDEBJERG: You've touched on the conflict with TV 2 about the final cut privilege. Were there any other difficult discussions about the film along the way, or in relation to the final stage of the editing process?

METZ: One very basic conflict emerged right towards the end, and the cause of it was TV 2's insistence on not wanting to broadcast a film that was longer than 45 minutes. Since the film was 100 minutes long, and we were contractually bound to produce a version of it for TV, we finally had to edit it down to 59 minutes. The cinema and DVD version is, however, the full, 100 minute-long one. TV 2 simply felt that it wasn't possible to show more of the film, because there also had to be time for a debate. TV 2's thinking about all this was very short-sighted, and nothing like this ever came up in the course of our dealings with the many TV stations that have shown the film internationally. Outside Denmark, we haven't had any problem showing the film in its entirety.

BONDEBJERG: In connection with the making of Christoffer Guldbrandsen's *Den hemmelige krig* (*The Secret War*, 2006), the Danish military revealed itself to be a very closed institution, with little interest, to put it mildly, in collaborating or communicating with outsiders. What was your relation to the military like?

METZ: There were several phases to our collaboration with the military. We were given quite unique permission to shoot in Afghanistan, and Kasper Torsting had actually already negotiated all that by the time I joined the project. I became part of it all just when the negotiations at the highest level were about to take place. Our military contacts were Frank Lissner (known to viewers from *The Secret War*) and Jens Rossen-Jørgensen. We were initially given permission to stay with the troops and to do our shooting over a period of nine weeks in all, and we were able to circumvent the usual rules and regulations that members of the press have to deal with. With time, however, we were virtually allowed to come and go as we wished in the military camp, and we even went home somewhere in the middle of it all so as to ensure that we didn't become too caught up in the milieu.

But in spite of the mutual trust that developed, we did experience a crisis when the Danish soldiers killed a group of Taliban and were accused of having simply executed them. The military wanted to see our images; they insisted that we'd been filming illegally and that they needed to look at everything so that we wouldn't run into any problems. They also showed us a contract that neither we, nor Fridthjof Film, had ever seen before. But we stuck to the line that they only had the right to see the finished film, with an eye to ensuring that it didn't contain things that might be a security threat. But we had, of course, learnt a lot from what happened with Guldbrandsen's *The Secret War*. So we were very well prepared, having already secured the support of people who could advise us about legal matters, and about how best to communicate with the military and handle a potential spin campaign against the film in the press. Although they threatened us, actually shut the film down, and insisted on our signing the contract, we stood our ground. The military finally backed down and we were allowed to carry on, but everything became just that much harder, and our access to the highest level of command was cut off. Those people simply refused to engage with us, so that's why that level simply doesn't figure in the film. When we'd finished shooting the film and started to edit it, the military leadership expressed a great deal of interest in being allowed to follow the process. But we managed to keep them out of it by means of various tactics. The whole process was actually rather dramatic, also because the case of the 'Hunter Force' book erupted in the midst of it all.[1] The military was suddenly being covered in a very massive and highly critical way by the media, and the last thing its leaders needed was another scandal, which is probably what they would have produced, had they decided to interfere with our film.

BONDEBJERG: Although your films have always been about issues with a clear global dimension, the making of a really tough and realistic film about war still seems like a bit of a leap. What was it about that story and the issues it raised that fascinated you? Why were you motivated to tell precisely that story?

METZ: I felt it was important to make a film that provided a really detailed picture of the reality of war, and of its consequences for the soldiers; and for the civilians for whose sake we are allegedly involved in the fighting in the first place. However, what I was really interested in was raising some big existential questions about our civilization, and our way of being human in the context of contemporary global realities. I think the reason people are surprised at my having made apparently very different films is that they, to a significant extent, forget that while I may examine different topics and issues, I always do so with the same fundamental questions in mind. The films often encompass a shared structure linked to travel, displacement, and various kinds of cultural exchange spanning various national borders. At the core of my films there's a concept of travel for the purpose of self-enrichment, and the whole mythology of adventure. In the case of *Armadillo*, the journey is very concretely that of the soldiers who go to war in a distant and unknown part of the world; but it's also a mental journey, on a national level, through our self-conceptions as a democratic nation. Why is it that we're now teaming up with the strong and powerful? Why are we building military bases in remote parts of the world in order to protect ourselves and to intervene in a quite different culture? The film is also about what this kind of active militarism does to our self-understandings as Danes, and, in a more extended sense, to the relationship between the West and other parts of the world. It's a film about the landscapes of globalization as they are reflected in the landscape of war. It's a film about what might be problematic about our new militant 'humanitarianism'; about the idea of a tough kind of tit for tat in a global game.

BONDEBJERG: With *Armadillo* you engage with a well-established international war film tradition. This tradition encompasses both fiction and non-fiction films, and films that are plot-driven, character-driven, and reality-driven. Where would you situate yourself in this tradition? How, quite concretely, did you go about developing the film's structure and story?

METZ: At a very basic level, the story is about this group of soldiers; about what they're like, how they prepare themselves for deployment in Afghanistan, how things turn out for them, and so on. So that's where I started my research for the film. Among other things, I talked to soldiers who'd already served in Afghanistan. What struck me after I'd done some initial research, after I'd had these conversations, was that nearly all of the soldiers wanted to go back to Afghanistan. What seemed to be motivating them was a sense of community – certain very intense experiences – and all the excitement that comes with being a solider on the front line.

Although many of them have experienced dreadful things and have seen friends die before their eyes, they still want to go back. That's really the starting point for the film and the story it tells. Certain initial intuitions were then developed and became more concrete when I met the group that we intended to follow in Afghanistan. At that point, the characters' background and psychology began to become clear. With that background in place, we were able to identify some spaces, scenes, and characters that we knew we would want to include in the film. After the first three weeks' of shooting, I joined forces with Rasmus Heisterberg, who knows a lot about fiction films and about war films. Together we looked at the material I had, and what we noticed was this clear dynamic that had to do with the way in which the characters' differences produced a number of typical contrasts. The most obvious contrast was the one between a cynical, hardened heart and an open one, which is most clearly personified in the film in the relation between Daniel and Mads. Daniel is drawn to the dark and dangerous sides of the war and tends to want to test limits, whereas Mads is considerably more sceptical about the military. The film's larger existential questions, its universal approach to war, and its probing of Danish mentalities related to Denmark's new role as a nation involved in the conduct of war, all of this is reflected in the relationship between the two main characters. In a sense, it's like capturing the world in a tiny grain of dramaturgical sand.

BONDEBJERG: Although *Armadillo* is a documentary film, it has a clear dramaturgical structure; one that resembles the sort of thing we expect to find in fiction films. At the same time, the film makes it clear that the material is organized chronologically. That is, we follow the soldiers' experiences as ordered in real time. How do you see the relation between chronology and dramaturgy in *Armadillo*?

METZ: They're actually pretty congruent, although certain scenes did get moved around because, psychologically speaking, it made more sense to place the relevant sequences elsewhere in the film. I have a motto: 'It's not what actually happened, but what really happened that is the guiding principle.' It's perfectly legitimate to edit things together in ways that are at odds with the chronology established while shooting if this helps to clarify the reality and story in question. But the changes the group and the characters undergo in the film actually occurred gradually – much as in the film – and the more dramatic moments occurred as they are depicted. But things could have worked out differently during the shooting, because this kind of film is unpredictable. I always have a strong sense of responsibility towards the authenticity of what I depict, but that doesn't mean that I feel constrained by chronology in terms of how I tell my story. It's quite possible that the right thing to do is to start with the end, or with something from the middle of the story. For example, the scene with Rasmus in the shower was shot before they left for Afghanistan, but it clearly illustrates his psychological condition after his return.

BONDEBJERG: What's your view on reconstructing and actually staging actions and events in documentary films?

METZ: I don't think it's possible to have a principled and general position on reconstructions and stagings. I think that approach is acceptable in a given situation if it's ethically defensible in terms of the film's relation to the authentic reality in question. That scene with the soldiers partying and cavorting with strippers just before their departure was picked up on by the press because it's a reconstruction of a party that the soldiers had organized without the crew being present. That scene is genuinely part of the story, part of the reality that the film is all about. If we hadn't organized a repeat of it, so as to be able to include it, the film's realism would have been compromised. There's no critical difference between how that scene came into being and how many of the other scenes in the film were made. For example, once I'd agreed with the soldiers that we'd come and interview them together with their families, I talked to them, ahead of the shoot, about what we were after and what we'd like to discuss. Making a documentary film is certainly all about capturing a reality in as authentic a way as possible, but the work involved in doing that requires planning, and encompasses preparations that also affect that reality.

BONDEBJERG: Any documentary is shaped by the director's stylistic and other choices. In *Armadillo*, your use of film language is very rich and varied; not just in terms of the film's visual style, but also its sound, music, and editing. Someone with a purist conception of documentary filmmaking might see *Armadillo* as a fiction film disguised as a documentary. What would your response to that kind of position be?

METZ: If I were to define documentary film through a contrast with pure journalism, then I'd say that it has an essayistic dimension. What's articulated is my interpretation of, and perspective on, reality, and I control this process through the various cinematic devices that I opt to use. One's conception of reality, as well as the cinematic style that one produces, do of course end up influencing the sound design, the selection of scenes, the editing, the visual language, and the general dramaturgical structure of the film. After all, a documentary film isn't supposed to be an extended news report, and *Armadillo* is a film that tries to grapple with some deep psychological issues, and to deal with some aspects of reality that just can't be captured by traditional journalistic means. Even in those moments when the film seems to be most intensely engaged with the brutal reality that it depicts, there are other far more universal psychological dimensions at work. At the same time, there are just so many mediatized images of war, and they're also at work in the film and undoubtedly influence our experience of the film's reality. As a filmmaker, I've clearly, for example, been influenced by the classic fiction film tradition of American war films. You just can't get around those, even as a documentary filmmaker. Feature fiction films like *Apocalypse Now* (dir. Francis Ford Coppola, 1979) or *Deer Hunter* (dir. Michael Cimino, 1978) are extremely realistic, truthful films, and their themes and perspectives on war are definitely discernible in *Armadillo*.

BONDEBJERG: The observational approach that you favour involves considerable intimacy, in terms of the depiction of people and their milieus. It's not hard to imagine conflicts between those in front of and behind the camera, about what can and cannot be shown. *Armadillo* offers a very intimate portrait of those young soldiers, just as your films about the Thai women depict aspects of reality that are very private and troubling. Do you see yourself as having a clear ethical stance in relation to the people you film?

METZ: Yes, I do. I talk to the people I'm filming a lot, and clearly explain to them what kind of story it is that I'd like to tell. But I have to say that initially I'd like to be able to film everything, without restrictions. Once the process of selecting scenes for the final film begins, there will clearly be things that have to be kept out of the final edit. I allow the participants to see a cut of the film before it is released, and I take their feedback seriously, even if I don't let them edit my film. I also tell the people I'm filming that it's fine for them to draw a line at any point during the shooting if they feel that we're crossing a threshold, in terms of privacy; and that actually happened quite a few times in *Armadillo*.

Note

1   In an article entitled 'Danish defence chief quits over Arabic book uproar' (4 October 2009), Reuters reported on this case as follows: 'The head of Denmark's defence forces quit on Sunday after the military was forced to admit its own officers had translated into Arabic a book describing Danish special forces' operations in Afghanistan and Iraq' (http://www.reuters.com/article/2009/10/04/idUSL4443356). In English the title of the book is: *Hunter Force: At War with the Elite*).

Chapter 13

Eva Mulvad

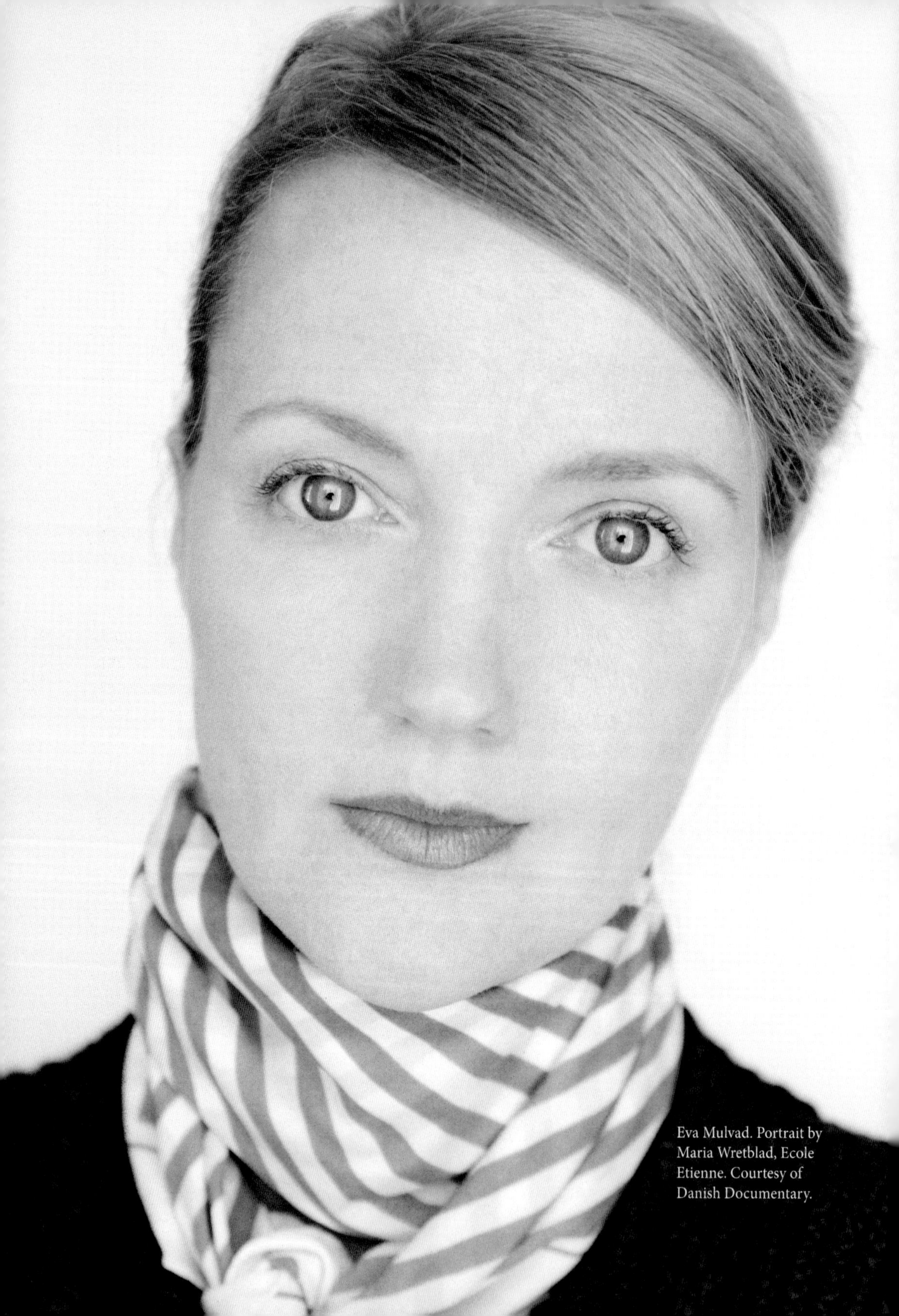

Eva Mulvad. Portrait by Maria Wretblad, Ecole Etienne. Courtesy of Danish Documentary.

B orn 1972. Mulvad trained as a documentary filmmaker at the National Film School of Denmark. Having graduated in 2001, Mulvad went on to make a number of films for TV. In 2005, she won the Nordvision prize for best documentary feature for *Den sidste dans* (*The Last Dance*, 2005), a poetic portrait of ageing. In 2006, Mulvad achieved international recognition with *Enemies of Happiness* (2006), which focuses on the female politician Malalai Joya's political campaign ahead of the first democratic elections in Afghanistan in 2005. The film won the Silver Wolf Award at IDFA, and subsequently the World Cinema Jury Prize at the Sundance Film Festival. 2006 also saw the release of *Kolonien* (*The Colony*), a film about a community of Danish expatriates living in a coastal town in Argentina, which Mulvad co-directed with Judith Lansade. Most recently, Mulvad spent three years working on a complex cinematic depiction of the relationship between a Danish mother and her daughter. Having enjoyed a jet-set existence as expatriates in Portugal, these women now find themselves bereft of means and with only each other for company. Entitled *Det gode liv* (*The Good Life*, 2010), the film was shown at IDFA, and went on to win the award for best documentary film at Karlovy Vary. While she was completing *The Good Life*, Mulvad made a courtroom drama entitled *Med døden til følge* (*The Samurai Case*, 2011), about the fate of a man who finds himself being tried for killing his best friend with a samurai sword. The film set a precedent in the context of Danish legal history, for no filmmaker had previously been granted permission to follow a court case closely, with a camera. Eva Mulvad co-owns the production company Danish Documentary. Her partners in the company are the directors Phie Ambo, Pernille Rose Grønkjær, and Mikala Krogh, and the producer Sigrid Dyekjær.

Documentary features:

2011   *Med døden til følge* (*The Samurai Case*)
2010   *Det gode liv* (*The Good Life*)
2006   *Vores lykkes fjender* (*Enemies of Happiness*)
2006   *Kolonien* (*The Colony*, with Judith Lansade)
2005   *Den sidste dans* (*The Last Dance*)
2001   *The Camp*

Television:

2007   *Kunsten at sælge* ('The Art of Selling,' DR TV)
2003   *Når vi skilles* (*Danish Divorce*, DR TV, six episodes)
2000   *Prinsesse for en dag* (*Princess for a Day*, DR TV)

REDVALL: How did you become interested in making documentary films?

MULVAD: Initially I wanted to become a librarian because there was quite a fine library in my little town. There was a big wide world to be found in that house, and the idea of sitting there with all those stories seemed really cool to me. Later I thought it would be more interesting to be a journalist or a foreign correspondent. I threw myself into writing, and ended up working for the monthly magazine *Press*. I did that for a few years. It was very interesting work and I learnt a lot. There was a commitment back then to bringing young people on board. There was a lot of unemployment, so there were many really talented journalists, and we had a huge editorial board because people weren't being paid. The good thing about the situation was that older, more experienced people took us in tow, and in exchange for that we had to do some of the dreary work, transcribe interviews, for example. It was hard, but I learnt a lot, among other things about being thorough, meticulous, and responsible. There was this well-established way of proceeding once we'd completed an article. We'd go to a café and ask some complete stranger to read it. The preference was to find someone who didn't resemble the author of the piece too much. I learnt to take the reader seriously, and speaking more generally, I do think you learn a lot from that kind of 'learning by doing,' certainly in the context of the creative and more practically oriented disciplines. What we do as filmmakers is very much like a craft, and there's something about the processes in question that makes it especially important to be part of a milieu where people work in a practical, hands-on way, but also share a language that articulates what they're doing. It's important to have some kind of intellectual framework for it all.

REDVALL: As I understand it, you hadn't worked much with moving images when you got into the National Film School of Denmark. What made you apply to the Film School?

MULVAD: As I moved up the ranks at *Press*, I ended up becoming one of the editors and also started writing articles myself. I'd written an article about a girl who'd had to change her identity because there was this man who kept pursuing her. The story worked just fine on the page, in part because I'd been able to draw on letters he'd written to her. But there were also messages he'd left on her answering machine. So I realized that the story also had this sound element to it, and so I asked the radio station P4 whether they might be interested. Mikala Krogh, with whom I now co-own a company, worked at P4 and became my mentor. They had a system that resembled that of *Press*, in that they also took in people who didn't have much experience and then assigned them a mentor. I ended up with a good radio montage, and in the process of producing it I discovered some new ways of telling stories.

Coincidence had a lot to do with my decision to apply to the Film School. A colleague at *Press* happened to mention the Documentary & TV Department, and I just figured their programme might be interesting. I was initially rejected, but then I was asked back for an extra test because a student had dropped out. The worry was that I didn't have a lot of especially visual experience, because I'd been involved mostly with writing and with producing material for radio. But they decided to give me a chance because the programme was just about to become a four-year course of study, and so the view was that there'd be plenty of time to teach me how to produce images! But the concerns were perfectly legitimate. It was really difficult in the beginning. The process of thinking in terms of images and of handling a camera is simply very different. It's hard to create interpretive layers with images, to ensure that you don't spell everything out and tell the viewer what to think. There has to be room to interpret a feeling, or a glance. In my view, a story becomes powerful when it's told through images that touch us on a more universal level; when it's a matter not just of mirroring reality, but of creating a layer of expression encompassing poetry, beauty, feelings. It took me a really long time to learn how to do that, to figure out how to make room for various feelings.

REDVALL: So how does one learn how to do that? Or rather, how did your film school teachers teach you how to do that?

MULVAD: The Film School is utterly unlike any other school I've ever attended. In other schools there's this expectation that everyone has to be good at the same things. There's a curriculum that everyone has to master. At the Film School, we were given this fine black notebook with blank pages, and then our teacher told us that it was the only book he expected us to read. The whole point was that we had to look deep into ourselves to discover what moves and drives us. Our teacher, Arne Bro, often evokes the distinction between what's somehow been given to us and what's been explicitly learnt or acquired. You can be good at learning something that everyone can learn, but there are other things that you, specifically, have been given. And the point is to connect and work with those specific gifts. This is a very private and personal process involving a lot of introspection, and that's why he defines documentary filmmaking as art.

And we did exactly what I've described. I worked with those things that are unique to me as a storyteller. We did this for four years, assisted throughout by various practical exercises. You learn a craft because you're taught cinematography and editing. But at the same time you also develop a language enabling you to articulate what you're doing with that craftsmanship because you're simply constantly discussing your work. It could be a matter of discussing whether some specific choice that you've made works or not, but also whether the imagery and psychological aspects as a whole feel right. Gradually you develop not only your own film language, but also an articulate understanding of that language. I had nothing resembling a film language when I arrived at the School, so I found it all both very difficult and very exciting. When you make that transition from a cool and collected world to a place where people read their diaries aloud to each other, there are moments when you feel it's all a bit much. I'd taken some Political Science courses at the University of Copenhagen before I embarked on the programme at the Film School, and during my first six months at the School I continued to take a course in International Politics because I found it hard to deal with what I saw as that tiny little world of inwardness.

But I'm just so glad to have attended the School. It's an incredible privilege to work with a teacher who is so good at helping you to discover your own artistic voice. Arne is alive to the world with all of his senses, and everything he does reflects that. In the beginning, I found his teaching very challenging because it was so different from anything I'd experienced previously. For example, he'd give lectures about his infidelity, which a lot of people find really provoking. But these stories helped to illustrate the point that everyone has flaws and that these flaws define you as a human being. They shape the character traits that make you unique. The idea was that you have to acknowledge and embrace your mistakes because they make you different. You don't hear that sort of thing very often, and it was interesting to step into the space that he opened up for us.

REDVALL: In terms of themes, your films seem to take up current social issues. *Enemies of Happiness*, with its focus on Afghanistan, is a case in point; and so is *The Samurai Case*, which takes a poetic rather than journalistic look at the Danish legal system. How would you describe the thematic focus of your work?

MULVAD: I think there are two recurring emphases in my work. On the one hand I'm interested in drawing people into certain discussions that are important in our society. Documentary films can be seen by a lot of people without a lot of prior knowledge or understanding. They allow you to bring some fairly complicated discussions about, for example, war in Afghanistan into people's homes. With *Enemies of Happiness*, I was looking for very human stories in the midst of war. What do the streets look like in Afghanistan? What's it like to go to school and to go to work in the middle of a war? Who are the local heroes? So that it's not always about us, us, and us again, that is, about the western world and our soldiers. I'm actually not especially interested in politics, but I am interested in the human stories that are caught up in the political discussions. I'm interested in stories that an audience can relate to emotionally and not only intellectually, even though they deal with serious current affairs issues.

Narrative material that's almost novelistic and about very basic human issues provides a second kind of thematic emphasis in my work. Good examples here would be *The Good Life* or *The Last Dance*. *The Last Dance* is, of course, about being old in an old people's home, which is a social issue, but the approach taken is more existential than political. And then there's someone like Anne Mette, the daughter in *The Good Life,* who's wonderful because she's complex; she's in many ways very irritating, but also has this novelistic way of understanding her own personal tragedy. I would like to be able to convey aspects of the world with far greater human poetry. Life, after all, is poetic in all sorts of ways, and that's something that documentary films sometimes forget. They're often about sociopolitical views and positions, and they tend to provide a thematic take on life. Yet film is very much a poetic medium – as is life – so there's room for a lot more poetry here.

I suppose I've always had a bit of a problem with journalism. In a way, journalism always provides a starting point for non-fiction storytelling. But during my years at the Film School there was an enormous amount of confusion about what a documentary actually is. As a result, I felt it was important to be able to say: 'I'm not doing journalism. I'm doing reality filtered through a gaze.' Generally speaking, I feel more inspired by fiction than journalism. If you make films based on a journalistic approach, you typically end up working with the alphabet of letters, whereas with fiction it's the alphabet of images that's in play.

REDVALL: You work with a number of film practitioners who have experience making both fiction films and documentaries. I'm thinking, for example, of the film editor Adam Nielsen. How important are these partnerships to you?

MULVAD: Finding an editor is all important. The discussions I have with Adam about a film are the decisive ones. He's the film's father, if I'm its mother, and his taste has a decisive impact on the final look of the film. In general, the editor is a central figure in a documentary filmmaking context because you come back with material that hasn't really got much of a shape to it. So a lot of decisions are made in the editing room. To some extent, the same is true of fiction, but with fiction the script is typically much tighter. With documentary material there are a lot of potential stories to be told, which is why it's so important to find the right creative partners.

I think that perhaps the most important reason why Danish documentaries are doing so well and have won so many prizes is that we've established these partnerships with the talented editors and cinematographers, who have experience with both fiction and documentary filmmaking. I see a lot of films at film festivals that just aren't finished yet. In terms of their visual aspect, these films just haven't been taken to the level that could have been reached, and

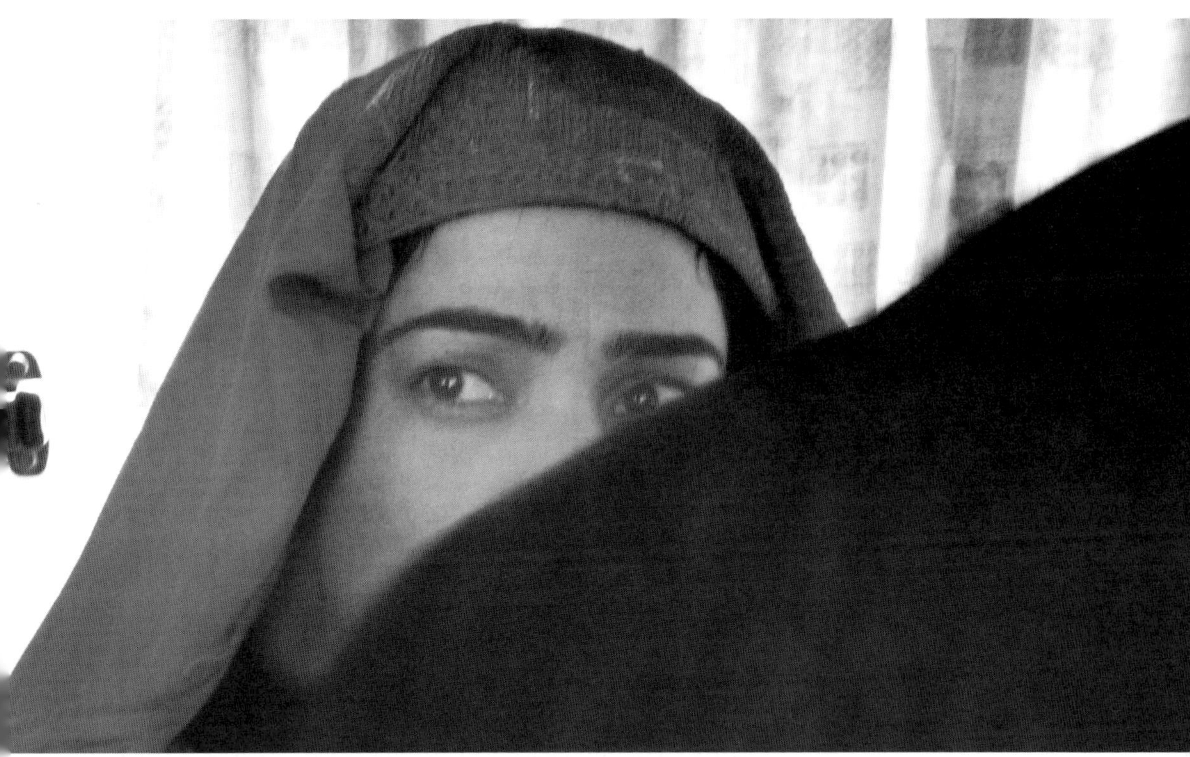

Malalai Joya during her 2005 campaign to get elected in the first democratic election after the war in Afghanistan (*Enemies of Happiness*, photo: Zillah Bowes. Courtesy of Danish Documentary).

often the sound and editing also need more work. The explanation is probably that a lot of countries just don't have the money to do what we're able to do here. But the difference in quality also has to do with the scale of the Danish film industry, which is small, and with the friendships that many of us developed during our years at the Film School. Many of the really talented editors think it's just as interesting to make a documentary film as it is to make a fiction film, so we never have to give the job to someone who's second best. And that really lifts the quality of the productions. We're able to make gorgeous cinematic works because we have these partnerships and speak the same language. A meeting with a cinematographer is never about journalism, but about questions like: 'How do we convey this in a visually powerful way?' A lot of cinematographers are looking for those sorts of challenges. They're tired of running around in order to produce reportage-like work in which no judicious choices about visual style ever get made. They're eager to be challenged by directors who are ambitious.

The partnerships are very important, and I'm really glad, for example, that our company, Danish Documentary, currently is owned by four directors and one producer. That constellation brings focus to the creative side because everyone is closely involved in the creative process, both with regard to their own works and the company's other films. For example, when I go to Portugal with my little camera, as was the case with *The Good Life*, I might discover that reality isn't quite doing what I want it do. My preference is to make what I call 'scenic' documentaries where, through clearly defined scenes, we get to experience a certain development of the characters who provide the film's focus. But this sort of thing takes a lot of time, and sometimes the film doesn't give you what you want. Being able to talk to other people who understand this process and are in it themselves is really wonderful because it makes everything a lot less lonely.

REDVALL: You made use of devices from the toolkit of fiction filmmaking as early as *The Last Dance*. And a lot of the younger documentary filmmakers in Denmark are doing something similar. What's the motivation for this approach in your case?

MULVAD: I think you're seeing the influence of the Film School here. We were taught that finding the most powerful form of visual expression is what's crucial; that moral or ethical deliberations about sincerity, authenticity, and purity aren't always that relevant. I suppose that this approach reflects an understanding of documentary film as a form of art; the idea that the material will always be filtered through the director's gaze and perspective. At that point you've already abandoned that very ascetic, truth-oriented way of thinking about documentary filmmaking. When I listen to veterans like Frederick Wiseman or the Maysles brothers talk about the concept of truth, I'm often puzzled because they're just as involved in this filtering process. Perhaps the American context helps to explain their stance. When you have people like Michael Moore making documentaries that are almost propagandistic, you might feel a greater need to hold onto the idea of being gentle with reality. But all their choices are also informed by their own background, by who they are. In Denmark, we've simply gone all the way with that idea of documentaries being shaped by a personal perspective. This is no doubt also the case because we work with editors who have a lot of experience with fiction films, and who are used to drawing on the relevant cinematic devices. I would like my films to have the feel of a fiction film. It's not that I want reality to disappear. But I want people to feel that they can really breathe the film in, so to speak; that they can sink into it, be seduced by it.

REDVALL: You often talk about 'scenic' documentaries, whereas others might talk about observational films or cinéma vérité. What's at stake for you in that term 'scenic'?

MULVAD: In my view there's an element of distance built into the cinéma vérité approach. I'm a great admirer of the godfathers of cinéma vérité. We're not actually producing cinéma vérité films, but we are working in that tradition. The term 'scenic' is meant to describe this commitment that we have to producing scenes that are sequentially linked. But it also captures our desire to use lots of music, and, more generally, as many cinematic tricks and devices as we can. So, for me, the term 'scenic' has less of an ascetic feel to it than cinéma vérité, but we're definitely talking about the same tradition. We're just a younger generation, and as far as we're concerned, it's absolutely fine to play with all the tools in the toolbox.

REDVALL: *The Good Life* provides an intimate account of a very human drama between a mother and her daughter. In an article about the film, Lars Movin notes the element of intimacy in your depiction of the mother/daughter relationship, and goes on to discuss the Kazakhstani director Sergei Dvortsevoy, who abandoned documentary filmmaking in favour of fiction filmmaking.[1] Apparently he did this because he felt that if he penetrated any deeper into the private lives of his protagonists, he'd either destroy their lives or his own soul. Does this way of reasoning make any sense to you?

MULVAD: Dvortsevoy is working in a very different society. What I've heard him say is that his films have had some pretty serious consequences for some of his characters because the political system simply persecuted them afterwards. We're not working in that kind of context in Denmark. Also, I don't actually feel that his films have quite the psychological intimacy that mine do. He's dealing with other sorts of problems, with issues linked to a very different part of the world. But of course we're always keen to protect the people we put in front of the camera. And it's always difficult. How far should we go? What's called for? When is a scene necessary, and when is it unnecessary? And what's the impact on people of seeing themselves filtered through my filter? I think it was Wiseman who once said that a good documentary filmmaker has to work on becoming a very fine-grained filter because otherwise the reality that ends up in the film will be sort of clumsy. And most important of all: the people you've put into a given film have to be able to live with the portrait that comes out of it all.

I understand why there's been some discussion about these sorts of issues in connection with *The Good Life* because that film involves a very intense portrait of a woman with a complicated relationship, not only to her mother, but to her surroundings more generally. The way she's depicted isn't entirely sympathetic, because what we have in the film is something like a chamber play for two women on a couch. The dramatic conflict is in this woman's head, and it's all about her fate. It's about how she finds herself in an impossible situation, yet can't take responsibility for it and instead blames the world and her mother for her plight. I find that her behaviour during those fights with her mother is extremely cinematic. She's poetic in her way of characterizing reality, and I do understand her logic. She's at her clearest as a character in those scenes where she's scolding her mother. But we did try to achieve some sort of balance because we didn't want her simply to be irritating. We wanted it to be possible to grasp her logic. I hope that the portrait we ended up with is a nuanced and complete one. We needed the intimacy because the film's focus is not some general theme, or some social issue, but what's going on psychologically within the characters. In a film like *Enemies of Happiness*, which is about Afghanistan and various social problems, you don't need the same kind of intimate depiction of the main character, of Malalai. Because the film is about a brave and strong woman who tries to change her country for the better, we need to show her strength. She's shown crying just once in the course of the entire film. And that's enough to evoke her vulnerability and humanity.

In connection with this question of just how far you can go in terms of intimate depictions, it has to be said that there are many different ways of making films about people's misfortunes, flaws, or vulnerabilities. In reality shows, the whole point is to put people's feelings and flaws on display. This is done in a very systematic way, and for the purposes of entertainment. I hope my films are entertaining, but I also hope that nobody will see the intimacy of my camera as a means of merely delivering entertainment. Hopefully the viewer feels that the intimacy is part of the film's deeper purpose, which has to do with one's own life, with wanting to convey the sorts of thoughts that prompt reflection and insight. The daughter's behaviour in *The Good Life* may, for example, prompt thoughts about childrearing, about the way one was raised oneself, one's own relationship with money, or about the relationship one has with one's own parents. If a film does all this – if it doesn't let you merely sit there, untouched, looking at other people's misfortune, if it involves you – then the practice of intimate depiction has a very different role. At that point, it's no longer intimidating.

REDVALL: You often refer to the people in your films as 'characters,' which is of course a concept we associate with the world of fiction filmmaking. How do you see yourself as working with the participants in your films as characters?

MULVAD: My view is that these people should be what we call 'characters.' The Anne Mette we see in *The Good Life* is of course a real person, but she's also very much a cinematic character inasmuch as my depiction of her involves cutting out all sorts of things. She has to become virtually a theatrical figure in order to be able to function in the film. This doesn't mean that the image the film presents lacks accuracy. But the editor and I have chosen to work with Anne Mette's most theatrical and dramatic aspects. It's definitely important to talk about needing to protect the people who are in your film, but you also have to have the courage actually to see reality, and to shape it to the point where it achieves cinematic clarity, and becomes touching or entertaining.

Being tried in a court of law is, for example, an incredibly intense experience, and it may well be one of the most serious things the person in question will experience in the course of his entire life. If you don't have the courage to show that, because of some concern about protecting people's feelings, you're just not depicting reality. You could say that your filter isn't refined enough. In Anne Wivel's *Ansigt til Ansigt* (*Face to Face*, 1987), which is about the Danish theological seminary, there's a scene where the young priests have to learn about different rituals. There are these scenes with re-enactments, with the aspiring priests being required to play different roles, one of them being that of pastor. One of the teachers takes on the role of someone with a serious illness, and then the woman who's playing the role of priest says something like, 'Well, I'm sure things will work out.' And the teacher's response is to say, 'You can't say that to a human being who's about to die. You're going to have to say something like: "It must be very difficult. It must be hard to live with."' Because when someone opens up to you to that extent and looks to you for help, almost as an act of desperation, you have to have the courage to tell that person that you really *see* his situation, that you acknowledge it. You can't just brush it all aside.

Film directors who turn off the camera, or point it in a different direction when people start to cry, have a narrow-mindedness that's entirely their own. They just don't have the courage to see the feelings that are part of the reality they're depicting. If you have a decent relationship to the people in the film – if you've worked on establishing trust and they then cry in front of the camera – it's because at some level they're authorizing you to see this. And so at that point, I feel that you have a kind of obligation actually to look at what's happening. When you get to the editing stage, you then have to make a decision about how to situate the moment in relation to a larger context, so you end up with the right portrait. There are no doubt those who would claim that *The Good Life* is far too interested in the fights, in the process of collapse, the aggression, and the denial of reality. I think it's also a question of how much intimacy you can take when it comes to other people. People have different limits in that regard.

REDVALL: Your company, Danish Documentary, offers workshops focusing on documentary filmmaking methods. Do you see yourself as working with a specific method?

MULVAD: The method changes from one film to the next. Some films I make on my own with just one camera, while others are made with a crew. There are different trade-offs. I like working with

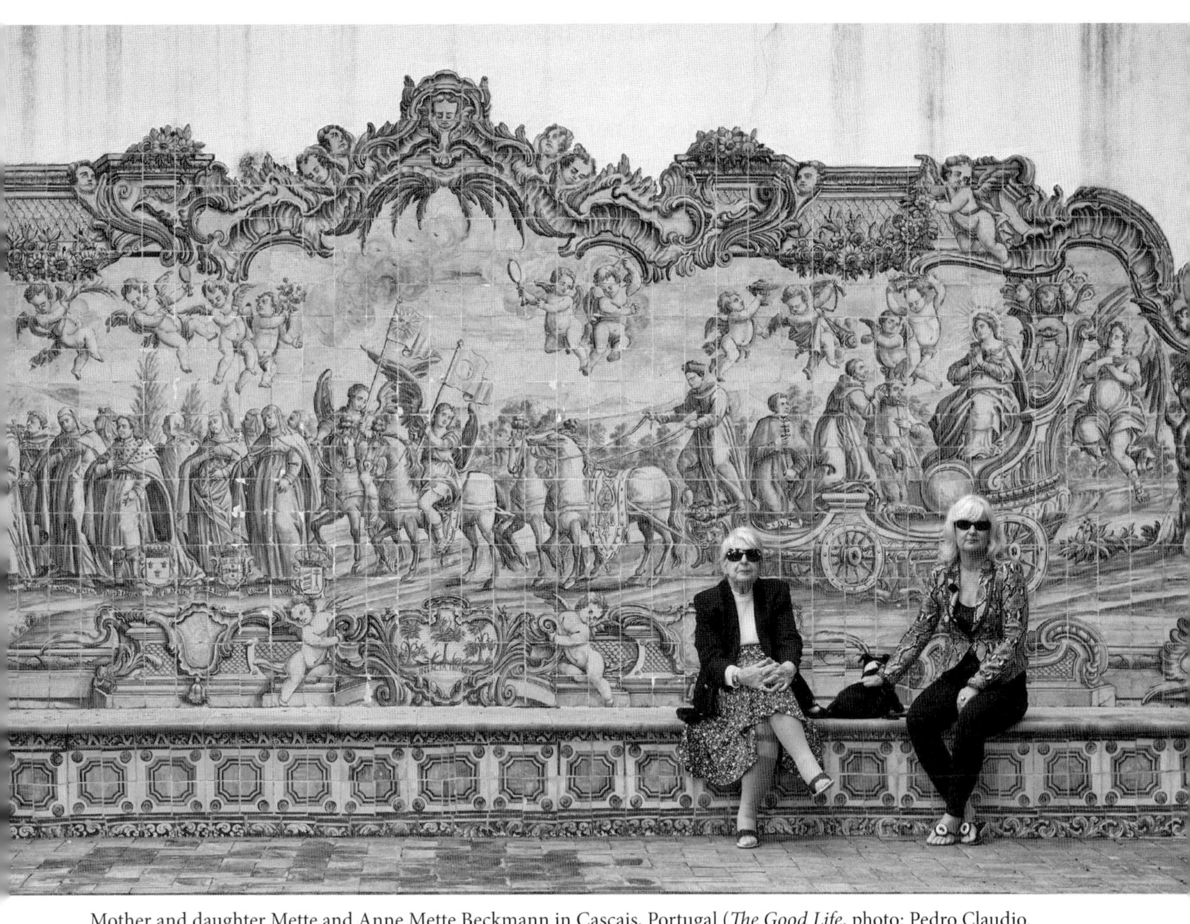

Mother and daughter Mette and Anne Mette Beckmann in Cascais, Portugal (*The Good Life*, photo: Pedro Claudio. Courtesy of Danish Documentary).

a cinematographer. But if it's a film like *The Good Life*, where it's a matter of being together with certain people over an extended period of time, and of having the patience just to sit there when nothing is happening, then I'd clearly rather be on my own. Some of the more intimate spaces work better if the director is alone. Other films, like *Enemies of Happiness* or *The Samurai Case*, have a much clearer framework, with three weeks of shooting just before an election, or three days in court. In those cases, it's really great to have a cinematographer, so that you're really able to play with the visual aspects of the film and don't have to deal with everything on your own. Sometimes everything feels a bit easier when other people are involved, but at the same time those films don't always achieve quite as much depth.

There are a lot of things you just don't see at first glance. For example, in *The Last Dance* there's a woman who's sitting at a window counting cars. She's one of my favourite characters, ever. But it took me about a month to figure out what it was she was doing. If you've had the patience and time to capture reality's nuances, the films become richer and mean more to you. The other films can also be good, and they can be sophisticated in all sorts of ways, but they tend to be the result of far more prompt decision making. There's a joyousness involved in penetrating the layers of those films you end up fiddling with for a long time.

Characters are simply crucial, and so, for example, the people you choose to work with have to enjoy being in front of the camera. I put a lot of energy into making sure that that's the case. You can have this really interesting story on paper, but that won't help you at all if people can't figure out how to occupy a space within the film. When I was at the Film School I made a film about a young girl who'd won 7.6 million Danish Crowns in the lottery. It was such a great story, but as a main character she just didn't provide any good material. So it's very important not to become too fascinated with the superficial pitch, and to ensure that it's actually going to work in front of the camera.

REDVALL: What's your position on staging in connection with documentary filmmaking?

MULVAD: Almost everything is staged. The mere fact of your standing in a room with a camera means that there's some sort of awareness of the process of something being filmed. But then some scenes are of course more staged than others. When the mother in *The Good Life* ends up in hospital, she clearly doesn't have a medical crisis for the sake of the film. I'm just there with my camera as this happens. You can't say that that's been staged. But then she starts to talk to the doctor about her daughter. I didn't ask her to do that, but she does of course know that I'm making a film about something very specific. If you work very thoroughly with your characters, and they know what it is you're looking for, my experience is that they often deliver precisely that. They'll do this when the opportunity arises, and often in a way that's much better than anything I could have staged. I hadn't expected to get a scene in which she'd get her own mental space to articulate how she felt, but she chose to give it to me.

I'd be interested in seeing whether I can make more room for the visual in my next film so that the images convey more than the words. But I've seen a lot of examples of films where the director had a specific visual project in mind and set up a framework that was supposed to facilitate it. But within that framework, everything then ends up somehow drying up because it's the director's idea that takes up most of the room, and there's no space left where reality can unfold, or where the characters can develop. That's what's difficult about documentaries, but also what's exciting; the film emerges in that connection between me and the participants, on the one hand, and something completely unpredictable, on the other hand. It's not shaped by my will alone, nor is it shaped entirely by their fate, for there's a synergy between these things. There has to be this natural exchange, a sense of an organic development, otherwise the film just dies.

Sometimes staging helps you to get at something that's far more 'documentary' in nature than if you just go with the flow. If you know what it is you need in order to create an integral story, it's fine to ask the character in question to produce the missing element, instead of having to sift through some 200 hours' worth of material with no real direction to it. Staging might mark the moment when you grasp what the story is really about, and thus find yourself looking for a very particular element. And sometimes this is so much the case that you simply ask people to enact the scene for you. Nobody is interested in making a bad film. The people participating in it certainly aren't. And if you end up missing some of the pieces you need to make a well formed film, then you just haven't done your job well enough.

REDVALL: A number of your films have an international dimension, or an encounter between something Danish and something foreign.

The Colony depicts life in a Danish colony in Argentina; *Enemies of Happiness* is about Afghanistan; and *The Good Life* focuses on two Danish women living in Portugal. Is there a particular reason why your films have this international dimension?

MULVAD: It's not entirely intentional, and I do believe that films can be genuinely international without being international in terms of their settings or themes. A Danish film like *The Last Dance* could have made its way internationally had I had more of an established reputation at the time. It's a question of getting at those universal stories. *The Colony* wasn't that clearly focused in terms of the universal aspects of its story, but that's because there was so much information that needed to be conveyed. The film was motivated by the desire to turn the Danish debate about immigrants around, by telling a story about Danes as immigrants from an historical perspective. But there was so much historical ground to cover, and it was very hard to pinpoint a clear story. *Enemies of Happiness* was a film that I inherited from another director, but I did feel that I was able to make it mine. And once you've had the experience of making a film like *Enemies of Happiness*, which makes its way internationally, well then you start to look for that international dimension. Because it's a whole lot more fun having a large audience and having your film be shown during prime time all over the world, as opposed to having it be seen by small numbers of people when its shown on Danish TV. If you've really got something you want to say, you want to get it out there.

REDVALL: Do you think the Danish documentary filmmaking milieu is unique in any way?

MULVAD: I have to say that I don't know the milieus in other countries that well. But looking at the films, I do think it's fair to say that the Danish ones seem to have been more professionally produced; they seem more polished. I think that our filmmaking milieu is especially important because our country is so small. You just can't afford to be an idiot. You depend on others, on people's willingness to help each other. I don't know whether people can afford to be idiots in France or the USA, but I imagine that a larger milieu makes it easier to think things like, 'I'll keep my secrets close to my chest, and I won't help anyone.' In Denmark we invite each other into the editing room; we help each other, share our experiences, and offer critical feedback on each other's work. We discuss the stories' possibilities. And we don't ask to be paid for any of this. And then we're extremely privileged because there's state funding for film and art, and because we're able to make films that are co-produced by the Danish Film Institute and TV.

REDVALL: What were your reasons for establishing your company, Danish Documentary?

MULVAD: The impetus was our desire to get our films out on DVD, and the production companies we'd worked with weren't interested in doing this. Pernille Rose Grønkjær and I would travel together – she with *The Monastery* (2006) and I with *Enemies of Happiness* – and we almost couldn't bear it, because we'd be at these festivals, where we'd sense that there was a demand for our films, and then we'd have no DVDs to offer, so people couldn't buy them. So Danish Documentary started out as a distribution company. The idea of also producing work grew out of conversations that Pernille and I had about what use we might be able to make of the festival screenings and the awards our films were getting. It turned out that we were pretty much on the same page, and the same was the case for the other directors, Mikala and Phie. We had had to fight hard over a long period of time to make our films. We were thinking something like: 'How can we make our work more fun? How can we capitalize on what we've managed to accomplish?' Our sense was that if we were going to keep on doing what we were doing, and if we were going to make more money doing it – and thereby achieve a greater measure of freedom to do what we wanted – we simply had to have more power. We needed to control the production process more fully.

Danish Documentary consists of four directors, and then we've been fortunate enough to be able to get a producer to join us – namely, Sigrid Dyekjær – who is someone we're all eager to work with. She is very strong in terms of the creative process, and has a lot of experience with international documentary filmmaking. We're a bit of a kamikaze company because we solve the problems as they arise. We don't have a fancy set-up or a bunch of assistants. Right now we have two other people working with us. They've been hired because we're involved in a number of productions, need their help, and are able to pay them. The concept is flexibility: if we're not producing anything, then we don't have any expenses, other than rent. We've emphasized this aspect a lot because we've had the experience of seeing money that was supposed to have gone into our films get spent on running a company instead. Nobody gets rich making documentary films, but as a director you're interested in making sure that the money that gets spent

REDVALL: has an impact on what you actually see on the screen, instead of having been used to finance a bunch of lunches.

REDVALL: Is it a coincidence that Danish Documentary consists of five women?

MULVAD: Yes, I think it is. The point was that we had the same needs, had spent time at the Film School together, had travelled together, and had worked with the same producer. A man could easily have been part of the mix.

REDVALL: The company's profile description says that your aim is to touch people and to entertain them. Why is it important to emphasize entertainment in connection with documentary filmmaking?

MULVAD: That's a battle we want to fight. My generation was simply carpet-bombed with black-and-white documentaries about WWII during secondary school. And those films created that dusty feeling of obligation that has been such a feature of the genre. We feel a certain obligation to try to shake that off. When my cohort from the Film School went to IDFA, we had an eye-opening experience watching films like *Grey Gardens* (dir. Ellen Hovde, Albert Maysles, David Maysles, and Muffie Meyer, 1975) or *Dark Days* (dir. Marc Singer, 2000). These were films that brought you into a genuinely cinematic universe, whether their focus was homeless people in New York or old ladies living out in the countryside in The Hamptons. What we sensed was that documentary film was about much more than information. A lot has happened since then. We now have CPH:DOX, and there's the TV programme called Documania on national TV. So there's a lot more diversity associated with the genre at this point, and then, of course, there's the Internet, which allows you to find all sorts of things. In the past that just wasn't possible. Things were secret and really inaccessible. But at the same time, my generation clearly dreams of making films that will be shown in the cinema. Our desire is to make films that are at once cinematic and entertaining.

Note

1   Lars Movin, 'Storhed og fald', in *Ekko* 51 (2010): 46–50.

Chapter 14

Michael Noer

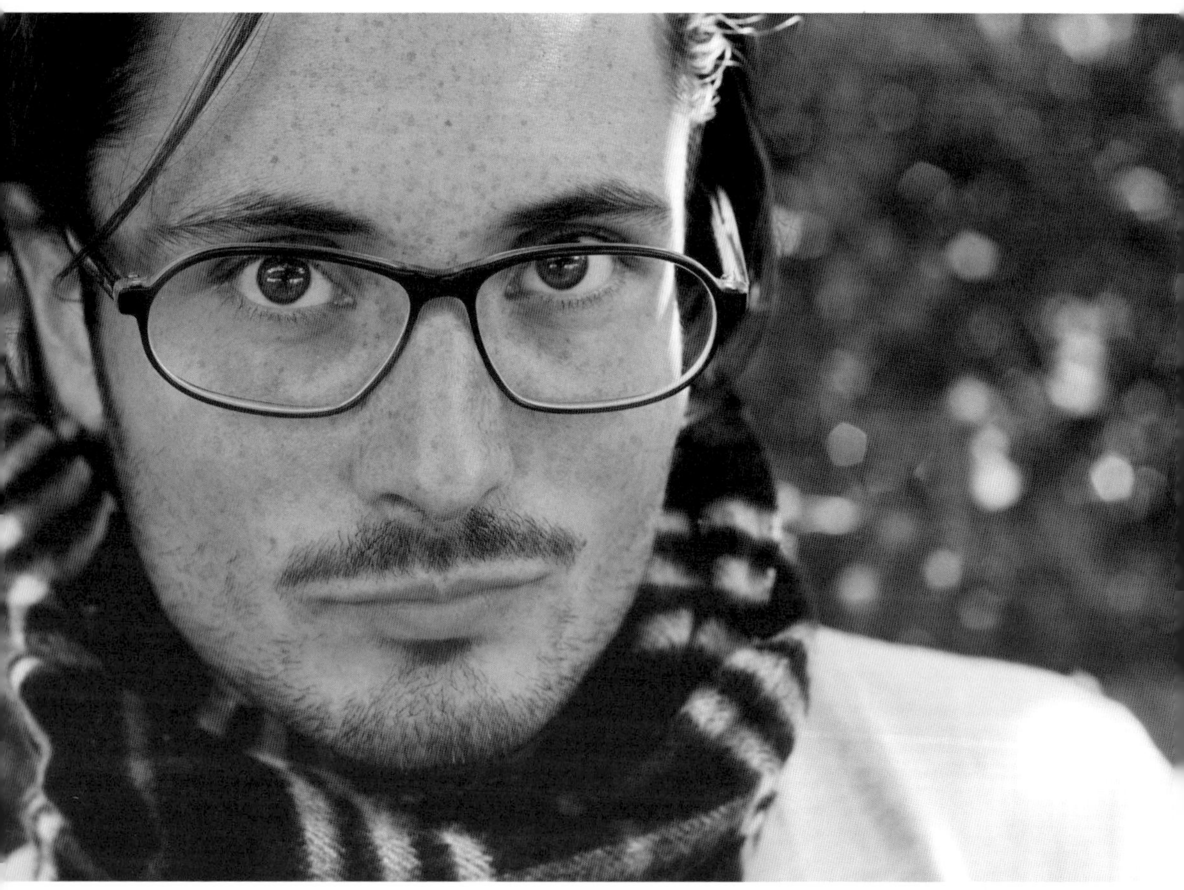

Michael Noer. Portrait by Jon Nyholm. Courtesy of Jon Nyholm and The Danish Film Institute Stills & Posters Archive.

orn 1978, in Esbjerg. Noer received his training at the National Film School of Denmark, and graduated with a documentary diploma film about Ole Ege. In spite of his young age, Michael Noer has already left his mark on Danish film, both fiction and non-fiction. His films are characterized by a strong sense of social and psychological realism, and often engage closely with male communities, with groups and their dynamics, and with couples. These tendencies are evident in his first feature film, *R* (2010), which he co-directed with Tobias Lindholm. The film is set in the tough environment of a Danish prison, which it depicts with an almost unrelenting documentary realism. *R* won almost all of the most important Bodil and Robert prizes in 2011. Noer's characteristic approach is also evident in *De vilde hjerter* (*The Wild Hearts*, 2008), which focuses on a group of men whose trip to Poland becomes an occasion for rituals of masculinity and wild behaviour, but also expressions of tenderness. A similar style description is also pertinent in the case of *Vesterbro* (2007), which is about the ups and downs of life as experienced by a young Danish couple. Noer has also played a pioneering role with his online documentary diary project, *Doxwise*, which provides an interactive context for video diaries shot by ordinary young Danes.

Documentary features:

2010   *Son of God* (with Khavn de la Cruz)
2008   *Doxwise* (*Doxwise Diary*; www.doxwise.dk)
2008   *De vilde hjerter* (*The Wild Hearts*)
2008   *Roskilde* (with Ulrik Wivel)
2007   *Vesterbro*
2007   *Jorden under mine fødder* ('The Earth under My Feet')

Documentary shorts:

2003   *En rem af huden* ('A Touch of the Same,' diploma film)

Television:

2005   *Mimis sidste valg* ('Mimi's Last Election')

Fiction films:

2010   *R* (with Tobias Lindholm)
2006   *Hawaii*

BONDEBJERG: You're from Esbjerg, a town on the western coast of Jutland. You grew up in the provinces, without a father and surrounded by women, and in other contexts you've often said that these circumstances have shaped both you and your films. But in spite of being from one of the more peripheral parts of Denmark, you managed to get into the European Film College in Ebeltoft in 1998, and then into the National Film School of Denmark in 1999. How did you end up choosing this path?

NOER: In a way, I was a very spoilt child. I was almost applauded out of bed in the morning by my mother and grandmother, both of whom really nurtured whatever creative talent I had. One experience that was decisive was seeing Lars von Trier's *The Element of Crime* (1984) as a young man, when I was living in the provinces. That film and other films shown by DR2 late at night really honed my appreciation for films that were strange and different. Those films gave me a powerful sense of what one could do with one's creativity, and I hadn't really had that before. I'd thought of film as mere entertainment, and there's nothing wrong with that, but those films taught me that film can do a lot more than entertain people. As a child and teenager, I'd always drawn and written things, and towards the end of my time in secondary school, I came across some promotional materials from the European Film College. I worked really hard to pull together the money I needed for the programme, and I got into it in 1998. The special thing about the European Film College is that you see a lot of films and hear a lot about film, but you also get to experience a milieu that is both creative and competitive. I made a lot of friends there, and they're now working in the film industry and remain friends to this day. But while I was at the European Film College, I also learnt how to work with my creative ideas in a more goal-oriented way. It was during that period that my first film projects started to take shape. I made a documentary film about a girl and her relationship with a 94-year-old person living in a nursing home, and a fiction film about a young girl who wants to commit suicide. I'd dabbled with film during my secondary school years, but entirely on my own, and these films were my first serious attempt at filmmaking.

BONDEBJERG: In 1999, when you were only 20-years-old, you got into the Documentary & TV Department at the National Film School of Denmark, which is quite an achievement. Your talent must have been really obvious to everyone involved in the selection process because the School tends to admit much older applicants.

NOER: To be honest, there was a bit of a hitch along the way because the year before, in 1998, I'd actually applied for admission to the film department, which focuses on fiction filmmaking. But I didn't get in because I was too young; and perhaps not good enough. What do I know? But then I heard about the Documentary & TV programme, which was fairly new at the time. Of course that didn't exactly impress all the film nerds at the European Film College, who worshipped the art of film and didn't think much of TV. But when I applied, I met Arne Bro and I immediately sensed that there was something special about the programme and that it suited me. I could tell that it would provide me with an opportunity to explore and develop my creativity, and that it had little to do with the distorted image, with which I'd been operating, of what a TV course was like. It was really perfect because, on the one hand, I was forced to work more directly with reality and with documentary modes of filmmaking, and on the other hand, I was allowed to do all this in a very personal way.

BONDEBJERG: What was your experience of the Film School like? What do you feel that you got out of your years there, both personally and professionally?

NOER: On a personal level I'd say that it was really quite overwhelming. Not only had I been admitted to a very prestigious school, but the Esbjerg lad that I was suddenly found himself in Copenhagen. When I started the programme at the National Film School of Denmark, I'd only spent the night in the capital on four previous occasions. My experience of the city was really a dramatic one because it felt a bit like a cultural revolution. For me, it was also almost a revolutionary experience to get into a programme where people were constantly being encouraged to work with their creative talents in a very personal way. To discover that there were people who actually took what we were doing seriously, and who challenged us, was simply amazing. The first time I met Arne Bro he gave us all a black Moleskin notebook, and he told us that this was the most important book he had to give us. I didn't know what sort of book it was, but I could see that it was a very fine one. But then I opened it and realized that the pages were all blank. And then Arne said that we ourselves would be writing the things that would become the most important part of our programme. Arne was very good at challenging us. In addition to Arne, there was Mogens Rukov, who was also a source of enormous inspiration. He was the kind of person people in Esbjerg would have steered clear of, but here in Copenhagen he was an oracle; a man who'd sit there mumbling strange truths or delivering offbeat lectures. I remember he gave a lecture on the difference between driving a car in European as compared with American films. His point was that in American films it's the car that drives the main character, whereas it's the other way around in European films. He was both a mystic and a great teacher.

BONDEBJERG: The relation between TV and film is often a source of conflict, and there's a lot of reciprocal prejudice in both of the milieus in question. At the National Film School, we've got this TV programme that aims to do something other than just train people to work in mainstream TV production. But if we look at the people who went through the programme, it quickly becomes apparent that they're actually doing quite well in the TV industry. A lot of them are managing to produce a mix of more mainstream as well as personal work. What was your experience of the relationship between TV and film during your years at the School?

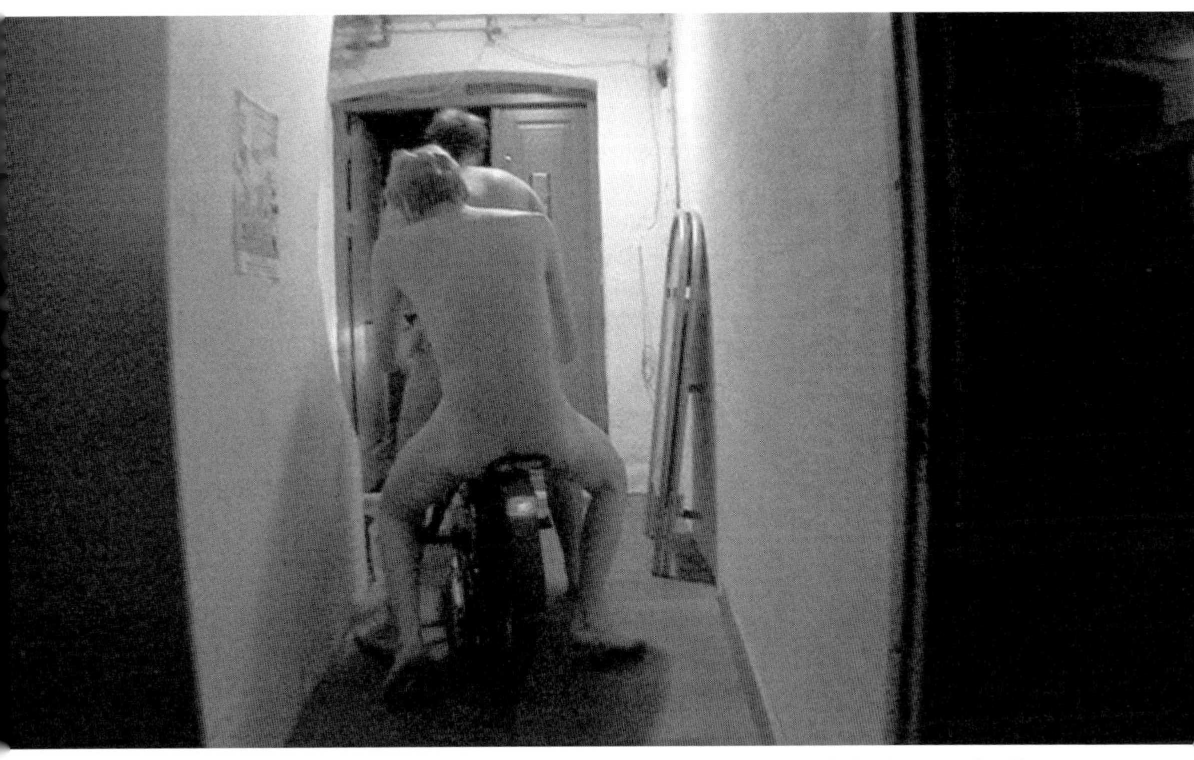

Showing off in the nude and on a motorbike (*The Wild Hearts*, framegrab, cinematography by Thomas Gerhardt).

NOER:
When I was at the Film School, the Dogme films had just met with massive success, so we were completely in awe of those film directors and the milieu to which they belonged. At the time, the field of documentary filmmaking probably lacked someone we could look up to in quite the same way. We did, of course, have Anne Wivel and Jørgen Leth, who were also involved in our programme. But even though they had a lot to give, both as persons and artists, what was missing was that sense of new beginnings, of a new generation making its mark. Ten years on, it's clear that the situation has changed completely. Now it's actually possible to talk about the impact that a new generation has had on the aesthetics and practices of documentary filmmaking. I was very young, and I didn't really feel that I was on the same wavelength as the people I was meeting from the older generation. We didn't talk about TV much, and if we did, it was seen mostly as an obstacle that had to be overcome, rather than as an opportunity. I suppose I felt that TV simply should be seen as a window, and that there are huge differences between the various windows that the Danish TV stations provide, between TV 2 and DR2, for example.

One thing that was really important was the 'open area' editing set-up that the School worked with. You couldn't shut yourself into a room with your own product, but were on the contrary encouraged to make good use of other people. We were encouraged to challenge each other and to learn from each other, and none of this was in any way incompatible with the idea of finding our own voice. I was especially close to Phie Ambo, who was almost like an older sister to me. But the whole group was important, and we really operated like a collective. That experience was really amazing, and it taught me some of the most important things I learnt at the School.

BONDEBJERG:
In an interview in *Ekko* that pits you and Erik Clausen against each other, you make a number of statements, one of which has to do with your relationship to fiction and non-fiction filmmaking.[1] Your assumption is that there's no problem at all with the idea of moving back and forth between these two types of filmmaking. I suppose that this idea is very much embedded in the Film School's programme, because while the differences between documentary and fiction filmmaking are acknowledged at the School, they're not seen as being inherent in specific cinematic devices. That is, one and the same device can be used to good

effect by both a fiction and a non-fiction filmmaker. How do you see the relationship between fiction and non-fiction, and the differences involved in working with the one as compared with the other type of filmmaking?

NOER: I believe the difference between documentary filmmaking and fiction filmmaking is very important, and I would be really unhappy if people mistook a film that I'd made as a documentary for fiction, for example. Actually, I also think that it's quite problematic to emphasize all sorts of aesthetic devices in a documentary film in order to get the look of a fiction film. But although it's important to keep the two types of filmmaking separate, there are lots of purely practical techniques and devices that are relevant in both contexts. Tightening a story, making it more focused, defining the characters better – these are tasks that are common to both types of filmmaking, although they're taken up in relation to different sorts of materials with quite different connections with reality. When you're making a documentary film it's important not to be too ambitious about formal issues at the outset. If you are, you may find it hard to access the reality you want to describe. As a documentary filmmaker, you have to do your research first. You have to find your reality and your characters first, and then work on finding the film form that is appropriate. In principle, fiction filmmaking provides a lot more freedom in that respect. But, in my case, the differences between the two may not actually be that great, because I also work a lot with realism, characters, and psychology in my fiction films.

BONDEBJERG: As a category, documentary filmmaking encompasses a lot of sub-categories: expository, observational, poetic, and performative types of documentary, to use some of Bill Nichols' influential terms. Your documentaries seem to be mostly observational in nature. Do you see yourself as drawing on the more anthropological or ethnographic approaches to documentary filmmaking?

NOER: Yes, the observational approach – and the formal properties that go with it – inform all of my documentary films. I have myself had some really negative experiences with certain stories I wanted to tell because I let my ambitions about film form get in the way of the reality I was interested in. What happened was that the people whom I wanted to depict were left with no room to express themselves. So, as far as I'm concerned, it's important that reality is allowed to unfold as it would before I start to stage things or to work in any systematic way with film form. My desire to make fiction films is closely connected to my desire to be able to control reality more, to process it creatively. But as a documentary filmmaker, I feel a lot more affinity for the observational approach to reality than I do for the poetic or more performative approaches.

BONDEBJERG: You made a few films during your film school years, before really establishing yourself with documentaries about some of the wilder aspects of youth culture. Your diploma film, *En rem af huden* ('A Touch of the Same'), is a portrait film focusing on Ole Ege, who is also the subject of Torben Skjødt Jensens *Den grimme dreng* (*The Naughty Boy*, 1996). Were you inspired by that film?

NOER: No, not in any direct way. I did see it, but I wanted to make a different kind of film, and I do feel that I found my own tone and perspective, and that I also developed a form that is very different from Skjødt Jensen's. What I found interesting about making precisely that film was that it depicts a man from a pretty tough milieu, whereas other portrait films typically focus on artists from more of a fine arts perspective. Here was this man who stood in the door and talked on the basis of his experiences in the porn milieu. But it turned out that he was a bit of a contradiction, and that provided an angle on the film's structure. He wanted to talk about his own porn films and about the porn milieu more generally, with all of the cynicism and commercialism that it entails. But at the same time he also wanted to talk a lot about love because he was really interested in that. His long-time involvement with the porn milieu had clearly had an impact on him, as had his very substantial consumption of alcohol. But he also felt a very real, albeit unhappy, love for his Ulla, the woman he'd always really loved. The film was shot over a period of several days, but we asked him to wear the same thing every day so that we could edit the takes into a dynamic, observational documentary film that looked as though it had been shot in a single day. The film has been shown at a lot of festivals and has also been sold to various TV stations abroad, including a Finnish one.

BONDEBJERG: You made your next film, *Hawaii*, through the Film Workshop. This fiction film also focuses on the porn milieu, and is set in a porn shop located in the Vesterbro area of Copenhagen. Why did you make your second film a fiction film, and why did you choose to tell the story you did?

NOER: I've always been drawn to both documentary and fiction filmmaking. So I was very comfortable with the idea of testing the porn milieu theme in the context of a more fictional form. With perfect hindsight, I'd say that it allowed me to try out some things before making my first feature film, *R*. With *R*, we tried to avoid all the mistakes we'd made in the first little film. *Hawaii* was a pure fiction film, but it had a powerful documentary core, and the idea was that the story would unfold over the course of a single day. I think that what I discovered was that it didn't have enough realistic or documentary content to it, and so that's something we tried to change in connection with *R*. It was a lot of fun being able to make *Hawaii*, which was really a stylistic exercise inasmuch as I didn't have to prove anything to anyone with it.

BONDEBJERG: In 2005, you made your first grand-scale portrait film for TV, namely *Mimis sidste valg* ('Mimi's Last Election'), which focuses on Mimi Jakobsen's exit from Danish politics and on the defeat that her party, which had been established by her father, ended up suffering. It's a dramatic and fateful story. How do you see that film today?

NOER: I think it was much more important for my subsequent career than my first two films, for it opened a lot of doors for me. I'm actually really happy with that film. It was the third time I opted to tell a story that unfolds in a single day and embodies a portrait with a very powerful dramatic dimension. The film ended up being a lot easier to make than it could have been because Mimi was very open during the various shoots that we did. It's a story with almost Shakespearean dimensions: a daughter caught between her father and her son. The film has the same kind of epic drive and drama that you find in *The Godfather* (dir. Francis Ford Coppola, 1972). Mimi had a lot to live up to and it was all very challenging, but she herself describes this in a very open and sensitive way in the film. The reason the film opened so many doors for me was that it somehow combined journalistic elements, archival images, and an observational approach to a politician's life and daily existence, with a psychological drama of the kind that we associate with fiction films. The film also proved that I was able to reach prime-time TV audiences. The film was made in collaboration with Lynx Media, a production company I'd worked for before. But what was really decisive for the film was the agreement that we reached with Mimi, which allowed us to follow her very closely. This meant that the TV stations were interested in buying the film. Of course it was also helpful that Christoffer Guldbrandsen's *Lykketoft finale* ('Lykketoft's Final,' 2005) appeared the very same year. I feel that 'Mimi's Last Election' proved that the graduates of the National Film School were capable of producing prime-time TV material.

BONDEBJERG: 'Mimi's Last Election' put you in a far more professional league at a still relatively young age. I take it that the film's success also meant significantly improved economic circumstances for you?

NOER: It's true that there were times when I only just managed to scrape by, had to work on other people's projects, and had to make do with very little. But I was fortunate enough, very early on, to receive a number of prizes and scholarships, which really helped a lot. Among others, I received the Nordic Film Award, which was worth 100,000 Danish Crowns. When you're as young as I was when I started out as a filmmaker, you can live on next to nothing, and I didn't have a lot of recurring expenses.

BONDEBJERG: In 2007, you made the first of a series of documentary films dealing with young people, namely *Vesterbro*. Copenhagen Bombay produced the film, which was supported by the DFI and TV 2. What prompted you to make this film?

NOER: Actually, it all began because Martin Zandvliet and Sarita Christensen had worked together at Zentropa. Sarita gave me a call because she was in the process of establishing a children and youth unit at Zentropa. That initiative eventually turned into the production company Copenhagen Bombay, which is very much oriented towards young people. And Copenhagen Bombay then produced not only *Vesterbro*, but also *Doxwise Diary* and *The Wild Hearts*. At the time, I wasn't really thinking along these lines, but I figured out that the people I lived next to on Vesterbro had excellent potential as characters in a youth documentary, so I leapt at Sarita's offer. Julie, who is one of the main characters in the film and part of the couple on which it focuses, would have these amazing parties, and since I was already part of that milieu, the project became a matter of exploring just how far it's possible to take the documentary depiction of the private sphere. My other documentaries about young people are also part of that same sociological and cinematic project. Above and beyond the idea of working very intimately with the young people in the film, there was another crucial element. And that was that we decided to let the characters shoot a lot of the material about their lives themselves. That's an approach I've used in all my films about young people.

BONDEBJERG: Through your focus on young people, and use of images or even video diaries produced by them (as in *Doxwise Diary*), you've managed to create a distinctive style, but also to capture something very contemporaneous. You capture some of the modes of expression that have been embraced by a younger generation that's very involved with new media and social networking. Were you aware of doing that? Or were you simply inclined to make use of these forms of expression and types of media because you're relatively young yourself?

NOER: In the case of *Vesterbro*, it was the first time I saw form and psychology as going hand in hand, and I think that's why there's that sense of capturing the spirit of the times. For example, the music in the film, which wasn't produced specially for it, is music we actually heard as we were doing the shooting. It's part of the film's authenticity and helps to reflect the way young people live today. And the same is true of the way they speak, of their way of being in the world. The film captures all of these things because of the way in which it was shot, through the pulse that it has.

BONDEBJERG: Although the film depicts young people with the kind of authenticity that you just mentioned, it's still very much your film. For example, your use of a whole range of dramaturgical and aesthetic devices is very clear. You begin in the past, then you develop a dramatic conflict, and then you go on to bring some of the typical traits of the road movie genre into play, and so on. I take it that you were very much the controlling force behind the film?

NOER: Yes, of course I was. However, the dramatic elements and actual events were also quite decisive, probably because I was almost at the same stage in my life as the young people depicted in the film. For example, for both Julie's partner and myself, the conflict surrounding her pregnancy and then the abortion was a really dramatic experience. That conflict was very consuming in reality, and that had an impact on the film. We really built the film around that conflict, which was one that could be unpacked at several different levels. It had to do with the differences between men and women, with decisions that can be taken either alone or together, with the way in which an existential crisis forces you to ask yourself a key question: 'What do I want to do with my life?' In a way, I didn't actually have to construct the dramaturgy myself. The film's documentary reality gave rise to the film's dramatic material. We just had to capture it and give it a cinematic shape. It was when Julie was completely beside herself that she started to use the camera in a more confessional or subjective way because it was very much her crisis. When I show the film to secondary school students, it's very clear that the girls side with Julie, while the boy's take Martin's side.

The response patterns almost suggest a kind of gender-based ur-conflict. I think this shows that the film really captures something very fundamental, and speaks to young people in a very direct way.

BONDEBJERG: Isn't *Vesterbro* a good example of how documentary film actually can surpass the fiction film? That film delivers a dramatic story, but it also provides an authentic experience of reality.

NOER: At the end of the film Martin says, 'I feel that I've learnt something, I'm just not sure what it is.' That's an utterance I'm very pleased with because I think it mirrors the attitude that young viewers have to the film. The film has an authenticity and honesty to it because we're not dealing with a story that we've simply invented. Although it's a documentary film, it easily stands its ground against films in the youth film category, which tend to tell fictional stories about young people's problems and their attempts to find themselves. That's been my sense when I've shown the film to young audiences and at film festivals. It really is a film with a very authentic, psychological story.

BONDEBJERG: As you said, your documentaries about young people were all to some extent a matter of testing just how far you could take your camera into an intimate private sphere. In *Vesterbro* you go deep into that sphere. Your camera follows the young people into the bedroom, and also depicts their innermost feelings and the conflicts that provoke them. The tendency in this day and age is to display what used to be seen as private; to bring what's backstage to the front of the stage. This does raise questions about where the limits lie. As a filmmaker, do you have an ethical line that you wouldn't want to cross?

NOER: I think I would have to say that when I'm shooting I don't feel there are any limits. In principle I believe that it should be possible to film and show everything. However, in the process of producing the final edit, there may well be some considerations that have to be taken into account. If I start by establishing limits during the process of shooting the film, I may end up introducing a lot of noise and confusion. If limits are to be established and certain scenes are to be occluded, this has to be done during the editing phase. But I actually talk to the film's participants about the film's central idea and premise and about what I'd like to film and how. And sometimes I'm met with a clear 'no.' That happened, for example, in the case of 'Mimi's Last Election.' I'd asked for permission to be there when she put on her make-up in the morning. But that's where she drew the line, although she otherwise was very open.

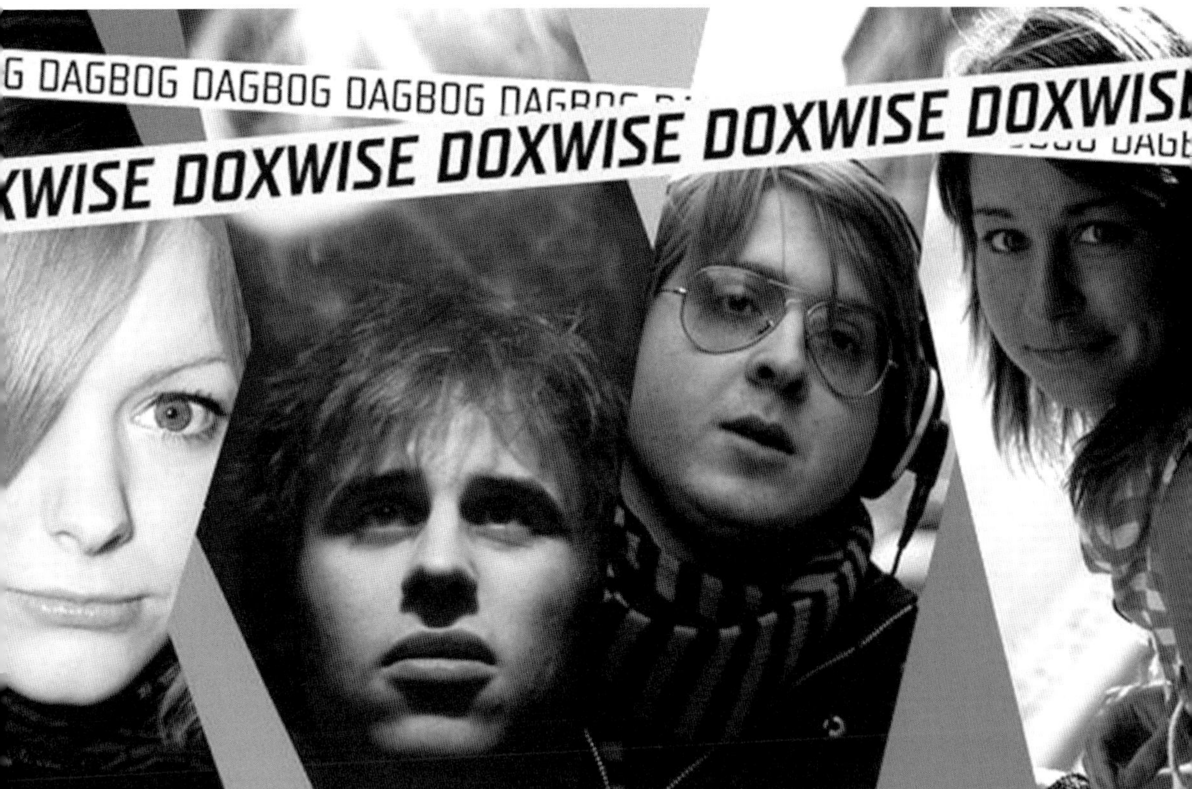

Four of the characters shooting video diaries (*Doxwise*, web-shot).

BONDEBJERG:

In *The Wild Hearts* there's a lot of extreme, masculine behaviour, but also a clear comic element. I think a lot of men are able to recognize themselves in that film, even if they haven't participated in all of the transgressive rituals that are depicted. Did your childhood amongst women make it personally important for you to make that film?

NOER:

Much of what I do involves a mix of coincidences, projects that just sort of come knocking, and which I become excited about and try to turn into something more personal. And this film was no exception. In this case, the impetus was that Julie, from *Vesterbro*, knew some of these wild guys and heard that they were planning this all-guys motorbike trip to Poland. It sounded ridiculous and absurd enough to spark my interest. And when I did some initial shooting, as a way of getting a sense of the milieu and the story, I ended up with what actually became the very first scene in the finished film: the one in which they all get branded with a red hot iron ahead of the trip. What struck me was the mad commitment these guys had to their project. That's what caught my interest, but I was also intrigued by the truly absurd and comic nature of their project. But it's of course also a film in which these men live out complexes having to do with their relationships to their mothers and fathers, and generally act out gender stereotypes. And that's also the way it was for me because we became part of the project and almost part of the group. For example, we were also naked when we shot those scenes in which the film's participants were naked. In terms of the film's characters, the point was clearly to learn more about themselves, to act out certain things, so that deeper truths beneath the surface of their lives could come to light. At the same time, the whole set-up is a massively staged one. There was one scene, which we actually shot but didn't include in the film, where the guys were talking about the significance of the camera's presence, about who was playing to it the most and thus was the least authentic. But the whole project was, of course, a staged event that you can only relate to as an absurd comedy. It you take it all too seriously, the film becomes incomprehensible, although the very fact of playing around with roles can be a source of deeper self-understanding.

BONDEBJERG:

The film was produced with support from the DFI and DR2. Was the production process a smooth one?

NOER:

Yes, I'd have to say that that's been the case for all my films. I've never had to deal with serious conflicts about money or ideology.

<table>
<tr><td></td><td>

My strategy has always been to shoot a fair bit before negotiating the financing. That way I can simply get going, without a lot of bureaucracy and paperwork, and without having to ask someone for permission first. When I then turn to the Danish Film Institute [DFI] or to the TV stations, I'm in a fairly strong position, in that I'm actually able to show them some actual cinematic material. That strategy has worked very well for me. A significant factor here is no doubt the fact that my films appeal to young audiences, and in a way that's fairly unique.

</td></tr>
<tr><td>BONDEBJERG:</td><td>

In your third documentary youth film, *Doxwise Diary*, you move into the online world as it's experienced by young people. The project, which involves a series, is based on the video diaries of four young people between 18 and 20 years old. *Doxwise Diary* was initially shown on MySpace, and in a way that facilitated a lot of interaction between the video diaries, the young people who made them, and the viewers. Up until now, there are very few Danish directors who have tried their hand at making documentaries for the Internet. How did the idea for this film occur to you?

</td></tr>
<tr><td>NOER:</td><td>

Here too it was a matter of opportunities that came my way, combined with an interest that I myself had in making that kind of film. In the context of Copenhagen Bombay, Sarita, Julie, and I had talked about how interesting it would be to mount a project that really gave young people an opportunity to express themselves. At the same time, the DFI was very eager to support Net-based documentaries. It's an entirely different process from that of making a film, and a separate budget had been established to support all this. I was already thinking about making a film with several characters; a kind of multi-plot film in which the characters would reflect and mirror each other. In a way, that idea worked better as a Net-based project than as a film because the Net is more like TV, where you can zap around. Julie and I got the process going by establishing profiles on MySpace, just to see what it was like, and it turned out to be really amusing. So MySpace became the platform we used. Our approach was to give each of the young participants a camera, and to edit what they produced as we went along and then upload it to their profiles. And that worked brilliantly. There were a lot of advantages to be had – both for us and for MySpace – from making use of an existing platform. MySpace was able to use the project for advertising purposes, and we got a technologically proficient platform, one that had been

</td></tr>
</table>

tried and tested. Once we'd chosen our four participants, we told them to develop their diary in relation to an issue or conflict that went to the core of their lives. And that turned out to be very different in each of the four cases. Esben was looking for a lover; Pierre had a problem with hash; Amanda's mother was sick; and Sabrina was about to come out of the closet as a lesbian. We'd placed an advertisement and received ten expressions of interest, and of those ten there were really only four that matched what we were looking for. The series was shown twice, and the second time it was *Politiken* that provided the necessary platform. The project was generally seen as interesting, and we ended up getting a media prize for it.

BONDEBJERG: *Roskilde*, which was made by a fairly large group of directors, is a classic rock film. You haven't really focused on music in your work, although there are clear connections between *Roskilde* and your other films inasmuch as it deals with a cult phenomenon that is part of a contemporary youth culture. What role did you play in the making of this film?

NOER: Yes, the Roskilde festival clearly speaks to me and the youth culture that I myself am part of. But it's very much Ulrik Wivel's film. He's the film's main director. I'm part of it all, as are the others who are credited as his collaborators.

BONDEBJERG: *Jorden under mine fødder* ('The Earth under My Feet') deals with a home for children and young people in Hundested, and appears to be linked to interests that have been constant throughout your filmmaking career. *Son of God* (2010), on the other hand, is about miracles in the Philippines, and seems to chart a new direction for you. How do you see these films as fitting into the body of work that you've produced?

NOER: There's a clear continuity between my earlier films and 'The Earth under My Feet,' which is an observational youth documentary. That was actually one of the most complicated and time-consuming projects I've ever been involved in. I only succeeded in making it because a lot of different foundations were willing to support it. The characters I depict are quite fragile, and so it took time to win their trust. Also, I had to follow them over a period of three years in order to get a developmental perspective on their story. The film is, of course, somewhat different inasmuch as it deals with young people who are handicapped. But at the same time, there's a clear thread back to my other films because it's also concerned with this issue of just how far into the private sphere you can take the camera. The film also depicts some rather big existential feelings and themes; perhaps a bit too big, in fact. A more down-to-earth approach might actually have been better. *Son of God* is a completely different kind of film. I just thought it would be amusing to make it. It was quite a challenge to shoot in a completely different country and in a different culture. I learnt a lot from making that film.

BONDEBJERG: You've made a significant contribution to the new Danish documentary cinema, yet you achieved your real breakthrough, both with the critics and the general public, with your first fiction film, *R*. The film won just about all of the most important Robert and Bodil prizes in 2011. Did you draw on your documentary filmmaking experience in making this film, or is fiction filmmaking simply something quite different, as far as you are concerned?

NOER: I worked very closely with Tobias Lindholm on that film, and he's incredibly good with language and dialogue, among other things. We were a great team in terms of developing the characters and their contexts, both psychologically and socially. We complemented each other really well, and we'd learnt a lot about what fiction filmmaking involves from having worked together on *Hawaii*. Our film came out around the same time as Thomas Vinterberg's *Submarino* (2010), which Tobias also wrote the script for. And I'd say that the films point to a heightened realism in Danish film, although they're also quite different.

BONDEBJERG: The film's realism and its excessive violence are certainly striking. I take it that the realism is informed by your work as a documentary filmmaker.

NOER: The realism is absolutely necessary in a film like that. The explosive violence is a direct result of violence that's always there, just beneath the surface of things. The film's story is actually very simple because it's basically about the main character's desire to survive and about how he doesn't make it. The choice of the prison world turned out to be a really productive one because that world is full of rules and routines, and they're a constant source of conflict. Our approach to realism was certainly informed by our documentary take on reality, but it was also influenced by the unrelenting realism of the Belgian Dardenne brothers. Our point of contrast was the many American prison films, in which the message is strident and where good and evil are very clearly defined. We tried to steer clear of black-and-white thinking, as we were looking for a much more subdued kind of realism.

BONDEBJERG: Do you see yourself as working with both fiction and non-fiction filmmaking in the future? Or does the success enjoyed by *R* make fiction filmmaking more appealing at this point?

NOER: I certainly have no intention of abandoning what I see as a profoundly realistic or documentary approach to reality. Right now, I'm most interested in pursuing fiction filmmaking, and I'll be doing precisely that in my next two films, which are set in a milieu involving criminal youths and in a nursing home. But I'm sure I'll return to documentary filmmaking at some point in the future.

Note

1   Synne Rifbjerg, 'I clinch om filmkunsten,' *Ekko* 49 (2010): 22–29.

Chapter 15

Katia Forbert Petersen

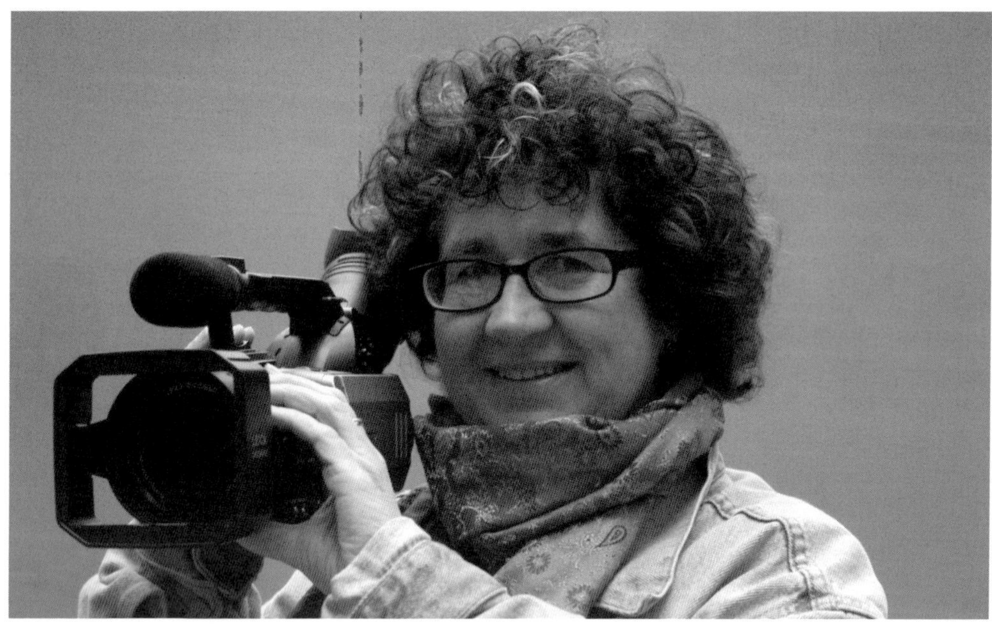

Katia Forbert Petersen. Portrait by Wojciech Kloczko. Courtesy of Wojciech Kloczko and Katia Forbert Petersen.

B orn in 1949, to a family with strong links to film over a period of 100 years, Forbert Petersen was trained as a cinematographer at the National Film School in Lodz, Poland. She completed her training in 1969, and has since worked as a cinematographer on more than 150 films, in Denmark and elsewhere. She has worked for ZDF and the National Film Board of Canada, among other organizations. In 1960, Katia Forbert Petersen and her family came to Denmark as political refugees from then communist Poland. During her years in Copenhagen, Katia Forbert Petersen has directed a significant number of documentary films and two short fiction films, in addition to her extensive work as a cinematographer. In her first Danish documentary film, *Polske piger* ('Polish Girls,' 1973), she already began to explore the women's issues that would become a central feature of her work. Her films depict the everyday lives of women (as, for example, in *Sammen med Lena* ['Together With Lena,' 1979]), but also women caught between different identities and cultures. Examples of this second tendency include her first film ('Polish Girls'), as well as *Kvinde i eksil* (*Woman in Exile*, 1988), a portrait of an Iranian immigrant, and *Gud gav hende en Mercedes Benz* (*God Gave Her a Mercedes Benz*, 1991), focusing on resilient African women. Both these perspectives are evident in *Mit iranske paradis* (*My Iranian Paradise*, 2008), which she made with Annette Mari Olsen. Katia Forbert Petersen has also depicted the thoughts and lives of children in several of her films. Focusing on two 6-year-olds in a hospital, *En uge uden smil* ('A Week Without Smiling,' 1980) provides insight into the everyday lives of children in Denmark. In *Min egen motorhest* ('My Own Motor Horse,' 2001), a film with a dynamic mode of narration, the focus is on young speedway drivers. In the films in which children play a central role, images of other countries and cultures are also important, as, for example, in *Bag bjergene* (*Behind the Mountains*, 2004) and *Fuglen der kunne spå* (*The Bird That Could Tell Fortunes*, 2007). Katia Forbert Petersen's films often feature documentary portraits, but she's also made three full blown portrait films, all of which are more experimental than many of her other films. An autobiographical dimension is clearly evident in the portrait that Forbert Petersen creates of her father in *Mand med kamera* (*Man With Camera*, 1995), a film that encompasses a variety of histories: family history, as well as media, cultural, and military history – the latter as seen through the eyes of her father. Two striking avant-garde artists provide the basis for cinematic portraits in *Von Triers 100 øjne* (*Von Trier's 100 Eyes*, 2000) and *Lyd på liv* (*Sound On Life*, 2006). While the former focuses on von Trier's production of *Dancer in the Dark* (2000), the latter looks at the composer Else Marie Pade at the age of 80.

Documentary features:

2012   *Mission Rape* (with Annette Mari Olsen)
2012   *Fangekoret* (*Prisoner's Choir*, with Annette Mari Olsen)
2011   *Sangbogen og de røde sko – om bombningen af Den Franske Skole*
        ('The Song Book and the Red Shoes: The Bombing of the French School')
2008   *Mit iranske paradis* (*My Iranian Paradise*, with Annette Mari Olsen)
2000   *Von Triers 100 øjne* (*Von Trier's 100 Eyes*)
1999   *Tiden før øjeblikket* ('The Time Just Before the Moment')
1996   *To kvinder på en flod* ('Two Women on the River', with Iben Haahr Andersen)
1995   *Mand med kamera* (*Man With Camera*)

Documentary shorts:

2007   *Fuglen der kunne spå* (*The Bird That Could Tell Fortunes*,
        with Annette Mari Olsen)
2006   *Lyd på liv* (*Sound on Life*, with Iben Haahr Andersen)
2004   *Bag bjergene* (*Behind the Mountains*, with Annette Mari Olsen)
2001   *Min egen motorhest* ('My Own Motor Horse', with Iben Haahr Andersen)
1991   *Gud gav hende en Mercedes Benz* (*God Gave Her a Mercedes Benz*)
1990   *Ønskebarn* ('Planned Child')
1988   *Kvinde i eksil* (*Woman in Exile*, with Annette Mari Olsen)
1987   *Mit søde barn* ('My Sweet Child')
1985   *Johanne fra Daugbjerg* ('Johanne from Daugbjerg')
1984   *Jeg vil have dig tilbage* ('I Want You Back')
1982   *Teknik for dig og mig* ('Technique For You and Me')
1980   *En uge uden smil* ('A Week Without Smiling')
1979   *Sammen med Lena* ('Together With Lena')
1976   *Havets lavvandsfauna* ('The Low Water Ocean Fauna')
1973   *Polske piger* ('Polish Girls')

Fiction films:

1989   *En fremmed piges dagbog* ('A Foreign Girl's Diary', short fiction film)
1988   *Jako*

BONDEBJERG: Could you talk about your Polish background, and your training at the National Film School in Lodz? How has your background shaped you and your work with film?

FORBERT PETERSEN: My film school experience is, of course, something that has been quite significant. Of even greater importance, however – although I didn't realize this until later on in my life – is the fact that I come from a good family, one that has given me a lot, and that has been deeply involved with film over a long period of time. Both my paternal grandfather and my father worked with film and photography, although in different ways. I never actually met my grandfather though, for he died in 1938. He was originally trained as an architect, but then in the early 1900s he started a photo atelier in Warsaw, where he came to specialize in portraits. My paternal grandfather, Leo Forbert, had Jewish roots, and around the time of WWI he became involved in the production of Jewish films. He had a great deal of success with those films. I only became interested in my Jewish background later on in my life, but my grandfather was one of these people who wanted to build bridges between cultures, so he also started making Polish films. But that didn't go well at all. He lost all his money and ended up having to flee to Australia with his family. He later returned to Poland and started making films again – with some success – but he died of a heart attack in 1938. Before my grandfather died, my father, Wladyslaw Forbert, had started working as a cinematographer and making films, and I've described all that in the film about my father, *Man With Camera*. So it's not strange at all that I should have developed an interest in film early on, and ended up deciding to pursue training in that area. It was all in the genes and in the family somehow. But my father wasn't at all happy about my decision. He was afraid it would be too hard, and too uncertain a life for a woman. But then he couldn't really stop me from pursuing my interest in film. Actually, I think I started taking photographs when I was 7. He eventually taught me everything, starting with the basics, and also how to work in a darkroom. Basically I grew up with photography and filmmaking. My father was also a photojournalist, but he didn't just work with still photography. As for his filmmaking, I can still picture his camera, which was part of the home I remember as a child. It was one of those famous Arriflex II cameras, in a silver box lined with red velvet.

BONDEBJERG: Although you grew up with film and were already technically quite skilled by the time you were a young adult, you chose to go to the Lodz Film School. The school is very famous, and many of its former students are now very well known directors. But what was the school like, and what was the milieu like during the communist period?

FORBERT PETERSEN: Well, I grew up in a communist country, so I learnt from a very early age that there were two worlds. There was what I could talk about at home, around the dinner table with my own family, and then there was what I could say outside the home and in public. It was like living in two parallel worlds that couldn't be united. Actually, the political and cultural climate in Poland changed quite a lot while I was still living there. I experienced the death of Stalin as a child, and how his picture, which had hung on the wall in my kindergarten, suddenly disappeared. Towards the end of the 1960s, while I was at the film school [1967–69], there was a kind of cultural thaw, a certain freedom in the midst of the more general oppression. I wasn't in the directors' stream at the school, but in the cinematographers' stream. We were trained in a very thorough and technical way, and you needed to have done well at school to get in. I was good at physics and chemistry, and that made a real difference.

But the school was also famous because Roman Polanski and Jerzy Skolomowski were trained there; that is, the directors who'd helped shape the new waves in Eastern Europe. Kieslowski was trained there too. Although it was very technical and skills-oriented, the cinematography programme required us to study philosophy, art history, and literature. It was, in many ways, a good all-round education; the teachers were open and eager to talk about art, and that provided me with a foundation that has stood me in good stead throughout my life. But I didn't complete the programme. I just did the first part because my family and I ended up having to flee from Poland, and that's how we came to Denmark.

BONDEBJERG: It can't have been entirely easy, this move to Denmark and having to start all over. How did you break into filmmaking in Denmark?

FORBERT PETERSEN: That's right, it wasn't. For example, I couldn't get any training at the brand new National Film School of Denmark. I couldn't even get into it, among other things because I'd already spent a couple of years at the school in Lodz. So I started a programme in Film Studies at the University of Copenhagen, with the aim of learning more about film and film history. Getting to know new people

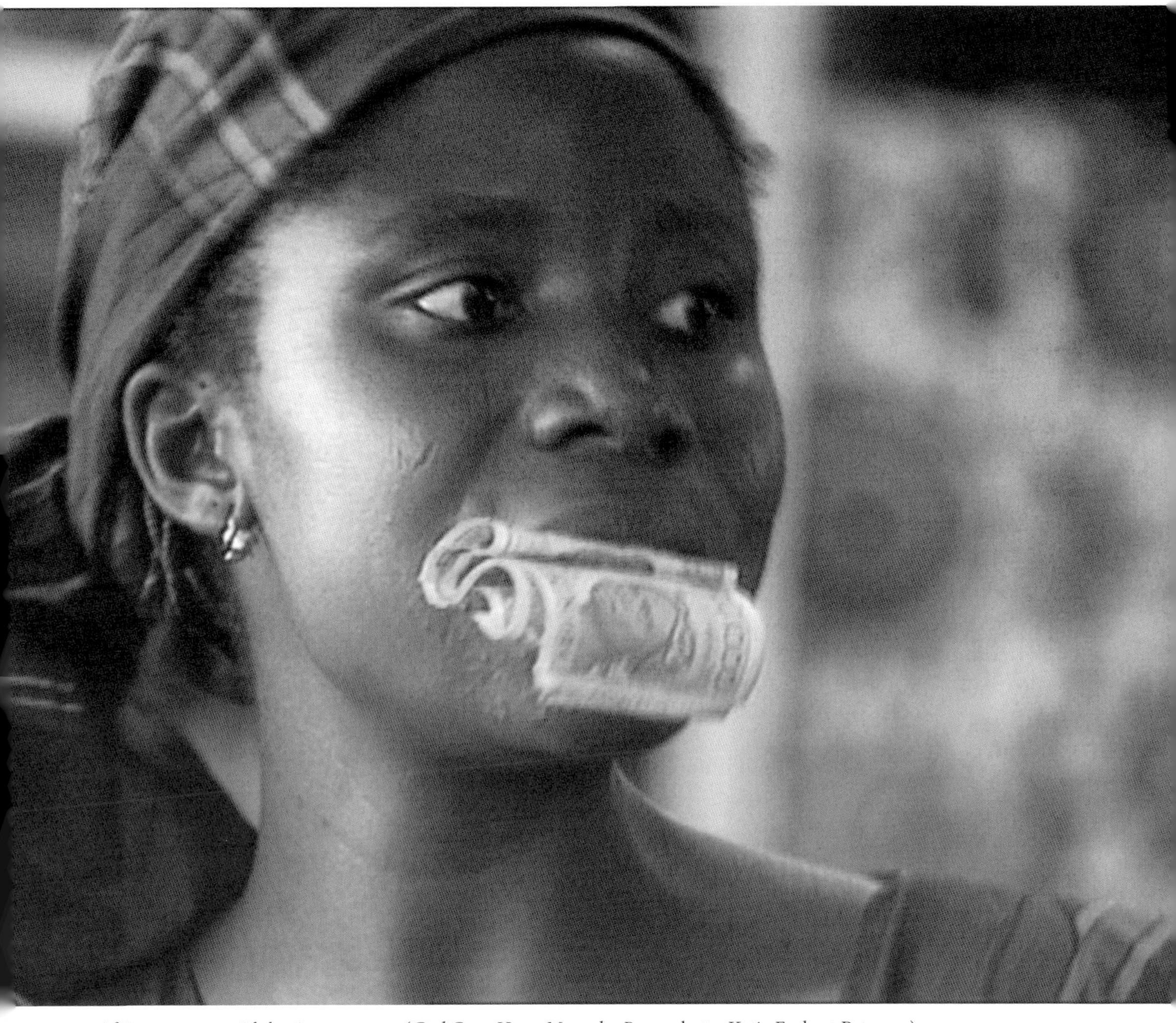

African woman with business success (*God Gave Her a Mercedes Benz*, photo: Katia Forbert Petersen).

and learning the language were also important to me. After all, I was from a very closed, communist country, a country that was also very traditional and where people didn't get any real information about the outside world, or, for that matter, about Polish society. I ended up at the University of Copenhagen right at the time of the student protests. There was a lot of left-wing critique in that period, which was all very different from what I was used to from Poland. I have to say that I became quite socially aware during my first years in Denmark. I was a stateless refugee, as my Polish citizenship had been taken away from me. So it was quite an overwhelming experience, especially considering that I also didn't know very much about Denmark or Danish culture.

BONDEBJERG: Although it must have been quite difficult, you nonetheless made your first Danish film in 1973, namely 'Polish Girls.' What motivated you to make precisely that film? How exactly was the choice of topic linked to your own life?

FORBERT PETERSEN: I made that film with the help of the Film Workshop, where I'd already made an experimental film called *Det uendelige rum* ('The Infinite Space'). Unfortunately, that film doesn't exist any more. In the meantime I'd married a Dane, and had also had my first daughter. The film was shot on Falster, which is where my husband is from. The English cinematographer Stuart McIntry was helping me, and we simply packed the car and headed off. It was learning by doing, especially when it came to editing. It's a little film about three Polish women, all of them around the age of 80, and of course the topic was one that I could identify with. During the process of shooting the film, I also learnt to respect the spontaneous or unexpected things that happen, the moments when something happens that wasn't quite planned. Initially there's a tendency to think that these things are a problem, but actually they're a gift. It's important to allow reality to unfold itself. Also, one should never interrupt people when interviewing them; they should be allowed to finish their thoughts.

BONDEBJERG: In *My Iranian Paradise*, which you made together with Annette Mari Olsen, you bring together a story about a specific woman and a story about having multiple identities, and a mixed cultural and social background. These are issues you've dealt with in several of your other films, and they're part of your own story too of course. How do you see *My Iranian Paradise*?

FORBERT PETERSEN: Having worked as a director for quite a number of years, I started to collaborate with other directors. Since I do the cinematography for all my films, I find there's an interesting and very creative dynamic – one that brings a lot to the film – when I work together with someone else, especially during the shooting. I could really see that in the case of *My Iranian Paradise*, which told a story that both Annette Mari Olsen and I were personally involved with. Both my father and Annette's mother were amongst the approximately 1.5 million Poles who were captured and sent to Siberia during the Second World War. Annette Mari Olsen's family has, just like my own family and many other families, been affected by war and political agendas that have sucked people into the merciless cog of history and changed their lives forever, as well as those of subsequent generations. In the film about my father, *Man With Camera* from 1995, Poland plays a pivotal role, as does war. *My Iranian Paradise* from 2009 tells a very personal story that points towards historical forces and events that can have a devastating impact on people's lives. The attempt to reconnect with a childhood paradise in no way obscures the film's interest in the Middle East, a part of the world that has been very much on the global agenda in recent times.

Bondebjerg:

It can't have been easy to make a film in Iran at that point, but the two of you actually made a few. Could you talk about the process of making *My Iranian Paradise*?

Forbert Petersen:

I started a production company together with Annette Mari Olsen, and that happened just around the time when the new digital cameras were beginning to be widely adopted. Also, this was when TV 2 was being established, and everyone was hoping that there would be a lot more work for everyone. In many ways these developments were good because it became a lot easier – both technically and money-wise – to make films; and so filmmaking became a lot less elitist. I liked that a lot. Annette Mari Olsen wanted to return to Iran, where she'd grown up, and I went along with her, although with some resistance and with a camera. We arrived in Iran on September 11, 2001. That day went on to become the day the whole world was shaken by events on the other side of the globe, and we found ourselves standing in Teheran thinking that the world would never be the same again. We stayed on for two months and established the basis for *My Iranian Paradise*, a film that finds its starting point in Annette's childhood in Teheran, and in various political changes and events. We shot most of the film using the two films for children – *Behind the Mountains* and *The Bird That Could Tell Fortunes* – as a pretext.

The regime had read the scripts for these two films and had approved them. But as we were doing the shooting for those two films, we were, of course, also shooting the sequences we needed for the other film. So *My Iranian Paradise* was made over a long period of time, from 2001–08. Although we had our pretext, we nonetheless encountered a lot of problems and obstacles along the way. I think the film is a very interesting and creative personal document that provides a modern European perspective on Iran's history over a period of some 60 years, as well as insight into the circumstances of the country today.

BONDEBJERG: Your experience of Iran must have resonated with your own personal history of living under another, equally authoritarian regime, in Poland?

FORBERT PETERSEN: Yes, you're absolutely right. If you replace the religious leaders with the communist party, you end up with clear parallels. In Iran you have wonderful people on the one hand, a culture of milk and honey, and then on the other hand you have the regime's iron fist and all of its repression. And in the Polish case, you similarly can't assume that all Poles and all Polish culture are like the political regime with which they're unfortunately imbricated. That conflict between culture, society, and people, over and against various forms of political power, plays an important role in my films.

My Iranian Paradise is a very concrete and human story about a particular period. It's an attempt to rediscover the lost world of a specific childhood, and to tell a very universal story about what people are like, even under the most repressive of regimes. Dramaturgically, it's quite a complicated story, perhaps because it was quite a complicated film to shoot, and because most people really don't know a lot about the historical context that the film is about.

BONDEBJERG: *Man With Camera* is the title of your portrait film about your father. The film is, of course, a portrait of your father, but it's also a story about the twentieth century as seen through photographs and film. I imagine that the title's similarities with Dziga Vertov's famous *Man with a Movie Camera* (1929) is anything but accidental. In that sense, your film's title implicitly evokes the truth-oriented *Kino-Pravda* movement with which Vertov was so strongly associated. Could you say a bit about the kind of portrait you were after, the kind of story you wanted to tell?

FORBERT PETERSEN: Yes, the echoes are clearly anything but accidental. My father was very interested in Vertov, and the Russian avant-garde more generally, inasmuch as the artists in question, soon after the

Russian Revolution, tried to break open the far too narrow understanding of art with which the communists were operating. My father was a documentary filmmaker, and much of his life he worked as a photojournalist, focusing on war and news reporting. His achievements have meant a lot to me, and I see his work as having in a sense been passed on to me. Inasmuch as he was involved in shooting in all of the world's hotspots, the film is about historical events of relevance to us all. I had at lot at stake personally in wanting to tell this story, but it was also important for me to pass it on to my own children and subsequent generations. It's very important to depict the horror and the tragedies that we human beings have inflicted on each other. At the same time, the film tells his story; a story about a human being who has documented all that horror, and who eventually was forced into exile. It's about a man who lost his citizenship and his identity, and who had to start from scratch as a refugee. The film manages to deal with a lot of the historical conflicts of the twentieth century, including the Vietnam War, as seen through my father's eyes. So, once again, the personal story becomes a much more wide-ranging, more universal story about developments that have shaped us all. We are all children of Europe's wars and crises.

BONDEBJERG: In the final credits, you write: 'Dedicated to my father and all film people.' At one point in the film we see you with a camera in your father's home, and he looks into the camera and notes with some measure of discomfort that he was always the one who filmed the family and the world more generally, but now he's the person being filmed. How did he feel about your film and your portrait of him?

FORBERT PETERSEN: He found being filmed very strange; also the fact that his daughter was now the director and cinematographer. I'd actually tried, many years earlier, to undertake a film about him, but he simply refused the idea. But I'd come to have a lot at stake in making a film that was also about how important film, and perhaps especially documentary film, is, as a modern art form. That's a story that I'm able to recount by telling my father's own, personal story. He really did experience and document a lot of world historical events. He was part of the group of photographers who followed the army into Berlin during World War II. He filmed the Nuremberg trials and he was in Vietnam when the French left the country, as well as later, during the war with the US. The films he made clearly show us just how important the documentary depiction of reality is.

BONDEBJERG:

The portrait of your father is not the only portrait film you've made. Quite a number of your films focus on specific people and provide either a portrait of an individual or of a group. In two of your other portrait films you similarly deal with artists, namely in *Von Trier's 100 Eyes* and *Sound on Life*. How did you end up making the von Trier film, and what did you mainly hope to achieve with it? You seem to be interested in both the cinematic and technical process, as well as in a more personal dimension; one that also has to do with the more dramatic aspects of *Dancer in the Dark*'s production history.

FORBERT PETERSEN:

The von Trier film began as a commissioned project. I was given very little lead time, and it wasn't a film that I myself had had the idea of making. Vibeke Windeløv called me up and told me that things weren't really working out with the director whom they'd hired to make a film about *Dancer in the Dark*. They were looking for someone else; someone who in a much more discreet and invisible way would move around and do the shooting needed to make a good film about the making of *Dancer in the Dark*. They wanted someone who had a better understanding of what was involved in making a film, and especially a film about the making of a film. Initially I had a few reservations because if the director they'd settled on in the first instance was having problems, then perhaps there were a lot of intrigues and power struggles going on. I was a bit worried about sticking my fingers into a hornet's nest. But of course I was also quite curious. When I first started working on the film, I simply proceeded in a very systematic and mathematical way. I planned, quite precisely, how much there should be of this or that aspect in the film. In *Dancer in the Dark*, von Trier worked with his now famous 100 cameras, and his approach more generally was very technical and experimental. I'm fascinated by that sort of thing because I've been intrigued by a similar approach to filmmaking. But there's also a very personal story to all of this, which is made clear in the beginning of the film when von Trier sits and reads from the Goldheart book that was an important part of his childhood, and which serves as a source of inspiration for his film. That personal story develops as the dramatic conflict surrounding the film unfolds, not least between Björk and von Trier. To make a film is in many ways to create a certain order from chaos. When I first started making that film, the only thing that had been clearly decided was that I was to follow the production of von Trier's film and make a film about it. The film's story ended

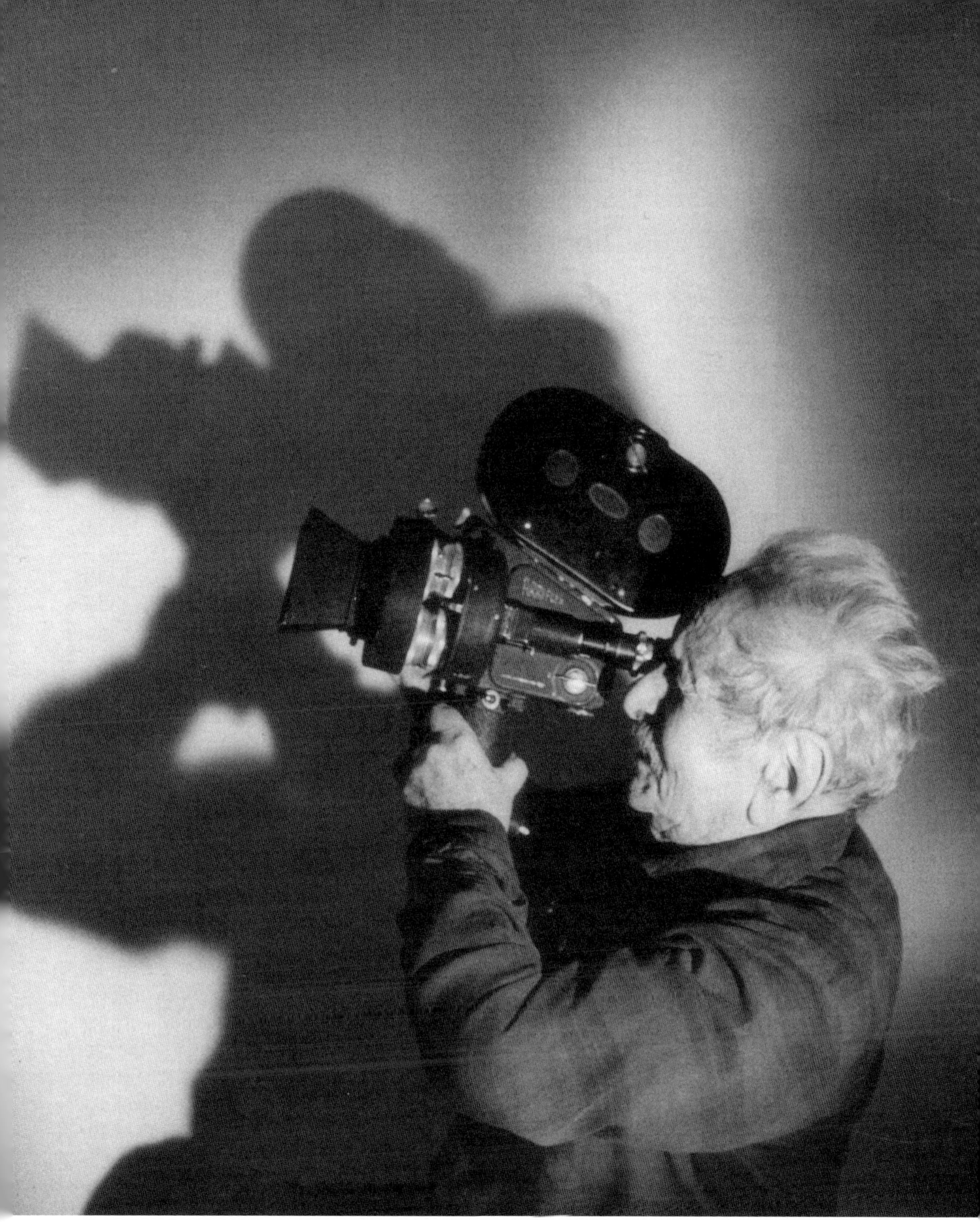

Katia Forbert Petersen's father, Polish photographer Wladyslaw Forbert, at the age of 80 (*Man With Camera*, photo: Katia Forbert Petersen).

up becoming quite chaotic in many ways, but I've been getting order out of chaos for 30 years, so that's what I did in this case too. I filmed and recorded everything, and I had all the equipment I needed in one bag. It simply wasn't possible to give too much space to the technical side of things, as I wasn't allowed to disrupt the shooting process. In fact, I had to develop a sound recording system myself, one that didn't take up too much room.

BONDEBJERG: The making of von Trier's film ended up becoming very dramatic, and you do to some extent capture that in the film when you show how Björk suddenly took off in the middle of a shoot. What kind of impact did all the conflicts between von Trier and Björk have on your film?

FORBERT PETERSEN: Yes, the conflict was very intense. All the difficult feelings and underlying tensions came to the surface. And the impact on my film was very direct indeed. Von Trier and Björk are both very sensitive people, and I have a lot of sympathy for Lars, who found himself in a truly impossible situation; at the same time, I also understand Björk. They finally worked things out, and the film went on to become a great success. But I ended up having a lot of problems with my film because Björk's lawyers, in the period leading up to Cannes, had to approve every single scene she was in. They would actually have preferred to shut the film down entirely. But a compromise was found, whereby Björk was allowed to appear in my film through clips from von Trier's film. All other scenes with her in them had to be cut. An additional requirement specified that Björk's music couldn't be used except in those instances where it accompanied clips from the film. I had to create my own Dogma rules and re-edit the film, so that the censorship in question became a kind of artistic challenge. That's why we don't see her as a person in her own right; she's always simply a character in von Trier's film. All this had the effect of making the film even more of a film about a director in the midst of intense chaos, and it's von Trier who becomes the character on whom my documentary focuses. The film also illustrates von Trier's unique qualities as a director: he works in a very intimate, involved, personal, and sensitive way; there's nothing of the great and rather distant superstar about him.

BONDEBJERG: Your most recent portrait of an artist, *Sound on Life*, focuses on the pioneering avant-gardist musician Else Marie Pade, who was 80 at the time. How did you end up making that film, and how would you describe your approach?

FORBERT PETERSEN: That was a subject I chose out of interest and curiosity after having read a portrait of Pade in *Politiken*. I made the film together with Iben Haahr Andersen, who has done a lot of work with sound, and who was also very keen on the idea of making a film about Pade. The film pushes a few boundaries, both on the sound side, and in terms of the visuals. I constructed a universe consisting of sound and staged spaces that together match the world and the time in which Pade grew up. You could say that I drew on the aesthetics of the expressionists and the Russian avant-garde because that's the world Pade comes from. At the same time, Pade's music is avant-gardist to an extreme degree. We had a tape recording, two hours long, with her own account of her life, and this gave me insight into her extraordinary experience of history, and into the impact her background had had on her and her work. I also got a sense of how her mind worked, and even of her dreams and aspirations. The film's music, soundscape, and images deal with all these dimensions of her life in a very expressive and complex way. The sound and images combine at all sorts of levels. It's the most avant-gardist film I've ever made, but it does shed quite a fine light on Pade's life and world. Her own narrative is expanded to the point where it becomes symbolic of a whole period. The film creates a mental universe that takes the viewer straight into her personal and artistic world.

BONDEBJERG: A lot of your films are portraits of specific women, or about women and women's issues. I'm thinking of 'Polish Girls,' *Sammen med Lena* ('Together With Lena'), *Johanne fra Daugbjerg* ('Johanne from Daubjerg') and *God Gave Her a Mercedes Benz*. The films are, of course, about different types of women, and about different kinds of issues, but at the same time there appears to be a certain agenda here.

FORBERT PETERSEN: Yes, it's clear that I've chosen to make films about things I know something about, and about things I'm interested in. As a woman who is also a refugee, I have a kind of dual identity, which helps to make the lives and experiences of these Polish women visible to me. The same probably holds for the other, very different portraits of women that I've made. 'Together With Lena' is a classic women's film about a Swedish girl from Stockholm, who ends up as a fisherman's wife on a small island. 'Johanne from Daubjerg' focuses on an old storyteller, and *God Gave Her a Mercedes Benz* is a story about African women who are successful, and who love to drive a Mercedes. I think that these films all reflect my interest in what it means to be a woman, and in the problems that women encounter, but I'm not interested in making journalistic problem films. I want to tell stories that allow us to understand how these women experience their everyday lives, and I want my films to convey their experiences by means of how we, as viewers, experience them and their lives. Sometimes my films are about women whom I don't know, as was the case, for example, with the film about the African women. But I'm almost always able to identify with them as women. There's something in their lives that reminds me of mine. Anthropologically, it's interesting that one is able to identify with something that, at least on the surface of things, appears to be foreign, 'Other.' Yet, I also think it's important to depict everyday life and, at least every now and then, to tell a 'feel-good' story. Journalists tell a lot of very negative stories, but there's a lot more to everyday life.

BONDEBJERG: Quite a number of your films focus on children, whether in Denmark or in other countries. I'm thinking of 'A Week Without Smiling,' *Tiden før øjeblikket* ('The Time Just Before the Moment'), *Mit søde barn* ('My Sweet Child'), 'My Own Motor Horse,' *Behind the Mountains*, and *The Bird That Could Tell Fortunes*. While the films are different in certain respects, also thematically, one senses a persistent interest in children.

FORBERT PETERSEN: I would say that one of the salient traits of my films about children is that they – much like my films about women – focus on everyday life. The films tell stories about the ups and downs of everyday life, but also about children's imagination and ability to do something worthwhile, even under quite difficult circumstances. Some of the stories have a quite critical dimension, as is the case with 'A Week Without Smiling,' which is about children's very negative hospital experiences. But just as I think it's important to penetrate the world of women and their experiences in it, and to articulate some of all that, I think it's important to depict the world of children. I listen with my camera, and I try to listen as the person I am; that is, I try to bring my own experiences into play. In 'The Time Just Before the Moment,' for example, I focus on women at a time when they're waiting to give birth. I made that film some 25 years after I myself had given birth to a child, but my starting point was nonetheless my own experiences and feelings. By listening to what they had to say, also about their dreams, I was able to get the material I needed for a story about everyday life; one that takes us close to the lives, thoughts, and expectations of women as they

pertain to giving birth and having children. I know that my films about both children and women are used quite a lot in various educational contexts; not as pedagogical films with a specific content that is to be absorbed, but as testimonials that provide insight into people's lived experiences.

BONDEBJERG: *Sangbogen og de røde sko* ('The Song Book and the Red Shoes') combines your interest in history, war, children, and women.

FORBERT PETERSEN: Yes, that's a film I'm very happy with, but I had a really hard time making it and then getting it distributed. It deals with the RAF's bombing of the French School in Copenhagen – by mistake, during the Occupation – and it shows just how dreadful the consequences of war are for children, even when the children in question are now 70-year-olds. The story is told through the eyes of several of the children who survived, so it's based on their own experiences and memories. And their testimonies are then combined with archival material and a depiction of the historical context. As a result, the film is much more of a classic expository/ educational film than any of my other films are. I strongly believe that historical documentaries such as this one should be part of the teaching of history, for history books often fail to depict truth as it manifests itself on a more personal or human level. Usually the history books only make room for the big political strokes and gestures. I'm quite interested in making a second film about what happened. The idea would be to focus on other aspects of the bombing, and on the role of Danish officials, the resistance movement, and the British. There are still a lot of things having to do with that event that haven't been brought to light. That's what's interesting about making documentary films – the digging around until you feel you've found the truth.

Chapter 16

Jeppe Rønde

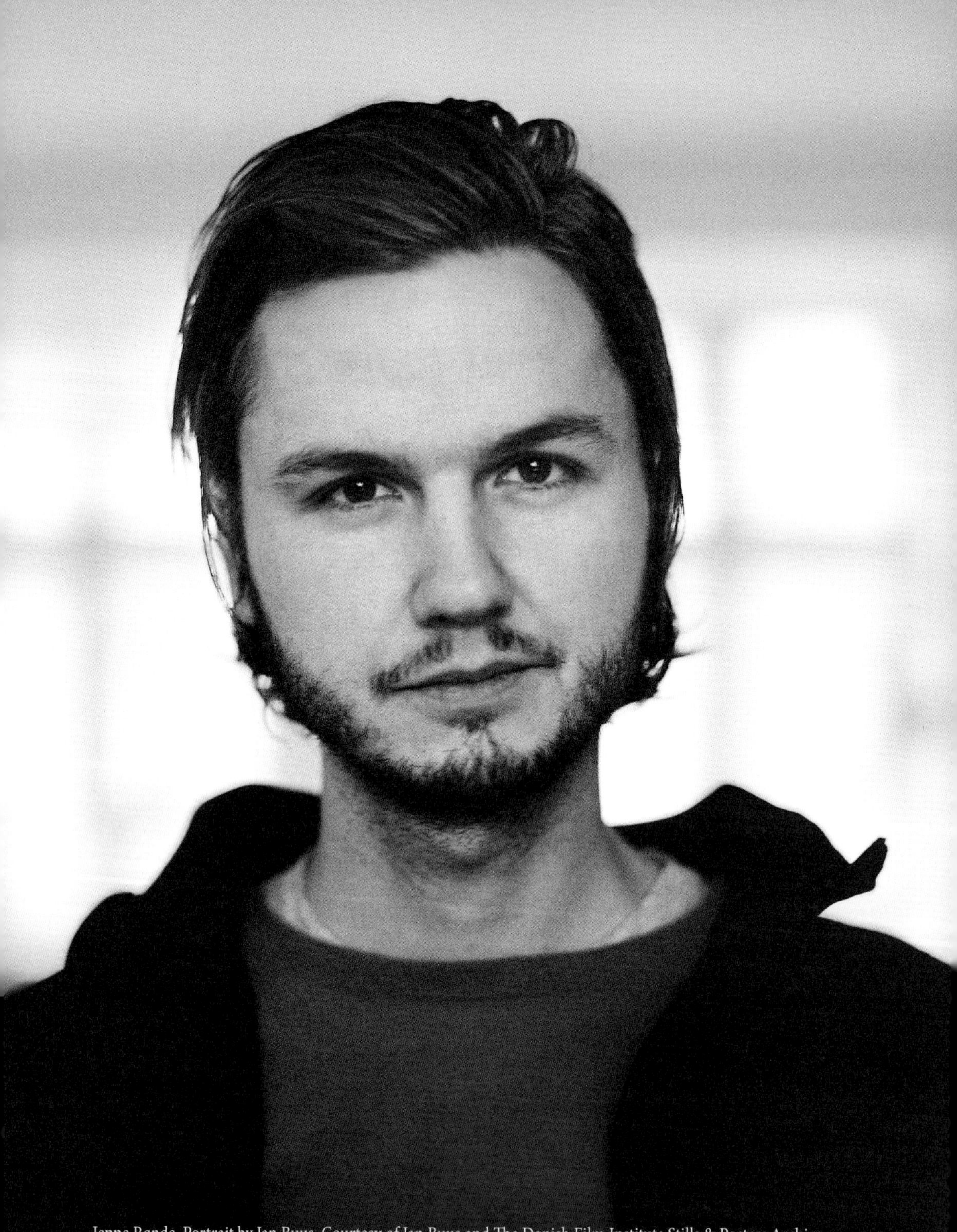

Jeppe Rønde. Portrait by Jan Buus. Courtesy of Jan Buus and The Danish Film Institute Stills & Posters Archive.

orn 1973. Jeppe Rønde holds a BA in Film and Media Studies from the University of Copenhagen, with a minor in Art History. He was active as a composer and musician before becoming a documentary filmmaker, and has composed original music for several of his films. Entitled *Dansen i brændpunktet* (*Dancing in the Midst of War*, 2000), Rønde's first documentary short focused on Danish dancer and member of the Tel Aviv-based Batsheva Dance Group, Jesper Thirup Hansen. Rønde's next three films – *Søn* (*Son*, 2001), *Jerusalem, min elskede* (*Jerusalem, My Love*, 2003), and *The Swenkas* (2005) – are formally complex works focusing on family dynamics, especially between fathers and sons. *The Swenkas*, which was filmed under difficult circumstances in the townships of South Africa, brought the director considerable critical acclaim, including awards such as best international director at the Toronto Film Festival. With directors Mads Brügger and Mikael Bertelsen in front of the camera lens, Rønde directed the critically acclaimed TV series entitled *Quatraro mysteriet* (*The Quatraro Mystery*) for the Danish Broadcasting Corporation in 2009. The eight-episode series investigates the otherwise unexamined death of Italian Antonio Quatraro, who fell from the European Union building on Rue de la Loi, in Brussels in 1993. More recently, Rønde directed *Girl in the Water* (2011) with the Malaysian filmmaker Woo Ming Jin, through CPH:DOX's DOX:LAB, which aims to create a space for artistic experimentation. The film, which is about a family that is torn apart by fateful circumstances, won the Danish Film Academy's Robert award for best short film in 2011. Jeppe Rønde's next project is a film entitled *Bridgend*, which is the name of a former mining town in Wales where a large number of young people have committed suicide, all by hanging themselves, mostly in public. Like many other members of his generation of documentary filmmakers, Rønde is interested in a productive relationship between fiction and non-fiction, and in issues and realities that take him well beyond the borders of Denmark.

Documentary features:

2014   *Bridgend*
2005   *The Swenkas*
2003   *Jerusalem, min elskede* (*Jerusalem, My Love*)

Documentary shorts:

2011   *Girl in the Water* (with Woo Ming Jin)
2001   *Søn* (*Son*)
2000   *Dansen i brændpunktet* (*Dancing in the Midst of War*)

Television:

2009   *Quatraro mysteriet* (*The Quatraro Mystery*, with Mads Brügger and Mikael
        Bertelsen, eight episodes)
2003   *Dansen i brændpunktet* (*Dancing in the Midst of War*)

HJORT: You're a musician and a composer, but also hold a BA in Film and Media Studies (with a minor in Art History) from the University of Copenhagen. The curriculum encompasses historical and theoretical courses, as well as internships and hands-on training. At what point did you decide to become a documentary filmmaker?

RØNDE: I've been a musician all my life really, and have also made a living that way. For me, the shift to film didn't feel like a shift at all. When you're playing or composing music, there's always a certain rhythm, there's a story, a certain mood, certain themes, all those things. The images you see are different, of course, because they're internal, but they're still images. So I found the shift to film very easy. It seemed like a very natural shift to me.

Film and Media Studies at the University of Copenhagen was something I ended up in by coincidence. I was involved with music and then I suddenly discovered that film was something you could study. It sounded interesting, and so I applied and embarked on the programme. But I have to say that I spent most of my time watching films. There was no Internet as we now know it, and there were hardly any DVDs; but the videotheque at the University of Copenhagen had a ton of films, and I started ploughing my way through them and finding all these things I'd never heard of before. I did, of course, learn about film at university, but what I learnt had very little to do with making films. It was all about desiccating films; that's to say, about analysing them and sucking the life out of them. So I quickly discovered that what I was really interested in was seeing the films.

There was this one course that was interesting. It was called 'Audiovisual Communication,' and it simply involved our making short films. So we were able to experiment with video cameras, and editing and so on, and I really enjoyed that. And there was this assignment that I worked on as part of a team, and I liked that because, as a musician, collaboration was familiar terrain for me. We received a lot of praise for our work, and so I decided to buy this new camera that had just come out. It was a SONY PD 100, a huge investment back then. And then I just started making films.

For me, film school is simply a matter of seeing a lot of films and then making them. All schools hone people and make them fit a mould. And this is true, whether we're talking about film schools or universities. Standardization through this process of polishing people has to be the very definition of a school. I was a musician, went to university more or less by accident, saw lots and lots of films, and then started making them. That was my film school.

HJORT: You've continued to work with music over the years, among other things by composing music for your films. Where does this passion for music come from?

RØNDE: I'm not a trained musician, but what happened was that my father died when I was seven. And before he died he told me that there were two things he wished he'd learnt how to do: play chess and play drums. He was a very intelligent man. He had all the books and all the LPs you could possibly want. And he would sit there and tell me stories about The Who's *Tommy* album or *The Brothers Karamazov* when I was 4 or 5 years old. He opened my eyes to that world. So clearly, when he died, the first thing I did was learn how to play chess and how to play drums. So that's how it all started. I then started playing the guitar, and that became my preferred instrument for many years, but I've also played the piano.

HJORT: Graduates of the National Film School of Denmark tend to see themselves as being able to draw on a whole network of contacts that were established during their four years at the film school. Is it harder to make one's way in the Danish film milieu without the networks that the Film School provides?

RØNDE: I haven't had any problems at all along those lines. It's true that the Film School's graduates emerge with this incredible network. They're so tightly connected during their film school years – almost the way you'd be at a boarding school – and they've spent a lot of time working in teams consisting of a director, producer, editor, sound designer, cinematographer, and so on. So they've got that history to draw on when they leave, and that's clearly an advantage. But I haven't had a problem finding people to work with, and it's also clear that you can't get around the Film School. That said, I actually quite enjoy working with people who haven't graduated from the School. The graduates are clearly different because they're individuals, but they've nonetheless been shaped in the same way, and so in a lot of situations you'll find that their thinking is quite similar, which can both be a strength and a weakness. There's that standardization I talked about, and sometimes it's just interesting to draw on others. But I've collaborated with some truly wonderful producers, scriptwriters, editors, sound designers, and cinematographers from the School.

It's not that I try to navigate around the Film School, because that's neither desirable nor possible, but I do find it quite natural to draw on people who aren't part of the film world. There's this priest whom I talk to on a regular basis, and there's also my psychologist, whom I also work with. I've also worked with writers. For example, when I was working on *The Swenkas*, I contacted this Norwegian author called Jan Kjaerstad because I felt he'd be able to help me develop the narrator's voice in a way that was light, but also a bit pseudo philosophical. I get a lot of my inspiration from novels and paintings, although I've also seen a lot of films and have been inspired by directors like Andrei Tarkovsky, von Trier, and Kieslowski. The history of film is so short compared to some of the other arts. A film itself is short. The language of film is only a bit over a century old, whereas the other arts are anchored in these ancient traditions, which sometimes makes the thinking deeper, more weighty.

HJORT: Your most recent films – *Jerusalem, My Love* and *The Swenkas* – have garnered a host of prizes. Both were produced by Cosmo Film and, more specifically, by Rasmus Thorsen and Anne Diemer. How would you describe the philosophy of this particular production company, and the nature of your relationship to it?

RØNDE: I ended up at Cosmo through a complex mix of things, including: support from the Film Workshop in Copenhagen, where I worked on the documentary short, *Son*; an unfortunate involvement with Bech Film, which folded while I was getting ready to make *Jerusalem, My Love* with them; and help from people like Jakob Høgel at the Danish Film Institute and Tue Steen Møller at The European Documentary Network.

Cosmo Film was fantastic. I was given an enormous amount of freedom, in the sense that nobody imposed any constraints on me. I was basically given a free rein. The most wonderful thing about the people at Cosmo was that they believed in all the ideas I put out there, no matter how bizarre they were, especially in connection with *Jerusalem, My Love*. What was decisive was that I was given time to become fully involved with my material, and to experiment with it. I think that's incredibly important when you're looking for, not necessarily a new film language, but a new way of telling your story. People say all stories have been told before, but what you can do is try to articulate them differently, with a different kind of sensibility. I was given the space I needed to really dig deeply into my material, and the peace of mind I needed to find my own voice. So I was able to think very carefully about the cinematic language I wanted to use in *Jerusalem, My Love*, and also about the story. Everything became a lot easier when that film started to win festival prizes and so on. But when you're starting out in that big real world of filmmaking, especially if you're as green as I was back then and if you haven't gone to film school, then Cosmo Film is exactly the sort of place where you'd want to be. I was incredibly lucky to end up there.

HJORT: In *Son* you turn your camera on your own family, interviewing relatives of your father, who died when you were seven. Your aim is to understand why he became an alcoholic and eventually a drug addict, and why he ended up failing himself but also you. In an almost detective-like manner, you slowly bring to light the neglect and abuse by which your father's life was shaped. At one point you describe yourself as feeling a sense of relief as you begin to see your father as having himself been the victim of different kinds of violence. It becomes clear to the viewer that the process of making the film is a therapeutic one for you. Is the idea of documentary filmmaking as a means of transformation or change a central element in your filmmaking?

RØNDE: I just want to say that you're free to ask anything you want about *Son*. I hope that, having seen the film, you know that. Being open about what happened was part of the very process you describe.

I knew my father was an alcoholic and smoked hash, which is not that uncommon. And I knew he'd been arrested, and that he'd often been found unconscious and had been revived by the medics who showed up when an ambulance was called. What I didn't know, until I made the film, was that he'd become addicted to harder drugs, and had started shooting heroin.

When someone hurts you – and I lived alone with my father and experienced all of the above – then what you can do to survive is invent stories, or you can change what you encounter in real life into stories. That's what I did. I fabricated these stories, these fantasies, so that reality could have a happy ending. I actually trained myself to come up with these narratives. So that process of telling stories about the real world started when I was very young.

And I like your question about the therapeutic aspect of the film because that's definitely part of the picture. Initially, I dealt with the issues I had with my father through music. And whether I'm playing music, or working with a text, with songs, or with film, it's all, for me, about processing reality in exactly the same way that I did when I was a young child. But of course, when I bought that camera, with money I didn't have, it seemed obvious to me that I would focus it on my family. I hadn't seen my father's family in twenty years, and the last thing I remembered my grandmother saying was that it was a good thing that he was dead. That had been pretty hard to understand. So of course I wanted to understand what the bloody hell that was all about. So the film becomes this crime drama, this investigation of family secrets. And, yes, it becomes a therapeutic project for me.

You mention how I discover that he was a victim himself, and that this somehow explains what he did. But that's just part of the story because the film doesn't end up exonerating him. Right at the end of it, we find out that he'd started shooting heroin. That's not something I can explain away. After all, he had a son. He had me. So why did he have to start doing that? I didn't want to believe he was a drug addict, and it takes the proof provided by the police's autopsy report to convince me.

It was a very therapeutic project. I've seen a lot of psychologists over the years – and that's helped – but it was playing music and making films that really helped. The process of making *Son* was a dynamic one because it got me to a point where I was able to begin to move on. And that dynamic aspect had to do with the fact that

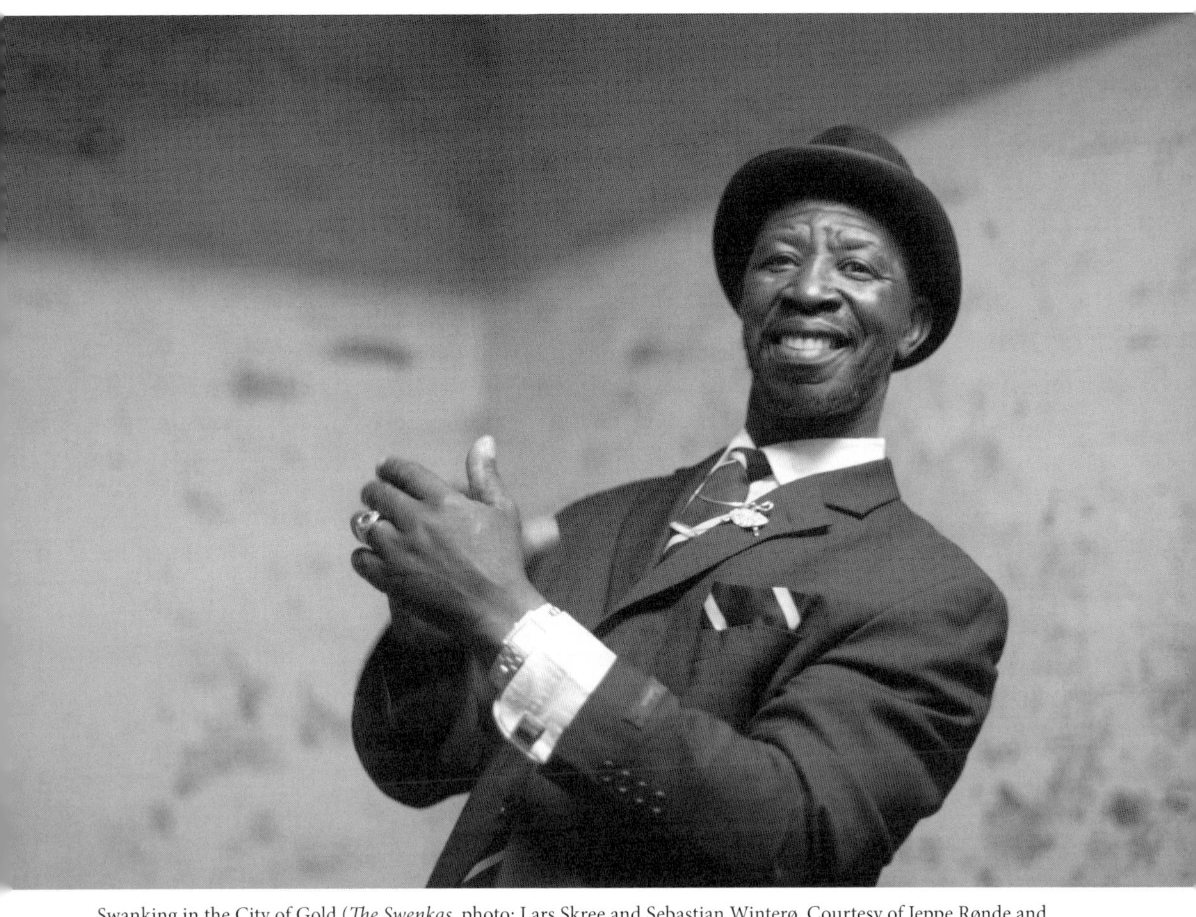

Swanking in the City of Gold (*The Swenkas*, photo: Lars Skree and Sebastian Winterø. Courtesy of Jeppe Rønde and Cosmo Film).

I didn't initially make the film for a wider audience, but just for myself. And that's still the case. I still make films just for myself.

I don't think you measure pain by the size of the sore. The pain of losing your first boyfriend can be almost unbearable too. But pain has been the motor that's driven my storytelling. I have a feeling that it's the same sense of necessity that's behind a lot of documentary storytelling. Among other things, storytelling is definitely also a means of surviving.

HJORT: *Jerusalem, My Love* and *The Swenkas* are the first two films in a trilogy entitled 'Faith, Hope, and Love.' What connects the two existing films and the third envisaged work to the point where they're best thought of, or marketed, as a trilogy? And which part of the world will you focus on in connection with 'Love'?

RØNDE: Well, what happens after *Son* is that I feel like I've now told my own personal story and how things were to the whole wide world. But I still find that I can't let go. And so I make a film about my father again and again. And if you look at the three films – that's to say, *Son, Jerusalem, My Love*, and *The Swenkas* – you'll see that maybe that's actually the trilogy: in a way it's my 'Father Trilogy.' The first film is very heavy; the second one is not light, but there's at least a dialogic dimension to what's going on; and then there's the third film, where I finally let go. It's really a trilogy about getting to the point where you can breathe again, and lift up those shoulders that have been held down by the weight of a dead father. It was actually Theis Schmidt, who worked on *Jerusalem, My Love* as my editor, who pointed this out. When he saw *The Swenkas* he said, 'So now you've made your trilogy. *The Swenkas* is the story about the good father.' And he was absolutely right.

When I'm making a film about something, I try to involve myself completely. And I haven't made that film about love yet. Because when you're making a film, there's this element of distance. And the thought of having to live at some distance from love for such a long period of time was too much at the time. I now have a wife and child, and that's why I haven't made that damned film yet. But I'm working on it now.

HJORT: Much like *Son, Jerusalem, My Love* has a strong personal or autobiographical focus. In the film, we hear the voice of a hypnotist who intends to help you regain your faith by taking you back to Jerusalem, where you lost it. The dialogue that emerges between you and the hypnotist gives a clear direction to the film, and helps to frame the visual material that depicts your encounters with

Jews, Muslims, and Christians in Israel and Palestine. Did you actually undergo hypnosis and say the things we hear in the film while in a hypnotic state? Put differently, how scripted or even staged are your documentary films?

RØNDE: Well, a film like *The Swenkas* is driven by a strategy that's designed to destabilize whatever might appear to separate fiction and non-fiction. But let me stick to *Jerusalem, My Love*. When I was making that film, I was hypnotized every Sunday over a very, very long period of time. This happened in front of three cameras, and I would then respond to questions that were put to me by my film commissioner, Jakob Høgel, my producer, Rasmus Thorsen, and my editor, Theis Schmidt. And I hadn't heard any of these questions in advance. If you've never tried being hypnotized, you might not know that there are degrees of hypnotization, different levels of it – at least for me. And the deeper I went, the less I was able to say; and I spoke more and more like a child.

I try very hard to make genre films, or at least to draw on certain genre conventions, and then to push the genre in question to the absolute limit. Genres are only interesting if you can find a way of articulating something personal, so that you shatter the formulae. What's funny is that my voice is the real thing. But I'd chosen a woman as my hypnotist because, goddamnit, I wanted the support of a mother during the process. And the woman in question spoke in a very dynamic, almost theatrical way, and when we test-screened the film I was shocked to find that people started laughing. So much to my dismay we ended up having to dub her voice, which I think is a real pity. But we didn't change the questions. We just needed to adjust the mood a bit! But I want you to know that, at the end of the day, it's all just film. I mean, I don't believe in some boundary separating fiction and documentary. As Theodor Adorno puts it: 'Art is magic freed from the lie of being the truth.'

HJORT: That's a position that's very common amongst younger documentary filmmakers in Denmark today.

RØNDE: Yes, it is. Clearly there are certain contexts where it makes sense to talk about differences between fiction and non-fiction. I'm thinking of the work that critics do, or the categories the Film Institute uses when it distributes funding. But as a filmmaker, I feel that ultimately what I'm doing is making a film. It may be short or long, and it may be more or less connected to some reality in, say, Jerusalem. I know what the story is because I can feel it.

From my earliest childhood, fiction and non-fiction were intertwined in my mind. On that point, I was touched by a conversation I once had with Abbas Kiarostami at a film festival. We went out for dinner and we talked, among other things, about truth and fiction. He put the point very incisively: 'The more I lie, the closer I get to the truth.' That's where I've been all my life. Because as I made up those little 'fictions' as a child – my truths – I found reality.

HJORT: What about differences having to do with ethics? In a documentary, you're depicting real people and their lives.

RØNDE: As far as I'm concerned, it's always and only about trust, trust, and trust. If people don't trust you, then you might as well forget about doing anything in life. If there's no trust, then there's no genuine relation to others, and that's what's most important to me. When I'm making my films, I give myself completely to the people I'm working with, and I expect them to do the same. I'm very opposed to this idea, which is quite popular amongst documentary filmmakers from my generation, that the participants should be given an opportunity somehow to vet the film afterwards. That doesn't happen with me, because we trust each other. Why should there be some unspoken notion of my just going ahead and doing something that can always be checked later? No, we look each other in the eyes and figure out who we're dealing with. And then we begin. And sometimes the trust is there within minutes, other times it takes a lot longer. With *The Swenkas*, Sabelo took my hand after just a couple of days and said, 'Jeppe, now you can do whatever you want with me.' It took me a year to win the trust of the Jewish man who is so central in *Jerusalem, My Love*. It can take two seconds, twenty minutes, or, for some, a lifetime. But that's true of life more generally.

HJORT: You first became interested in making a film about the South African 'Swenkas' when you saw an exhibition of photographs by the South African T.J. Lemon. Your desire to make a film about the Swenkas took you to a dangerous part of Johannesburg. How did you deal with the risks, and why did you choose not to evoke them in the film?

RØNDE: Violence is uninteresting when you know in advance that it's there, especially in an African context. Representations of Africa almost always focus on war, illness, poverty, starvation, and exploitation. A countless number of films like that have already been made. And I just wasn't interested in making yet another

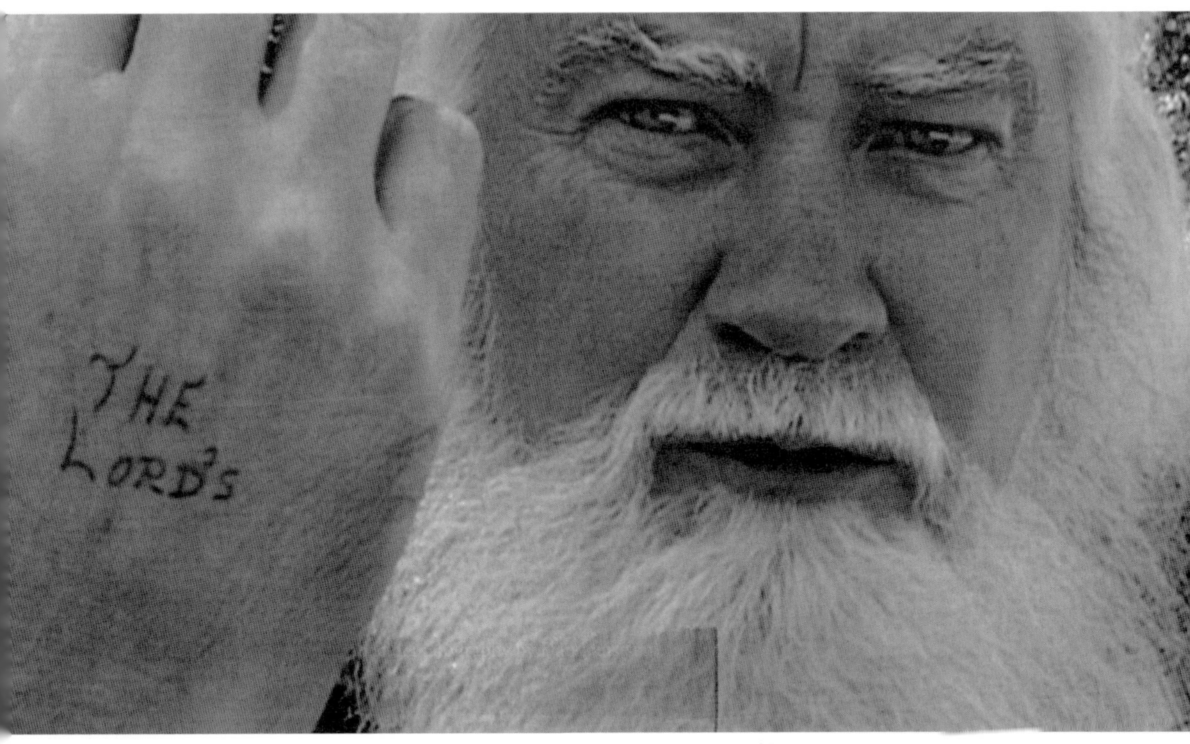

A modern-day prophet in Jerusalem (*Jerusalem My Love*, photo. Jeppe Rønde and Nadav Neuhaus. Courtesy of Jeppe Rønde and Cosmo Film).

one. What I found interesting was homing in on realities that in some sense provided a clear contrast to all that – and as such pointed to it anyway, but also to a new story. And I really mean that because when I saw that photo exhibition in London, those eight photographs in a corner of the room, I felt like I'd suddenly stumbled across a completely different image of Africa. The Africa that I saw depicted in them was so different from the one that's normally described to us. I wouldn't go so far as to say that violence and conflict aren't there in the film. After all, I have the narrator say that there are holes and fissures in his story, just as there are in his country. And that sort of utterance should prompt viewers to draw on everything that they already know about South Africa and the history of Apartheid. But I didn't feel the need to go into any of that explicitly, because it was already there.

What I found fantastic was how the Swenkas, in the midst of a lot of hopelessness, used clothes and these public displays as a source of self-respect, and as a means of building respect for others. They talked about being clean, and initially, especially if you have a family background like mine, you might think they were referring to drugs. But they weren't. They really had soap and water in mind. It was beautiful. We all know that you need to put decent clothes on if you're going for a job interview. Well, they take that thinking a whole lot further, and it's beautiful. Essentially they step into their own fiction and grow in their own eyes, and in those of others, as a result. This is what Sabelo said to me: 'When I swank it's like I hear a nice slow foxtrot inside my head that nobody else can hear.' There's also something in the swanking that has to do with taking on and appropriating certain symbols associated with the culture of white people. It's quite a complicated thing, and clearly very powerful.

HJORT: But the actual process of making the film must have involved quite a number of risks, including threats to your personal safety.

RØNDE: Well, yes, I was shot at. My car got smashed. Most of my crew members, all of whom were black South Africans, were attacked on their way home from the shoots. They were completely stripped of everything, and they were just glad they hadn't been raped, which is common even if you're a man. But I have to say that Mr Dangerous – the new father of Sabelo in the film – is someone who's earnt his name. He's a former street fighter, and made a living as such when he was younger. And he knew everyone. After a while it became known that he was part of this film that we were making. I can't say the danger disappeared entirely, but he did command a certain amount of respect. The Swenkas generally command a lot of respect in those neighborhoods.

HJORT: In *The Swenkas*, you make use of a narrator. Yulo Mooitong's narrative appears to draw on rich and still vital oral storytelling traditions in Africa, and lends enormous energy to the film. How did you approach the whole issue of narration in this film?

RØNDE: After a few conversations with Jan Kjaerstad, I decided to move on and ended up working with Mogens Rukov, specifically on the narrator's role. But unfortunately, Mogens got sick, so I continued working on the narration with Kim Leona. One thing we wanted to do was to have this shift in the narration at a certain point, as a means of getting the audience to ask questions. So we start with the narrator, who seems to be fictional, sitting in an empty basement, talking about how the story that's to be told takes place in Johannesburg, The City of Gold. And then, towards the middle, we find the narrator amongst the Swenkas, sharing their space. And the Swenkas start to interact with him as they would with someone they know well. Because of that interaction, the stage turns, so to speak. What you think is one thing turns out to be something else, although it's also still the same thing: it's still a story about the same group of Swenkas, in the same city. Yulo Mooitong is an actor, not a Swenka, and I found him through a casting. In the film he's a little bit dirty, and he's clearly someone who travels around a lot, observes things, and tells stories about what he sees. The idea is to suggest that if I'm there as a director telling this story, then I'm some sort of vagabond. The fascination we have him demonstrate for the Swenkas is, of course, very much mine, and his role and the things he says convey that. He is me.

You're right, African storytelling traditions were important. I did a lot of research on those traditions, and was very interested in how African storytelling works. What I discovered is that the focus keeps shifting from the storyteller to a man, to a woman, and so on. That's how *The Swenkas* is structured, so I see the film as being very African in terms of its narrative approach. But then there are also elements in the film that are archetypically western, so there's a tension, which I see as productive, at various levels: between fictional and documentary elements; between African and western elements. People in Europe don't always see that, but when I traveled around Africa with the film, people would often say that the film reminded them of the stories they'd tell around the fire at night. At the same time, it's also just a Christmas fairytale.

I script things 100 per cent. But I'm always just waiting for the moment when I can crunch up the paper, throw it in the bin, and move 180 degrees in the other direction. I wait for that moment when the material somehow looks back at me; like when you're looking at a painting and suddenly someone or something is looking back at you. Perhaps you notice a detail that makes the painting seem completely different, and you feel the impact of this, although you might not fully understand it. That's the moment I'm always looking for because I don't want to be imposing my story on the material. So I dig and I dig and I dig, until the story's direction suddenly becomes clear to me. In the case of *The Swenkas*, I obviously realized that this was a story about a father and a son, about a father who dies. And I knew that I could tell that story, and that I could tell it well.

HJORT: *The Swenkas* was very positively received in South African. What are some of the most moving responses you received to the film?

RØNDE: I was in South Africa for the premiere and was interviewed for TV. And it was great to have the Swenkas there, who of course did some swanking. There was a slightly difficult moment because the photographer, T.J. Lemon, seemed to have a strong sense of ownership. He said that my film was basically just fiction because normally, for example, the Swenkas would travel home by combi, whereas in my film they take the train. I didn't quite know what to say, because it doesn't make a difference to me. The train just has this aura to it, with the tracks carving up countries and leaving huge scars across continents. But then Sabelo intervened, and he was seeing the finished film for the first time, and said: 'Mr T.J. Lemon, everything that happened here is true. I have come through the loss of my father in a way that otherwise would have been impossible.' The film had narrativized his loss, and he stood by it because we'd created the reality that the film depicted together. It was a very touching moment, and it reflects a lot of the things I was saying earlier on about trust.

The Swenkas and I also went to New York together, where there were these swanking competitions in a museum context, mostly with people from the black community, but there were also whites who joined in. But the most incredible experience was when the Swenkas flew up here, to Copenhagen, for the Danish premiere. They'd never been outside South Africa before, nor had they flown before. So it was really amazing to be standing in the Grand Cinema in Copenhagen with them. And they were on TV, both on DR and TV 2, where they had make-up done (by white people) and felt like kings.

HJORT: Danish documentary filmmakers are enjoying a lot of success these days. What are the factors that are allowing documentary filmmaking to thrive more generally, but also in the Danish context?

RØNDE: Yes, things are going really well. It's not just the prizes, because they are what they are. You never know what's going to happen with prizes, because it all depends on who you're up against that year and who's in the jury. But there's so much interest in Danish documentaries. You sense it at the film festivals. People are writing about the films, and you also sense the energy in the milieu itself. But what's even more important is this gradual awakening of an interest in documentary film in the population more generally. My sense is that the people I meet who are not part of the film world are seeing far more films – and far more interesting films – than they were just ten years ago. The whole idea is, of course, for us all to learn to see and appreciate better and better films, and it seems like that project is really taking off.

HJORT: What's your take on the question of distribution?

RØNDE: I've been lucky because my films have been released theatrically, and without any special terms or clauses. As far as I'm concerned, a theatrical release is what's optimal right now. *Jerusalem, My Love* was shown in the cinemas in Denmark and Italy, and *The Swenkas* was shown throughout Europe, Africa and the US, for example. A theatrical release gets the film a lot of attention because of all the reviews and interviews. The main alternative right now is TV, and as a platform or window, TV is just incredibly fragmented. So we really need that Net-based platform devoted to documentary film, which many of us are hoping to see developed. I do think that's going to happen. The cinemas are drawing fewer and fewer people, but there will always be this 'dark church' where there's room to contemplate things with others. But doing something major on the Net afterwards is the way to go. That way, as many people as possible will see the films.

HJORT: Where do you see yourself as working in the near future? Are the realities you wish to explore mostly in Denmark or well beyond its borders, as was the case with *Jerusalem, My Love* and *The Swenkas*?

RØNDE: I don't believe in the nation state. The stories I tell are universal ones. The lovers I've had have not been Danish. My wife is part Ugandan, part Slovak. I've lived in other parts of the world, in Prague, for example. At best I'm a European. I made *Son* in Denmark, and the other stories I have to tell will be told from outside Denmark. Whether I'm here or somewhere else, I'm basically just Jeppe.

HJORT: You mentioned that you're now working on that story about love.

RØNDE: I'm in the process of writing a script for a film that will also tell a story that really happened. In 2008, there was a suicide epidemic in this town called Bridgend, in Wales. Over a period of about a year and a half, 30 young people hanged themselves. Some of them had been in touch on the Net, some were related, some were friends; but nobody's been able to prove that there was a suicide pact. I've been over to Bridgend to investigate this, and the idea is to make a film about what happened. That's my next film, and, yes, it will be about love.

Chapter 17

Sami Saif

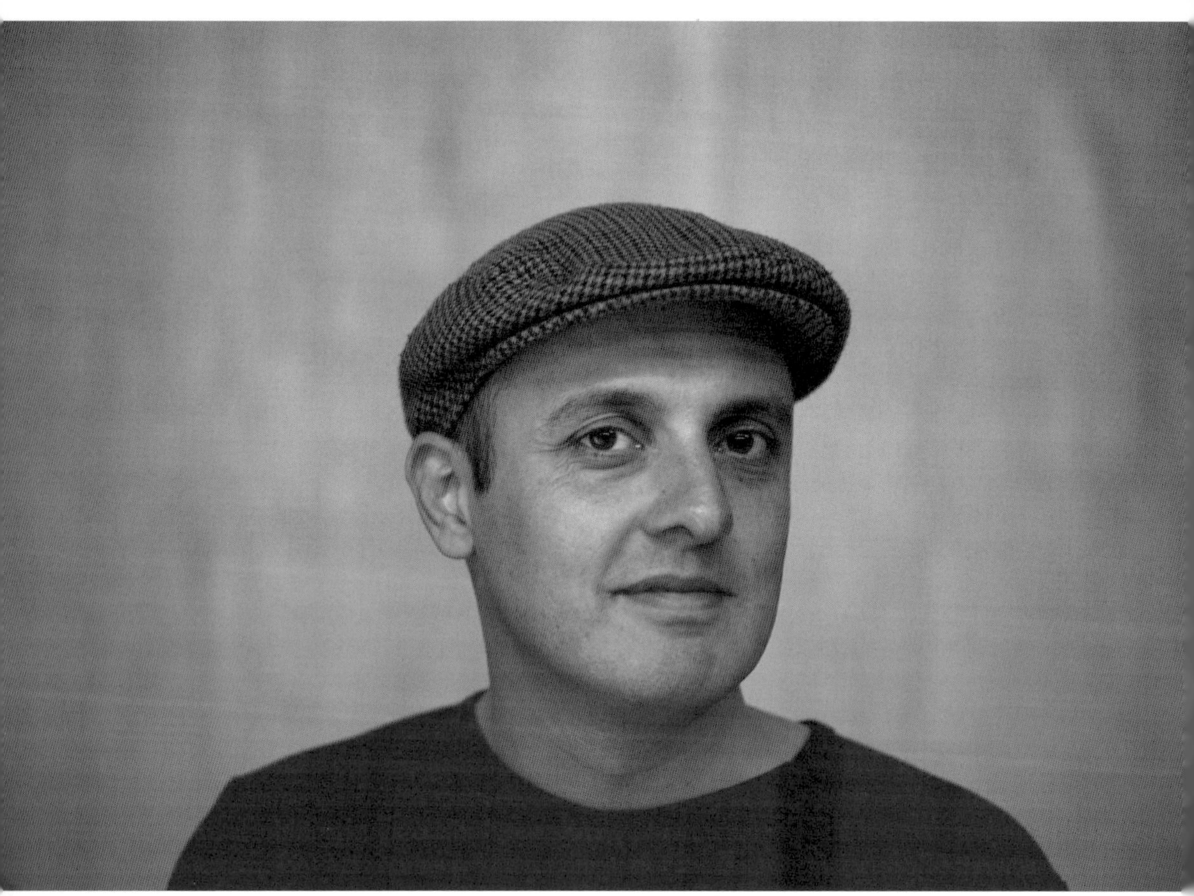

Sami Saif. Portrait by Thomas Vilhelm. Courtesy of Thomas Vilhelm and Sami Saif.

Born 1972. Saif trained as a documentary filmmaker at the National Film School of Denmark, graduating from the Documentary & TV programme in 1997. Before film school, Saif used the opportunities provided by a media centre to produce a documentary short about the various processes – institutional and other – that death unleashes. Entitled *Sidste rejse* ('Last Journey', 1993), the film became a stepping stone to the Film School, and provided an early indication of Saif's commitment to focusing intensely on the serious and difficult aspects of human reality. This commitment is especially evident in Saif's attempt to counter the dehumanizing effects of mass media depictions of so-called 'Björk stalker' Ricardo Lopez, who killed himself on camera at the age of 21. Working closely with well-known editor Janus Billeskov Jansen, Saif edited the documentary material that Lopez left behind, and this in ways quite different from the sensational reporting on TV. Entitled *The Video Diary of Ricardo Lopez* (2000), Saif's film looks for the psychological causes driving Lopez's actions, documenting his deepening state of depression and the suicidal process leading to his death. Death – this time in his own family – was the driving force behind Saif's next film, *Family* (with Phie Ambo, 2001), which won the prestigious Joris Ivens Award at IDFA. Saif's mother died of alcohol-related causes, and his brother Thomas committed suicide, and these two deaths prompted the filmmaker to look for his Yemeni father, whose whereabouts had been unknown to him since early childhood. With its strong narrative drive, clear interest in making good use of the toolkit associated with fiction film, and proven capacity to draw audiences to the cinemas, *Family* is a landmark film in the Danish context, and an almost paradigmatic example of new tendencies in Danish documentary filmmaking.

In the wake of the 'Cartoon Crisis' that erupted in 2005, Saif became involved in a collaborative initiative mounted by the Danish Broadcasting Corporation (DR) and Al-Arabiya, *Mit Danmark* (*My Denmark*, 2006), providing a brief portrait of Iraqi refugee Muniam Alfaker (2006). *Paradis* (*Paradise*; with Jens Loftager and Erlend E. Mo, 2008) is a serious and thought-provoking response to the much touted research findings that proclaim Danes the happiest nation on earth. The film develops its arguments through a series of contrastive portraits, one of them of an Iraqi refugee family living at a Danish asylum centre. Saif has at various times been affiliated with Lars von Trier's production company Zentropa and the Film Town in Avedøre, most clearly in connection with the 'making of' film entitled *Dogville Confessions* (2003). Providing insight into the unorthodox processes involved in shooting Lars von Trier's *Dogville* (2003) in Sweden's Trollhättan, Saif's film won a FIPRESCI award (Honourable Mention). Saif's most recent documentary feature is

Tommy (2010), a film that once again uses the camera to find the humanity behind the reductive depictions that circulate as true through the mass media. In this case, the focus is on the once popular musician Tommy Seebach, and on the implications, for those who loved him, of the alcoholism that killed him. Saif completed a six-episode TV series about the free town of Christiania for DR2 in 2012.

Documentary features:

2010	*Tommy*
2008	*Paradis* (*Paradise*, with Jens Loftager and Erlend E. Mo)
2008	*Roskilde* (with Ulrik Wivel et al.)
2003	*Dogville Confessions*
2001	*Family* (with Phie Ambo)

Documentary shorts:

2006	*Awaiting*
2004	*American Short*
1993	*Sidste rejse* ('Last Journey')

Television:

2012	*Christiania – fristad i frigear* (*Christiania: Freetown Full Throttle*, DR2, six episodes)
2006	*Muniam Alfaker* (film nr. 9, *Mit Danmark* [*My Denmark*], DR & Al-Arabiya/ O3 Production)
2000	*The Video Diary of Ricardo Lopez* (DR)
1995	*UFO-krigen* (*The UFO War*, TV2)

HJORT: It is very difficult to get into the National Film School of Denmark. Your family background – with an alcoholic mother and an absent father whose whereabouts were unknown to you – was hardly a supportive one. How did you end up deciding you wanted to go to film school?

SAIF: I was left to my own devices a lot as a child, and basically had to figure out how to amuse myself on my own. I read a lot of books, but I also went to the cinema a lot. I liked the idea that there was this world to be discovered that was different from that of everyday life, a world of fantasy. I was really intrigued by Michael Ende's *The NeverEnding Story*, for example. To me, the whole idea of parallel worlds was fantastic. One of my friends had a VHS camera which we were always playing around with. We filmed all sorts of things with it, and then spent time editing what we'd shot. Already then there was a documentary aspect to what I was doing. I became much more serious about all this when I moved away from home and into student housing offered by DKIK [Danmarks Internationale Kollegium] in Albertslund. I left home when I was quite young. DKIK offered opportunities to become involved in local TV production, which I found really exciting. I was placed with a media centre at one point because I'd been unemployed for an extended period of time. And while I was there I made this film called 'Last Journey,' a very serious film about what happens when you die. The film follows an old man, all the way through the system, until he's cremated and buried.

And then one day I decided to contact Thomas Heurlin, who was producing documentaries for TV 2's new programme, *Reportageholdet* ('The Reportage Unit'). What he was doing was really fresh and different. For years there'd been what DR had to offer, and then TV 2 was established, and their approach was just completely different. The DR documentaries were typically very heavy and serious, and then suddenly there was this playful approach being adopted by TV 2, with 'The Reportage Unit.' They were exploring these really amusing stories. So I called Thomas Heurlin and told him that I'd be interested in doing something like that. He then asked me to meet with him and his team, which included Jens Ulrik Pedersen and Lars Seidelin. They now co-own Koncern TV & Film Production. Before I knew it I'd been told I could have a go at something myself. That was really a fantastic day for me. I then made this short TV documentary about UFOs called *The UFO War*. Among other things, it was about the dynamics between these two rival organizations that insist on the existence of UFOs. When I applied to the Film School, which I did while I was working with Thomas Heurlin, I sent along 'Last Journey,' and that got me in.

HJORT: In terms of your future career as a filmmaker, what would you say was most important about the experience of being a student at the National Film School of Denmark?

SAIF: I think it was quite a complex programme. Back then, it was just a two-year programme. It's since been expanded. What made it all quite complex was that there was this emphasis on a larger developmental project, on this cultural project. I found all that very difficult to handle. We had to learn about the visual arts more generally, and I had a lot of trouble understanding why that was the case given that we were all interested in film and attending a film school. What I found helpful was the thinking about dramaturgical issues; that is, the encounter with Mogens Rukov. There was so much about the programme that was abstract, but the dramaturgical aspects were wonderfully concrete. We spent a lot of time thinking and talking about what it was that we were doing, so I found it quite a relief to focus on something concrete. I was quite jealous of the cinematographers and editors because they were working on concrete tasks all the time. Mogens Rukov helped me to systematize things. I began to see what I had to do, quite concretely, if I wanted to communicate something in such a way that people would actually be able to feel it and understand it. The dramaturgical concepts and models helped me to clarify what I wanted to say, and to identify *which* emotions I wanted people to be feeling, and *when*. So I wouldn't hesitate for a second to say that it was that encounter with Mogens Rukov that was especially important to me. But the film school experience was also about meeting colleagues. I'm still working with people from my film school days. People discovered that they had these interests in common and were driven by some of the same desires. So I'd say that, for me, the Film School was about two things: it gave me a point of entry to thinking about how storytelling works, and it facilitated these professional friendships, which then became the basis for further collaboration. I appreciate that dimension a lot; that is, that filmmaking is something we do together with other, like-minded people. As I see it, that's very important.

HJORT: Like many graduates from the National Film School of Denmark, you've worked for the Danish Broadcasting Corporation's Children

& Youth Department. What role did your work for DR play in your development as a filmmaker?

SAIF: Yes, I spent over a year at DR. I was involved in this project called *U-land*. It was quite interesting initially, but it ended up becoming overly complicated because there was this emphasis on working with three media all at once: the Internet, radio, and TV. I found that incredibly frustrating because it meant that you could never get deeply involved in whatever you were doing. I had a very strong need to be involved in something that allowed for a lot more depth. So I ended up making *The Video Diary of Ricardo Lopez* while I was at DR, and that film then gave me an opportunity to travel a lot because it was shown at a lot of festivals.

HJORT: *The Video Diary of Ricardo Lopez* is a film with a strong ethical impulse. It's also a film that took a lot of courage to make, and one that demonstrates what independent documentary filmmaking has to offer a world where TV reporting is dominated by media conglomerates. It's not an easy film to get hold of, and my sense is that you're not particularly keen to see it distributed widely and prefer to be present when the film is shown. Why is that?

SAIF: I have a lot at stake in being able to stand by what I've done with the material. I want to be able to explain why I edited it the way I did, why I saw it as important to make the film, and how I understand Ricardo Lopez. My desire to engage very directly with the audiences who see the film has to do with the fact that Ricardo Lopez is dead. That is, it has to do with just how serious a process it was for me to make the film and to try to understand this person who'd killed himself. I want to be there when people see the film because there are all sorts of things about Ricardo Lopez on the Internet. I like to be able to talk to people about what it is they've actually seen. People are often very surprised by the film.

HJORT: What prompted you to make the film?

SAIF: What motivated me was this intense awareness of just how quickly the media can create their own reality. The Ricardo Lopez material was seen as being sensational, so it was picked up by TV stations all over the world. And they were editing it in ways that were deeply distorting, so what we were getting was a series of lies. A lot of what was said by the police was false. That bomb that Lopez tried to send to Björk was defective and wasn't about to go off. The media coverage focused on the elements in the story that were sensational, and nobody was asking about any of the deeper reasons that might have led him to do what he did. The media just showed the actions and didn't consider what might have motivated them. I was interested in the psychological aspects. Who was the person who did this? What were his actions really about? I remember seeing brief excerpts from the video material on TV, with Lopez saying: 'She's fucking a nigger. I just have to kill her.' It was pretty clear to me that what I was seeing was really bad acting, and I just started to feel that the media depictions of Lopez were all wrong. I then got hold of all the tapes, and as I started to watch them I could see that there was something quite different going on in them. So my aim became to understand who Lopez was, as a human being.

The questions I wanted to answer were: 'Who was this young man? And what went wrong?' I wanted to tell his story in such a way that the audience would be very alone with the material in the beginning. So we had this very simple rule, which was that during the first 15 minutes of the film, audience gratification would be based on the story's sensational aspects. But once those 15 minutes were over, it would become clear that the rest of the film wasn't going to be gratifying in that way. We wanted the audience to realize that something else was going on in this film. We also wanted them actually to decide that they were going to continue to watch this film, and were willing to engage with it in a thoughtful way. We wanted to make it crystal clear, after 15 minutes, that the sensational part was well and truly over, and that the story was moving onto terrain that was psycho-analytic and heavy. In the last part of the film, the focus is on the incredibly complex suicidal process that engulfs Lopez; and here the aim was to encourage spectators to analyse the young man's mental states so that they'd become emotionally involved with his life.

HJORT: You did a fair amount of research in connection with the film. What were some of the questions that you saw yourself as needing answers to in order to be able make the film?

SAIF: What happened was that Janus [Billeskov Jansen] and I started to edit the material and quickly had this really strong feeling of not quite being able to understand the deeper issues that were reflected in it. We could see that there was something about the mother that was key. She was very possessive, which had clearly made it difficult for Lopez to break out of his shell and to become his own person as an adult. But we knew that we needed a far deeper psychological understanding of Lopez, so we got in touch with Peter Elsass, whom Janus knew. Peter is a psychologist, and he's

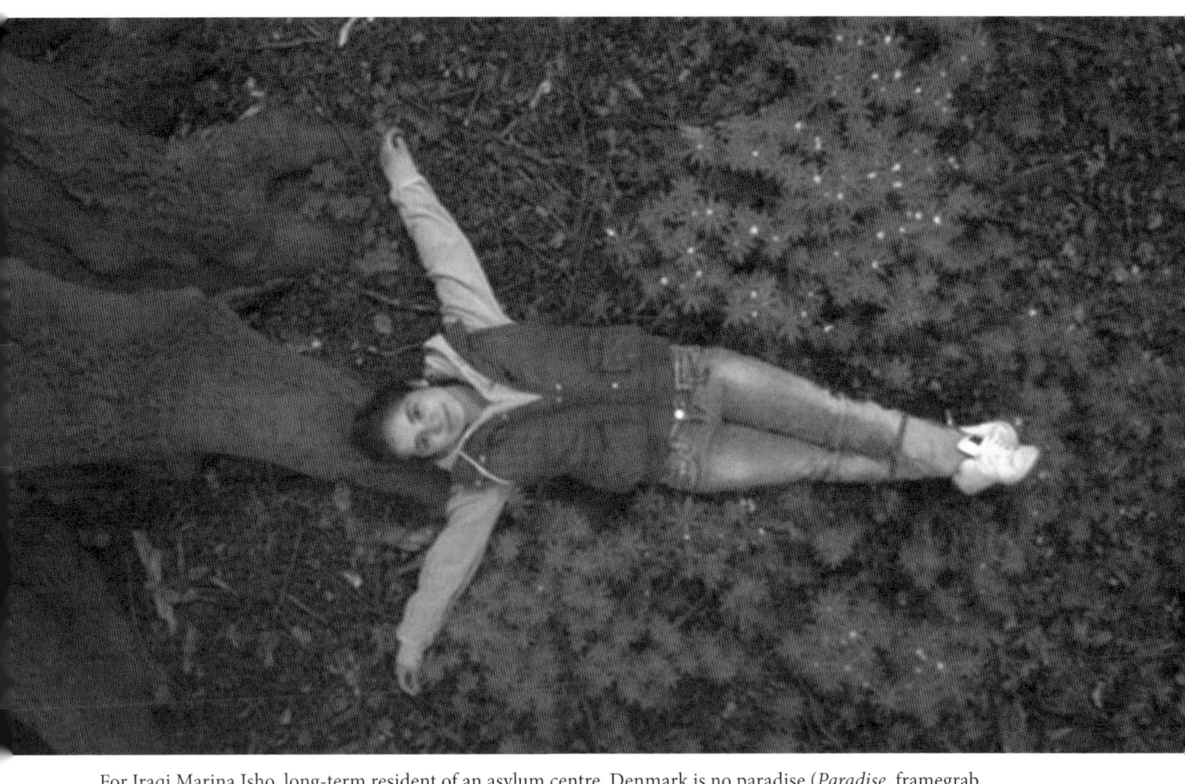

For Iraqi Marina Isho, long-term resident of an asylum centre, Denmark is no paradise (*Paradise*, framegrab, cinematography by Lars Reinholdt, Rasmus Heise, Anthony Dod Mantle, Erlend E. Mo, and Sami Saif).

also done some filmmaking, so we asked him to watch the material and to give us his take on it. Peter's view was that Lopez had had this sexual drive, which was completely natural, and that it had been blocked. He'd slept in his mother's bed over a long period of time, for example, and during those crucial years when his sexuality should have been developing, his mother had created obstacles, which had trapped him in some kind of pre-pubescent phase. And because of all this, sexuality had become something very complicated for this young man. So there was this excessively strong connection to the mother, one of the effects of which was that Lopez projected his 'dirty' sexuality into a realm of fantasy. In that fantasy world, the sexual drive somehow became acceptable because the love was pure and the object of it, namely Björk, was seen as different from everyone else. Adding to the complexity of the issues with the mother was Lopez's state of depression. What Peter also helped us to understand is that the video material documents a very typical suicidal process that includes a certain ambiguity; with thoughts about the necessity of dying, but also about not dying. Because Lopez started to isolate himself, nobody noticed that he was doing things that are characteristic of a suicidal process. Circumstances didn't intervene to push him in the other direction, and he ended up playing with his thoughts and fantasies to the point where they became his reality. He then constructed that bomb, which didn't actually work. But the fact of having sent it meant that he now had to die. In his mind it's all over and his death is necessary. Peter's insights helped us to clarify the nature of the story that we were trying to tell, and it was very much focused on this investigation of the psychological process that led to Lopez's suicide.

HJORT: The project of humanizing Ricardo Lopez hinges on your editing, on the information that you provide in brief textual inserts, and on your decision to organize the video material into chapters with titles such as 'Big Brother George,' 'Ricardo's Friend Ralph,' 'The Phone Call from Mother.' How would you describe your approach? Why did you opt to be so minimally present in the film?

SAIF: There were all sorts of ideas about how to expand on the material. The thing is, we're basically presenting this incredibly intimate space, and I think the form reflects that. He only shoots in his own home, within the four walls of his personal space. So there's this contract, from the very beginning, about how we're seeing something incredibly private and intimate. Every time we tried to bring in something that was external to that space, it was just sort of pushed away by the material. Because the space that Lopez had created with his camera was so insistent and so intimate, anything we brought to it from the outside just had the effect of scrambling the cinematic logic of it all. But the form we chose also reflects my view that, in a story like this one, it's not the director's task to try to please the audience. The film tells a story about a very difficult and tough reality, and so, as a filmmaker, you have to make it clear that watching it is going to be demanding. It's a long and heavy journey, and it ends with him dying. We did a few things with music, just to remind the audience to think about what it is they're watching. We wanted them to be asking questions throughout the film. 'Who is this person? What's his state of mind like right now? What is it exactly that's happened up until this point?' The music creates a space that allows the viewer to think about those sorts of questions, and then we're back with Lopez again. But the short answer to your question about the film's form is that Lopez himself had established a frame for the story, through the camera's insistence on that intimate space.

HJORT: *The Video Diary of Ricardo Lopez* must have been a very tough film to make. And you made it very early on.

SAIF: I think the seriousness of the project was what was important to me. I'd lost my mother to illness caused by alcoholism, and my brother had committed suicide. I've always felt that it's really important to insist on seriousness, and to be willing also to focus on the ugly aspects of reality. Life includes a lot that's very serious and not especially pleasant. I think the stories that tell us that life isn't one big party have an important role to play. I don't like stories that try to get us to believe that life's an endless party, because that's just not true. Life is often incredibly hard, intense, and violent. All sorts of things happen to people, and they have to find a way of dealing with them. So seriousness is important. Loss is important. Death is important. Life is fragile, and stories that insist on its serious side require me to live mine in a decent way.

HJORT: *Family* was a major breakthrough for you. The film has often been discussed in terms of your use of various fictional devices such as the three-act structure associated with storytelling with a strong narrative drive. What gets somewhat lost as a result of such discussions is the extent to which this film documents a deeply personal process of genuine discovery that is linked to deep psychological needs of yours. There is talk in the film about your need to find your father, or information about him, in order to 'be whole.' In this sense the film is part of a therapeutic process. Is it fair to say that the film makes it possible for you to carry out a very difficult search, by providing a framework and by requiring a certain level of commitment from you?

SAIF: There's no doubt whatsoever about that being true. I'm really not sure I would ever have gone on that trip, in search of my father, had it not been for the film. But I also remember thinking: 'OK, now I've made that Ricardo Lopez film, which involved making use of a lot of very intimate material. How can I justify having done that if I'm not willing to do something similar with my own life?' After all, I also had a story to tell. So there was this sense of it now being my turn! And right from the beginning I decided that if I was going to tell my story, then I was going to tell it incredibly well, and in such a way that it would elicit a lot of sympathy. I wanted the audience to cry in response to my story because I actually felt really, really sorry for myself!

With *Family* my approach was to say, 'OK, you're this important director and you're the main character in your film. And you're fully in control of that character, but only during the editing phase.' I knew I needed a really good editor, so I was glad to be able to work with Janus Billeskov Jansen again. Phie [Ambo], who was my partner at the time, shot the film. My agreement with her was that she would shoot whatever she wanted to shoot; that is, I wasn't allowed to refuse to be filmed. We also agreed to emphasize the visual qualities of the film. So she'd shoot medium shots, close-ups, and so on, and I'd allow myself to be placed wherever she wanted me to be. And she'd keep coming back to that basic agreement of ours, which was that she was allowed to film everything. It was important to know that we were both bound by that agreement. The reason the film works so well is that we ended up having all these unexpected experiences that are simply perfect in terms of the story. I really enjoyed being both the director and the main character in the film because it was very easy to control the process. Making *Family* was a very playful, pleasant, and happy experience.

HJORT: You worked as a consultant for Zentropa Real at one point. What did this job entail?

SAIF: I've been involved with Zentropa on different occasions. The idea with Zentropa Real was to explore the possibility of making documentaries for TV. But things never really fell into place.

Things were going incredibly well for Zentropa back then, around 2003. So I was at Zentropa for a while, along with some other people with an interest in documentary filmmaking, and our job was to listen to people's ideas and to think about how they might be developed. It was especially Peter Aalbæk Jensen who was interested in getting this off the ground. But the idea of expanding Zentropa's activities onto the terrain of documentary filmmaking hadn't been developed in any kind of systematic way, so it didn't really go anywhere.

HJORT:

Dogville Confessions is a Zentropa Real production. It won a FIPRESCI prize (Honourable Mention) for its 'valuable illustration into the temperamental, sometimes childish relationship between Lars von Trier and his actors in the making of the film *Dogville*' [IMDb]. With its emphasis on truth-speaking – in the context of a confession booth that was ultimately anything but private – the making of this film must have been a potentially explosive affair. I'm sure you have a lot of material that didn't end up in the film! How constrained/free were you in making the film, and what did you see yourself as trying to achieve?

SAIF:

It was all incredibly complicated; interesting, but also completely insane. Authenticity is really important to me. If I sense that there's an element of feigning in someone's behaviour, I turn the camera off and try to talk things through. With *Dogville Confessions*, I suddenly found myself with a huge number of actors whose lives are all about feigning. So there I was with my camera, and everything I was shooting with it was so extreme. I was either shooting something that was completely exaggerated or something that was utterly banal. Nicole Kidman would see the camera and say, 'Oh, it's a wonderful day.' If I'd just had Nicole Kidman and one other person to focus on, then the situation would have been completely different, because then I'd have been able to get to know them. My method is all about getting to know people, and the intimacy that's part of that process is very important to me. So I found it all very confusing. I was allowed to be present with my camera all over the place, but the thing is that there are also things that are private on a film set. People work all day and then they live their private lives. I don't actually think it's OK to film what's private. My approach was to emphasize honesty and intimacy, but not what's completely private. I'm not interested in filming people when they're drunk, for example. I found myself in this strange gossipy world that I didn't really understand, so I was very much out of my comfort zone. A lot of the actors reacted to my camera as though I were some paparazzo, whereas for me it was all about trying to get at the humanity of those film stars. I was quite interested in the challenge that was involved in the documentary project, in this idea of somehow making the stars human. But I wasn't able to achieve what I set out to do, and I realize now that my thinking about the film was naive. Reality doesn't work that way. As for the confession booth, that was von Trier's idea, and I quite liked it too.

HJORT:

What's said in a confession booth is normally strictly confidential. That wasn't the case here.

SAIF:

Yes, and the problem was that the actors would go into that booth, and be drunk out of their minds, and do all sorts of very private things. When I got the tape, I found myself looking at all this paparazzi shit. And when I tried to use some of the material, some agent or other would intervene and tell me that I really couldn't do that, which was of course true. So the confession box became a very strange thing. But there were other problems. For one thing, there were simply too many people involved, so it was impossible for me to keep track of everything and I couldn't really get close to anyone. Getting access to the stars was simply too complicated. I suppose I could have approached the documentary in a completely different way. I could have made something like *Lost in La Mancha* (dir. Keith Fulton & Louis Pepe, 2002), where the filmmakers followed director Terry Gilliam closely as he tried to make *The Man Who Killed Don Quixote*. But that wasn't the approach we'd agreed on, so I have to say I think there was something wrong with the premise of *Dogville Confessions*. It might have been better just to focus on von Trier, although that would have been hard too because he's so changeable. I could be there with my camera and suddenly have von Trier telling me to 'go away.' 'Why?' I'd ask, because there seemed to be no good reason to ask me to leave. It was all very strange and very chaotic. I never felt that I really understood what we were trying to achieve. The only bit of guidance we had to work with came from von Trier himself, who kept saying: 'We don't know what we're doing.' That was his premise with *Dogville*, and that had implications for what I was trying to do with *Dogville Confessions*. Nobody understood what was going on. It was really strange.

HJORT:

You contributed the portrait of Iraqi Muniam Alfaker to the collective film project entitled *My Denmark*, which was coproduced by DR and Al-Arabiya/O3 Productions in the wake of, and in

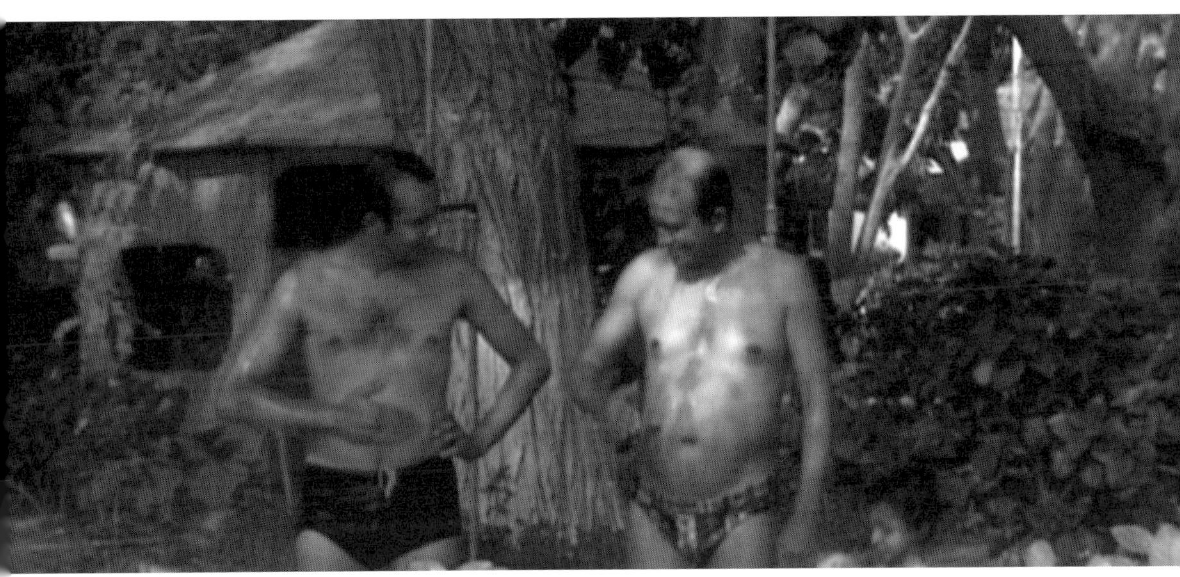

Sami Saif and his newly discovered half brother find evidence of a shared gene pool in their baldness (*Family*, framegrab, cinematography by Phie Ambo).

response to, the 'Cartoon Crisis.' The introductory segment that prefaces the portraits refers explicitly to how '12 caricatures of the prophet' created 'a new frontline between the West and the Middle East.' It also foregrounds the idea of '10 Danish Arabic voices, 10 directors, 10 stories, and 1 common reality.' The Beirut-born filmmaker, film critic, and film producer Mohamad Soueid travelled to Copenhagen in order to get this project off the ground. How collaborative was this project, and what exactly was the brief given to you as a director?

SAIF: The directors weren't really given a brief. I found it a bit problematic because it was such a direct response to the 'Cartoon Crisis.' So there were these entrenched positions, with people for and against this and that. I always have trouble with that sort of thing because I never see myself as a spokesperson for anything other than a basic human project. What I found interesting was the opportunity to work with Muniam, who was writing these messages to his brother, whose reality was the war in Iraq. Although Muniam is living in a part of the world where things more or less work, there's this powerful split in his reality. And that sense of being cut off from something is always there in the life of a refugee. Refugees don't just flee, find themselves a safe place, and become happy. They're human beings with families, many of whom are living in parts of the world where there's war, and where all sorts of atrocities are happening all the time. And refugees are constantly in touch with family members about these horrifying realities. War is part of the reality of anyone who is aware of its existence, and refugees are. That was the phenomenon that I was interested in. The media don't provide images of that reality, and if they did perhaps we'd take war a little more seriously. But the project itself was irritating at some level, because the thinking, however well intentioned, seemed to be to convey the idea that Arabs living in Denmark also are human beings.

We did meet as a group. The project had the best of intentions. But it would have been better to start with a broader investigation of society, of its institutions, of how we relate to each other. And if we'd ended up discovering institutionalized racism, then we could have talked openly about that. When it comes to racism and refugees, Danish society sometimes seems pretty unenlightened to me, and as a result of that, projects of this type easily become a bit unfortunate. So in terms of the parameters, we basically knew who was involved in the project, and that we were responding to the 'Cartoon Crisis.' And then there was this subtext which was that everyone was supposed to like each other. It was a bit strange.

HJORT: *Paradise*, which you made together with Jens Loftager and Erlend Mo, provides a fascinating counter-narrative to the research findings of happiness experts, who see Danes as the happiest people in the world. The contrast established between the plight of an Iraqi refugee family (and especially the young girl, Marina Isho), and the ultra-privileged young Danish couple consisting of the pregnant Sofie Egmont-Petersen and Thomas Garth Grüner is telling. Even more thought-provoking, however, is the portrait– highlighting small-mindedness, a sense of entitlement, and a striking lack of joyousness – that the film paints of Egmont- Petersen and Garth Grüner. How do you handle the ethical issues that necessarily arise when the picture being painted of people who have lent their support to your filmmaking project is negative?

SAIF: Something that's very important to me is that I don't film people I don't like. I spend time with the people I film, and I get to know them. I chose Sofie and Thomas because there was a fragility to their relationship that I could relate to. I was interested in Sofie's wish to have a child, and in her sense of certainty about that decision. And then there was Thomas' sense of lots of issues as having been somehow settled by that decision, as requiring little or no discussion. But life isn't like that, because the decision to have a child involves a lot of emotions, and it's also a question of figuring out what kind of life you're going to live as a family. I found all the tensions that came to the surface as a result of that decision to establish a family fascinating. And then, of course, there was the issue of wealth. Even if you have a lot of money, there are still going to be these very human dilemmas having to do with relationships. As we were making the film, Jens, Erlend, and I talked a lot about the issue of opportunity. Are people who have lots of opportunities available to them actually able to see them, and to make use of them? The contrasts we established in the film are our attempt to raise questions about consumerism, about the reasons we have for having children, and about what's involved in being a parent. One of the contrasts is between children who are allowed to be children, and children who aren't. The point of the film is to get us to look at ourselves, at our values.

HJORT: Has Sofie Egmont-Petersen seen the film?

SAIF: Yes, and she felt the portrait of her and Thomas was very hard-hitting. I don't think it is. I think it shows things the way they are. They're both from the kind of social background where a lot is expected of you. You're supposed to be successful all the time. He's inherited this huge estate and is supposed to run it, but maybe that's not what he really wants to do. But it's not easy to opt out either; so at a basic human level it's all quite confusing, in spite of all the privileges.

HJORT: *Tommy* looks closely at the life of the musician Tommy Seebach, who died in 2003 at the age of 53. Among other things, the film shows the costs that changing musical tastes had for Seebach and his family. Seebach and Lopez were clearly very different people. Their stories are, however, both tragic. Also, your films about these two people are very much about using the truth-finding power of documentary filmmaking to restore some dignity to their lives. Is this part of the appeal of documentary filmmaking, as you see it?

SAIF: Yes, dignity is partly what it's about. Seebach had been this hugely popular musician, and then suddenly he was reduced to being nothing more than an alcoholic in the newspapers. There was this sense of 'to hell with the human being.' So there's a very strong drive in the film to defend this human being, and to give him a certain dignity, some humanity. There are lots of people like Tommy Seebach, and lots of families like his. In Denmark, there are a lot of children growing up with parents who are alcoholics. Once again, it's about insisting on the seriousness of things. It's almost more normal than unusual for someone to go to the dogs. I don't accept the narrative that says Seebach was a star, became an alcoholic, and now deserves to be forgotten. That's not fair. He was doing his best. But, yes, he drank far too much and he wasn't in control of his life. I think it's important to show that because the effect of seeing the impact of his alcoholism on his wife and three children in a film is very different from seeing a picture of him in a drunken condition in some newspaper.

HJORT: The film draws on a lot of home movies that his wife, Karen Seebach, made available to you. One of the most heart-breaking scenes in the film shows the family trying to celebrate the birthday of one of the children, with Tommy Seebach unable to participate on account of his drunken condition.

SAIF: Yes, that's the way it was. Those are the sorts of things that Karen and the children experienced. I didn't know I would have all those home movies to work with, but then Karen suddenly told me about them, and said I could use them. It was incredible.

HJORT: You worked very closely with Karen and the children, all of whom are now adults.

SAIF: Yes, I always become very involved with the people I work with. It's a very big part of what I do. I don't work with trick questions, and I don't have a hidden agenda. I put everything on the table so they understand what I'm trying to do. In the case of the Seebach film, I began by saying that we'd only talk about the bad things that had happened, right from the start. Honesty was really crucial. So we talked things through, and then we did some very long interviews, where it was also a matter of talking about what the project was all about. So there was room to ask why a certain question was necessary. Or someone might say that he or she didn't want to respond to a given question. And then I'd be able to follow up, and ask why. So these interviews became exchanges about lived experiences, and they allowed us to work out what it was we were trying to do. Karen and the children got a sense of what was driving me, and they also came to see that they were very much part of the process of shaping the film. That's incredibly important. I don't do anything on my own. And then once we'd arrived at a shared understanding about the project, we went on to shoot these really long interviews. The family was involved throughout the entire process of making the film, including the editing. They would come in and look at what we'd done while we were editing, and we'd call each other and talk on the phone, and so on.

HJORT: Did their input during the editing phase change anything?

SAIF: No, it didn't, and that's because I'd been so open about my intentions right from the start. I wouldn't want a situation where they'd suddenly find something very different from what they'd expected in the editing room. The grown-up children might have felt it was strange to see themselves as children again, but there were no objections to how we'd depicted the family's experiences.

HJORT: What are you currently working on?

SAIF: I'm making a TV series about Christiania. In a way it's the same issue all over again. You have these two positions, and neither of them really do justice to the reality of the situation. There's the state, and then there's Christiania. The state's view is that Christiania is nothing but trouble. And the people who are part of Christiania keep saying, 'Freedom! Freedom!' Either way, it's a lie.

So the idea is to look closely at Christiania, and to figure out what it's really all about. And the terrible truth that you discover when you do that is that Christiania isn't that different from the suburb of Brønshøj! So it's about getting to the truth of things. It's been a lot of fun, and it's been great to be doing a TV series. The approach is very playful, and we're working in a very grass-roots sort of way, with cheap cameras in a bag. We're working closely with the people in Christiania, who'll give us a call if something comes up. We'll have a cup of coffee together and ask them what's happening, and what they feel we should be shooting. It's all very playful. In Christiania, there's this huge emphasis on consensus. If two people are quarrelling in some street in Copenhagen, people will just walk on by. But in Christiania, people will intervene, and say, 'OK, what's the problem here? How do you see the problem? And now it's your turn to explain the problem.' And then everything's written down and printed in their weekly publication. There's an emphasis on behaving decently towards other people. Certain things just aren't OK. I like the collectivist aspects of that very human project of trying to be authentic. There's something very family-like about it all. At home if you forget to buy milk, you may need to talk about whether your excuse is good enough. Well, it's the same sort of dynamic in Christiania; it's just happening in a much larger context. I find that fascinating.

Chapter 18

Anne Wivel

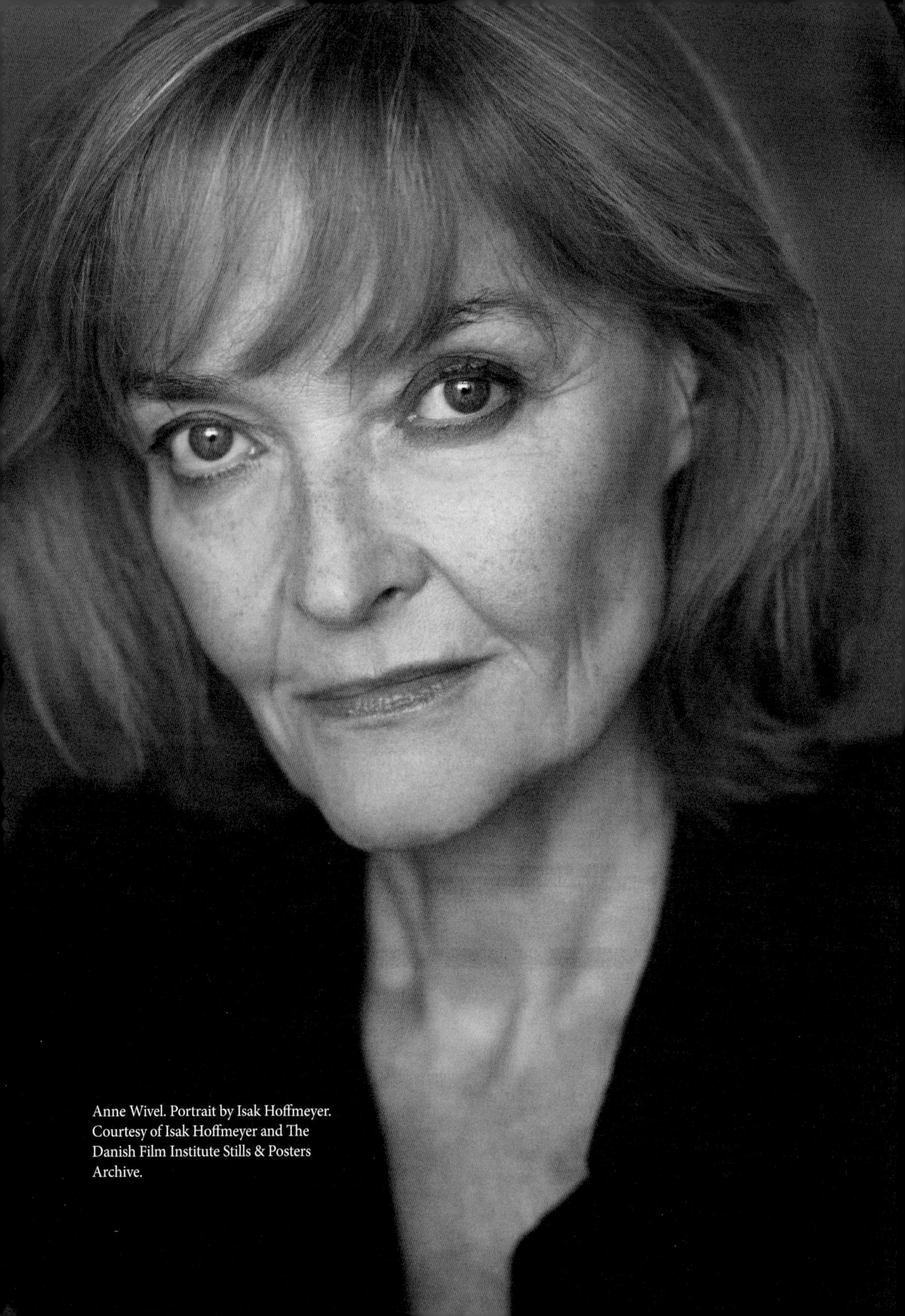

Anne Wivel. Portrait by Isak Hoffmeyer.
Courtesy of Isak Hoffmeyer and The
Danish Film Institute Stills & Posters
Archive.

B orn 1945. A graduate of both the Royal Danish Academy of Fine Arts (1977) and of the National Film School of Denmark (1980), Wivel's contributions to the Danish art scene are wide-ranging, encompassing poetry, painting, and essays, in addition to film. For more than three decades, Wivel's main focus has been filmmaking that is at once essentially documentary, yet driven by a powerful desire to blur the boundaries between the domains of fiction and non-fiction filmmaking. Wivel's commitment to finding compelling and engaging ways of making reality's stories visually articulate has never entailed a neglect of the ethical dimension that must be central to documentary filmmaking. Her filmmaking reflects a fine sensitivity and an especially well-developed capacity to establish the trust that is required if some of the more authentic aspects of human lives are to be captured on-camera. Wivel has made a significant number of documentary films, many of which have won Danish, Nordic, or international awards. Tellingly, her work is featured in David A. Goldsmith's *The Documentary Makers: Interviews with 15 of the Best in the Business*,[1] alongside that of figures such as Errol Morris, Wu Wenguang, Jean-Marie Teno, and Anand Patwardhan.

Wivel first won recognition for her filmmaking early in her career: *Motivation – nærbilleder fra en ungdomsskole* (*Motivation: Close-ups from a Youth School*; co-directed with Arne Bro, 1983) won a Robert for best documentary short from the Danish Film Academy in 1984, as did *De tavse piger* (*The Silent Girls*; co-directed with Arne Bro, 1985). Wivel is a two-time recipient of the Nordic Film Prize: for her first feature documentary, *Ansigt til Ansigt – en film om tro, håb og kærlighed* (*Face to Face: A Film about Faith, Hope, and Love*, 1987), and for *David eller Goliath* (*David or Goliath: A Film about the World Press in Jerusalem*, 1988). Focusing on the Beit Agron International Press Centre in Jerusalem at the time of the first Intifada, *David or Goliath* reflects Wivel's respect for documentary practices associated with cinema direct. The film won the Frederick Wiseman Special Prize at the Filmer à Tout Prix festival in Brussels in 1989. *Giselle – en film om drøm og disciplin* (*Giselle: A Film about Dreams and Discipline*, 1991) is concerned with romantic love and devotion to art, and with beauty and seduction. Featuring remarkable cinematography by Dan Laustsen, inspired by German Romantic landscape painting, *Giselle* won numerous prizes, including the Silver Medal at the Dance on Camera Film Festival in New York.

Wivel's oeuvre includes films of considerable intimacy, such as *Johannes' hjerte* (*The Heart of Johannes*, 1998), *Slottet i Italien* (*The Castle in Italy: An Elegy*, 2000), and *Svend* (2011), all of which focus on prominent Danes at a time of personal crisis. *Face to Face* and *David or Goliath* are examples of Wivel's interest in the energies of a more institutional reality, whereas films like *Søren Kierkegaard* (*Søren Kierkegaard*, 1994) and *En gal, en elsker eller en poet* (*A Madman, a Lover, and a Poet*, 2005) reflect a desire to bring to light the humanity that rests within figures belonging to the canons of Danish national culture. In *Menneskenes land – min film om Grønland* (*The Land of Human Beings: My Film about Greenland*, 2007), Wivel expresses a deeply personal appreciation for Greenland, and one that is well attuned to the political issues that its people face. Wivel's role in the landscape of Danish documentary filmmaking is not limited to that of filmmaker. She is the artistic director of Barok Film A/S, a company that plays a crucial role within the ecology of Danish documentary film production. Wivel's approach to documentary filmmaking is reflected in the work of an entire generation of younger directors for whom she has served as a mentor and teacher, through her involvement over many years with the National Film School of Denmark's Documentary & Television Department. Anne Wivel is the daughter of the well-known writer Ole Wivel. Her son is the dancer and filmmaker Ulrik Wivel.

Documentary features:

2011   *Svend* (*Svend*)
2006   *Menneskenes land – min film om Grønland* (*The Land of Human Beings: My Film about Greenland*)
2005   *En gal, en elsker eller en poet* (*A Madman, a Lover, and a Poet*)
2000   *Slottet i Italien* (*The Castle in Italy: An Elegy*)
1998   *Johannes' hjerte* (*The Heart of Johannes*)
1994   *Søren Kierkegaard*
1991   *Giselle – en film om drøm og disciplin* (*Giselle: A Film about Dreams and Discipline*)
1988   *David eller Goliath* (*David or Goliath: A Film about the World Press in Jerusalem*)
1987   *Ansigt til Ansigt – en film om tro, håb og kærlighed* (*Face to Face: A Film about Faith, Hope, and Love*)

Documentary shorts:

1996   *Tobacco* (part of omnibus film *Danske piger viser alt* [*Danish Girls Show Everything*])
1988   *Vand* (*Water*)
1985   *Den lille pige med skøjterne* (*The Little Girl with the Skates*)
1985   *De tavse piger* (*The Silent Girls*, with Arne Bro)
1984   *Gorilla gorilla* (*Gorilla gorilla*)
1983   *Motivation – nærbilleder fra en ungdomsskole* (*Motivation: Close-ups from a Youth School*, with Arne Bro)
1980   *Arbejde mod frihed – En film om et statsfængsel* (*Work Towards Freedom: A Film about a State Prison*)

HJORT: You graduated from the Royal Danish Academy of Fine Arts in 1977, and from the National Film School of Denmark in 1980, and this institutional trajectory marks your shift from painting to filmmaking. What drew you to filmmaking?

WIVEL: I was the kind of person who was always drawing and painting, so I was fortunate to get into the Academy of Fine Arts, where I was initially trained as a painter and as a graphic artist. I then went on to pursue a graduate programme in visual arts, which the Academy offered, and which included courses in photography and video. At the time, video was a completely new medium. I had this wonderful professor called Albert Mertz, who was a Fluxus artist and a very internationally oriented person. He was just as intrigued by video as I was, and since we were both fascinated by avant-garde artistic experimentations, we were constantly playing around with this new medium. At some point in his past, Albert Mertz had made some films together with Jørgen Roos, so he had one experimental leg firmly planted in the world of documentary film. He felt that I should be trying to position myself in that same space, so he told me about these short, introductory courses that the Film School offered. I ended up being granted leave from the Academy, where I was still enrolled, and I then spent about 12 weeks at the Film School. I made a lot of friends there and had a really good time. And by the end of that short course, the thought that I could actually apply to the School as a full-time student started to occur to me. And so I did, and got in.

For me, quite personally, the Film School offered an opportunity to rebel against this rather heavy artist's persona that was very much part of the visual arts milieu and that just didn't appeal to me. There were a lot of youth revolts at the time, and we were all rebelling against something or other. This was also the case for me personally. I just couldn't handle the very clearly defined path to which the Academy had somehow led me. I experienced the Film School as a milieu that was wonderfully unencumbered by tradition and history because the art of film was so young compared with the other arts. That was very much part of the School's appeal as far as I was concerned. And I suppose it's fair to say that I held on to that sense of personal rebellion by situating myself, rather quickly and quite radically, in the field of documentary filmmaking. Nobody had done that before, at least not in the context of the Film School, because the focus of its efforts was very much fiction filmmaking. I did, of course, do some of that, but I couldn't help but feel that the cinematic language that was the norm for Danish film at the time was very uninteresting. The language in question was so dominant, so pervasive, that it would have been almost impossible for me, as a lone woman, to break with it to the point where I'd be able to express something that I'd actually find meaningful. I simply realized that the field of documentary filmmaking was where I'd best be able to do something more personal with the medium of film. And that's still how I see it.

I entered the world of film as a slightly shy person with this inner world that wasn't always that easily expressed. Film is quite a healthy tool to be working with if you're the kind of person who doesn't quite know how to motivate people to come together to do something. In a different era I might have become a somewhat lonely artist. I'm quite sure I would have become some kind of artist, perhaps a painter or a writer. As far as my becoming a filmmaker is concerned, I have to say that it was very liberating to be drawn into a social world where the expressive needs that I have could be met through creative processes that are deeply collaborative. Film made being together with other people a whole lot easier.

HJORT: You've been involved in teaching initiatives at the Film School, and at this point quite a number of its graduates see you as an important mentor figure. How do you see your role as a teacher at the School?

WIVEL: My view was that since reality – and all the material it has to offer – can be grasped, interpreted, and filmed in such endlessly different ways, there was no reason why the Film School shouldn't relate to it in a thoughtful and considered way. It made no sense to think that documentary approaches would only end up on the School's radar when someone, for some reason that would never even become clear to anyone else, decided that she didn't want to make a fiction film. So I and a number of like-minded friends – including Arne Bro, who was my partner for many years – came up with the idea of establishing an entire programme devoted to documentary film. It's Arne who's been the driving force behind the programme, in terms of shaping and developing it. I've been part of the process during specific periods, when my filmmaking commitments have allowed it. I'm always part of the admission's process, together with Arne, for one of the Documentary & TV Department's two programmes. I'm at the School on a regular

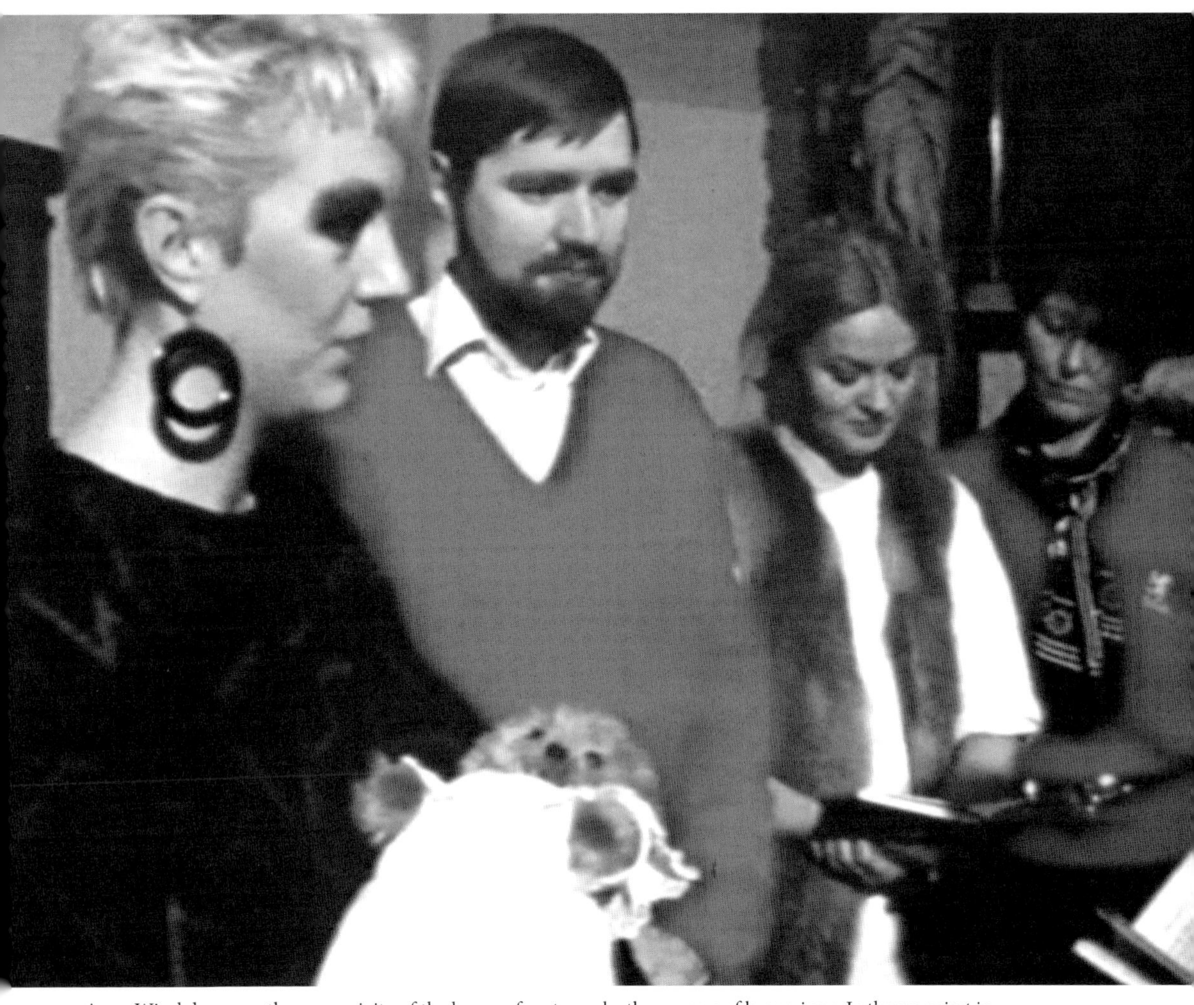

Anne Wivel draws on the expressivity of the human face to evoke the process of becoming a Lutheran priest in Denmark (*Face to Face*, framegrab, cinematography by Dan Laustsen).

basis, as a teacher, and I do think I have something to offer. It's very exciting to be involved in certain processes. The students may, for example, have thought about what they want to do, but may be unclear about what approach to take. I also like to return to the School when the students have reached the editing phase and face the challenge of having to articulate the potential that's in their material.

HJORT: What do you see as being decisive during the highly competitive admissions process?

WIVEL: I'm involved in admitting the six students who get into the documentary filmmaking programme every second year. The aim is to give these people the opportunity to spend several years in a place where they're really able to make good use of their time. We look for applicants who have an original eye and certain abilities that we'd like to see developed over a period of years. It's really about defending people who clearly have an original way of seeing things, and about giving them a framework or a context in which they can develop the unique, personal perspectives that they have.

HJORT: The Documentary & TV Department requires its students to spend a month making a film more or less on their own in a Middle Eastern or North African country. Why is it important to challenge the students in this way?

WIVEL: This is a challenge they're presented with about halfway through their programme. The idea is for them to experience what it's like to be completely on their own with a camera, somewhere in the world where they can't rely on their usual networks or assumptions. They have to orient themselves in a new place; at the same time, they've been taught to think of themselves as having a unique way of perceiving the world; and they find themselves in environments that are often intense and thought-provoking. Together, these elements usually become the basis for a really good film. The students also grow a lot as a result of this assignment. There's really no other way of putting it.

HJORT: You're one of the co-founders of the production company Barok Film A/S and you serve as the company's artistic director. How did this company end up getting established?

WIVEL: That happened well over a decade ago. Erik Stephensen from Skandinavisk Film Kompagni got in touch with me and said something along the lines of: 'We've got this surplus and want to do something interesting with it.' SFK was quite mainstream, and was involved in the production of all sorts of TV programmes, including morning talk shows. But Stephensen was a staunch supporter of the kind of films I stood for, and so he wanted me to establish a production unit within SFK. Initially the idea struck me as a bit odd, so I needed a bit of time to think about it, but I eventually agreed. I got in touch with a former student from the Film School, Mette Ann Schepelern, whom I thought was really good, and she helped me to get the initiative off the ground; and then later I got Vibeke Vogel to join us. After about a year, I had a long talk with Erik Stephensen, who's also a good friend. I told him that I was having a hard time understanding why Barok Film had to answer to SFK's senior managers, given how independent we actually were. I looked him straight in the eyes and explained that Barok Film was never going to become a profit-making undertaking, because that's just not how I think. I told him that I didn't want to be thinking in terms of the bottom line all the time, which was more the thinking in SF. We ended up agreeing that it made more sense for Barok Film and SFK to go their separate ways, and so we became an independent company. We rented office space from Nordisk Film for a few years, and after that we moved to Zentropa's Film Town. Now we're in Farvergade, which is a good, central location for us, and I expect we'll stay there.

HJORT: What were the years in the Film Town like?

WIVEL: The Film Town and Zentropa were created by good friends of mine from my film school days; Peter Aalbæk, Lars von Trier, and I were all at the Film School together. Once you've spent four years at the School, you really do think of yourself as belonging to a kind of clan. Some of the School's graduates end up in Avedøre, at Zentropa. Others end up in Farvergade, at Barok, and some end up at Nimbus Film. The friendships get established during the Film School years, but persist well beyond them because people realize that there are still all sorts of projects they'd like to undertake together. Peter and Lars have enormous drive and energy, and an incredibly productive way of interacting with each other, and that's enabled them to create this extraordinary Film Town, which is really a huge operation. Personally I prefer a smaller milieu. I would, for example, never want Barok Film to become as big as Zentropa. Barok Film has worked with a lot of different directors at this point, so it's not actually that small. But, still, the scale is very different from that of Zentropa. Zentropa is the main artery in Danish film, certainly in the area of fiction filmmaking. It's a different story when it comes to documentary filmmaking.

HJORT: Is this where Barok Film comes into the picture?

WIVEL: With Barok Film, the driving force has always been my own active involvement with documentary filmmaking. I never stopped making my own films. Once Barok Film was established, it basically became the place where I produce all my films. And then over the years, my colleagues and I managed to create an identity for the company that made it natural for graduates from the Film School to look to us when they were trying to find a producer for their first film. We've also produced fiction films, so we're not genre specific in that sense. For example, we produced Jytte Rex's *Silkevejen* (*Silk Road*, 2004). But it's clear that my strengths and interests lie in the area of documentary filmmaking. I think that over the years, Barok Film has produced a lot of films we can be really proud of.

HJORT: What are some of the current projects that you're especially excited about, in your capacity as Barok Film's artistic director?

WIVEL: Ole Roos is in the process of developing a film he'd like to make about the legendary documentary filmmaker Theodor Christensen, who's a really big name. There's this mythical aura surrounding Theodor Christensen, and it consists of this strange mix of something heroic and something a bit tragic. But the fact is that most people don't actually know much of anything about him. He spent time in what was then Ceylon, and in Cuba, and he played a pivotal role in the founding of the National Film School of Denmark. He was apparently an extraordinary teacher, someone who had a huge and very positive impact on everyone who became part of his magical sphere of influence. And Ole Roos knew him. Karl Roos, Ole's father, and Theodor Christensen were both film theorists and filmmakers, and they were good friends. So Ole sat at their feet as a child, and later ended up working as an apprentice filmmaker for Minerva Film – a company associated with Theodor Christensen and Karl Roos – as well as with Jørgen Roos, Ole's uncle. There are even sequences with Ole dancing on a beach as a child, as Theodor Christensen was shooting one of his films. So Ole Roos is definitely the right person for this film. He has all of Theodor Christensen's letters and diaries, and he has the rights to all of his films. So that's one of our larger documentary projects and we're very excited about it.

            We're also working on a film by my son, Ulrik Wivel. He was a ballet dancer for many years, and got involved with film when he was in New York with the New York City Ballet. He got his film training here in Copenhagen though, through the alternative film school, Super 16. Ulrik has made quite a lot of films at this point, and won a Robert for *This is Me Walking* (2004). Although he's my son, I have no hesitation whatsoever in saying that he's a very talented filmmaker. His approach to staging is quite unique because he's got such a strong choreographic sensibility. I also think that, as a documentary filmmaker, he's very good at exploring a given space because he's got this intuitive sense of its sculptural, but also malleable dimensions. Some of his films actually focus on the world of dance, where these elements are very strongly present. But no matter what he does, he'll always be acutely attuned to those sorts of qualities.

Ulrik's current project is a film about two brothers, one of whom is autistic. It's a story about two brothers who are very different, and who haven't had a lot of real contact with each other. The older brother begins to take an interest in his autistic younger brother when the decision is made to move him to a new place that raises questions about his future, and about what his life is going to be like. The older brother takes an active part in this whole process, and begins to explore the possibility of having some sort of intimacy with this autistic younger brother of his, who in so many ways is excluded from anything like a shared reality. I think it's going to be a very powerful film about two brothers.

HJORT: Danish documentary filmmaking is thriving these days. Why do you think that is?

WIVEL: Things are going incredibly well, it's true. I can't help but feel a measure of pride when I think about what's happening. Some of that pride has to do with Arne Bro and what he's achieved, but part of it also has to do with my own contributions. So many of the developments and tendencies that are current today are exactly what Arne and I hoped for when we first started to plan that programme in documentary filmmaking many years ago. I've always refused to draw a line between fiction and documentary filmmaking because I've never wanted to be locked into a very issues-oriented, pedagogical universe – with all due respect for pedagogy. I wanted to make space for all sorts of elements that were typically associated with fiction filmmaking. If you look at the younger generation of Danish documentary filmmakers, many of whom are enjoying a lot of success these days, it's clear that this refusal to trace a boundary between fiction and non-fiction filmmaking comes very naturally to them. They're very proud to be making documentaries that have a strong narrative drive, and that draw on visual styles resembling those of fiction films. I think that's just wonderful.

It's important to make sure that the ambition that gets fuelled by a certain kind of success doesn't end up changing the way we assess the quality or value of a documentary film. While a theatrical release may be appropriate in some cases, we don't want a situation where we think of a film as having fallen short of some required standard if it doesn't get shown in the cinemas. Denmark is a small country, so there's a real limit to how many tickets a film will ever be able to sell. Measuring a documentary film's quality or legitimacy in terms of box office criteria simply makes no sense. There are parallels to this in the publishing industry, where you don't measure the quality of a collection of poems in terms of book sales. I think it's important to make sure that there's money available to support the production of a lot of documentary films, and that policy-makers understand that the filmmakers can't all be aiming at a theatrical release. TV channels remain an excellent window for documentary films, and the Internet is also very promising in terms of new forms of distribution. You end up in a dead end if you think that a theatrical release and box office figures provide the criteria of success. We need policy-makers who understand that we all benefit when excellent films get made, and that excellence can't be measured in a narrow, market-driven way.

HJORT: You draw on a number of quite different documentary film traditions in your work. In *Face to Face*, for example, you appear to be inspired by direct cinema, for the filmmaker is invisible, the scenes are relatively long, and there is a strong sense of simply being a 'fly on the wall.' In films such as *The Land of Human Beings* and *The Heart of Johannes*, on the other hand, you're clearly present in the film. In *The Castle in Italy*, we hear you instructing the painter Per Kirkeby and his interlocutor, the author Ib Michael, to move in a certain direction or to do certain things. In *The Heart of Johannes*, we know throughout that Johannes Møllehave, and at times his wife, are talking to you, Anne Wivel, a person with whom they are well acquainted. What are the challenges and advantages of these quite different approaches to documentary filmmaking?

WIVEL: I feel there's an element that's common to all my films, however different they may seem. To put it very simply, I think I'm very interested in looking at other people's faces, and that this is evident in all my films. There are a lot of different ways of approaching faces if that's what you're interested in. There's a huge distance, for example, separating the way in which I've tried to get faces into my films and what we see on TV, on a daily basis. Just think of all the faces we see on TV, all the time. But we don't see these faces the way I try to show the face in my documentaries. My films involve a real process of investigation. They're based on a lot of questions, and also elicit questions from the viewer: When do you see a face that's listening? What is that face listening to? When do you see a face that's speaking? And why do you see it when it's speaking? Why did the filmmaker cut to the face of the person who was speaking? Or why did the filmmaker focus on the face of the person who wasn't speaking? Was it perhaps because the person whose face you see was listening to something that your ears are hearing? For me, the process of studying people's faces is genuinely an investigative one, but not in some abstract, theoretical sense. That process is always driven by something I really want to understand.

HJORT: In some of your films – *The Castle in Italy* and *The Heart of Johannes*, for example – your presence is crucial, whether it's a matter of your being implicitly present in the responses that are given to questions you must have asked, or of your being briefly glimpsed in an image, or heard on the film's soundtrack.

WIVEL: I think the differences you're driving at have to do with technological developments, but also my own personal development as a filmmaker. Quite a number of my early films were shot on 35mm film, which involves a completely different way of making films, as compared with how I worked with *The Castle in Italy* and *The Heart of Johannes*. If you've been given a big budget and a large crew to work with, it becomes important to investigate some very specific aesthetic aspects of the images you're hoping to capture on that very fine celluloid, on that 35mm film. *Giselle*, for example, is a very beautiful film. I made that film together with some very, very talented people, including the cinematographer Dan Laustsen, and in my view, it's one of the most beautiful black-and-white films to have been made in Denmark. I then went on to shoot the Kierkegaard film on 35mm, where I focused on those faces in an attempt to press some life out of what is really very heavy philosophical material. After that, I could feel that it would be liberating to try a different approach; one that didn't involve the cumbersome machinery of filmmaking, all the money, the large crew, and so on. I had a strong desire to be in charge of the process myself, so I chose to make a number of films that were well suited to that approach. *The Castle in Italy*, *The Heart of Johannes*, *Svend*, and *The Land of Human Beings* are all films that I shot myself with a modest little camera. Yet, the substance of these films is such that they ended up being transferred to 35mm and shown in the cinemas. That's not an uninteresting way to go, and that route is always available to you, provided the material itself has some real authenticity to it.

HJORT: It's true that *Giselle* is an astonishingly beautiful film. What sorts of stylistic concepts were you working with?

WIVEL: There's this very basic timeline in *Giselle*. There's this choreographer, Henning Kronstam, whose job it is to stage *Giselle* for the Royal Danish Theatre. We follow him and his dancers, especially Heidi Ryom [as Giselle] and Lloyd Higgins [as Albrecht], from the beginning of that process until the curtain goes down on the night of the opening performance. In the last sequence, we see the dancers walking out of the frame, like Chaplin into the sunset. But the film isn't really about this timeline at all. I'd go so far as to say that, for me, the film is a poem. Like a poem, it's extremely subjective, and meant to touch you, to unleash something in you. My desire as a filmmaker was to connect with romanticism, which I'm very interested in. What is it that the choreographer-dreamer sees? What is his vision? We often see Henning Kronstam from behind, staring out over some kind of dreamscape, much as in a Caspar David Friedrich painting. The idea was really to pursue this idea of longing or dreaming, and to have this recurring visual return to that moment when someone is sitting and staring with longing at something. These were the sorts of things I'd discuss with my cinematographer. And then I used a theme from *Don Giovanni* as a musical thread. I wanted it to be crystal clear that the film was about desire, longing, and seduction.

As we started to shoot the film, we realized that we needed to come to terms, quite quickly, with an entire ballet that we didn't really know that well. Having been given access to the rehearsals and so on, I had to say what it was I was interested in. So I said I was especially interested in the scene where Giselle loses her mind, which was not a bad choice. Since love is also is a form of madness, I think there's a sense of dizziness to the film. What's beautiful about it too, is that real people had to try to express or show all that. And in doing so, they were motivated by a quite different kind of love,

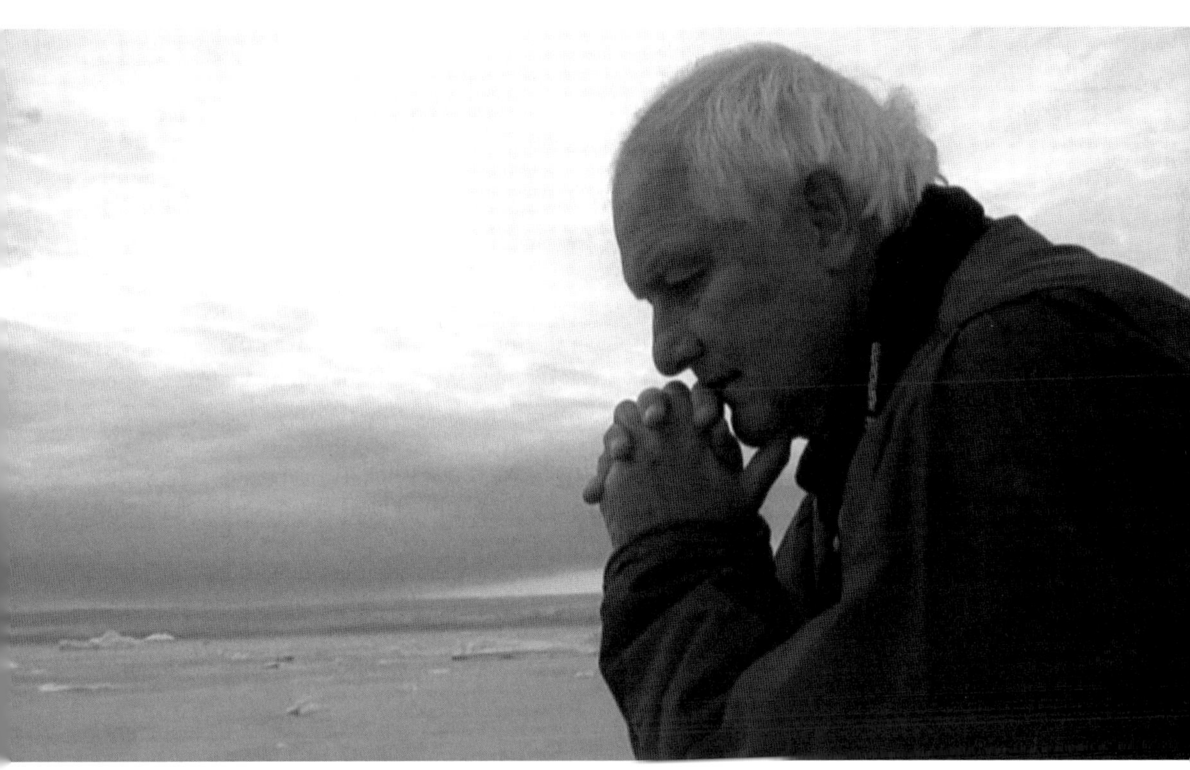

Svend Auken, former Danish Minister for the Environment, discusses the threats of climate change during a trip to Greenland (*Svend*, framegrab, cinematography by Anne Wivel).

	namely devotion. That, in turn, makes them beautiful. That's the kind of dynamic that's at work in the film, I think.
HJORT:	*The Castle in Italy* and *The Heart of Johannes* both focus on well-known Danes –Kirkeby and Møllehave – during periods of great vulnerability or crisis. Kirkeby was grappling with depression and with the collapse of his marriage, and Møllehave with the risks and implications of heart surgery. What role do you see the collaborative filmmaking process as having played in these two men's lives at the time?
WIVEL:	The element of friendship was vital. I've been friends with Per Kirkeby for a very long time. I'm someone who has a very strong drive towards an authentic life. So the crisis that Per was experiencing was one that I could really relate to, at a very deep level. That crisis was all about shutting the world out in order to produce authentic art. It was about the problem of how to become involved in the world again, following that process of seclusion and exclusion, and about trying to understand how the other, or others, fit into all of this. Friendship is what made it possible for Per to open up to the extent that he does in the film. He went through a kind of euphoric explosion over a period of days. The film facilitated a process that allowed him to rethink, revisit, and relive things that went to the heart of the crisis he was experiencing. With Johannes Møllehave, the situation was similar. We established a friendship during the making of the Kierkegaard film. *The Heart of Johannes* is based on friendship and mutual trust, which are also a very important part of what the film has to share with the viewer.
HJORT:	Having clear ethical principles is perhaps especially important in situations of friendship and trust, where scenes might be shot that are ultimately best excluded from the final edit. How do you see your ethical obligations as a documentary filmmaker?
WIVEL:	Much of what passes for documentary filmmaking involves violating people's dignity, and thus also certain ethical principles. I have a very powerful sense of what counts as an infringement along those lines. I can barely stand to watch that sort of thing, but it's so pervasive as to be almost inescapable. I categorically refuse to engage in that kind of filmmaking, and I can honestly say that I'd be deeply ashamed of myself if I were to receive praise and lots of awards for a film that's somehow predatory or exploitative. So I have no choice but to pursue a very different path, and I think that this is something that the people in my films have noticed about me. They could tell, from my earlier films, that I respect

certain limits, but also have the ability to move quite deeply onto the terrain of feelings, vulnerabilities, and previously undepicted mental realities. This sense of where the ethical limits lie, in a given case, is something you develop in the course of the collaborative process, and especially through exchanges with the editor. We have some exceptionally gifted editors in Denmark, and I've worked with a number of them. What we look for is those moments where there's a certain nakedness and vulnerability, or cracks offering glimpses of a deeply personal reality. But there are also places we wouldn't dream of going with the film, even if we had all the material that might be needed. So some of the ethical principles have to do with what you see yourself as looking for.

Let me give you an example. I started shooting *Svend*, about my husband, the politician Svend Auken, about two and a half years before he died. By then I'd been accompanying Svend on work-related trips for some time. He was very internationally oriented as a politician, and involved in all sorts of things having to do with climate change, energy, and so on. I felt that the internationalism of the social democratic project in Denmark wasn't especially well understood, and that Svend, whom I was close to, somehow personified it. So that was one of the reasons I wanted to make the film. Svend was then diagnosed with cancer, and we thought that he'd be able to survive it, but that turned out not to be true. Instead it became clear – while I was still in the process of shooting the film – that he was going to die. What then happened was that some of the people who'd invested money in the film started to insist that it would make good sense to have the camera follow him into the hospital, and so on. My response was: 'That's not at all where this film is headed. There's no need whatsoever for this film to show scenes from a hospital.' When I was asked to explain myself, I said something along the lines of: 'Well, a hospital, a nurse, and a doctor. If there's anything we're capable of seeing in our mind, they're it. And if we have some need to see that sort of thing again, all we have to do is turn the TV on. There all sorts of emergency room dramas, with weird people croaking, on TV all the time. That's just not the kind of story that needs to be told. You've trusted me enough to fund my film, so now you have to trust that I'll tell a story that we haven't already seen and heard a million times.' So those ethical limits are also related to this commitment I have to exploding clichés, and to telling stories that provoke our curiosity, but in a good way that's ultimately defensible.

HJORT:

You've made several films about canonized Danish figures, living and dead, and most recently about Hans Christian Andersen. *A Madman, a Lover, and a Poet* evokes the person that Andersen was, as well as his stories, through a conversation between Kathrine Lilleør [a theologist], Niels Birger Wamberg [a literary scholar], and Johannes Møllehave. Before the title of the film appears, we see a fairly dismal building site with a big puddle in the foreground and an abandoned shopping cart. As we contemplate this image, we hear the following words being spoken off-screen: 'May my eye never glimpse the home that can only see my faults – but has no heart for the great thing that God has given me. I hate what hates me. I curse what curses me. As always, cold breezes come from Denmark – that petrify me outside. They spit on me. They trample me underfoot. I am, after all, by nature a poet, of whom God has not given them many.' The next sequence reveals the voice as Wamberg's and the words as part of a letter by Andersen that causes some mirth when Wamberg proceeds to comment on it. Why did you choose to begin the film in precisely this way?

WIVEL:

A Madman, a Lover, and a Poet was commissioned in connection with the bicentennial of Andersen's birth. The idea was that I'd make a film that would somehow round things off. In other words, it was hard *not* to have a whole year's worth of banal chatter about Andersen ringing in my ears, as I began thinking about what approach to take. I wanted, as always, to make a film that would really last. But that text of his is really excellent because there's so much frustration in it. Andersen is an incredibly subjective artist. He's not just this great figure, surrounded by children who love his stories. He was also very much a prisoner of his own idiosyncratic hell, and that's what that short text expresses. He hates everything because he's not sufficiently loved. It's narcissism, pure and simple. At the same time, Andersen is one of our most wonderful writers, and capable of bringing genuine tears to our eyes. He's such a great figure that it becomes interesting to encounter him, not in all of his greatness, but in those moments when he's just a small-minded man. The excerpt from the letter is incredibly childish, and we used it as a way of getting at Andersen's temperament.

I have to say that I think Kathrine Lilleør, Niels Birger Wamberg, and Johannes Møllehave are pretty extraordinary. The scene where Kathrine paraphrases *The Little Mermaid* is incredibly beautiful. Here's this woman who's completely made the story her own, and retells it in her own words. The authenticity is palpable, and it's really as if time suddenly stands still. A scene like that is utterly different from anything you'd see on TV. And you don't get that kind of material without a lot of effort. It's not just a question of resources in the sense of money, but of time, commitment, sensitivity, and technical skill. We're not all equally good at everything. And if you've grasped that, and approach filmmaking with the necessary respect and standards, then sometimes you end up with material that's very different from what you'd otherwise get.

HJORT: In *David or Goliath: A Film About the World Press in Jerusalem* and *The Land of Human Beings* there's more of a sense of explicit argumentation than in your other films. In both cases we're geographically remote from Denmark, yet dealing with political realities that have implications for Denmark. Did you see yourself as intervening in ongoing political debates through these films?

WIVEL: I've always followed my heart, and I've always been driven by curiosity. Also, sometimes it's important to situate yourself in a completely new context. In the case of *David or Goliath*, I certainly remember feeling very drawn to the idea of making a film outside Denmark. But more specifically, the reason I ended up making that film was that my partner at the time was a journalist, and he was working in Jerusalem. I accompanied him to Jerusalem, and was doing a lot of writing for *Information*. I then discovered the Beit Agron International Press Centre in Jerusalem, and something simply clicked for me. At the very heart of Beit Agron was this man, Rafi Horowitz, a journalist by training, who was now in the government's service. I thought he was incredible, although his political views as an Israeli were certainly towards the right. Horowitz was in charge of Beit Agron at the time, which was just months after the eruption of the first Intifada. So he had all these problems he had to solve. The government imposed restrictions on the press, and Horowitz was constantly being challenged by all these extraordinary journalists from the BBC and elsewhere. My dream would have been to shoot the entire film in Horowitz's office, and to extract meaning from that closed space until there was simply no oxygen left. As you can tell, Frederick Wiseman is someone I find very inspiring. As it turned out, I was able to get permission to shoot my film within the Centre, but not just in Horowitz's office. I felt that what went on within that space shed light on the whole world, and did so in an incredibly lively way. I think of the film as a reflection on journalism at its absolute professional best.

David or Goliath is the only film I've ever made that was seen as controversial. Although TV 2 paid for it, it's never been shown in Denmark. I've had enormous success with the film internationally, and it's won all sorts of prizes. But somehow the position I'm seen as taking in the film is touchy. There was some concern – strong enough to block the film from being shown on TV – about the issue of whose side I'm on. I actually believe that the film achieves a very fine balance in this regard. I think it places itself on the side of certain progressive, democratic forces, while focusing on people with real depth on both the Palestinian and Israeli side of things. Maybe it's time to have another go at getting it shown!

Note

1   David A. Goldsmith, *The Documentary Makers: Interviews with 15 of the Best in the Business* (Hove, UK: RotoVision SA, 2003).

Chapter 19

Anders Østergaard

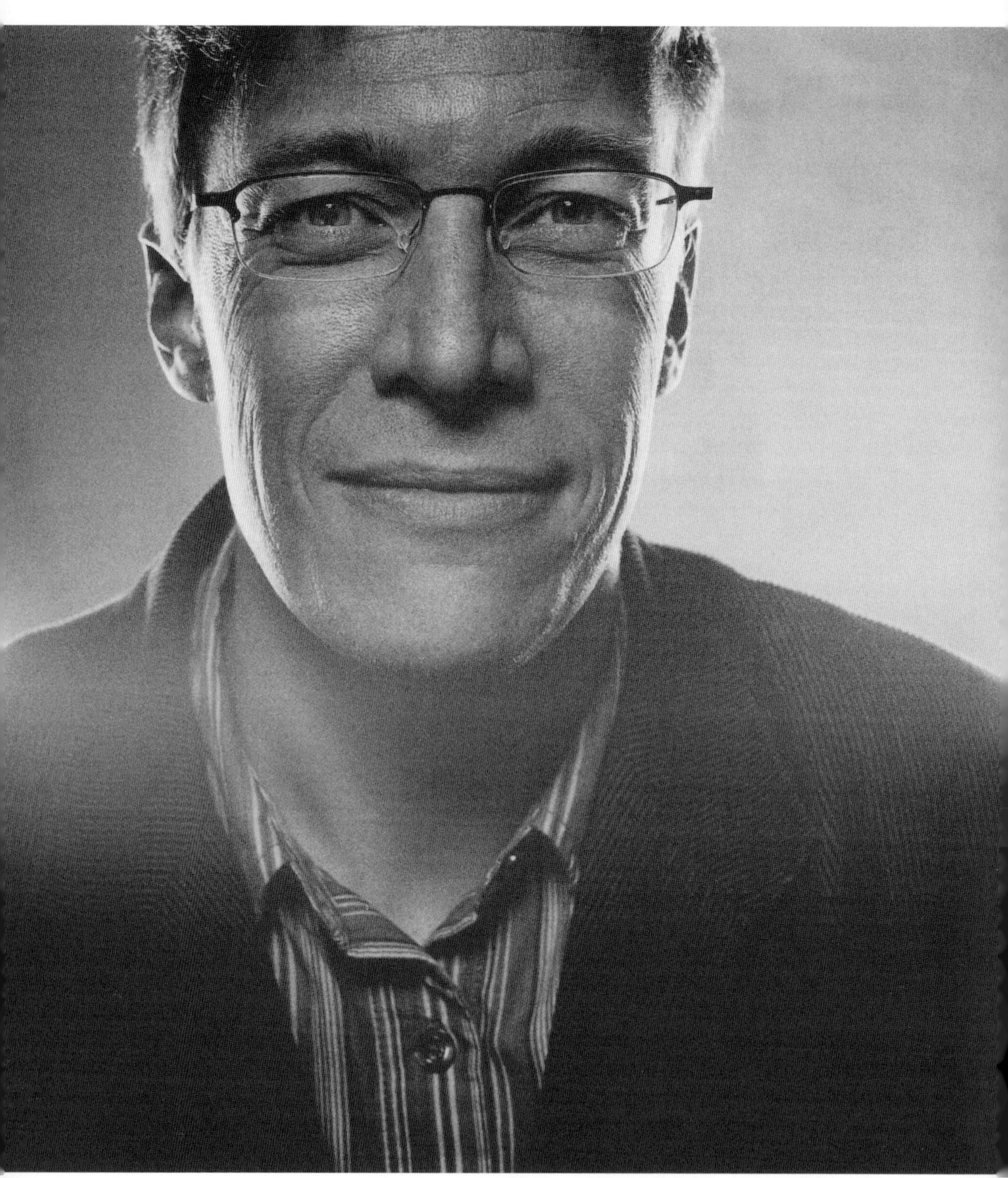

Anders Østergaard. Portrait by Jan Buus. Courtesy of Jan Buus and The Danish Film Institute Stills & Posters Archive.

Born 1965. Østergaard graduated from the Danish School of Media & Journalism in 1991. Before embarking on a career as a film director, Østergaard worked in advertising and as a researcher for documentary TV programmes. With only a few notable exceptions, most of his documentaries are portrait films with a clear cultural focus, defined by a striking mix of documentary authenticity and psychological intimacy. In these films, the documentary depiction of a given individual is combined with historical and contextual elements, the result being a dual portrait of a significant cultural figure and of the period in question. Østergaard's preferred approach involves both observational and expository documentary types, and draws on various sorts of archival materials, in addition to material that he himself shoots. Terms such as 'poetic', 'expressive', and 'symbolic' are, however, also pertinent in his case, for in his cinematic depictions of various figures we find reconstructions, visual or symbolic effects, and a striking use of sound or music. Together these devices help to evoke a certain mood, or even a particular mental space.

Although most of Østergaard's documentaries are portrait films, he has also achieved considerable recognition internationally with work of a more social or political nature. *Malaria* (2002) is an example of such work, as are *Magtens billeder – Diplomatiets fortrop* ('Pictures of Power: The Vanguard of Diplomacy', 2004) and *Burma VJ – reporter i et lukket land* (*Burma VJ: Reporting from a Closed Country*, 2008). 'The Vanguard of Diplomacy' focuses on a front-line diplomat in Iraq. *Burma VJ*, which has won no fewer than 18 international prizes, provides a unique account of the monks' Saffron Revolution against the military dictatorship in Burma in 2007.

Østergaard emphasized the genre of the documentary portrait as early as his debut film, *Gensyn med Johannesburg* ('Johannesburg Revisited', 1996). The film's title makes reference to Henning Carlsen's legendary film *Dilemma* (1962), which was set and shot in Johannesburg, with Østergaard's documentary capturing the reunion, after a period of many years, of the actors who were part of it. His second film, *Trollkarlen* (*The Magus*, 1999), focuses on the jazz pianist Jan Johansson, who died at a young age. Østergaard's poetic depiction of the musician's life was seen as masterful, with the film winning the award for best documentary at the Odense Film Festival (1999). Østergaard achieved his international breakthrough with *Tintin og mig* (*Tintin and I*, 2004), in which he made use of various animation techniques to provide a poetic take on the Belgian Hergé's life and world. In a Danish context, Østergaard's film about a much loved Danish rock group, *Gasolin'* (2006), made him a household name. *Gasolin'* sold around 250,000 tickets, and was thus seen by more cinema-going Danes than any other documentary film since 1960. Here too it was a matter of creating a cinematic portrait of key cultural figures while also providing a portrait of Denmark. With reference to the film's depiction of Denmark, the focus is clearly on the post-1960s era; that is, on the period when the small nation state of Denmark began to encounter and to engage with various globalizing energies. In his most recent film, *Så kort og mærkeligt livet er* ('How Short and Strange Life Is,' 2008), Østergaard takes up yet another Danish icon, namely the poet Dan Turèll. In keeping with Turèll's outlook, the filmmaker made use of a number of surreal visual effects to stage encounters between the living and the dead.

Documentary features:

2008   *Burma VJ – reporter i et lukket land* (*Burma VJ: Reporting from a Closed Country*)
2006   *Gasolin'*
2004   *Tintin og mig* (*Tintin and I*)
2004   *Magtens billeder – Diplomatiets fortrop* ('Pictures of Power: The Vanguard of Diplomacy,' with Anders Riis-Hansen)
1999   *Trollkarlen* (*The Magus*)
1996   *Gensyn med Johannesburg* ('Johannesburg Revisited,' with Jesper Strudsholm)

Documentary shorts:

2008   *Så kort og mærkeligt livet er* ('How Short and Strange Life Is')
2002   *Malaria* (with Simon Plum)

BONDEBJERG:	You were trained as a journalist, and worked in advertising and TV before becoming an independent filmmaker. What kind of impact has this background of yours had on your film career?
ØSTERGAARD:	I think the most important thing is that I learnt to think in terms of target audiences, which probably wasn't especially common in the film industry back in the early 1990s. When you work with target audiences in the commercial context of advertising, you come into contact with the more cynical aspects of what's involved in being aware of an audience. But I've nonetheless been able to use the awareness I acquired in my artistic work with film. My ability to identify with the viewer in no way undermines my integrity as a filmmaker. As I see it, art is a form of communication. In this sense, I see it as helpful to have concepts and tools available to me that allow me to think in terms of films that aim to communicate a story to an audience.
BONDEBJERG:	Would you say, then, that you haven't experienced any kind of tension, whether internal or external, between your work as a journalist and your work as an independent documentary filmmaker? I ask because many of the people I've spoken to in the film industry point to all sorts of conflicts between film and the more journalistic world of TV, perhaps partly because the two are reciprocally dependent to a considerable degree.
ØSTERGAARD:	No, I haven't personally experienced that kind of conflict, nor do I see any deep schism here. I've often commented on this alleged conflict as involving a less than fruitful contrast between what's art and what's not. When I moved into the film industry and started working with Film & Lyd, the view was that we didn't much care whether we were producing art, journalism, or something else. We simply made films about particular issues, and we did this in the way that we felt was most appropriate, and with reference to relevant considerations having to do with communication and audiences. Whether what we produced was art or not wasn't important to us; we saw that as being for others to decide. In that context, the fact that I hadn't been trained at the National Film School, but at a school for journalists, served me well. I feel no need whatsoever to label myself a film artist. Art is not just a matter of special talents, but of particular practical skills. Although I refer to myself as a filmmaker and not as a journalist these days, my training in the context of what some would see as the more instrumental and cynical world of journalism has perhaps been rather helpful. I do understand that the way in which the

relationship between film and TV has developed in Denmark over the last ten years is problematic. The tendency, in the TV milieu, to cater to the lowest common denominator does mean that certain films and projects get caught between the two cultures. But the film milieu is not entirely innocent in all of this, because of its rather too relaxed, even arrogant, stance on the issue of audiences and how best to communicate with them.

BONDEBJERG: You've been active as a filmmaker since 1996, and you've made eight rather different documentaries, in addition to having been involved in productions for TV. How would you describe the conditions for documentary filmmaking during this period? Has it become easier or harder to pursue documentary filmmaking?

ØSTERGAARD: I started out making a small nationally-oriented film, but then quickly went on to make internationally financed films. So it's probably a bit difficult to talk generally about the conditions under which all my films were made because these conditions were actually different from film to film. But perhaps this move from the national to the international is quite characteristic of documentary film production in that period. The idea of making Danish films for a national market ceased being taken for granted, and the topics with which filmmakers engaged also changed a lot. It became clear that where you come from isn't really that important. More precisely, if you're good enough, you can, as a Danish film director, make films about all sorts of topics. Also the opportunities for collaboration and co-financing became a lot better. At least that has been my experience during the period in question.

BONDEBJERG: But how do you see the Danish part of the system? I'm thinking here of the Danish Film Institute's [DFI] involvement in documentary film production, and the activities of the DFI's film commissioners.

ØSTERGAARD: I did catch the tail end of the 'old days' of the National Film Board of Denmark [SFC]. I remember the decision-making process as relatively swift, and the film commissioner as someone who relied, to a great extent, on gut feeling. Since then the system has become a lot more complicated and bureaucratic, even legalistic. There are a lot more levels to the process now, and in my opinion this hasn't necessarily been a positive development. I'm probably a bit arrogant, as I generally feel that I know what I'm trying to do with my films. I don't feel I've been involved in any especially creative sparring process with the different film commissioners. I remember that the DFI's initial response to the idea for the Gasolin' film was quite negative, and *The Magus* was actually a project that started in Sweden. In my view they're not always good enough at dealing with, or at nurturing, creative talents who've already proven that they can deliver. My sense is that there's too much editorial involvement as far as the topics are concerned: 'It would be good if so and so could make this or that kind of film because we need a film about this particular topic.' I've always had to fight a fair bit for my projects, although at the end of the day, I've been able to get most of them made. The most recent example of this is a film that I'd like to make together with Peter Bastian, but I couldn't even get anyone to agree to a meeting about that one. I'm not saying that I should simply be allowed to do what I want, but I do feel that there's a problematic tendency to think in terms of topics, as opposed to talent or someone's track record as a filmmaker. But at the same time, I can't complain about the financing and support that I nonetheless ended up getting for my films. I also think it's important not to scoff at the professionalization that has taken place at the DFI, in the area of distribution, for example. I feel well served by all this, so the last thing I want to do is bite the hand that feeds me. There have been positive as well as negative developments. The negative aspects having to do with the need to conform to specific rules and procedures are related more to developments in society generally – and to preferences regarding the management of publicly funded institutions – than to anything else.

BONDEBJERG: In the film industry, the general impression of the documentary filmmaker's working conditions seems to be that it's hard to make a living from filmmaking; that filmmakers have to supplement their income by working on other people's films, or by involving themselves in TV production, or even in activities outside the fields of film and TV. Your CV suggests that you haven't had any problems along these lines. You seem to have been able to support yourself with your own films.

ØSTERGAARD: Yes, that's more or less true. I've never been wealthy, but I've been able to generate a fairly decent, steady salary over the years. I've usually been able to generate enough money with a given film to finance the first stages of the next one.

BONDEBJERG: Some directors regularly have a lot of trouble making the films they really want to make, and so they end up taking on commissioned projects. You've clearly pursued two tracks: the one involving portrait films about cultural figures, such as authors and musicians, and the other involving films about social and political issues and events. You've made more of the former kind of film than of the latter. Do you see yourself as having been able to make the films you wanted to make in both categories, or has it, for example, been easier to make portrait films?

ØSTERGAARD: For me there's a clear difference between the projects that I've been really passionate about and see as my own personal work, and the projects that I've carried out because someone approached me about undertaking them. *Malaria* and 'The Vanguard of Diplomacy' are, for example, projects that I was approached about, whereas my main portrait films are ones that I feel very strongly about. But I've never felt obliged to make films that I couldn't defend just to put food on the table. And I don't have any sense at all of not having been able to make certain films that I really wanted to make. My sense, on the contrary, is that I've been treated very, very well, whether I was working on a commissioned project or on a more personal one. I feel I've been allowed to realize the projects I've been passionate about.

BONDEBJERG: I'd like to take up the question of film style, in the first instance, with reference to your portrait films focusing on various cultural figures, both Danish and international. With *The Magus*, which is your first real portrait film and one of your finest and most original works, you already seem to have discovered your own distinctive personal style. Perhaps we could begin by talking about how you came to make that film.

ØSTERGAARD: I actually went to Sweden to see the commissioning editor at SVT about this idea that I had for a film about Jan Johansson. The people at SVT were excited about the idea right from the start, as they could see that this was a film that really needed to be made. I actually think that my being from Denmark was an advantage because I had a more external, and thus a somewhat fresh perspective on this Swedish figure. It was almost as though they found it flattering that I, a non-Swede, could be so involved with a Swedish figure, and so committed to making a film about him. I experienced a similar situation in connection with one of my other portrait films about a non-Danish cultural figure, namely *Tintin and I*, which focuses on Hergé. In that case, it turned out that there were actually different schools of thought about Hergé in his own native country; different factions, each with a distinct position on him. I had none of the baggage in question, and so I was able to take up the challenge of making a film about him

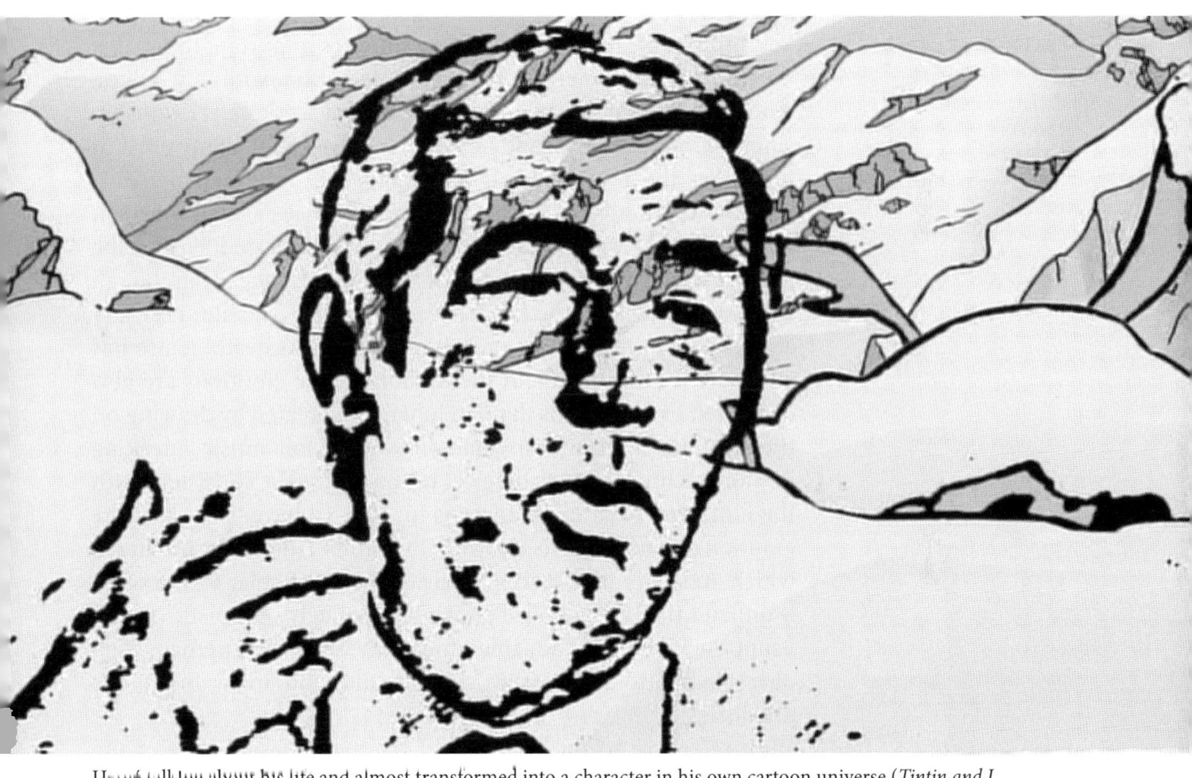

Hergé talking about his life and almost transformed into a character in his own cartoon universe (*Tintin and I*, framegrab, cinematography by Simon Plum).

with fresh eyes and a new perspective. In both cases, the films were produced with financial support from several countries. *Tintin and I* had a budget of about 1 million Euros, which is unusually large for a documentary film.

BONDEBJERG: *The Magus* really has a lot of the features that define the style of your portrait films. I'm thinking of how you depict Johansson and his artistic practice by creating a symbolic universe that breaks with the expository approach in poetic ways. What is your take on the style of this film?

ØSTERGAARD: Yes, I think that's right. At the same time, it's important to say that the film's form emerged through interaction with my editor, Anders Villadsen. We've had a very special working relationship since my very first film, and he's been involved in all of my portrait films. Yet the film's form is also shaped by my own personal relation to the subject matter. In depicting that particular person and his times, I was also depicting my own childhood. For me the film is about the 1960s as an era of hope and change. Even though I was only a child at the time, I sensed all that. The film is clearly about these things, but as a result of Johansson's death, it also has an element of sadness and melancholy. These emotions are also expressed in the sounds that Jan Johansson created by drawing on the blues, on jazz traditions, and on Swedish folk music. Speaking in more technical, musicological terms – which is consistent with the film's approach to Johansson's music – I'd have to say that the emotional tenor has to do with the shifts from flats to sharps which are so dominant in his music. That particular form makes it difficult to say whether the tone is ultimately optimistic or sad. I suppose it's both at the same time, in the same way, perhaps, that our relation to the lost world of childhood lives on in our memories.

BONDEBJERG: With reference to the editing and the actual visual style of the film, how would you describe the way in which you and Villadsen worked together?

ØSTERGAARD: First of all, our approach was clearly shaped by the technological possibility of non-linear editing. It's easy to forget just what a revolution it was to be able to work with the material in a much less constraining way. Torben Skjødt Jensen, Jacob Thuesen, and Tómas Gislason were really pioneers as far as this issue of exploring the new possibilities is concerned. In the late 1990s, it simply became possible to rework material in a way that was unconstrained by an initial interpretation, to move sequences and frames around, to play with the film's visual expression. We had a lot of fun doing all of these things with *The Magus*. We shot on 16mm, but did the editing digitally, which gave us an entirely new expressive freedom. Also, we'd worked out a specific conceptual approach to the portrait we were making, one that involved turning the conventions for that type of musical portrait upside down. Tradition has it that the musical work is sort of untouchable, in the sense that you're not supposed to investigate it in any kind of analytic way. Instead, the idea is to dig into the musician's personal history and into the times in which that person lived. We invert that: we provide a very detailed analytic account of how his musical universe is to be understood and explained, and we make the connection to the human being Jan Johansson in a very poetic and suggestive way.

I have, in several different contexts, characterized my documentary method as a kind of mental documentarism, as involving documentaries of the mind. That method is characteristic of my artists' portraits, and it involves an attempt to enter a given person's subjective and artistic world, and to provide an empathetic portrait of it. Visually and aesthetically speaking, the style and form of my portrait films are defined by devices that are intended to bring this dimension to life and into focus. I'm not that keen on a deconstructive, analytic angle, so I tend to opt for a poetic approach to the artist as a human being, and to that person's artistic work. The process of beginning to understand the work and the person is, for me, a matter of grasping the person's thoughts, of getting inside a certain mental space. And then the point is to express all this through the language of the film, and through the approach that it evidences. I suppose that the tendency these days is really quite different because people tend to want to see the person's private life in social terms. But my intent is to capture the mental dimension: the psychological aspect, the person's consciousness.

BONDEBJERG: In your subsequent portrait films, you essentially return to the method and style of *The Magus* again and again. This is certainly true of *Tintin and I*, which you made immediately after the film about Jan Johansson. Much as in the case of *The Magus*, you're the outsider from another country who decides to make a documentary portrait of an internationally established figure. Of all of your portrait films, *Tintin and I* has the most international and also the most costly production history. Where did the idea for this film come from, and what was the production process like?

ØSTERGAARD: Part of the story here is, of course, that I've been a Tintin fan since childhood, and so I'm fascinated by that universe. But just before I began to articulate a precise concept for the film, I happened to discover that Hergé had experienced a life crisis around the time of *Tintin in Tibet*. I saw that as the tip of an iceberg in a very interesting story that I now wanted to tell. More formally, it all began with my sending a letter to the Hergé Foundation with a description of the film that I wanted to make. I also sent along a copy of *The Magus*. They liked my proposal, and it turned out that I'd approached them at a time when they themselves had been discussing the timeliness of making a film about Hergé and his work.

BONDEBJERG: In *Tintin and I*, you once again take us deep into an artistic world, into Hergé's mental space as a person and as an artist. But the film is also defined by the unique material you got access to through a very long interview with Hergé that the unknown French student, Numa Sadoul, had done. Sadoul had won Herge´s confidence to the point where he really took stock of his life; as it happens, towards the end of it. So even though the method and style are reminiscent of *The Magus*, there are also clear differences between the two films.

ØSTERGAARD: Clearly that interview material is the film's scoop, for it provides a unique point of access to Hergé's world, and to his personality. At the same time, the film's agenda is much more ambitious than that of *The Magus*. Allow me to be pretentious for a moment. *Tintin and I* is a film that doesn't merely depict a concrete individual and a specific artistic universe: the film is about what it's like to be human in the twentieth century, and it's also about the history of that century. Hergé's life mirrors some of the key developments in a very dramatic and striking way, and that's all reflected in the world of his cartoons. Hergé's story is the story of this very proper Catholic Boy Scout who feels the need to change, to free himself, and he then does this slowly, and over a period of time. And while this is going on, he stages his own existential dilemma, his relation to the world, in the universe of his cartoons. The scope of this story, which is not merely a personal one, but one about culture and history, is quite significant. And that's why his private story became such a central and intimate source for the larger story. But otherwise, the method we used is the same as in *The Magus*. It's very much a matter of telling Hergé's story from the inside, with his own voice and through his own cartoon universe. In *The Magus*, we allow a musical world to unfold, along with explanations of it. In *Tintin and I*, the aesthetic and narrative approach is to bring the language and figures of the cartoons to life in an almost magical way, as a kind of extension of the personal and cultural-historical story. The film's style is also partly defined by the desire to pass on this fascinating artistic universe, by the desire to recreate that world in a cinematic form. The cultural-historical dimension of the film ends up being situated in a more general context because there are these archival images that link it to social history, and to Hergé's relation to that history.

BONDEBJERG: How would you describe the film's production history? Was this a difficult film to make?

ØSTERGAARD: The process was actually quite a difficult and complicated one, and there were a lot of negotiations and discussions. For example, it took almost two years to get a final cut agreement with the Hergé Foundation. They're absolutely not used to relinquishing the right to the final cut. But I was finally granted an exclusive final cut right, after having made some compromises regarding distribution rights. A key factor here was the worry that Foundation members had about just how direct and open I was going to be in my depiction of Hergé's life, and about where I stood on his alleged sympathy for Nazism. It was a matter of convincing them that it was better to be open and to go on the offensive than to wait for others to provide incorrect interpretations.

BONDEBJERG: *Tintin and I* won a Bodil prize for best documentary, as well as a number of international awards. Several countries were involved in financing the film, but how well has the film fared on a global basis?

ØSTERGAARD: Strangely enough the film didn't get much of a response in the French-speaking part of the world, nor was it widely distributed there. But it's done very well in the Anglo-Saxon world, both in England and the US. I've also had a lot of success with it in Spain, for some reason or other, and Scandinavia has of course been a significant market for it. I think that the film's form and genre have a lot to do with its not being especially well received by the French- and German-speaking markets. The French and German documentary film traditions are very didactic, and don't provide a propitious context for a film with a decidedly experimental and expressive form. Several TV stations have of course shown the film, including in the French-speaking world. And France 2 also broadcast it, but not at a particularly good time.

BONDEBJERG: *Gasolin'*, your next film, is also a portrait film, but the focus in this case is on a group with cultural-historical significance, rather than on an individual. Your film about the iconic Danish band is legendary, if only because it sold more tickets [250,000] than any other Danish documentary since 1960, the year when the practice of screening documentaries before the main feature film was abandoned. I take it that it was easy to get this film financed and produced?

ØSTERGAARD: It certainly wasn't! The DFI actually turned down the project the first time around, and the film commissioner I was dealing with simply couldn't understand why on earth we wanted to make a film about a burned-out rock band. There was also this attitude that Gasolin' represents commercial popular culture, so I'd have to say that to start with the position taken on this film was very negative indeed. But apparently someone at the DFI had second thoughts. My sense is that the distributor Loke Havn, among others, made a case for the film. Something happened in the corridors, and we ended up being given another chance.

BONDEBJERG: *Gasolin'* depicts both the group and the period that they were part of. The story you tell presents the rock band as an expression of some of the crucial developments that occurred in Denmark from around 1960 onwards. You articulate the musicians' contradictions in such a way that the story of the band ends up also being about different forms of Danish culture, or about Danish culture as it responds to the globalizing forces that are very much part of the period in question. I'm thinking of the wonderful contrast between Franz Beckerlee's personal story and his roots in American rock, in Jimi Hendrix, for example. Or of Kim Larsen's roots in the Danish folk song tradition as it's somehow incarnated by Osvald Helmuth [1894–1966], the popular actor and king of the beloved Copenhagen revue song tradition. How would you describe the story you're trying to tell in the film?

ØSTERGAARD: One of the reasons I'm so fascinated by the story of Gasolin' is that they're an incarnation of both Hendrix and Helmuth. Both these tendencies in our culture are important; I certainly wouldn't be able to choose one of them at the expense of the other. What's fascinating about Gasolin' is that you find both tendencies, and all of the tensions between them, in one and the same rock band. In a way, Gasolin' fuels globalization through music that brings together the national and the global. This has to do with the unique combination of very different personalities, and with the musicians' ability to get the best out of each other, in spite of all the differences and even, at times, real conflicts.

We chose a mythological framework for the story; one with roots in well-established literary traditions and fairy tales. On the one hand there's Hans Christian Andersen's Clumsy Hans, and the figure of Aladdin. Together they represent the natural genius and embody the qualities that characterize Kim Larsen. On the other hand, we have the more sophisticated princes that we're familiar with from Andersen's tales, or the figure of Noureddin in Adam Oehlenschläger's play, who help us to define Franz Beckerlee as a character in the film. Actually you see the same kind of contrast in Milos Forman's *Amadeus* (1984), where Mozart is the natural genius, and Salieri the person who has to give way to the genius he doesn't really understand. It simply made a lot of sense to situate the two main characters, Kim Larsen and Franz Beckerlee, within this larger mythological framework. Also, since they were quite brilliant at telling their own stories and also understood the nature of the roles they were playing, they actually ended up taking on a mythological dimension. I really don't feel we imposed some pre-existing template on the film and its story. The film's story grew naturally out of the musicians' own way of telling and understanding their story. But their story turned out to be integrally connected to a much bigger story about Danish culture at that moment in time, and so the film ended up also being about the encounter between what's 'out there' and what's 'here'; between the international and the national. In the case of Gasolin', that encounter was a genuinely productive one that ended up enriching Danish rock music in quite a unique way.

BONDEBJERG: Were you surprised by the extent of the film's success?

ØSTERGAARD: I believed in the film, and our aim was certainly to make a film that would reach a broad audience. But it's not as though we were thinking strategically about this while we were making the film. Yes, I suppose I was surprised by the extent of its success.

BONDEBJERG: The portrait provided by the film involves several different narrative strands. There's the strand focusing on the musicians, as persons and individuals, and then there's the focus on the group's history, and a third strand devoted to the history of music and key musical developments at the time. Finally, there's the element of Danish cultural history, which functions as a kind of backdrop, and as the connective tissue tying all the strands together. What was your thinking about the film's narrative structure?

ØSTERGAARD: The film's core is clearly the relation between the first three strands that you mentioned. The larger history of Denmark is important, but given our overall approach, it was crucial to avoid an authoritative and detached tone. The larger story is typically linked quite naturally to a given individual's story or to that of the group, thereby providing those stories with another dimension. For example, at one point in his account, Kim Larsen suddenly says, 'That was the summer they walked on the moon.' In this way, a specific story, with all of the memories and recollected experiences that it involves, becomes anchored in a larger, shared story. In the film, we made constant use of this sort of connection, so the bigger story ends up being woven into the images, but also into the music, which points to a particular era.

BONDEBJERG: In your next portrait film, 'How Short and Strange Life Is,' you focus on another popular figure in the Danish cultural landscape: the poet, crime novelist, and musician, Dan Turèll. In the subtitle of the film, you refer to the film as a 'film by Dan Turèll, made by Anders Østergaard.' What's the point of doing that?

ØSTERGAARD: On the one hand it's of course a gimmick, but it's also intended as a gift to Dan Turèll, who himself was full of tricks and gimmicks. Also, the point is to draw attention to the film's basic form: the film's story is told in the form of a monologue delivered by Dan Turèll himself, and not as some external analysis of him. It's not, of course, the case that Turèll controls the film's story, because I'm the director and I orchestrated and put together the film. Anyone can see that the film and the story it tells are highly staged, for the relationship, for example, between images and sound is very much a creative one. Of all the films I've made, this is probably the one that's most experimental and gives the greatest weight to staging and dramatization. And I have to say that I think those aspects of the film fit very nicely with Turèll's quite surreal and whimsical world. I had several reasons for adopting this particular strategy. Although quite a lot of archival material pertaining to Turèll exists, it's not always the sort of thing that is cinematically interesting or that corresponds to the mood of his literary and personal world. What is more, there's actually a DVD with nothing but archival materials about him, and I really felt that it was important to avoid merely repeating all that. So it became especially important to make use of dramatization and staging because this was the best way of getting into Turèll's world and of reaching him as a person. The idea was to let him do the talking himself, but also to allow him to somehow see himself and to experience an encounter with other figures, and with the fictional world that he'd created through his books. That approach produced quite an extreme version of the expressive and poetic style that I always use, and I see it as marking a kind of expressive limit in terms of my work as a whole; that is, I don't see myself as taking that strategy any further in the future. The Turèll project required the sort of formal experimentation I've just described, but I don't plan to work along similar lines again.

BONDEBJERG: You've also made a number of documentary films that are more journalistic in nature and focused on society. An example would be 'The Vanguard of Diplomacy,' which is part of the 'Pictures of Power' series. And then there's *Burma VJ*, which has generated considerable interest internationally. What's striking is that these films have a global theme, in the sense that they're not about social contradictions within the small nation state of Denmark, but about global conflicts in which the country may be involved. Was that a conscious decision on your part?

ØSTERGAARD: Yes, I think my generation is much more interested in a global perspective than earlier generations were, which makes sense given the extent to which globalization now shapes our everyday lives. Technology and the media are also part of the explanation though: we simply see and hear a lot more about the global through various media, and at the same time, new technologies have made it a lot easier to film from a global perspective. *Burma VJ* would have been impossible to make without digital technologies and the Internet. The fact is that it's based on contributions made by people who found themselves in the very midst of the conflict with the military junta, and who were able to get images they'd shot out of the country. In the past these things would have been intercepted and would never have reached their destination. But I'd made other films with a global perspective before *Burma VJ*, perhaps because I've spent periods of time working in England. I've no doubt absorbed some of the internationalism of various English traditions.

BONDEBJERG: You made 'The Vanguard of Diplomacy' in collaboration with Anders Riis Hansen, as part of the 'Pictures of Power' series. This project has been described as fairly conflict-ridden by some of those who were involved in it. As they see it, a tension between the production cultures of the TV and film milieus was especially problematic. Was this your experience too?

ØSTERGAARD: No, I don't feel that I personally had any problems with this project. Anders Riis-Hansen and I have experience working in a more journalistic as well as a more cinematic way, and we have a good understanding of both approaches, so we worked very well together. I experienced the process of making 'The Vanguard of Diplomacy' as relatively unproblematic. That said, I do think that as a general rule these quite ambitious, large-scale concept- and topic-driven projects can be problematic. I have a lot more faith in the idea of nurturing talent and letting people make the films they're really passionate about. It's not usually especially productive to say, 'We need a film about walruses. Perhaps you'd like to make one?' But every now and again something interesting comes out of these thematic collaborations between people in the film and TV milieus.

BONDEBJERG: *Burma VJ* appears to represent quite a stylistic shift, as compared with your earlier work; although you had of course made documentaries about political and social issues before. How did you end up making this film?

ØSTERGAARD: Yes, when compared with my portrait films, *Burma VJ* clearly represents a departure. But, in a way, I also drew on some of the same strands that characterize my other films. The commitment to journalism is a constant in my work, and in *Burma VJ* we do have a person who is absolutely central to the whole project. *Burma VJ* isn't a straightforward portrait film, because, for security reasons, we couldn't actually film the first-person narrator. Instead we see things along with him inasmuch as the images represent his perspective on the unfolding events. In that sense, art and journalism are brought together in the film, which was something I'd been interested in attempting for quite some years. So I'd have to say that I don't actually think of this film as being that different from my earlier work. I think people tend to forget that *Burma VJ* wasn't just a matter of editing what the video journalists in Burma had shot. The film is chock full of reconstructions. Our problem was that we wanted to tell two stories. There was the macro story about the revolution, and we had a lot of images dealing with that. We were well covered in that respect. But then there was the micro story that we also wanted to tell, which was about the people who produced the uprising. And that was a problem. We simply didn't have the material we needed about these people, nor did we have much of anything about what they actually did to produce the revolution. So we had to improvise in order to reconstruct both the images and the sound that we needed.

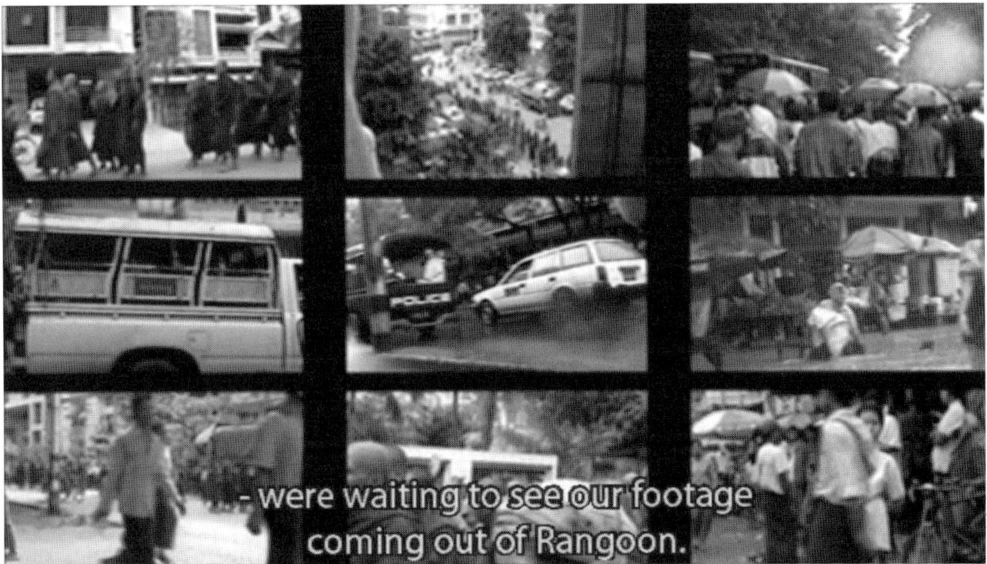

Collage of films made by the Burmese photo-journalist who filmed the political protests in Burma and worked hard to get information out to the rest of the world (*Burma VJ – Reporting From a Closed Country*, framegrab, cinematography by Simon Plum).

BONDEBJERG: *Burma VJ* is in many ways a work that points to new ways of filmmaking in an era of digital and global developments. In a sense, 'Joshua' and the Burmese video journalists who risked their lives to smuggle images across the border are your co-authors. Could you say a bit more about the making of the film, in terms of the basic material you had to work with, but also the editing of it? What sorts of ethical issues did the particular production process in question give rise to?

ØSTERGAARD: The film grew out of a much smaller project that I'd initiated long before the uprising in 2007 occurred. I wanted to produce a portrait of Joshua, and of his, at the time, rather quiet daily life as a video journalist. He didn't have a whole lot of video material at the time, so we came up with this conceit, which was 'the camera that's never turned off.' The idea was to reconstruct what happened with Joshua before and after the shooting of something that could be seen as inherently critical of the regime. So the idea was that he'd use his camera to capture not only the things he'd normally shoot, but also the response of the police to what he was doing. We then transferred that conceit to the much larger project that the film ended up becoming. The Burmese video journalists shot about 60 per cent of the material in the film, and I shot the remaining 40 per cent. Their material was of course by far the most important. The reconstructions that I produced played a supporting role, in the sense that they were designed to provide something like a silver platter for theirs. It was very important to be forthright about the film's production history, precisely because it involved this mix of original and staged materials. So that's why there's that 'disclaimer' in the text at the beginning. I had no desire whatsoever to mislead viewers. My goal was to use elements of the docudrama genre to provide viewers with an experience that would get Burma under their skin.

BONDEBJERG: Has *Burma VJ* been shown in Burma and the wider region, whether legally or as an underground film? If so, how did the authorities respond?

ØSTERGAARD: Yes, it was shown on the very same satellite channel that the young revolutionaries used during the rebellion. And you can buy it on the black market. But that takes courage, especially before the recent changes in the country. The Burmese regime's only response was an indirect one. They blocked the transmission of the Oscars ceremony the year the film was nominated. But the film functions as an underground film in other parts of the world where there's opposition to authoritarian regimes.

BONDEBJERG: Of all your films, *Burma VJ* is the one that has won the most prizes, although you've also received awards for some of the others. Also, *Burma VJ* has received more prizes than any other contemporary Danish documentary film. It would be easy to assume that these awards have implications for the distribution of your work, and thus for the economic success of your films. What's your own sense of the significance of these awards for your films, but also for you as a director?

ØSTERGAARD: Clearly all that recognition means a lot to me, and I'm sure it's opened doors for me, both here in Denmark, and elsewhere. But, at least so far, it hasn't had any impact on my bank statements. Even a film like *Burma VJ* has yet to produce a profit. Part of the picture here is that the film industry is a highly competitive one. Also, it's become a lot more difficult in recent times to make sure that the rights one has as a filmmaker aren't violated, and that one gets the monies to which one is entitled. Sometimes it's as though the film just disappears into a big black hole once it's finished – economically speaking. Even though you know it's probably being seen by people all over the world, you just don't have a clear picture of all that. I find that quite problematic, and

	nobody is really doing anything about it. In fact, nobody knows how to deal with the problem. I've had a perfectly good relationship with the different producers I've worked with, but none of them have been on top of this aspect of things either.
BONDEBJERG:	I take it that your success to date means that you don't have to worry about whether you'll be able to make the films you want to make. How do you see your future right now?
ØSTERGAARD:	Yes, I won't have any problems making more films, but there is an issue having to do with the kinds of films I'll be making. I really don't want to repeat myself, and I'd like to be part of the process of renewing documentary filmmaking. I'm not especially interested in the idea of making fiction films, as I'm still most fascinated by stories drawn from reality. But I'm spending a lot of time thinking about what my next project should be – and about how I'd like to proceed with it – because I don't want automatically to continue working in the areas in which I have a proven track record. I established my own company, Everest Pictures, in 2008, as a means of enhancing the control I have over my own film productions. But what I've learnt is that it can be very difficult to find time to do everything that needs to be done yourself, and my relationship to the producers in the companies I've worked with in the past has actually been perfectly alright. Clearly it's best to have a long-lasting and somewhat symbiotic relationship to a producer. That's certainly true if the aim is to take advantage of some of the opportunities that the new media seem to be creating. As for my next film, I fear that I may find myself being encouraged to do what I've already proven myself capable of doing, as opposed to being encouraged to pursue new angles in which I'm interested. I hope I can avoid being pigeonholed.

Glossary

Association of Danish Film Directors (Foreningen af Danske Filminstruktører, DF) was created in 1956 as a union of directors, and with the aim of protecting and developing rights for film directors. The organization was initially devoted to cultural and political issues pertaining to film, and was granted representation at the National Film Board of Denmark (Statens Film Central, SFC) and later also at The Danish Film Institute (Det Danske Filminstitut, DFI). In 1990, DF became a formal union of film directors, involving itself in the negotiation of film directors' contracts. DF is a member of the Nordic Association of Film Directors (Sammenslutningen af Nordiske Filminstruktører, SNF), the Federation of European Film Directors (Fédération Européenne des Réalisateurs de l'Audiovisuel, FERA) and the International Association of Audiovisual Writers and Directors (Association Internationale des Auteurs de l'Audiovisuel, AIDAA).

Bodil Danish award established in 1948 and named after the actors Bodil Kjer and Bodil Ipsen. Winners are identified by an association of film journalists and critics, which has around 40 members (Filmmedarbejderforeningen, FMF). Awards are distributed across a number of categories, including best Danish film, best actor, and best actress. Documentaries have been eligible for a Bodil award from the outset. From 2007 onwards, a best documentary award has been given on an annual basis, following a decision to depart from earlier practices, which saw documentaries recognized on a more sporadic basis.

Bro, Arne Born in 1953 and educated as a film director at the National Film School of Denmark (Den Danske Filmskole), Bro has made several documentary films, among them *Motivation – nærbilleder fra en ungdomsskole* (*Motivation: Close-ups from a Youth School Motivation*, 1983; with Anne Wivel) and *De tavse piger* (*The Silent Girls*, 1985; with Anne Wivel), and is much used as a consultant for documentary film projects. His main contribution to the new Danish documentary cinema is closely linked to his role as the charismatic founding head (since 1992) of the Documentary Film & TV Department (TV-uddannelsen) at the National Film School of Denmark. In 2006, he received the important Jørgen Roos award for his dedication to documentary filmmaking, and for his contribution to the education of documentary filmmakers.

Camre, Henning Born in 1938 and trained as a cinematographer at The National Film School of Denmark (Den Danske Filmskole), Camre went on to serve as its head from 1975–92. He subsequently became head of The National Film and Television School in Beaconsfield, UK (1992–97), returning to Denmark in 1998, when he was recruited for the position of CEO (1998–2007) of the newly reorganized Danish Film Institute (Det Danske Filminstitut). He currently serves as the director of The European Think Tank on Film and Film Policy. Between 1969 and 1988 Camre shot several fiction and documentary films, but his most important contribution to Danish film culture is as a both visionary and efficient director of its two most important institutions, and as a link between European and national cinemas.

Carlsen, Henning Born in 1927, Carlsen is one Denmark's most accomplished and internationally recognized directors, with a career encompassing both documentary and fiction films. He was employed by Minerva Film (1948–53) and Nordisk Film Junior (1953–57), two of the most significant documentary film production companies during the years in question. Carlsen was the founding owner and director of Henning Carlsen Film (1962–73) and the owner of the Dagmar Cinema (1968–81). He currently runs Dagmar Film Production (since 1981). His most important documentary films created a new wave of Danish documentaries, inspired by innovative tendencies in French and British documentary filmmaking. His trilogy *De gamle* (*Old People*, 1961), *Familiebilleder* (*Family Portraits*, 1964) and *Ung* (*Young People*, 1965) are classics of early modern documentary cinema. Also, his first fiction film, *Dilemma* (1962), based on a book by Nadine Gordimer and to some extent clandestinely shot in South Africa, has a typical documentary style. Carlsen achieved his international breakthrough as a director of fiction films with *Sult* (*Hunger*, 1966), a film based on the Norwegian author Knut Hamsun's well-known eponymous novel.

Children & Youth Department, DR (Børne- og Ungdomsafdelingen, B&U; see Danish Broadcasting Corporation, DR) was created in 1968 and went on to become one of the most important and successful departments of the main public service broadcaster, DR. Before 1968 the production of programmes for children and young people belonged to the portfolio of the Department for Actuality & Information. The Children & Youth Department represented a break from the more traditional and paternalistic programming philosophy of the early public service period. Indeed, the Department's programming strategy became a creative engine for the development of innovative TV production, often with a critical, social profile. A number of documentary filmmakers in Denmark gained initial practical experience with production in the context of this department. The B&U's documentary programmes and series explored a full spectrum of types, including ones involving a significant emphasis on staging, and reflexive genres on the very border of fiction and non-fiction. Mogens Vemmer headed the department from 1968 to 2000, and people sometimes speak of having attended the 'Mogens Vemmer school.'

Cosmo Doc is an independent sister company founded in 2003, under the production company Cosmo Film. Cosmo Film was started in 1990 by Rasmus Thorsen and Tomas Hostrup-Larsen, but until 2003 the company was mostly dedicated to feature film production. Jakob Høgel was one of the driving forces behind Cosmo Doc, which existed as part of Cosmo Film from 2003–09. From May 2009 Cosmo Doc started operating under the new name, Upfront Film.

CPH:DOX was established in 2003 as a Copenhagen-based international documentary film festival. Since 2003 the festival has grown to become the largest in Scandinavia, and one of the most important festivals for documentary film in Europe. CPH:DOX focuses its efforts on providing support for independent and innovative documentary films. The festival screens in the vicinity of 200 films during each edition, and aspires to bring the latest tendencies in documentary filmmaking, including art cinema and experimental film, to audiences. The festival also organizes CPH:FORUM, an international financing forum for documentaries, and the cross-cultural production programme DOX:LAB. CPH:DOX answers to the Copenhagen Film Festivals Board. Tine Fischer has been head of the festival since 2003.

Danish Broadcasting Corporation (DR) was the first public service TV station in Denmark, and enjoyed a monopoly from 1951 until 1988, when TV 2 was established, soon to be followed by other more commercially funded TV stations. DR has been from the outset one of the key channels for the production of TV documentaries, for the distribution of documentary films, and, from the late 1960s onwards, also increasingly for the co-production of documentaries in partnership with the Danish Film Institute (DFI). In 1975, DR created TV-Aktuelt, which became the first important producer of critical documentaries in a journalistic vein. In 1988, DR afforded TV documentaries considerable autonomy and latitude in the context of the DR Documentary Group (Dokumentargruppen, 1988–). Structural changes were, however, made in the post-2000 period. With the split of DR into several channels (e.g. DR K and DR2), documentaries were produced for and shown on many different channels. DR2 does, however, have a distinct and dedicated profile as a platform for both Danish and international documentaries.

Danish Documentary Production is a production company specializing in documentary filmmaking. The company was established in 2007 by directors Phie Ambo, Pernille Rose Grønkjær, and Eva Mulvad, initially as a distribution platform for their award-winning films *Enemies of Happiness* (2006), *The Monastery: Mr. Vig and the Nun* (2006), and *Mechanical Love* (2007). Producer Sigrid Dyekjær and director Mikala Krogh subsequently joined the company.

Danish Film Institute (Det Danske Filminstitut, DFI) was established in 1972, and since 1997 has been an umbrella institution embracing the previously autonomous National Film

Board (Statens Filmcentral), the Danish Film Museum (Det Danske Filmmuseum), and The Danish Film Institute (focusing exclusively on fiction films up until 1997). Since 1998 the Danish Film Institute has been organized into three main sections, focusing on production and development (of all types of films); audiences and promotional matters; and the DFI archive and cinematheque. Henning Camre was the DFI's CEO from 1998–2007, with Henrik Bo Nielsen assuming the position from 2007 onwards.

Dogma 95 (Dogme 95) is both the name of a film collective consisting of four Dogma brethren – Lars von Trier, Thomas Vinterberg, Søren Kragh-Jacobsen, and Kristian Levring – and a manifesto-based, rule-governed film initiative underwriting the four original Dogma films by the brethren. Dogma 95 went on to become a global phenomenon, and was officially brought to a close ten years after it was first announced, by another flamboyant statement by von Trier. In 2002, von Trier launched a so-called Dogumentary manifesto aiming to bring Dogma rules to the area of documentary filmmaking. The idea was to establish a stronger connection between documentary filmmaking and reality. Three Danish directors (Sami Saif, Klaus Birch, and Michael Klint) and two Scandinavian filmmakers (Swedish Pål Hollender and Norwegian Margreth Olin) made films according to these dogumentary rules.

European Documentary Network (EDN) was established in 1996 as a global network for professionals working with documentary film and TV. By 2012 more than 1000 professionals from more than 60 countries had joined EDN. EDN provides documentary consulting and information about various possibilities in the areas of funding, financing, development, co-production, distribution, and collaboration across borders. EDN publishes *DOX Magazine* and the *EDN Financing Guide*.

European Film College (EFC, Filmhøjskolen i Ebeltoft) was established in 1995, based on a vision to create a European, as well as globally oriented, place for filmmakers and film education. The first principal of the college was Kjeld Veirup (1995–2000), followed by Jens Rykær (2000–06), Søren Høy (2007–10), and Mette Damgaard-Sørensen (since 2000). Following the traditions of the Danish Folk High School, the EFC does not offer a formal education leading to a degree, but offers a space where new talents can emerge and develop.

Film & Lyd (1972–2002) was one of the most productive and important production companies in Denmark in the area of documentary film. The company started as a small, experimental production company, but became more established in the 1980s. Key figures associated with the company are: Rumle Hammerich, Jørgen Flindt Petersen, Erik Stephensen, Lise Roos, and Anders Østergaard, among others.

Film commissioners (filmkonsulenter) provide a central channel for film support administered by the Danish Film Institute under the Commissioner Scheme (konsulentordningen), and up until 1989 they oversaw the only available funding scheme. Currently the scheme allows for six commissioners, each appointed for three years, with the possibility of a two-year extension. Three of these commissioners focus their efforts on fiction film, and the other three on documentaries. Of the six commissioners, two of them (one in the feature film area, the other in the non-fiction area) have a special responsibility for children and youth film production. In 1989, the 50/50 and later 60/40 scheme (60/40-ordningen) – now called the Market Scheme (Markedsordningen) – was introduced as a new, market-oriented support scheme, but only for fiction film. In 2003, another scheme, New Danish Screen, was established (see below), with documentary film being included at a later stage of its development. Support is allocated for short documentaries, as well as feature-length documentaries.

Film Studies, University of Copenhagen (Film- og Medievidenskab, København Universitet) Established in 1967, the film programme (BA, MA and PhD level) focuses on the historical, aesthetic, psychological, and sociological aspects of film. Although its offerings incorporate a component of practical filmmaking, these do not amount to the kind of full range of practice-based film training characteristic of film schools. Yet many film practitioners currently working in the Danish film industry have taken courses through the programme. In 1988, Film Studies was merged with Media Studies, and in 2012, the BA and MA curricula became Film & Media Studies programmes.

Film Workshop (Filmværkstedet) Established in 1972 and housed in The Danish Film Institute. It provides aspiring filmmakers with access to equipment, and also offers small grants to successful applicants to help them cover basic production costs.

Filmstriben is a digital film streaming service for Danish public libraries, established in 2008, in collaboration with, and with support from, The Danish Film Institute. The developer and distributor is DBC, a company run by the Danish State and by the Association of Municipalities in Denmark (Kommunernes Landsforening). The service is available to anyone with a Danish IP address, through their local library. The site offers access to more than 500 films. Using its rights to non-commercial distribution, the DFI makes all documentaries available on this site.

Guldbrandsen, Christoffer Born in 1971, Guldbrandsen has a degree in journalism from The Danish School of Media & Journalism and City University London. Before becoming an independent documentary filmmaker, he worked as a news journalist for the Danish TV station TV 2. Since his debut film, *De første* ('The First', 2002), Guldbrandsen has gone on to become one of the new generation's most prolific political documentary directors. Inspired by the American direct cinema tradition of the 1960s, he has developed his own observational, dramatic form, often with close-up portraits of political conflicts, parties, or central political characters. *Fogh bag facaden* (*The Road to Europe*, 2003), which follows the Danish Prime

Minister and EU President Anders Fogh Rasmussen during negotiations towards the Union's enlargement, won the Golding Link Award, a prize awarded by the European Broadcasting Union. In 2011, Guldbrandsen made *Præsidenten* (*The President*), which provides a candid look at the European Union's political processes, and at the election of its first president. *Den hemmelige krig* (*The Secret War*, 2006), about Denmark's military presence in Afghanistan, was one of the most intensely debated documentaries of the decade.

Høgel, Jakob Born in 1967, Høgel has an MA in anthropology from the University of Copenhagen and a degree in visual anthropology from Manchester University. In 1999, he became a documentary film commissioner at the Danish Film Institute (1999–2004). In 2004, Høgel was involved in establishing and running Cosmo Doc, a film production company that has produced films by some of the most important filmmakers currently contributing to the new Danish documentary cinema (e.g. Christoffer Guldbrandsen, Anders Østergaard, and Simone Aaberg Kærn). In 2007, he became head of New Danish Screen (see below).

International Documentary Festival Amsterdam (IDFA) Founded in 1988, with the aim of fostering creative documentary filmmaking and an international documentary film culture, IDFA may be the most important documentary festival in the world. IDFA encompasses a number of initiatives: the IDFA Forum, which is focused on facilitating co-productions; DOCS for Sale, which provides a marketplace for the documentary film trade; the IDFA Academy, through which documentary filmmakers receive training; and finally, the IDFA Fund, which supports documentary filmmaking in the developing world. The festival awards a number of prizes, foremost amongst them the prestigious IDFA award for best feature documentary.

Jansen, Janus Billeskov Born in 1951, Billeskov Jansen works in the areas of both fiction and documentary film, and is one of the most respected and most frequently employed film editors in Denmark. In 2005, he was given an honorary Bodil for his role in Danish cinema. He has edited documentary films for such directors as Lise Roos, Jørgen Leth, Anders Østergaard, Sami Saif and Phie Ambo, Anne Wivel, Jesper Jargil, and Max Kestner.

Kanal 2 The first local, commercial TV channel in Denmark, started in 1984 by two private entrepreneurs, Baron Otto Reedtz-Thott and Klaus Riskær Pedersen. The station could only be seen in the Copenhagen area, and went bankrupt within a year.

Laterna Film Danish film production company, established in 1955 by one of the most important figures in modern Danish film culture, Mogens Skot-Hansen (1908–84). The company mostly made short and documentary films, among them films by influential directors like Børge Høst, Ole Roos, Astrid Henning-Jensen, and Theodor Christensen. The company had to close in 1970 after having lost a lot of money on expensive fiction film productions.

Leth, Jørgen Born in 1937, Jørgen Leth is one of Denmark's most accomplished and productive filmmakers, and one of its staunchest defenders of film as art. *The Jørgen Leth Collection*, released by the Danish Film Institute, provides insight into his cinematic oeuvre. It consists of five boxed DVD sets: 'Anthropological Films' (01–05); 'Sports Films' (06–11); 'Travel Films' (12–18); 'Fiction Films' (19–21); and 'Film Portraits' (22–29). Leth has been a teacher at the National Film School of Denmark (Den Danske Filmskole) for many years, and has inspired generations of filmmakers working with both fiction film and documentary film. Leth introduced the concept of creativity under constraint to the school's curriculum, through the so-called 'penneprøver,' a rule-governed approach also found in the Dogma 95 initiative. The same approach informs Leth's collaborative work with Lars von Trier, the award-winning festival hit entitled *De fem benspænd* (*The Five Obstructions*, 2003).

National Film Board of Denmark (Statens Filmcentral, SFC) Established in 1938, the National Film Board of Denmark originally focused its efforts on distributing documentary films to the general public and schools. The original mission of SFC was clearly defined in the 1938 Film Accord. However, in later years the SFC also shouldered responsibilities, associated with other semi-public and public institutions, in the area of documentary film production. With the new 1972 Film Accord, all public support for documentary films in Denmark, and tasks related to their distribution, were formally brought together under the auspices of SFC. In 1997, SFC was closed and support for documentary filmmaking was integrated into the new Danish Film Institute.

National Film School of Denmark (Den Danske Filmskole) Founded in 1966 and supported by the Danish Ministry of Cultural Affairs (Kulturministeriet), the School offers programmes in the areas of film, TV (documentary), scriptwriting and animation. The first head of the School was I.C. Lauritzen (1966–69). Henning Camre was head from 1975–92 and professionalized the programmes by introducing more structured curricula. He was followed by Poul Nesgaard (see below).

Nesgaard, Poul Born in 1952, Nesgaard became a well-known figure through his creative productions at the Danish Broadcasting Corporation's (DR) Children & Youth Department (B&U) in the 1970s and 1980s. The dramatized documentary series *I sandhedens tjeneste* (*In Honour of Truth*, 1984, 1987, & 1990) played with fiction and reality, while also making good use of social critique and satire. In 1992, Nesgaard was appointed head of the National Film School of Denmark (Den Danske Filmskole).

New Danish Screen Established in 2003 as a talent development scheme under The Danish Film Institute, co-funded by the Danish Broadcasting Corporation DR and TV 2. The scheme has funds of roughly 15 million Euros through the 2011–14 Film Policy Accord. The purpose of the scheme is to give new generations of filmmakers the opportunity to push their limits, and to create new experiences for cinema and TV audiences. The scheme supports new talent working on a professional level, as well as less experienced filmmakers. The emphasis is on facilitating experimentation through low budget filmmaking of all types, and through digital game production.

Nordic Film and TV Fund (Nordisk Film & TV Fond, NFTF) The NFTF was founded in 1990, with the primary purpose of promoting film and TV productions of high quality in the five Nordic countries (Denmark, Finland, Iceland, Norway, and Sweden), by providing support for top-up financing of feature films, TV fiction / series, and creative documentaries. The fund also supports a range of other initiatives. These include support aimed at facilitating the wider distribution of Nordic productions throughout the region (distribution and dubbing); and assistance for Nordic professionals, focusing on the development and improvement of their knowledge and skills through master classes and workshops. Through its Film Cultural Initiatives programme, the Fund also supports a range of film events with Nordic significance: festivals, seminars, or forums, for example. The NFTF administers the prestigious Nordic Council Film Prize (Nordisk Råds Filmpris), and arranges and hosts the annual Nordic Talents event each autumn. Nordic Talents aims to put graduating students from the Nordic film schools in touch with relevant producers, through, among other things, a programme of pitches. The NFTF is based in Oslo, Norway, and the CEO is Hanne Palmquist.

Nordic Panorama (Nordisk Panorama) With a first edition in 1990, Nordic Panorama is the most important Nordic festival for short films and documentaries. It is closely linked to the Nordic association of independent shorts and documentary filmmakers, Filmkontakt Nord ('Nordic Film Contact'). This association was established in 1991 to create a professional Nordic network, and to strengthen co-production activity and other forms of collaboration between the Nordic countries and the international film community.

Robert Danish film award granted for the first time in 1983 by the then newly established Danish Film Academy. Prizes are awarded in a number of categories, including documentary shorts and feature-length documentaries.

Roos, Jørgen (1922–98) One of the most important and productive documentary filmmakers of his generation, Roos made more than 100 films spanning a wide range of genres and themes. He was one of the first Danish filmmakers to engage with Greenland, giving rise to a tradition of making documentary films about this part of the North. Like his older brother, Karl Roos (1914–51), and Theodor Christensen (1914–67), Jørgen Roos is often considered one of the founding fathers of the classical, documentary film movement in Denmark.

Rukov, Mogens Born in 1943, Rukov is a charismatic and influential teacher of scriptwriting at the National Film School of Denmark (Den Danske Filmskole), where he has taught since 1975. He has also written scripts for many Danish fiction films. His emphasis on the concept of a 'natural story' and on the idea of creativity under constraint is seen as having shaped the new Danish cinema – be it in the area of fiction or non-fiction film. Documentary film directors regularly refer to his influence as especially formative.

Sheffield Doc Festival is an international documentary film festival established in 1994. The vision of Peter Symes from BBC Bristol informs its goal to celebrate the creative dimensions of documentary filmmaking (both TV and film). In recent years, the festival has developed a strong focus on digital documentary filmmaking.

SVT (Sveriges Television) is the oldest and biggest Swedish public service television broadcaster, established in 1957 with the creation of the first channel, SVT1. In 1969, SVT2 was added. Unlike Denmark, Sweden has long emphasized collaboration between film and TV in the area of documentary production.

Trier, Lars von Born in 1956, Lars von Trier is a central figure in the landscape of New Danish Cinema, and one of the most internationally acclaimed directors of his generation. His own oeuvre includes experimental low budget films, as well as big international co-productions. Von Trier has influenced Danish film culture greatly through his production company Zentropa, which he established in 1992, together with film producer Peter Aalbæk Jensen. Besides producing von Trier's own films, the company has also provided a creative space for many other directors, especially in the wake of Dogma 95. Zentropa Real, which specializes in documentary film production, is part of Zentropa. Von Trier's 'Dogumentary Manifesto' (2002) was an attempt to create a Dogma movement for documentary film (see Dogma 95).

TV 2 National public service broadcaster, established in 1988, based on the model of British Channel 4. TV 2, which is based in Odense, has a strong regional profile, and is authorized to make in-house productions focusing on news and sports, whereas it must commission all other programmes. The station was originally financed through a mix of licence fees and commercials, but is currently funded through commercials and viewer subscriptions. From 1988–2000, TV 2 had a significant documentary presence through programmes such as *Fak2eren* and *Reportageholdet* ('The Reportage Unit'). Today its documentary profile is oriented towards more entertaining documentary programmes and reality television.

TVSyd One of the eight regional stations under TV 2.

Vemmer, Mogens Born in 1935, Vemmer is a charismatic and influential figure, whose leadership as head of the National Broadcasting Corporation DR's acclaimed Children & Youth Department (B&U) from 1968–2000 is seen as having been decisive. Among other things, Vemmer created room for creative experiments, and defended programmes when they gave rise to controversy both internally and within a larger arena.

Video Workshop Haderslev (Det Danske Videoværksted, Haderslev) Founded in 1977, and since 2003 an independent institution, the Video Workshop in Haderslev receives subsidies from the Danish Film Institute. These enable it to support amateur and professional filmmakers with equipment and production funding.

YLE Founded in 1957, YLE is the main Finnish public service broadcaster. YLE is known for its strong commitment to documentary filmmaking, and is often involved in both Nordic and European co-productions.

ZDF (Zweites Deutsches Fernsehen) Established in 1963 and located in Mainz, ZDF is one of the most important German public service television stations. ZDF collaborates with the French-German channel Arte, and has a strong profile in the documentary area. An entire channel, ZDF Dokukanal, is dedicated to documentaries. ZDF is very active in European co-production activities, and as a distributor of documentary films and TV programmes.

Zentropa Founded by Lars von Trier and Peter Aalbæk Jensen in 1992, Zentropa went on to become one of the largest production companies in Scandinavia. Developed in a flamboyant manner and in a spirit of oppositionality, Zentropa joined forces with its former rival Nordisk in 2008. Nordisk now owns 50% of Zentropa's shares. Zentropa is located in the Avedøre Film Town, south of Copenhagen.

Index of Titles and Names

A

Aalbæk, Peter, 135, 216, 351, 367, 409, 410

The Abyss (*Afgrunden*), 147, 161

Adorno, Theodor, 331

Air, 207, 208

Alfaker, Muniam, 341, 342

'Allan Hagedorf: A Dane in Hitler's Germany' (*Allan Hagedorf – En dansker i Hitlers Tyskland*), 146

Amadeus, 393

Ambassador, The (*Ambassadøren*), 84, 90, 99, 103–5

Ambo, Phie, chapter 1, 17, 25, 109, 114, 184, 192, 201, 265, 290, 341, 342, 350, 353, 403, 406

American Short, 342

'Anatomy of Thought, The' (*Tankens anatomi*), 51, 52, 60–61

Andersen, Hans Christian, 376, 393

Andersen, Iben Haahr, 306, 317

Andersson, Roy, 194

'Angelface' (*Englefjæs*), 145, 147, 148–9

Antonioni, Michelangelo, 103

Apocalypse Now, 261

'Are We in a Hurry, Mum?' (*Har vi travlt mor?*), 184

Are You Afraid? (*Er I bange?*), 53

Aristide, Jean-Bertrand, 227, 232, 234, 236

Armadillo, 245, 246, 250, 253–56, 258–61

'Art of Selling, The' (*Kunsten at sælge*), 266

Auken, Svend, 25, 373, 375

Awaiting, 342

B

'Bailiff, The' (*Kongens Foged*), 31, 32, 44

Balling, Erik, 127, 129,

Ballroom Dancer, 202

Banks, Elizabeth, 227

Bastian, Peter, 385

Bauer, Mette, 52

'Beauty' (*Smukke*), 70

Beckendorff, Ghita, 156

Beckerlee, Franz, 392

Behind the Mountains (*Bag bjergene*), 305, 306, 311, 318

Behind the Scenes: Accused, 184

Bejmar, Magnus, 206, 207, 219

Bell, Jamie, 227

Berliner, Alan, 191

Bertelsen, Mikael, 89, 90, 102, 323, 324

Beth's Diary (*Beths dagbog*), 183, 184, 189, 192, 195, 201

Bierlich, Ann, 227

Billeskov Jansen, Janus, 38, 341, 346, 350, 406

Birch, Klaus, 404

Björk, 314, 316, 341, 345, 348

Bird That Could Tell Fortunes, The (*Fuglen der kunne spå*), 305, 306, 311, 318

Blair Witch Project, The, 119

Blue Collar White Christmas (*Nede på
    jorden*), 165, 166, 167–9, 172, 251
Bomholt, Julius, 13
Bonaventura, Lorenzo di, 227
Bonfils, Dola, chapter 2, 4, 23,
Bonke, Christian, 202
Bonnén, Kaspar, 184
Borderliners (*De måske egnede*), 71
Brask, Dorte Høeg, chapter 3, 15, 192
Bridgend, 323, 324, 338
Bro, Arne, v, ix, 3, 17, 18, 33, 73–4, 111–12,
    185, 268, 287, 288, 361, 362, 364, 369,
Bro, Sara, 183, 184, 185, 195
Brothers Karamazov, 325
Brügger, Mads, chapter 4, 15, 84, 323, 324
Brydesen, Lars, 174,
Burma VJ, 7, 11, 19, 46, 381, 382, 395–99
Burstein, Nanette, 172

C
Cairo – Garbage, 183, 184, 198–201, 202
Camp, The, 266
Camre, Henning, 12, 22, 57, 63, 402,
    404, 407
'Can an aesthetic be gendered?' (*Kan man
    give æstetikken et køn?*), 52
Carlsen, Jon Bang, 3
Carlsen, Henning, 3, 16, 51, 53, 381, 402
Carl Th. Dreyer: My Metier (*Carl Th. Dreyer –
    min metier*), 145, 146, 151, 152, 155
Carstensen, Claus, 213
Castle in Italy: An Elegy, The (*Slottet i Italien*),
    361, 362, 370, 371, 372, 374
Celebration, The (*Festen*), 138, 140,
Chaplin, Charlie, 220, 372
Christensen, Bo, 129
Christensen, Pernille Bech, 113
Christensen, Sarita, 294
Christensen, Theodor, 368, 406, 408
*Christiania: Freetown Full Throttle
    (Christiania – fristad i frigear)*, 342
Cimino, Michael, 261
'Cities on Speed', 24, 183, 184, 198–201

City Slang Redux, 146,
Clandestine (*Eventyrerne*), 245, 246, 248–251
Clarks, 165, 166
Claro, Manuel Alberto, 183, 188, 194, 197
Clausen, Erik, 290
Clemmensen, Carl Henrik, 183
C-Memorandum (*K-Notatet*), 51, 52, 57–60
Colony, The (*Kolonien*), 265, 266, 280
Complicated Family Life, The (*Det
    komplicerede familieliv*), 110
Copenhagen Dreams (*Drømme i København*),
    165, 166, 176–9
Coppola, Francis Ford, 261, 293
Cruz, Khavn de la, 286

D
Damgaard-Sørensen, Mette, 404
Dancer in the Dark, 305, 314
Dancing in the Midst of War (*Dansen i
    brændpunktet*), 323, 324
Danes for Bush, 89, 90, 94–8
Danish Divorce (*Når vi skilles*), 266
Danish Documentary, 21, 31, 44–5, 109,
    112–3, 120, 183, 184, 194, 201–2, 265,
    272, 276, 281–2, 403
Danish Girls Show Everything (*Danske piger
    viser alt*), 362
'Danish Images' (*Danske Billeder*), 174
Dark Days, 282
*David or Goliath: A Film about the World
    Press in Jerusalem* (*David eller
    Goliath*), 361, 362, 377–8
D Day (*D-Dag*), 135, 138
Deer Hunter, 261
Denmark (*Danmark*), 174
Detour to Freedom (*Omveje til frihed*), 183,
    184, 192–95, 201
Dibbern, Erik, 127, 129
Diemer, Anne, 326
Dilemma, 381, 402
Diver Inside Me, The, 32, 37, 39
Dog Day Afternoon, 241
Dogville Confessions, 341, 342, 351–2

Don Giovanni, 372
Doxwise Diary (*Doxwise*), 286, 294, 299
'Dr Dante: Playground of the Stars' (*Dr. Dante – Stjernernes legeplads*), 146
'Dreams with Deadlines' (*Drømme med deadlines*), 51, 52, 60–1
Drouzy, Martin, 148
Dvortsevoy, Sergei, 273–4
Dyekjær, Sigrid, 9, 21, 31, 45, 109, 113, 116, 184, 193, 201, 265, 281, 403

E
'Earth under My Feet, The' (*Jorden under mine fødder*), 286, 300–1
Ege, Ole, 145, 146, 152, 154, 156, 158–9, 285, 292
Egmont-Petersen, Sofie, 355, 356
'Eighteen Holes' (*Atten Huller*), 165, 166
Ejbøl, Jørgen, 135
Element of Crime, The, 135, 286
Elkatsha, Sherief, 199
'11th Hour, The' (*Den 11. Time*), 89, 90
Eliasson, Olafur, 127
Elling, Tom, 148
Ende, Michael, 343
Enemies of Happiness, 18, 19, 25, 265, 266, 269, 271, 274, 278, 280, 281, 403
Engberg, Marguerite, 148
Epilogue (*Epilog*), 183, 184, 185
'Erik and Karl' (*Erik og Karl*), 70
'Erland Josephson: Are You Playing Tonight?' (*Erland Josephson – Spelar du i kväll*), 146
Everything is Relative (*Alt er relativt*), 116, 183, 184, 186, 188, 192, 194, 195, 196–9, 201, 202
'Everything is Yours' (*Alt er dit*), 147
Exhibited, The (*De udstillede*), 127, 128, 136
Exit Through the Gift Shop, 44

F
Face to Face: A Film about Faith, Hope, and Love (*Ansigt til Ansigt – en film om tro, håb og kærlighed*), 276, 361, 362, 365, 370
Fall of the King, The (*Kongens Fald*), 130
Family, The (*Familien*), 110
Family, 31, 32, 34–6, 37, 38, 40, 73, 113, 192, 341, 342, 349–50, 353
Family of Man, 186
Family Portraits (*Familiebilleder*), 16, 402
'Farmer Niels' (*Bondemand Niels*), 32
Fauli, Søren, 183, 184, 193
Fever: A Film about Julie Nord (*Fever – En film om Julie Nord*), 32
'Film/Art: Art Moves #1' ('Film/Kunst – Art Moves #1'), 109, 110
'First, The' (*De første*), 405
First Annual Anti Anti Fashion Video Performance, 145, 146
Fischer, Tine, 403
Fish out of Water (*Fisk uden vand*), 183, 184, 190–1
Five Obstructions, The (*De fem benspænd*), 5, 25, 227, 230, 232, 407
Flaneur I-III, 145
Flaneur II – Dandy, 146
'Flaneur III – Benjamin's Shadow' (*Flaneur III – Benjamins skygge*), 146
Fledelius, Karsten, 91
Forbert, Wladyslaw, 307, 315
'Foreign Girl's Diary, A' (*En fremmed piges dagbog*), 306
Forman, Milos, 393
Fraser, Nick, 158
Frederiksen, Jonas, 36, 114
Freelancer, 147
Free the Mind, 31, 32, 39, 41
Friedrich, Caspar David, 372
Fulton, Keith, 352
Furtado, Jorge, 172, 199

G
Gabold, Anne-Lise, 128
Gambler, 31, 32, 38, 39
Gammeltoft, Thomas, 150

Gasolin', 22, 381, 382, 385, 391–93

Geertsen, Anders, 64

Genz, Henrik Ruben, 185

Ghosts of Cité Soleil, 227, 231, 232–40

Gilbert, Dalkia, 104

Gilliam, Terry, 352

Girl in the Water, 323, 324

Giselle: A Film about Dreams and Discipline (Giselle – en film om drøm og disciplin), 361, 362, 371, 372

Gislason, Tómas, 183, 185, 388

Glass, Philip, 159

Glawogger, Michael, 198

Godfather, The, 293

God Gave Her a Mercedes Benz (Gud gav hende en Mercedes Benz), 305, 306, 309, 317

Good Life, The (Det gode liv), 25, 265, 266, 269, 272–9

Gordimer, Nadine, 402

Gorilla gorilla (Gorilla gorilla), 362

Graduate, The, 252

Greenaway, Peter, 169

Grey Gardens, 282

Growing Up in a Day, 32

Grønkjær, Pernille Rose, chapter 5, 25, 31, 184, 191, 201, 265, 281, 403

Grüner, Thomas Garth, 355

Guldbrandsen, Christoffer, 18, 19, 25, 248, 256, 257, 293, 405–6,

'GURPS' (*Gurps*), 52

Graabøl, Niels, 193

Grunnet, Henrik, 58

Grunwald, Morten, 161

Grønkjær, Pernille Rose, chapter 5, 25, 31, 184, 191, 201, 265, 281, 403

H

Haiti: Untitled (Haiti – Uden titel), 185,

Hammerich, Rumle, 161, 404

Hamsun, Knut, 402

Hans Henrik Lerfeldt – It's a Blue World, 146, 149

Hansen, Bente, 51, 55, 62

Hansen, Dino Raymond, 149

Hansen, Erik Molberg, 171, 188, 197

Hansen, Helle, 51, 62

Hansen, Jesper Thirup, 323

Hansen, Kim G., 89

Harris, Ed, 227

Hartkopp, Christian, 53, 54

Hassing, Anne Louise, 137

Havn, Loke, 392

Hawaii, 286, 292–93

'H. C. Andersen meets Carl Nielsen' (*H.C. Andersen møder Carl Nielsen*), 146

Heart and Soul (Fra hjertet til hånden), 185

Heart of Johannes, The (Johannes' hjerte), 361, 362, 370–72, 374

Heide-Jørgensen, Vibeke, 184

Helmuth, Osvald, 192

Helsøe, Jesper, 60

Henning-Jensen, Astrid, 406

Henningsen, Poul, 174

Herdel, Steen, 152, 159

Herzog, Werner, 233

Heurlin, Thomas, 343, 344

Higgins, Lloyd, 372

Hollender, Pål, 404

Holst, Per, 127, 130

Home Front, The (Hjemmefronten – fjenden bag hækken), 31, 32, 39, 43

Horowitz, Rafi, 377

Hostrup-Larsen, Thomas, 403

House Inside Her, The, 109, 110

Hovde, Ellen, 282

'How Short and Strange Life Is' (*Så kort og mærkeligt livet er*), 382, 394

Humiliated, The (De ydmygede), 127, 128, 135–37, 139

Hunger (Sult), 402

Høeg, Peter, 71

Høgel, Jakob, 193, 248, 327, 331, 403, 406

Høst, Børge, 406

Høy, Søren, 404

I

I am Fiction (*Fiktionstyveriet*), 166

Idiots, The (*Idioterne*), 127, 135, 136, 138, 139, 140

Ilha das Flores, 172, 199

'Images for the Times' (*Billeder til tiden*), 51, 52, 54, 55, 61–3

In Honour of Truth (*I sandhedens tjeneste*), 407

'In Search of a Future' (*Fremtid søges*), 52, 54

Inside Rooms: 26 Bathrooms, 169

'In the Service of Truth: A Journey through the Unknown Europe' (*I sandhedens tjeneste - En rejse i det ukendte Europa*), 94, 102

'In the Shadow of Death' (*Med døden inde på livet*), 51, 52, 54, 56, 60

Ipsen, Bodil, 401

Ipsen, Henrik, 251

Isho, Marina, 347, 355

Island of Flowers (*Ilha das Flores*), 172, 199

It's a Blue World, 145, 146, 149, 153, 154, 155

'I Want You Back' (*Jeg vil have dig tilbage*), 306

J

Jack, Jesper, 251

Jacobi, Frederik, 231, 233, 237

Jako, 306

Jargil, Jesper, chapter 6, 4, 406

Jargil, Mira, 25, 140

Jean, Wyclef, 236–9

Jenny's Big Sister (*Jennis storesøster*), 166

Jensen, Astrid Kruse, 109, 110

Jensen, Dunja Gry, 174

Jensen, Johannes V., 130

Jensen, Mariella Harpelunde, 71, 86, 191

Jensen, Torben Skjødt, chapter 7, 4, 14, 63, 292, 388

Jeppesen, Ida Holten, 192

Jepsen, Christian Sønderby, 25, 140

Jerusalem, My Love (*Jerusalem, min elskede*), 323, 324, 326–27, 330–31, 332, 333, 337

'Johanne from Daugbjerg' (*Johanne fra Daugbjerg*), 306, 317

'Johannesburg Revisited' (*Gensyn med Johannesburg*), 381, 382

Johannsen, René Sascha, 95, 101

Johansson, Jan, 381, 386, 388, 389

Joya, Malalai, 18, 265, 271

'Just a Touch' (*Som et strejf*), 146

Jørgensen, Elith, 94

Jørgensen, Simon Jul, 95, 98

K

Kam, Søren, 183

Kampmann, Christian, 154–5

Kestner, Max, chapter 8, 15, 17, 18, 27, 199, 248, 251, 406

Kiaorostami, Abbas, 332

Kidman, Nicole, 351

Kid Stays in the Picture, The, 172

Kierkegaard, Per K., 193, 201

Kieslowski, Krzysztof, 308, 326

'Kingdom of Credibility, The' ('Troværdighedens rige'), 127, 135, 137

Kirkeby, Per, 127, 128, 130, 132, 133, 134–5, 138, 216, 370, 374

Kirstein, Stine, 207, 208, 211, 216

Kisses Right and Left (*Kys til højre og venstre*), 53

Kjer, Bodil, 401

Kjærsgård, Pia, 176

Kjaerstad, Jan, 326, 335

'Kleinrock's Cabinet' (*Kleinrocks cabinet*), 89, 90

Klich, Kent, 183, 184, 189, 195

Klint, Michael, 404

Knudsen, Mette, 52

Knudsen, Nina Steen, 62

Koefoed, Andreas, 25, 202

Koester, Joakim, 213

Koether, Jutta, 214

Kragh-Jacobsen, Søren, 127, 138, 404

Krogh, Leila, 184, 186

Krogh, Mikala, chapter 9, 31, 109, 116, 403, 265, 267

Krogh, Torben, 184, 186
Kronstam, Henning, 372
Kræmmer, Lars, 127
Kærn, Simone Aaberg, chapter 10, 21, 406

L
Landgreen, Malene, 127
Land of Human Beings: My Film about Greenland, The (*Menneskenes land – min film om Grønland*), 362, 370, 372, 377
Larsen, Kim, 392–94
Larsen, Peter, 159,
Last Dance, The (*Den sidste dans*), 18, 265, 266, 269, 272, 278, 280
'Last Journey' (*Sidste rejse*), 341, 342, 343–4
Laustsen, Dan, 361, 365, 371
Lemon, T.J., 332, 336
Lerfeldt, Henrik, 145, 146, 149, 150, 153–5, 156, 159
Leth, Asger, chapter 11
Leth, Jørgen, 3, 5, 25, 165, 174, 183, 185, 227, 228, 242, 290, 406, 407
Leth, Karoline, 227
Leth, Kristian, 227
Levring, Kristian, 127, 404
'The Life-giving Relation' (*Den livgivende relation*), 146
Life in Denmark (*Livet i Danmark*), 16, 174
'Life of Our Youth, The', 238
Lilleør, Kathrine, 376
Lindholm, Tobias, 285, 286, 301
Lissner, Frank, 256
Little Girl with the Skates, The (*Den lille pige med skøjterne*), 362
Little Mermaid, The, 376
'Little Yellow Airplane, The' ('Den lille gule flyver'), 208
'Living Words 1–3' (*Levende ord 1–3*), 51, 52, 54
'Living Words 1: Community and Democracy' (*Levende ord 1: Fællesskab og demokrati*), 51, 52, 54

'Living Words 2: The Environment and Development' (*Levende ord 2: Miljø og udvikling*), 51, 52, 54
'Living Words 3: Encounters with the Other' (*Levende ord 3: Mødet med de fremmede*), 51, 52, 54
Loftager, Jens, 341, 342, 355
Lomholt, Nils, 148
Lončarević, Miloš, 231, 233, 237
Lopez, Ricardo, 341, 342, 345–49, 350, 356
Lost in La Mancha, 352
Love Addict: Stories of Dreams, Obsession and Longing, 25, 109, 110, 117–20, 121, 122
'Love and War', 254
Love on Delivery (*Fra Thailand til Thy*), 245, 246, 249, 250, 252–53
'Low Water Ocean Fauna, The' (*Havets lavvandsfauna*), 306
Lumet, Sidney, 241
'Lykketoft's Final' (*Lykketoft finale*), 293

M
Mackie, Anthony, 227
Madman, a Lover, and a Poet, A (*En gal, en elsker eller en poet*), 361, 362, 376
Magus, The (*Trollkarlen*), 381, 382, 385, 386, 388–89, 390
Malaria, 381, 382, 386
Man on a Ledge, 227, 240–41
Man Who Would Live Forever, The (*Manden som ikke ville dø*), 361, 362, 376
Man With Camera (*Mand med kamera*), 305, 306, 307, 311, 312, 315
Matador, 100
Max by Chance (*Rejsen på ophavet*), 165, 166, 169–72, 199
Maysles, Albert, 273, 282
Maysles, David, 273, 282
McLuhan, Marshall, 93
Me and My Twin (*Mig og min tvilling*), 183, 184, 202
'Me and You' (*Mig og dig*), 166, 172–73
Mechanical Love, 25, 31, 32, 35, 39, 403

Megacities, 198–99
Melancholia, 84
Mertz, Albert, 363
Messerschmidt, Morten, 97
Metz, Janus, chapter 12, 19, 22, 201
Meyer, Muffie, 282
Mifune (*Mifunes sidste sang*), 138
'Mimi's Last Election' (*Mimis sidste valg*),
    286, 293–94, 296
Mission Rape, 306,
MK, 183, 184, 194, 196
Mo, Erlend E., 341, 342, 347, 355
Models, The (*Modellerne*), 110
Monastery: Mr Vig and the Nun, The, 109,
    110, 114, 115, 116–67, 118–19, 120,
    122, 123, 202, 281, 403
Mooitong, Yulo, 335
Moore, Michael, 273
More Sex Please, We're from Scandinavia
    (*Tugt & Utugt*), 145, 146, 158–59
Morricone, Ennio, 103
Morris, Errol, 361
Motivation: Close-ups from a Youth School
    (*Motivation – nærbilleder fra en*
    Ungdomsskole), 361, 362, 401
Movin, Lars, 273, 282
Mozart, 393
Mulvad, Eva, chapter 13, 4, 10, 17, 18, 19, 25,
    31, 109, 122, 184, 201, 403
Mum is Coming (*Mor kommer snart*), 69, 70, 71
Muniam Alfaker, 341, 342, 352, 354
'Mutual Involvement' (*Gensidig berøring*), 147
'My ...' ('Min   '), 69, 70, 76 7
My Denmark (*Mit Danmark*), 341, 342, 352
My Father's Choice (*Min fars valg*), 184, 186,
    191–92
My Grandfather's Murderer (*Min morfars*
    morder), 183, 184, 192, 193
My Iranian Paradise (*Mit iranske paradis*),
    305, 306, 310–12
My Love (*Min elskede*), 341, 342, 352
'My Own Motor Horse' (*Min egen*
    motorhest), 305, 306, 318

Myrick, Daniel, 119
'My Sweet Child' (*Mit søde barn*), 306, 318
'My Yellow Airplane' (*Min gule flyver*),
    207, 210
Møllehave, Johannes, 370, 374, 376
Møller, Nanna Frank, 176
Møller, Tue Steen, 327

N
Nameth, A'a'me, 183, 192
Nam June Paik, 213
Naughty Boy, The (*Den grimme dreng*), 145,
    146, 152, 156, 292
Nesgaard, Poul, 94, 102, 407
NeverEnding Story, The, 343
New Scenes from America (*Nye scener fra*
    Amerika), 227, 230
'Next Time We'll Be Birds' (*Næste gang bliver*
    vi fugle), 166
Nichols, Bill, 291
Nichols, Mike, 252
Nielsen, Adam, 270
Nielsen, Allan Berg, 58
Nielsen, Asta, 146, 153, 157, 159, 160, 161
Nielsen, Carl, 146, 176
Nielsen, Henrik Bo, 404
Nielsen, Miriam, 196
Noer, Michael, chapter 14, 4, 17
Nord, Julie, 31, 32
Normal Life, A, 183, 184, 195, 202
Nossel, Jacob, 95, 98
Notes on Silence (*Notater om tavshed*), 69,
    70, 74
'Nothing has Changed' (*Alt er som det plejer*),
    147
Nyholm, Kristoffer, 136
Nøhr, Rasmus, 173

O
Oehlenshläger, Adam, 393
Old People (*De gamle*), 402
Olin, Margreth, 404
Olsen, Annette Mari, 305, 306, 310, 311

'Open Sky', 207, 208, 218
'Out of the Borderlands' (*Ud af
	grænselandet*), 146

P
Pade, Else Marie, 305, 316–7
Page One: Inside New York Times, 203
Palmquist, Hanne, 408
Paradise (*Paradis*), 341, 342, 347, 355–56
Passenger, The (*Professione – reporter*), 103
Patwardhan, Anand, 361
Pedersen, Jens Ulrik, 343
Pedersen, Jørgen Flindt, 404
Pedersen, Katia Forbert, chapter 15
Pedersen, Klaus Riskær, 406
Per Kirkeby: Winter's Tale (*Per Kirkeby –
	Vinterbillede*), 127, 128
'Personal History of the Danes, The'
	(*Danskernes egen historie*), 78
Pepe, Louis, 352
Perfect Human, The (*Det perfekte menneske*),
	25
Philp, Adam, 119
'Pictures of Power' ('Magtens billeder'), 23,
	51, 52, 57–8, 59, 381, 382, 395
'Pictures of Power': *C-Memorandum*
	('Magtens billeder': *K-Notatet*), 51,
	52, 57–60
'Pictures of Power: The Vanguard of
	Diplomacy (*Magtens billeder –
	Diplomatiets fortrop*), 381, 382, 386,
	395–6
'Planned Child' (*Ønskebarn*), 306
Polanski, Roman, 308
'Police as They Are, The' 1–3 (*Politiet i
	virkeligheden 1–3*), 51, 52, 54, 56–7, 60
'Polish Girls (*Polske piger*), 305, 306, 310, 317
President, The (*Præsidenten*), 18, 19, 406
Princess for a Day (*Prinsesse for en dag*), 266
Prisoner's Choir (*Fangekoret*), 306
'Psychomobile: The World Clock'
	(*Psykomobile #1 – Verdensuret*), 127
Purified, The (*De lutrede*), 127, 128, 137–8

Pusher 2, 31, 38
Pusher 3, 31, 38

Q
'Quartermaster, The' (*Kvartermesteren*), 183,
	184
Quatraro Mystery, The (*Quatraro mysteriet*),
	89, 90, 102–3, 323, 324
Quatsiluni, 146,

R
R, 285, 286, 293, 301, 302
Rasmussen, Anders Fogh, 406
'Real Man in the Moon, The' (*Le véritable
	homme dans la lune*), 147
Red Chapel, The (*Det røde kapel*), 89, 90, 95,
	97–102, 103, 104
Reedtz-Thott, Otto, 406
Refn, Anders, 228
Refn, Nicolas Winding, 31, 38–9, 228
Repeating Grandpa (*Min morfar forfra*), 109,
	110, 114
'Reportage Unit, The' (*Reportageholdet*), 69,
	72, 343, 409
Restless Heart (*Hvileløse hjerte*), 147
Reuter, Ursula, 62
Rex, Jytte, 3, 368
Riefenstahl, Leni, 220
Rifbjerg, Klaus, 174
Rifbjerg, Synne, 302
Ripples at the Shore, 31, 32, 44
Road, to Europe, The (*Fogh bag facaden*), 405
Roos, Gerd, 150
Roos, Jørgen, 156, 363, 401
Roos, Karl, 368
Roos, Lise, 404, 406
Roos, Ole, 368
Roskilde, 286, 300, 342
Rossen-Jørgensen, Jens, 256
Rossi, Andrew, 203
Royal Greenland, 207, 208
Rukov, Mogens, 137–8, 196, 198, 288, 335,
	344, 408–9

Rupture, 246
Ryom, Heidi, 372
Rykær, Jens, 404
Rønde, Jeppe, chapter 16, 90, 248

S
Sadoul, Numa, 390
Saif, Sami, chapter 17, 17, 31, 32, 36–7,
 113–4, 192, 404, 406
Saint-Exupéry, Antoine de, 220
Salieri, 393
Samurai Case, The (*Med døden til følge*), 265,
 266, 269, 278
Sánchez, Eduardo, 119
Scattering Clouds: When Mom and Dad Have
 Wronged (*Et hul i himlen – Når mor*
 og far er i fængsel), 69, 70, 75,
 78–80
Scent of Beirut, The (*Duften af Beirut*), 69, 70,
 77–8, 81
Schepelern, Mette Ann, 367
Schepelern, Peter, 148
Schmidt, Theis, 193, 196, 330, 331
'Secondary School: A Kind of School'
 (*Gymnasiet – en skoleform*), 51, 52,
 54, 56
Secret War, The (*Den hemmelige krig*),
 256–57, 406
Seebach, Tommy, 342, 356–57
Seidelin, Lars, 343
'Seize the Sky', 208
Sejer, Niels, 119
Shargawi, Omar, 3
Sharma, Arun, 247
'Sheer Bliss?' (*Lutter lagkage?*), 52
Silk Road (*Silkevejen*), 368
Silent Girls, The (*De tavse piger*), 361,
 362, 401
Skot-Hansen, Mogens, 406
Spies, Simon, 146, 153–54, 159–60
Simon Spies: Simon's Film (*Simon Spies –*
 Simons film), 146, 159
Singer, Marc, 282

'Sisters in the Sky: A Road Movie from the
 Air' (*Sisters in the Sky – en roadmovie*
 fra luften), 207, 208, 211, 215–18,
 220, 221
'Sketches for a Portrait of a Painter (*Skitser*
 til et portræt af en maler),
 127, 128
'Skjoldhøj Archive, The' (*Skjoldhøjarkivet*),
 89, 90, 92–3
Skolomowski, Jerzy, 308
Skree, Lars, 201
Smiling in a Warzone, 21, 207, 208, 210, 211,
 215, 216, 218, 219, 220, 221–22
Smith, Frede, 157, 160, 161
'Society Ladies' (*Selskabsdamer*), 70
Son (*Søn*), 323, 324, 327–30, 338
Son of God, 286, 300–1
'Song Book and the Red Shoes: The
 Bombing of the French School, The'
 (*Sangbogen og de røde sko – om*
 bombningen af Den Franske Skole),
 306, 319
Songs from the Second Floor (*Sånger från*
 andra våningen), 194
Soueid, Mohamad, 354
Sound On Life (*Lyd på liv*), 305, 306, 314,
 316–17
'Sound Pictures: Six Variations on a Theme'
 (*Lydbilleder – 6 variationer over et*
 tema), 51, 52, 54, 61, 62
Spider Sisters, 208
Stalin, 308
Stausholm, Sidse, 183, 184, 192
Steen, Rasmus, 248
Stensgaard, Molly Malene, 220
Stephensen, Erik, 366–67, 404
Storyville, 158
'Strike First, Frede' (*Slå først, Frede*), 129
'Sundholm Reading Group, The (*Læsegruppe*
 Sundholm), 89, 90
Surrational Cityscaping I: De Rerum Natura,
 146
Svend (*Svend*), 25, 361, 362, 372, 373, 375

Swenkas, The, 323, 324, 326, 329, 330, 331, 332, 334–37
Submarino, 301
Søren Kierkegaard (*Søren Kierkegaard*), 361, 362

T
Tabloid Newsroom, The (*Avisredaktionen*), 184, 203
Talking Muse, The (*Den talende muse*), 146, 153, 154, 157, 159, 160–1
Talk Radio (*Radiofolket*), 69, 70, 76
Taraneh heading for the Stars, 208
Tarkovsky, Andrei, 326
'Technique For You and Me' (*Teknik for dig og mig*), 306
Teno, Jean-Marie, 361
This is Me Walking, 369
Thomsen, Knud Leif, 128, 129
Thorsen, Rasmus, 326, 331, 403
Those Were the Days (*Der var så mange glæder …*), 110, 114, 118
Thuesen, Jacob, 3, 38, 193, 388
Thygesen, Erik, 150
Ticket to Paradise (*Fra Thy til Thailand*), 245, 246, 250–51, 252–53
Times Goes By, 147
'Time Just Before the Moment, The' (*Tiden før øjeblikket*), 306, 318
Tintin and I (*Tintin og mig*), 19, 361, 362, 386–8, 389–91
Tobacco, 362
To Be or Nothing to Eat, 147
Togeby, Lise, 57
'Together With Lena,' (*Sammen med Lena*), 305, 306, 317
Tommy, 342, 356–7
Torsting, Kasper, 254, 256
'Touch of the Same, A' (*En rem af huden*), 286, 292
Township Boys, 245, 246, 247–8
Turèll, Dan, 382, 394–5
'TV Happy' (*TV-Glad*), 110

2Pac, 231, 233, 234, 235, 236–9, 240
'Two Painters, Two Studios' (*To malere – to værksteder*), 51, 52, 62
'Two Women on the River' (*To kvinder på en flod*), 306
Tøjner, Vibeke, 127, 128, 138, 140

U
UFO War, The (*UFO-krigen*), 342, 343–4
U-land, 89, 345
Ulsteen, Helle, 222

V
Vahradian, Mark, 227
Vasulka, Steina, 213
Vehkalahti, Iikka, 253
Veileborg, Henrik, 251
Veirup, Kjeld, 404
Vemmer, Mogens, 72–3, 402, 409
Vertov, Dziga, 312–3
Vesterbro, 285, 286, 294–6, 298
Video Diary of Ricardo Lopez, The, 341, 342, 345–6, 349
Villadsen, Anders, 388
Villesen, Gitte, 209–10
Vilstrup, Li, 52
Vinterberg, Thomas, 127, 138, 301, 404
Viola, Bill, 186, 213
'Visual Arts Practice 1–2' (*Billedkunstnerisk praksis 1–2*), 51, 52
Vium, Christian, 248–50
Vogel, Vibeke, 367
von Trier, Lars, 5, 25, 84, 127, 128, 135–9, 212, 227, 286, 305, 314, 316, 326, 341, 351–2, 367, 404, 407, 409, 410
Von Trier's 100 Eyes (*Von Triers 100 øjne*), 305, 306, 314

W
Wamberg, Niels Birger, 376
Wanna Fly, 207, 208
'War of the Small, The' (*De smås krig*), 166
'War in Art' ('Krig i Kunsten'), 207, 208

Water (*Vand*), 362
Wayfarer – 8900 Randers, 146
'Ways of Memory, The' (*Indretninger i hukommelsen*), 184
'Week Without Smiling, A' (*En uge uden smil*), 305, 306, 318
'We Got our Lives Back' (*Vi fik livet tilbage*), 184, 194
'We Need to Help Each Other' (*Vi skal jo hjælpe hinanden*), 146
Who, The, 325
'Why Democracy?', 24
'Why Poverty?', 24
Wiedemann, Vinca, 196
Wild Hearts, The (*De vilde hjerter*), 285, 286, 289, 294, 298–99
Will, The (*Testamentet*), 140
Wilson, Jane, 186
Wilson, Louise, 186
Windeløv, Vibeke, 216, 314
Windfeld, Kathrine, 191
Wiseman, Frederick, 51, 54, 273, 274, 361, 377
'Witnesses of a Century' (*Århundredets vidner*), 194
Wivel, Anne, chapter 18, 4, 5, 18, 25, 276, 290, 401, 406

Wivel, Ulrik, 286, 300, 342
Woman in Exile (*Kvinde i eksil*), 305, 306
'Women and the Common Market' (*Kvinderne og fællesmarkedet*), 51, 52, 53–4
Woo Ming Jin, 323
Work Towards Freedom: A Film about a State Prison (*Arbejde mod frihed – En film om et statsfængsel*), 362
World in Denmark, The (*Verden i Danmark*), 165, 166, 173–6, 178–9
Worthington, Sam, 227
Wu Wenguang, 361

Y
Young People (*Ung*), 16, 402
'Youth Guarantee, The' (*Ungdomsgarantien*), 183, 184, 185, 186

Z
Zandvliet, Martin, 294
Ørsted, Claus, 174
Østergaard, Anders, chapter 19, 7, 11, 19, 22, 23, 46, 248, 404, 406

Index of the Institutional Landscape and Central Topics

A

adaptations of annual reports, Jesper Jargil
    on, 131

addiction, different forms of, 118

advertising agency, of Gutenberghus,
    131, 145

aero-feminism, 207

Afghanistan, first democratic elections in,
    65

AIDS-Fondet, 56

aesthetic form, 14, 46, 291, 295

Al-Arabiya, 341, 342, 352

American film industry, working within and
    artistic integrity, 242

American films, Mogens Rukov's
    understanding of, as compared with
    European films, 288

Apartheid, 334

archive material, 159

AROS Museum, Aarhus, 207

Arriflex II camera, 307

Art History, minor in, 324

art, intuition and material expression,
    132

ARTE, 19, 410

Asbæk Gallery, 207

Association of Danish Film Directors, 69, 71,
    78, 85, 140, 401

audience, broad, Phie Ambo on, 44

autodidact, 52, 147

Avant-garde, Russian, 312-13, 317

B

Barok Film A/S, 17, 170, 362, 366, 367,
    368–69

Bastard Film, 17, 173–74

BBC, 24, 158, 186, 377, 409

Bech Film, 327

Beit Agron International Press Centre, in
    Jerusalem, 361, 377

Bellevue Studio, 127, 131

Berlin International Film Festival, 148

Bikuben Fund (BG Fonden), 173

black market, and *Burma VJ*, 398

box office criteria, and documentary film's
    quality, 370

brain-scanning, 60

C

cameras, hidden, 104

Cannes Advertising Film Festival, 127

Cannes International Film Festival,
    135, 245, 316

'Cartoon Crisis', the, 200, 341, 354, 355

cartoons, universe of Hergé's, 390

Casablanca Society, and experimental and
    popular art, 63

chance, Phie Ambo on, 42

Chief of Defence, 60

children, Katia Forbert Petersen's interest in
    depicting world of, 318–19

children's film, and edgy stories, 82–3; as
    practice area, 82

Children's Media Think Tank, 86
children's TV channel, 83
Christiania, free town of, 342, 357–58
cinemas, documentaries being seen in, 22, 31, 140, 337, 370
cinéma vérité, 13, 16, 273
Cineworks, 103
Cité Soleil, Haiti, 232, 234, 238
collaboration, across the fiction/non-fiction divide, 37–8; between film and TV, 15; culture of, 112–13
commercials, director of, 127, 128, 227; and experimentation, 129–35
commissioning editor, Dola Bonfils as, 63–4
company, establishing of, 45, 127, 281
conflicts, seen from perspective of women, 221
consensus, emphasis on, in Christiania, 358
cooperation, with the filmmaker, 56
Copenhagen Bombay, 294, 299
Copenhagen revue, song tradition, 392
Cosmo Film, 326–27, 403, 406
CPH:DOX, 22, 183, 245, 248, 250, 282; and DOX:LAB, 323, 403
cultural exchange, 98, 258
cultural thaw, in Poland, 308

D
Dagmar Theatre, 53
Danish International Development Agency (Danida), 183
Danish Broadcasting Corporation (DR), 15, 403; and Al-Arabiya, 341; and Children & Youth Department, 69, 70, 71, 89, 91, 94, 101, 165, 402, 407, 409; and collaboration with, 60, 210; and gift from, to North Koreans, 100; and hidden cameras, 104; and *Horisont*, 250; and Klub 12 (DR1), 185; and making of *Danes for Bush*, 96; and outreach programme, 89; and power struggles, 58; and radio

productions, 248; and Ramasjang, 202; and Reportage Unit, 69; and stance on the US, 97; and *U-land*, 345
Danish Confederation of Trade Unions (LO), 165
Danish Documentary Production, 21, 31, 44, 112–13, 183, 194, 265, 403; as distribution company, 281; and workshops, 276
Danish documentary filmmaking, interest in, 13, 46, 337
Danish film, and crisis, 84
Danish Film Academy, and Robert award for best short film, 323, 360
Danish Film Institute (DFI), 403–4; and *Armadillo*, 254; as central funding body for fiction films, 13–4; and 'Cities on Speed', 24; and collaboration with DR and TV 2, 23; and digital distribution, 65; and distribution of *Township Boys*, 248; and fiction film, as doing poorly, 84; and Film Act (1997), 21; and film art, development of, 120; and film commissioners, 15, 51, 58, 63, 76, 134, 196, 198, 384; and freedom, 251; and *Gasolin'*, 392; and Henning Camre, 22, 57, 63; and 'Megacities', 199; and net-based documentaries, 299; and online film site, Filmstriben, 405; and production of *A Normal Life*, 202; and professionalization, 385; and subsidy system, as dependent on collaboration with TV, 64; and support from, 19, 167, 170, 172–73, 178, 294, 298
Danish Film Museum, 20, 148, 405
Danish Health and Medicines Authority, The, 56
Danish Nurses' Organization, 56
Danish military, 19, 51, 59, 60, 256, 258–59
Danish People's Party, 97

Danish rock music, 393
Danish School of Media & Journalism, 89,
        91, 111, 381, 405
Danmarksfilm, 173–75
de-film-schoolification, Phie Ambo on, 38
DFDS Canal Tours, 128
dictaphone diary, and Lars von Trier's *The
        Idiots*, 136–37
dignity, restoring of, to lives, through
        truth-finding power of documentary
        filmmaking, 356; violating of,
        374–75
distribution, new digital modes of, 47
Direct Cinema, 13, 405
director, self-taught, 51, 159, 201, 208
Directors Guild of America, and
        Outstanding Directorial Achievement
        prize, 227, 233
DKIK (Danmarks Internationale Kollegium),
        in Albertslund, 343
DocPoint, Helsinki, 202
docudrama, 160–61, 398
Documania, 282
documentaries, of the mind, 389
documentary film, narrow, and audience, 47;
        and formal issues, 291
documentary filmmaker, and research, 38,
        43, 60, 61, 79, 80, 103, 118, 119, 130,
        155, 159, 161, 169, 172, 178, 191, 196,
        198–99, 203, 215, 232, 248, 250–51,
        258, 291, 335, 346, 381
documentary filmmaking, as different from
        fiction filmmaking, 331; ethics of,
        111, 112, 183, 192, 332; ethnographic
        approaches to, 291; as a means of
        transformation, 327; and role of
        film school graduates, 201; and
        subcategories, 291
'docutale,' Simone Aaberg Kærn on
        documentary fairy tale, 218, 221
Dogma, 'The World Clock' as precursor to,
        136
Dogma brethren, 404

Dogma rules, Katia Forbert Petersen's
        creation of her own, 316;
        transgression of, 138
dramaturgical concepts, 344
dramaturgical structure, and *Armadillo*, 259

E
Egmont Fund, 54
Ekstra Bladet, and newsroom, 184, 203
Englefilm, 148
essayistic dimension, documentary, as
        compared with pure journalism, 260
EU Media programme, 103
European Documentary Network, The, 202,
        327, 404
European Film College, in Ebeltoft, 286–87,
        404
European Union building, on Rue de la Loi,
        in Brussels, 323
Everest Pictures, 399
expository documentary, 61, 291, 319,
        381, 388
Expressionists, aesthetics of, 317

F
Fantask, 147
father trilogy, Jeppe Rønde's, 330
female aesthetic, and Dola Bonfils, 62
fiction, and non-fiction, productive
        relationship between, 323
Film Act, introduction of, in 1972, 14
Film & Lyd, 151–52, 404
Filmer à Tout Prix festival, in Brussels, 361
Film i Väst, 103
film language, and articulate understanding
        of it, 268
film school, experience of, 38–9; impact of
        teachers at, 112; Jeppe Rønde's, 325;
        transition from, to the film industry,
        113–14
film style, 7, 15, 18, 61–3, 93, 145, 149, 152,
        154–56, 160, 165, 168–69, 172, 173,
        174, 175–76, 194, 221, 245, 251–52,

260–61, 272, 285, 294–95, 370, 386,
388–91, 395
Film Town, in Avedøre, 367, 410
Film Workshop, 14, 23, 145, 148, 149–52,
156, 185, 246, 247, 292, 310, 326–27,
405, 410
Finnish Film Foundation, The, 103
Fipa d'or Grand Prize, Biarritz, 183
FIPRESCI award, 341, 351
Fluxus, 363
fly on the wall, Pernille Rose Grønkjær's lack
of belief in, 117
France 2, 19, 391
freedom, of director, 12, 18, 43, 44, 56, 166,
229, 239, 251, 281, 327
Freemasons, 102
full-step outline, 169

G
Gammel Strand art association, 127, 136
gangs, in Haiti, 232–36
Gangsted Fund, The, 56
garbage dumps, Cairo, 199
Genlyd, 145
genre conventions, 103, 331
globalization, 4, 11, 17–21, 25, 245, 251, 253,
258, 392, 395
globally relevant films, 51
global perspective, interest in, 198,
250, 395
global themes, 24, 245, 247
Goldsmiths College, 207
Grand Cinema, in Copenhagen, 228
Gutenberghus, 131, 145

H
Hergé Foundation, 390–91
home movies, 78, 356–57
'Hunter Force' book, case of, and Danish
military, 257
'hurrah films', Jesper Jargil on, 131, 136
Hvidovre Hospital, 60
hypnosis, 331

improvisation, as compared with planned
scenes, 96–7
illegal immigrants, from Africa, in Europe,
245, 248
industry training, as opposed to film school,
127, 129
International Documentary Film Festival
Amsterdam (IDFA), 105, 109, 158,
183, 253, 282, 406; and Joris Ivens
award, 31, 109, 114, 341; and Silver
Wolf Award, 265
Internet, 24, 76, 282, 299–300, 324; and
Burma VJ, 395; and development
of, 93; and impact on investigative
journalism, 203; and new forms
of distribution, 370; and Ricardo
Lopez, 345

I
Interpresse, 145–147
intimacy, and Anne Wivel's oeuvre, 361; and
depiction of North Korea, 101; and
diary film, 31; and *Gambler*, 39; for
its own sake, lack of interest in, 37;
and observational approach, 261; and
Repeating Grandpa, 109; and Sami
Saif's approach, 351; and *The Good
Life*, 273–76; and transgression of
boundaries, 136
inspiration, 10; and *Armadillo*, 19; and art
as a source of, for Mikala Krogh,
186; and Dola Bonfils on, 54; and
the 'Goldheart' book, 314; and Mads
Brügger on, 93–4, 102; and Max
Kestner on, 172, 175; and Mogens
Rukov, as source of, 288; and Phie
Ambo on, 44; and Sine Plambech, as
source of, 250
Insurance Denmark, 56
Intifada, 361
Iran's history, modern European perspective
on, 312
Italian mafia, 102

J

jazz traditions, 388

Johannesburg, the City of Gold, 335

Joris Ivens Award, 31, 109, 114, 341

journalism, Mads Brügger on, 91–3; new, 93; and traditional conception of, 93

journalistic problem films, Katia Forbert Petersen's lack of interest in making, 318

journalists, and negative stories, 318

K

Kanal2 Rapporten, 91

Karlovy Vary, 265

Kino-Pravda movement, 312

Kino Valde, 51, 53

knowledge society, 60

Koncern TV & Film Production, 17, 167, 343

Koreans, as accepting of Mads Brügger's stories, 98

Kryger prize, 89, 92

language of film, as compared with other arts, 326

L

Laterna Film, 16, 53, 406

learning by doing, 52–3, 229, 247, 310

Louisiana Museum of Modern Art, 207

Lynx Media, 167, 293

M

mainstreaming, 218

Malmö Konsthall, 207

mass media, dehumanizing effects of, 341

media conglomerates, and TV reporting, 345

Ministry of Defence, 60

Ministry of Education, 19, 54

mix, of documentary and fictional elements, 140

'Mogens Vemmer school', 402

monopoly, enjoyed by state-funded channels, 56, 403

MTV, and music hits, 239

multi-plot stories, 39, 179

Museum Erotica, 156

Museum of National History, Hillerød, 207

music videos, and visual style, 61

MySpace, 21, 299

mythological framework, 393

N

narration, 61, 124, 172, 175, 305, 335–36

National Film Board of Canada, 305

National Labour Market Authority, The, 167

nation state, Jeppe Rønde's lack of belief in, 338

National Film Board of Denmark, The (SFC), 14, 20, 150, 305, 384, 407; and distribution system, 63–4

National Film School, Lodz, Poland, 305–8; and communist period, 308

National Film School of Denmark, 407; and admissions process, 366; and Anne Wivel, 361–63; and Arne Bro, 401; and Asger Leth, 229–30; and creation of a Documentary & TV programme, 17; and curricula, 3, 5; and Dorte Høeg Brask, 69; and dramaturgical aspects of training, 344; and Eva Mulvad, 265, 267; and focus on inner selves, 74; and founding of, by Theodor Christensen, 368; and training of a generation of documentary filmmakers, 124; and graduate destinations, 367–68; and graduates of, and method/network, 188, 325–26; and graduates of, being in demand, 201; and graduation films from the Documentary & TV programme, 33; and Henning Camre, 402; and Katia Forbert Petersen, 305, 308; and Max Kestner, 165–66; and part-time teacher, 74; and Michael Noer, 285–90; and Mikala Krogh, 183, 185; and Mogens Rukov, 408;

and networks, 325; and Pernille Rose
Grønkjær, 109–10; and Phie Ambo,
31; and philosophy of, 187–90; and
Sami Saif, 341, 343–44; teaching, as
compared with other film schools,
112; and transition from DR's
Children & Youth Department, 73–4;
its way of doing things, as the only
way, 212
Nazism, Hergé's alleged sympathy for, 391
Netto films, 132
network, 325–26
New Danish Screen, 23, 64, 405,
406, 407
new militant 'humanitarianism', 258
new tendencies in Danish documentary
filmmaking, paradigmatic example
of, 341
New waves, in Eastern Europe, 308
Nikolaj Church, Stockholm, and exhibition,
183, 195
1960s, as era of hope and change, 388
Nordic Film and TV Fund, 19, 103, 170,
253, 408
Nordic Panorama, 408; and best Nordic
documentary award, 89, 102
Nordisk Film, 15, 127, 128, 129, 367, 402
Nordisk Reklamefilm, 127
Nordvision prize, 265
Nuremberg trials, 313

O
observational documentaries, 16, 18, 19, 51,
54, 58, 60, 61, 92, 173, 175, 245, 248,
261, 273, 291–3, 300, 381, 405
observational documentary filmmaker, Dola
Bonfils as, 54
Occupation, The, of Denmark, during
Second World War, 319
Odense Film Festival, 154, 381
openness, new strategy of, and Danish
Military, 60

Oscars ceremony, and *Burma VJ*, 398
outsourcing, Phie Ambo on, 43

P
pain, as motor for storytelling, 330
Panum Institute, 213
parental abuse, effects of, 183
participatory stance, 94
performative documentary, 90, 93–4, 220,
291, 292
Petra Film, 127, 130, 131
pirate student, Simone Aaberg Kærn as, 213
pitches, Phie Ambo on, 42
poetic and reflexive documentary
filmmaking, Max Kestner as central
figure, 165
Point of No Return, 151
Poland, as a communist country, 308
political documentary filmmaking, 18, 53
porn milieu, 292
portraits of female pilots, exhibition of, 215
Potemkino, 103
Press, monthly magazine, 266–67
principles of filmmaking, Griersonian, 58
'pseudo-scientific' film, Max Kestner's *Max
by Chance* as, 172
Public Service Agreement, 15, 254
public support for documentary filmmaking,
in Denmark, Phie Ambo's views on, 43

R
racism, 354–55
Radio24syv, 89, 91
radio montage, Danish tradition of, 92, 267
Radio, P4, 185–86, 193, 267
RAF, and bombing of the French School in
Copenhagen, 319
Ramadan, 200
Rampen, 227, 230
Rantzausminde Efterskole, 185
reality, and Jeppe Rønde's fabrication of
stories, 328; of war, 354

Red Cross, the, 124
re-enactments, 7, 276
responsibility, of documentary filmmaker, 77, 80, 123, 259
Rheumatism Association, 131
risks, Zentropa's willingness to take, 116
Robert prize, for best short documentary, 69, 76, 127, 285, 301, 361
Romanticism, 372
Roskilde Cathedral School, 147
Roskilde Festival, 254, 300
Roskilde University, 19, 70, 245
Royal Danish Academy of Fine Arts, 207, 208, 212, 361, 363
Royal Danish Theatre, 198, 372
Runepress, 145
Russian Revolution, 313

S
Saffron Revolution, 19, 381
SAGA Basement, 214
sanctions, 101
Sankt Annæ Gymnasium, 128
'scenic' documentaries, 272
science documentaries, Dola Bonfils' move towards, 61
scripted, documentary films as, 104, 331
scripter, Dola Bonfils as, 53
See Docs, Dubrovnik, 183
'Semaine de la Critique', and Grand Prix, 245
September 11, 2001, 230, 311
seriousness, and insistence on ugly aspects of reality, 349
Seville International Film Festival, 183
sexuality, history of, 145, 156–58
SF Film Production APS, 194
Sheffield Doc/Fest, 40, 409
Siberia, and 1.5 million Poles sent to, during Second World War, 311
Sisyphuz Film, 247
sociology of knowledge, 60

SONY PD 100, 325
soundscapes, 110
South Africa, townships of, 245, 247, 323
sparring, Anders Østergaard, 384; Asger Leth on, 230; Mikala Krogh on, 198; Pernille Rose Grønkjær on, 113
staging, 102, 117, 130, 260, 278, 279, 369, 394, 402
State funding for film and art, 281
stateless refugee, Katia Forbert Petersen as, 310
storytelling, standard for, 46; oral traditions, in Africa, 335
student helper, Dola Bonfils as, 53
student protests, Pernille Rose Grønkjær's interest in, 310
success, indicator of, 11; meaning of, 123; of Danish documentaries, 337, 369–70
Sundance Film Festival, 89, 102, 109, 265; and World Cinema Jury Prize, 265
Svensk Filmindustri AB, 194
SVT, 19, 386, 409
Sydney Film Festival, 109

T
Taliban, and Danish soldiers' killing of, 256
technological developments, Jesper Jargil's embracing of, 138
Tegneværkstedet, 145
tension, between African and western elements, in *The Swenkas*, 335
Thai community, in Jutland, 250
therapeutic aspect, Mikala Krogh on, 195; of Jeppe Rønde's *Son*, 328
Third Cinema, 53
Tju-Bang Film, 184, 192–94, 202
Toronto Film Festival, 323
trailers, Pernille Rose Grønkjær on, 116; Phie Ambo on, 42
Trollhättan, 341
True/False Film Festival, Memphis, 222
trust, 9, 72, 113, 136, 242, 256, 276, 300, 332, 336, 361, 374, 375

truth, and fiction, 331–32
TV Aalborg, 110, 114
TV sector, and commercial channels, 15, 56
TV stations, and sensational material, 146
TV Stop, 62–3
TV 2, 19, 23, 131, 254, 311, 337, 378, 405; and 'The Reportage Unit' (Reportageholdet), 69, 72, 343, 409
TV production, milieu of, and clash with artistic world of the Film School, 111

U
university background, as unusual, 246
University of Copenhagen, 405; and Asger Leth, 227; and Dola Bonfils; and Eva Mulvad, 268; and Dorte Høeg Brask, 86; and Jakob Høgel, 406; and Jeppe Rønde, 323–24; and Jesper Jargil, 130; and Katia Forbert Petersen, 308–10; and left-wing critique, 310; and Mads Brügger, 89–91; and Phie Ambo, 31–2; and Simone Aaberg Kærn, 213; and Torben Skjødt Jensen, 145, 147–48

V
video diaries, 285, 294, 299
video-on-demand sites, 65
Video Workshop, Haderslev, 14, 145, 148, 185, 410

Vietnam War, 313
Villumsen Museum, Frederikssund, 186
visual art, Dola Bonfils' interest in,
Visual style, as poetic and symbol-laden, and Dola Bonfils, 62–3
voice, and children, 71

W
war films, and classic fiction film of American, 261
websites, directors' creation of, and DVD purchase, 65
women, as actively engaged in war, 221; and documentary filmmaking, 11, 85, 113, 120, 282; and how they experience their everyday lives, 305, 318
working conditions, of documentary filmmaker, 16, 79, 199, 210, 385

Y
Year of the Brain, 60
YLE, 19, 24, 253, 410
Young British Artists scene, 186

Z
ZDF, 19, 24, 305, 410
Zentropa, 101, 103, 116, 135, 216, 294, 341, 350–51, 367, 409, 410
Zentropa Real, 350, 351, 409